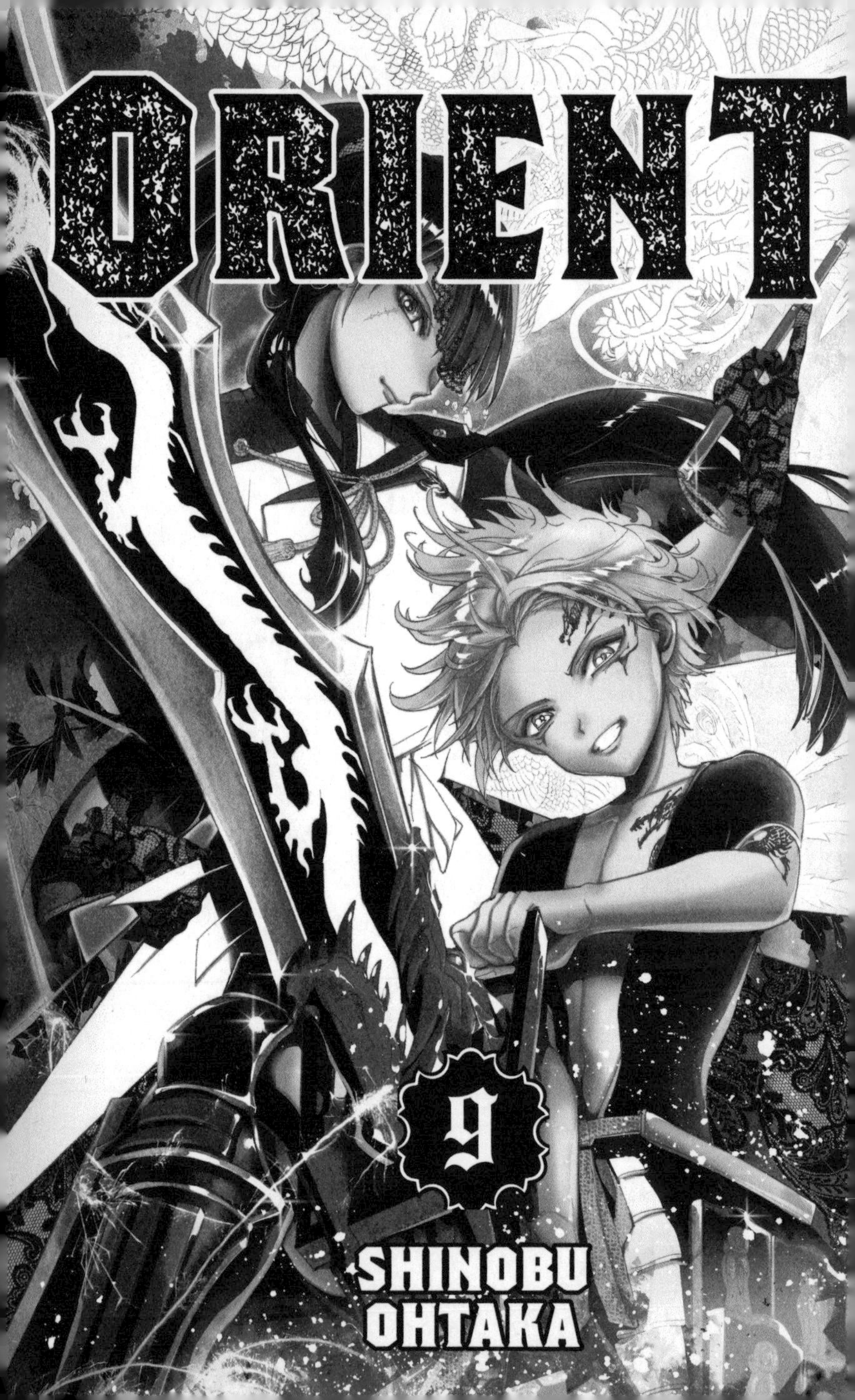
ORIENT
9
SHINOBU
OHTAKA

ORIENT

9

SHINOBU OHTAKA

CONTENTS

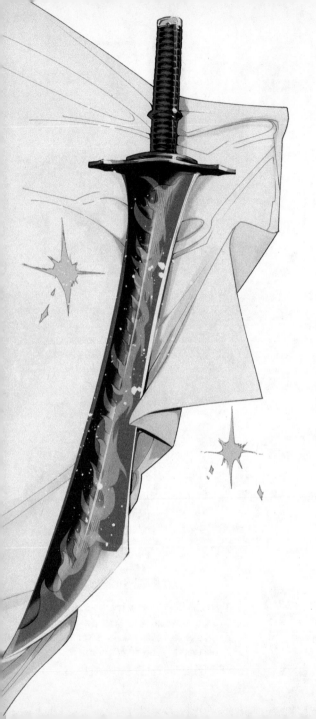

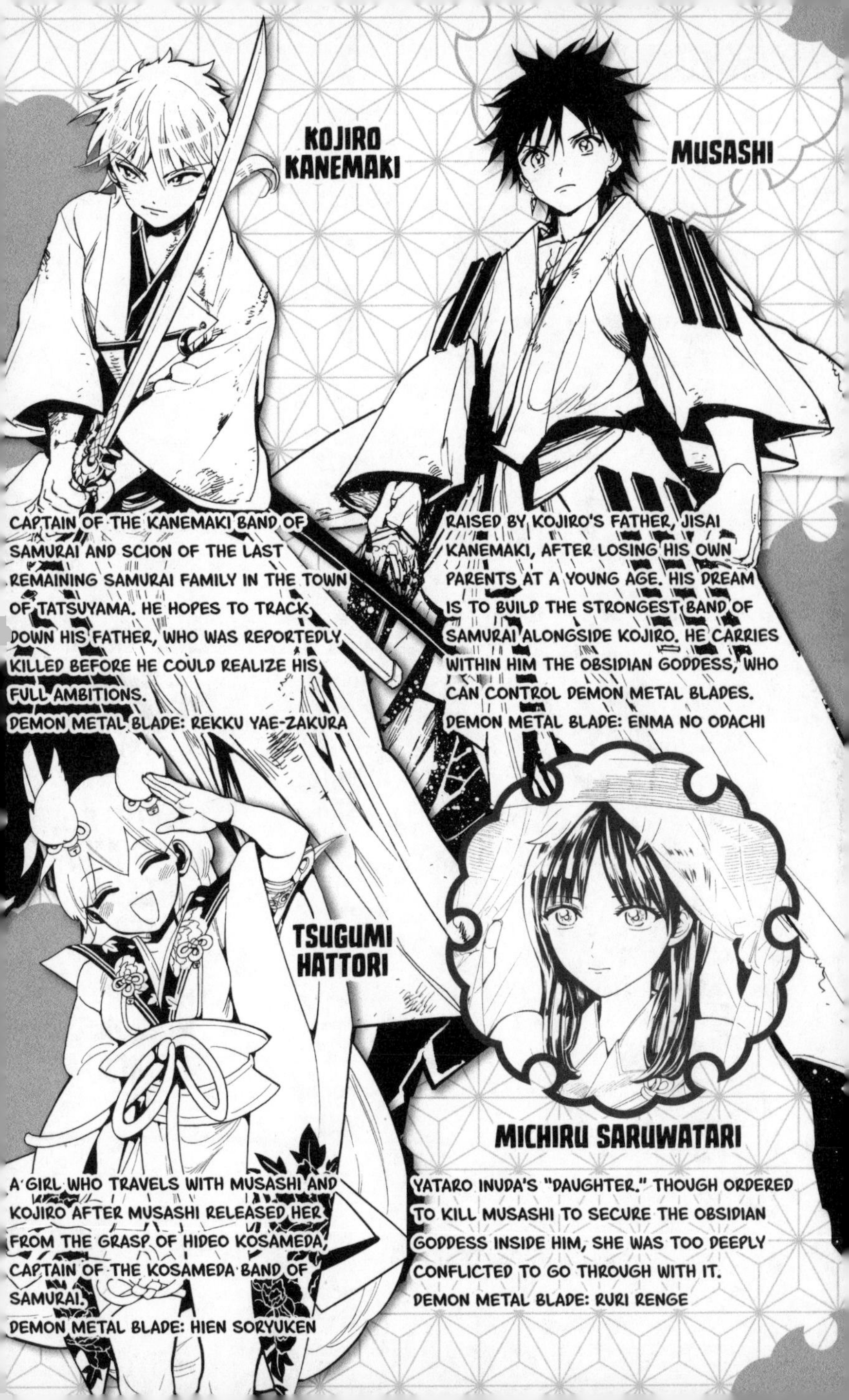
MUSASHI
RAISED BY KOJIRO'S FATHER, JISAI KANEMAKI, AFTER LOSING HIS OWN PARENTS AT A YOUNG AGE. HIS DREAM IS TO BUILD THE STRONGEST BAND OF SAMURAI ALONGSIDE KOJIRO. HE CARRIES WITHIN HIM THE OBSIDIAN GODDESS, WHO CAN CONTROL DEMON METAL BLADES.
DEMON METAL BLADE: ENMA NO ODACHI
KOJIRO KANEMAKI
CAPTAIN OF THE KANEMAKI BAND OF SAMURAI AND SCION OF THE LAST REMAINING SAMURAI FAMILY IN THE TOWN OF TATSUYAMA. HE HOPES TO TRACK DOWN HIS FATHER, WHO WAS REPORTEDLY KILLED BEFORE HE COULD REALIZE HIS FULL AMBITIONS.
DEMON METAL BLADE: REKKU YAE-ZAKURA
MICHIRU SARUWATARI
YATARO INUDA'S "DAUGHTER." THOUGH ORDERED TO KILL MUSASHI TO SECURE THE OBSIDIAN GODDESS INSIDE HIM, SHE WAS TOO DEEPLY CONFLICTED TO GO THROUGH WITH IT.
DEMON METAL BLADE: RURI RENGE
TSUGUMI HATTORI
A GIRL WHO TRAVELS WITH MUSASHI AND KOJIRO AFTER MUSASHI RELEASED HER FROM THE GRASP OF HIDEO KOSAMEDA, CAPTAIN OF THE KOSAMEDA BAND OF SAMURAI.
DEMON METAL BLADE: HIEN SORYUKEN

CHARACTERS

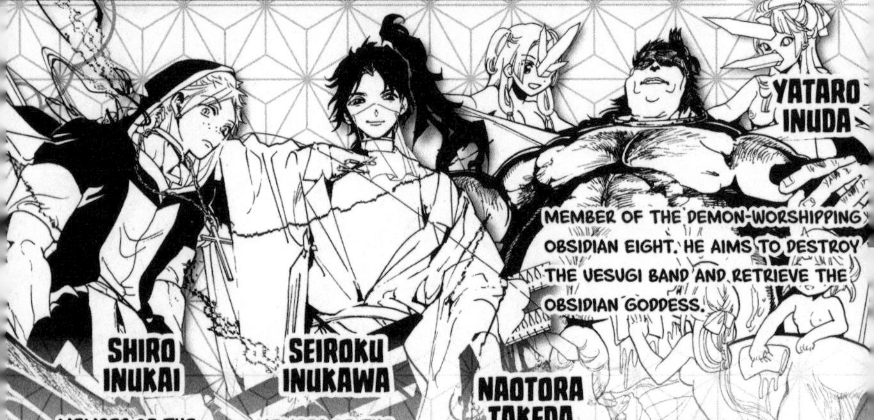

YATARO INUDA

MEMBER OF THE DEMON-WORSHIPPING OBSIDIAN EIGHT. HE AIMS TO DESTROY THE UESUGI BAND AND RETRIEVE THE OBSIDIAN GODDESS.

SHIRO INUKAI

MEMBER OF THE OBSIDIAN EIGHT. HE DOGGEDLY PURSUES THE OBSIDIAN GODDESS.

SEIROKU INUKAWA

MEMBER OF THE OBSIDIAN EIGHT. HE IS CAPABLE OF SEVERING BLADE-SPIRIT TIES BETWEEN SAMURAI.

NAOTORA TAKEDA

CAPTAIN OF THE TAKEDA BAND OF SAMURAI AND ONE OF THE FIVE HEROIC GENERALS. HE IS AS MATCHLESS AS TATSUOMI UESUGI HIMSELF.

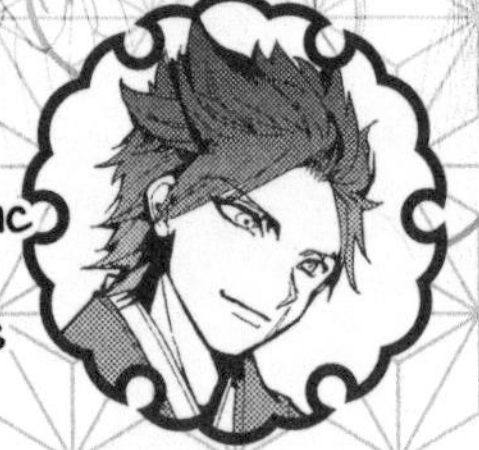

KANETATSU NAOE

A TOP MINISTER IN THE UESUGI BAND. REFERRED TO REVERENTLY AS THE DRAGON GOD, HE IS ONE OF THE STRONGEST IN HIS FORCE.

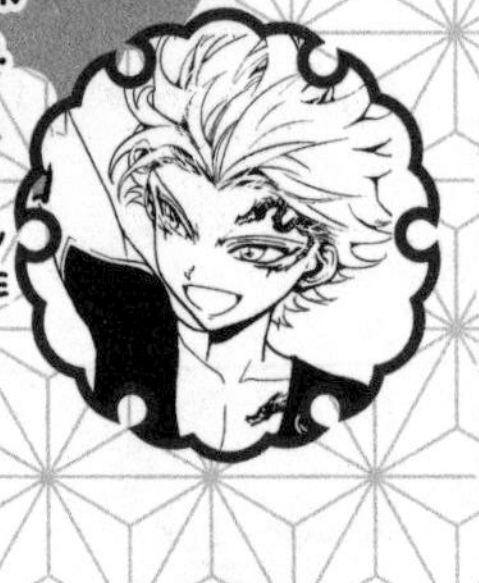

KUROKO USAMI

CHIEF TACTICIAN OF THE UESUGI BAND. SHE WIELDS HER DEMON METAL BLADE ONLY TO PROTECT HER COMPANIONS.

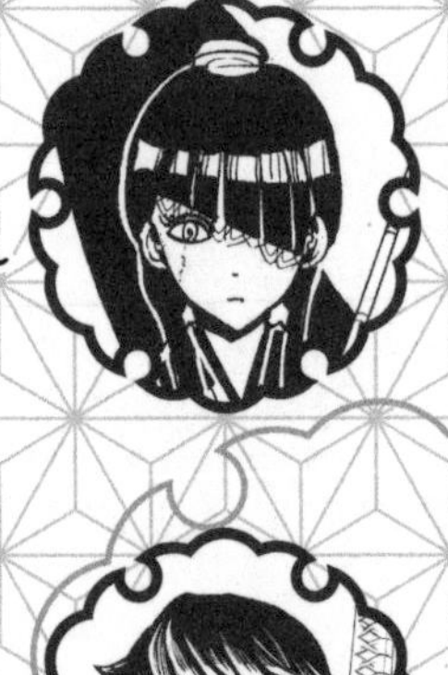

AKIHIRO SHIMAZU

SON OF THE HEAD OF THE SHIMAZU BAND. HE MOPPED THE FLOOR WITH MUSASHI IN A BATTLE TO DECIDE THE LEADER OF THEIR PLATOON. DEMON METAL BLADE: TENRO TEKKYAKU

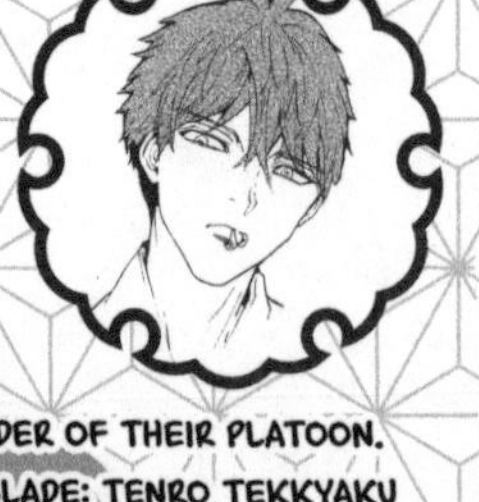

KATSUMI AMAKO

SON OF THE HEAD OF THE AMAKO BAND. HE TAUGHT MUSASHI THE BASICS OF FIGHTING WITH BLADE SPIRIT.

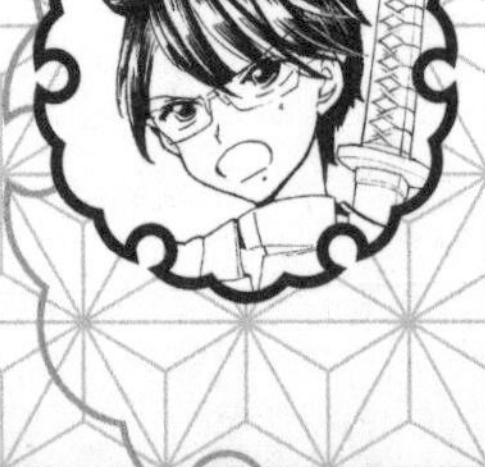

ORIENT

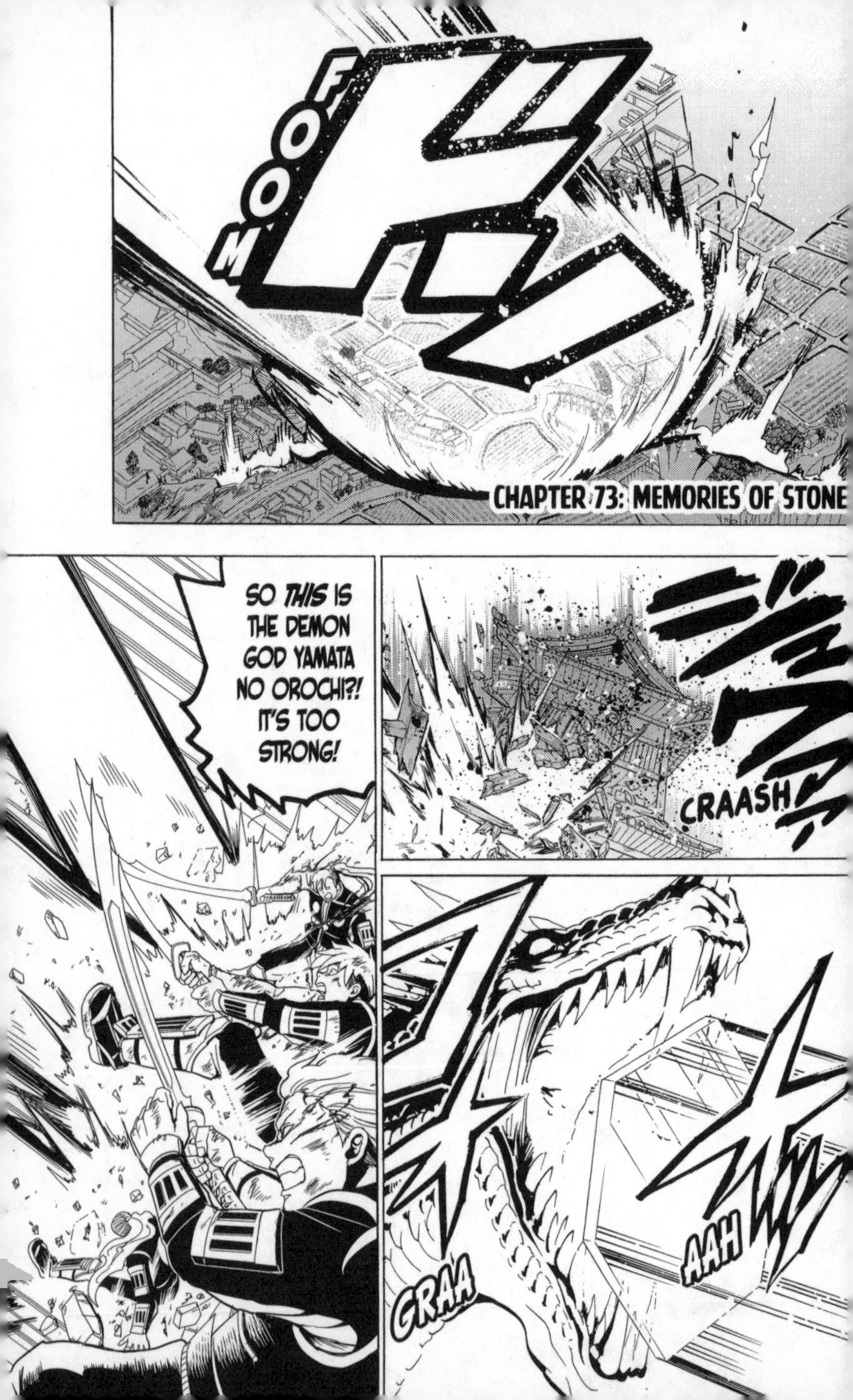
FOOM
CHAPTER 73: MEMORIES OF STONE
CRAASH
AAH
GRAA
SO THIS IS THE DEMON GOD YAMATA NO OROCHI?! IT'S TOO STRONG!

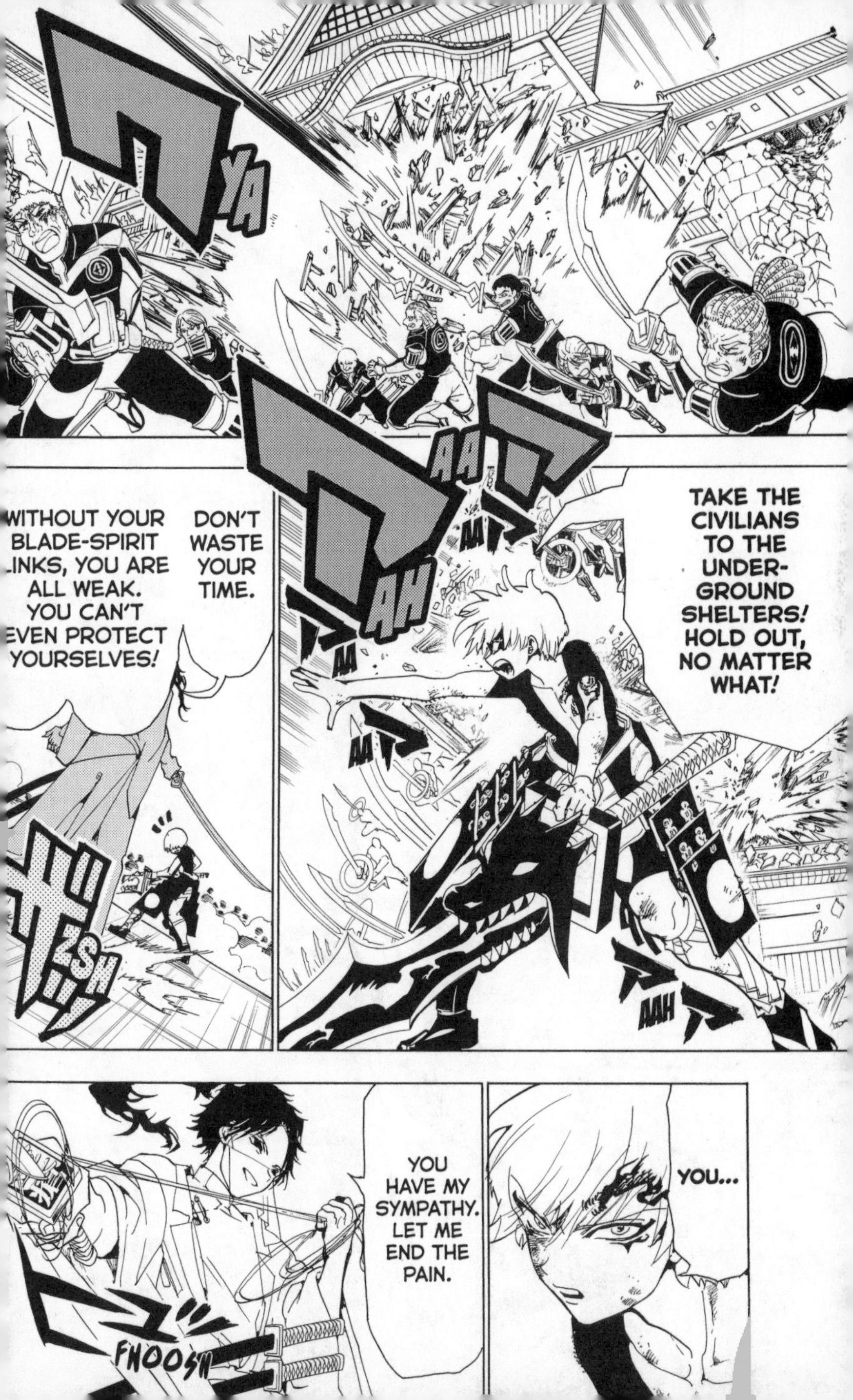
YA
AA
AA
AH
AA
TAKE THE CIVILIANS TO THE UNDER-GROUND SHELTERS! HOLD OUT, NO MATTER WHAT!
AA
AAH
DON'T WASTE YOUR TIME.
WITHOUT YOUR BLADE-SPIRIT LINKS, YOU ARE ALL WEAK. YOU CAN'T EVEN PROTECT YOURSELVES!
ZSH
YOU...
YOU HAVE MY SYMPATHY. LET ME END THE PAIN.
FHOOSH

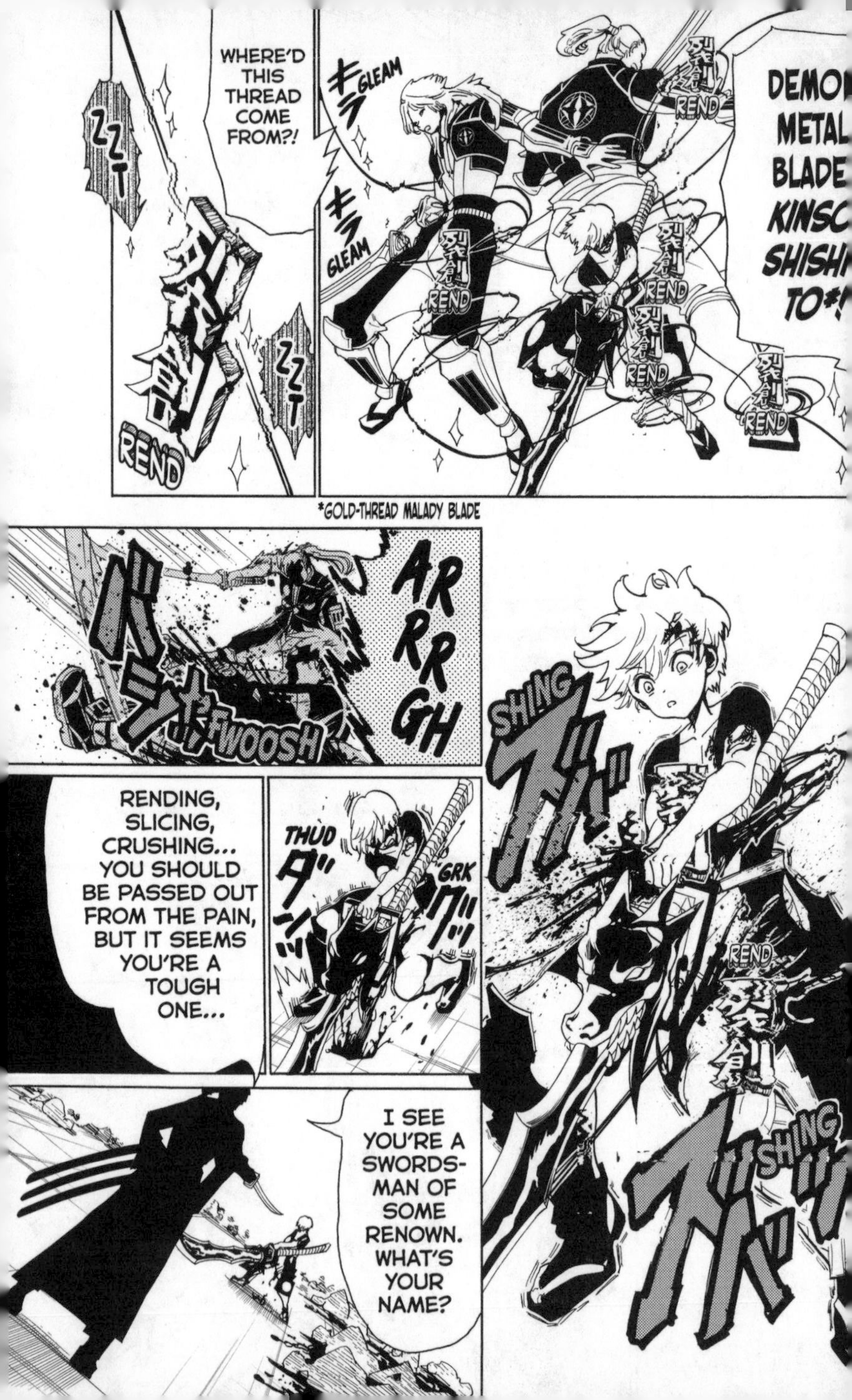
DEMON METAL BLADE KINSC SHISH TO*!
GLEAM
GLEAM
REND
REND
REND
REND
REND
WHERE'D THIS THREAD COME FROM?!
ZZT
ZZT
REND
*GOLD-THREAD MALADY BLADE
SHING
REND
SHING
ARRRGH
FWOOSH
THUD
GRK
RENDING, SLICING, CRUSHING... YOU SHOULD BE PASSED OUT FROM THE PAIN, BUT IT SEEMS YOU'RE A TOUGH ONE...
I SEE YOU'RE A SWORDS-MAN OF SOME RENOWN. WHAT'S YOUR NAME?

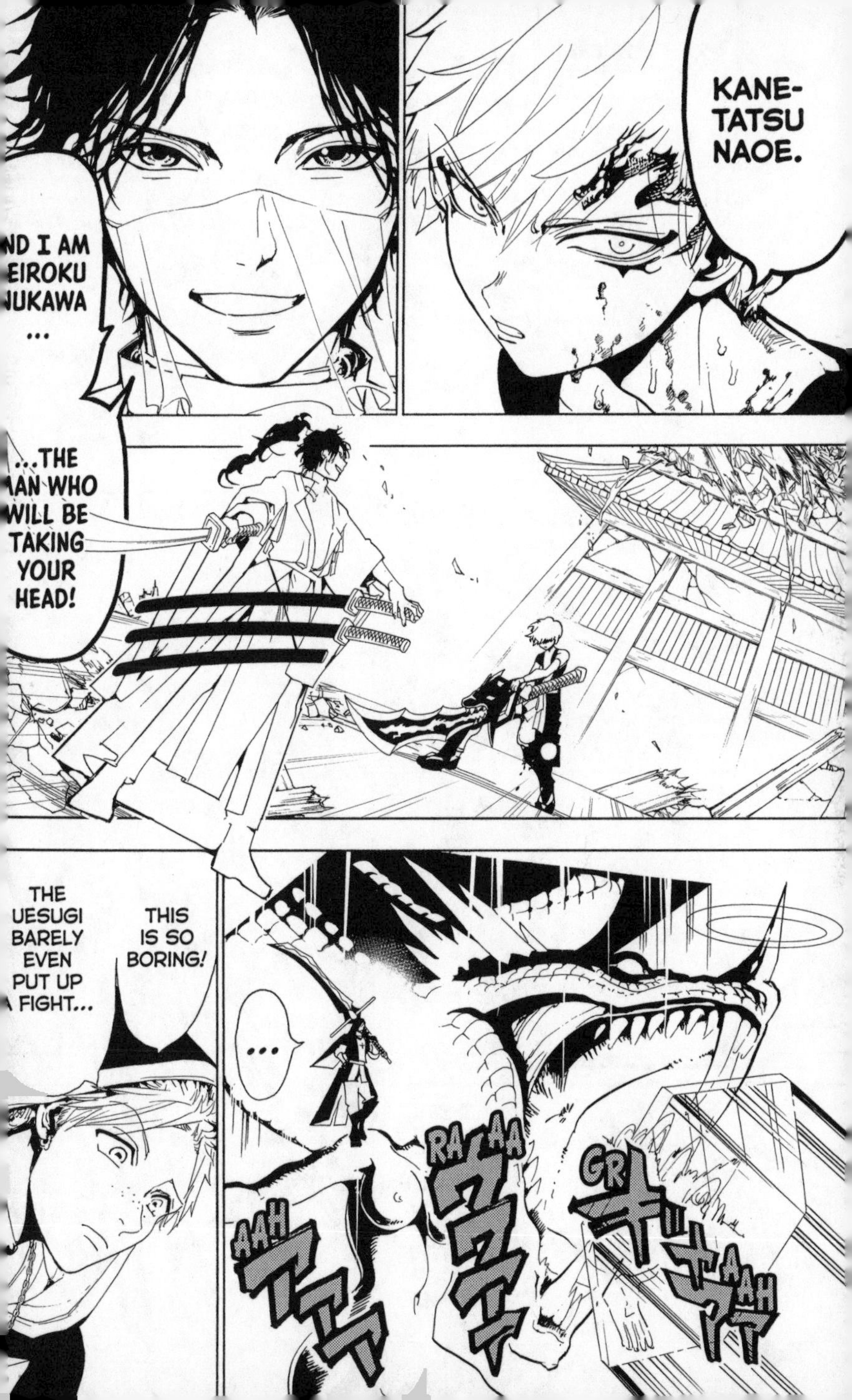
KANE-TATSU NAOE.
ND I AM EIROKU NUKAWA ...
...THE AN WHO WILL BE TAKING YOUR HEAD!
...
RAAAA
GR AAH
AAH
THIS IS SO BORING!
THE UESUGI BARELY EVEN PUT UP FIGHT...

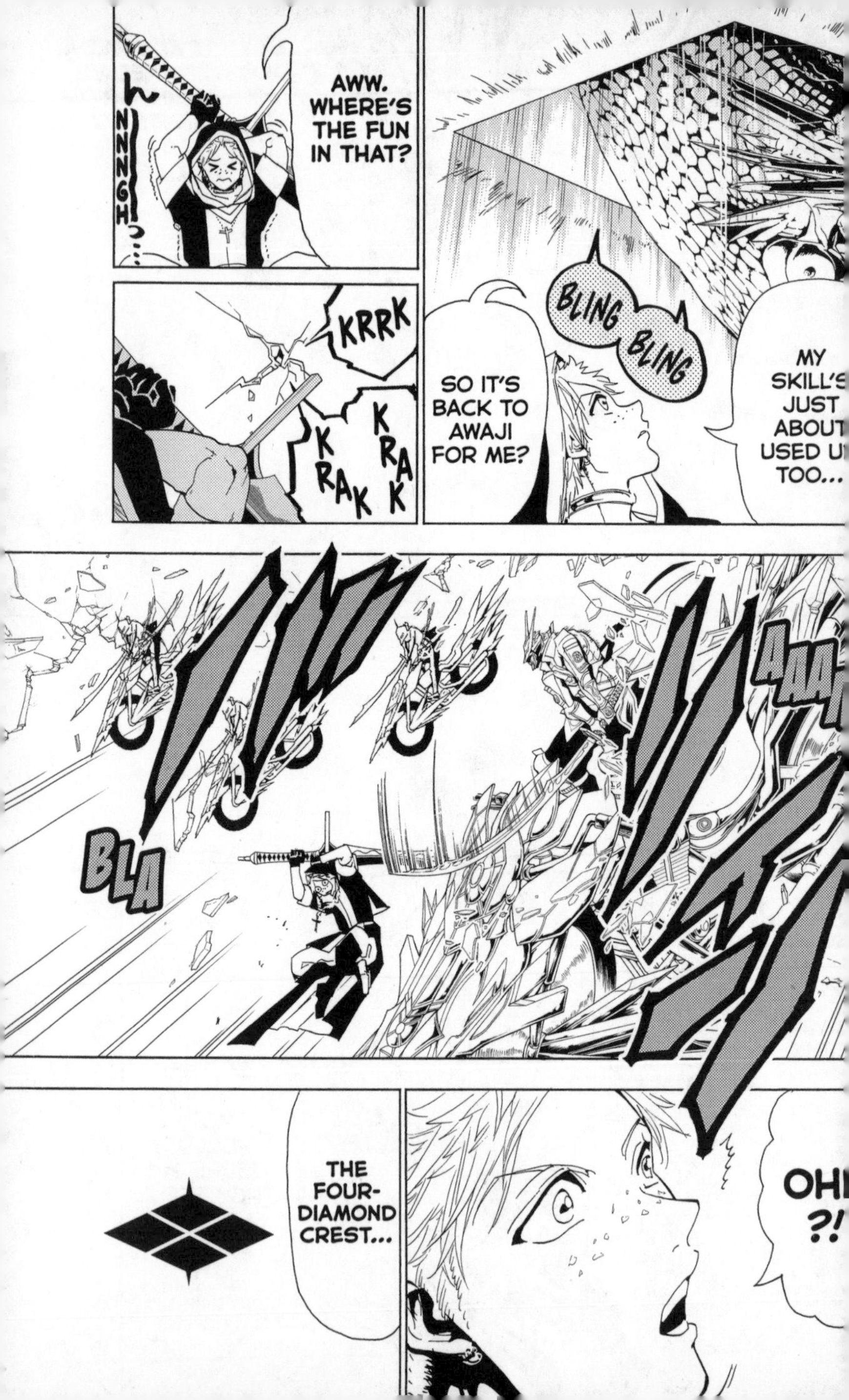

MY SKILL'S JUST ABOUT USED U TOO...
BLING BLING
SO IT'S BACK TO AWAJI FOR ME?
AWW. WHERE'S THE FUN IN THAT?
んNNNGHっ...
KRRK
KRAK KRAK
AAA
BLA
OH ?!
THE FOUR-DIAMOND CREST...

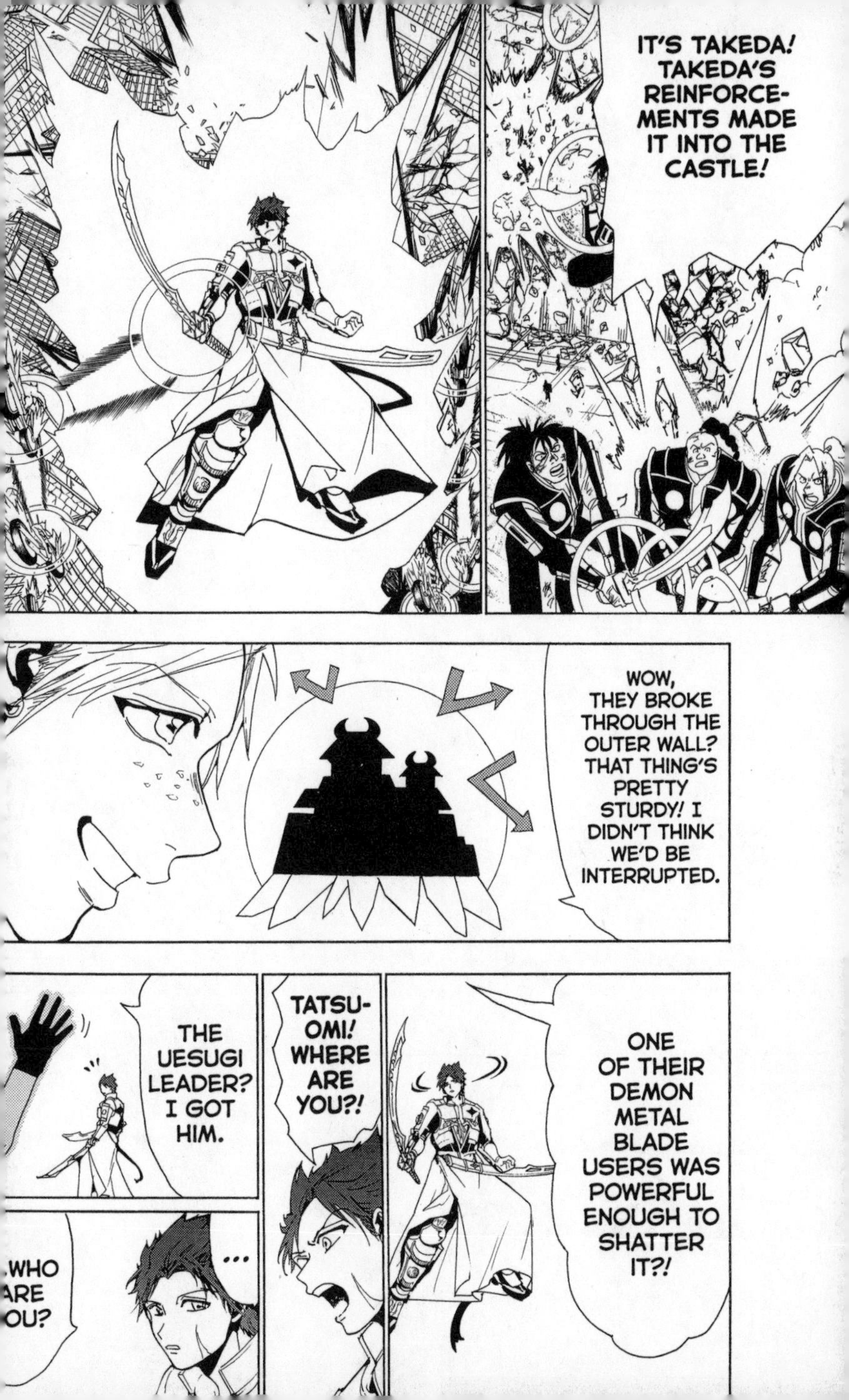
IT'S TAKEDA! TAKEDA'S REINFORCEMENTS MADE IT INTO THE CASTLE!
WOW, THEY BROKE THROUGH THE OUTER WALL? THAT THING'S PRETTY STURDY! I DIDN'T THINK WE'D BE INTERRUPTED.
ONE OF THEIR DEMON METAL BLADE USERS WAS POWERFUL ENOUGH TO SHATTER IT?!
TATSUOMI! WHERE ARE YOU?!
THE UESUGI LEADER? I GOT HIM.
...
.WHO ARE OU?

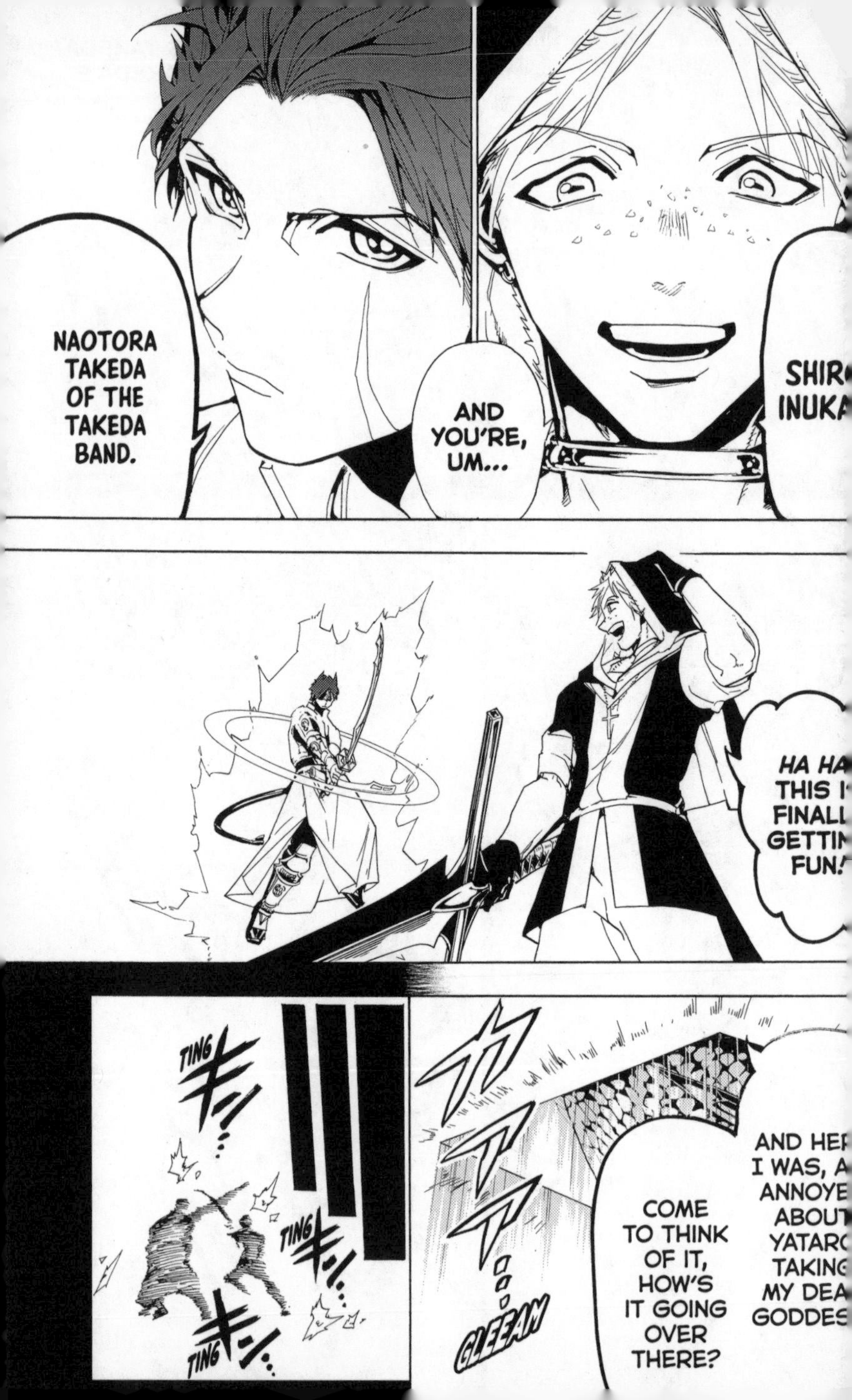
SHIR
INUKA
AND YOU'RE, UM...
NAOTORA TAKEDA OF THE TAKEDA BAND.
HA HA THIS I FINALL GETTIN FUN!
AND HEF I WAS, A ANNOYE ABOUT YATARO TAKING MY DEA GODDES
COME TO THINK OF IT, HOW'S IT GOING OVER THERE?
GLEEAM
TING
TING
TING

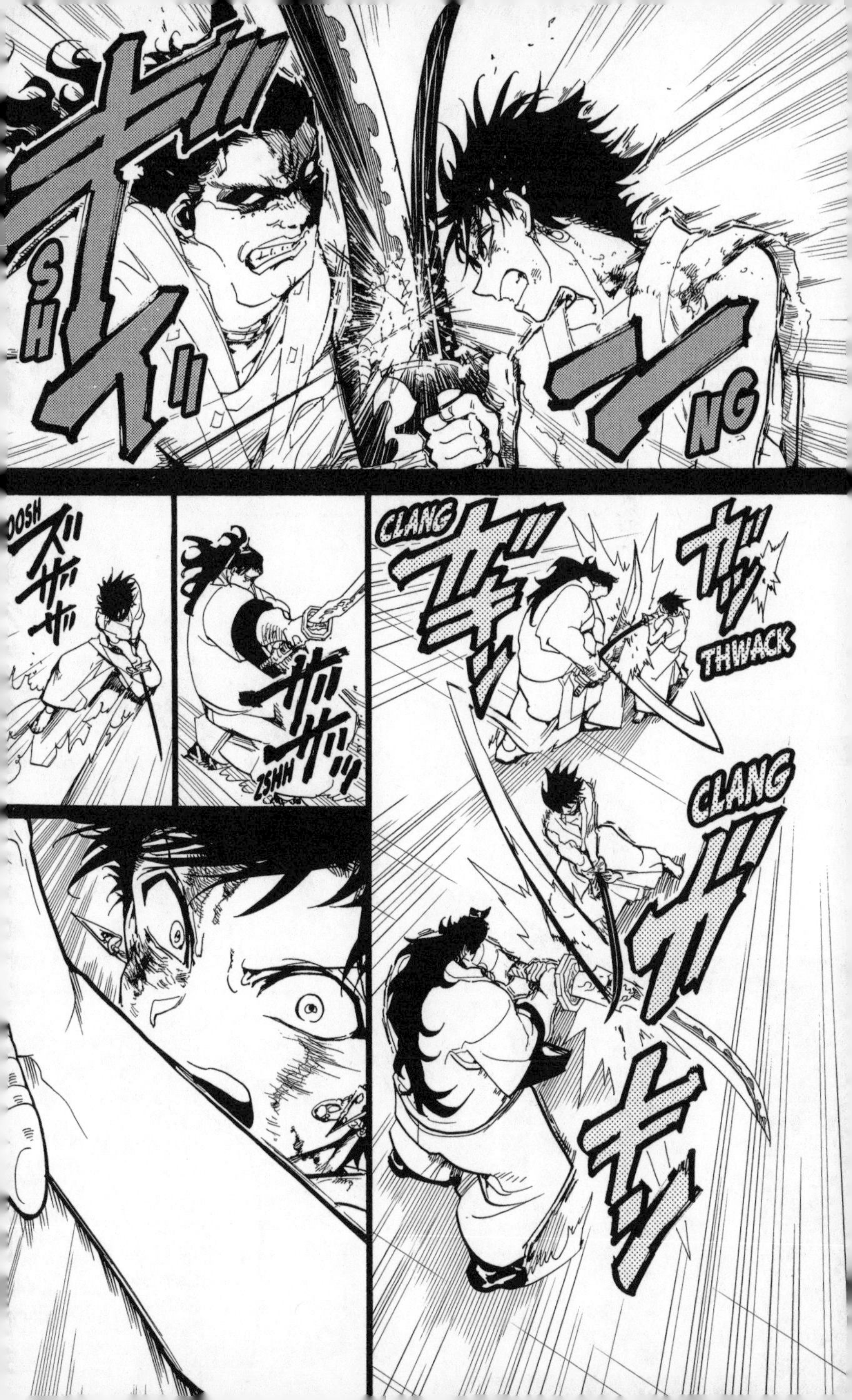
SH
NG
CLANG
THWACK
CLANG
ZSHH
OOSH

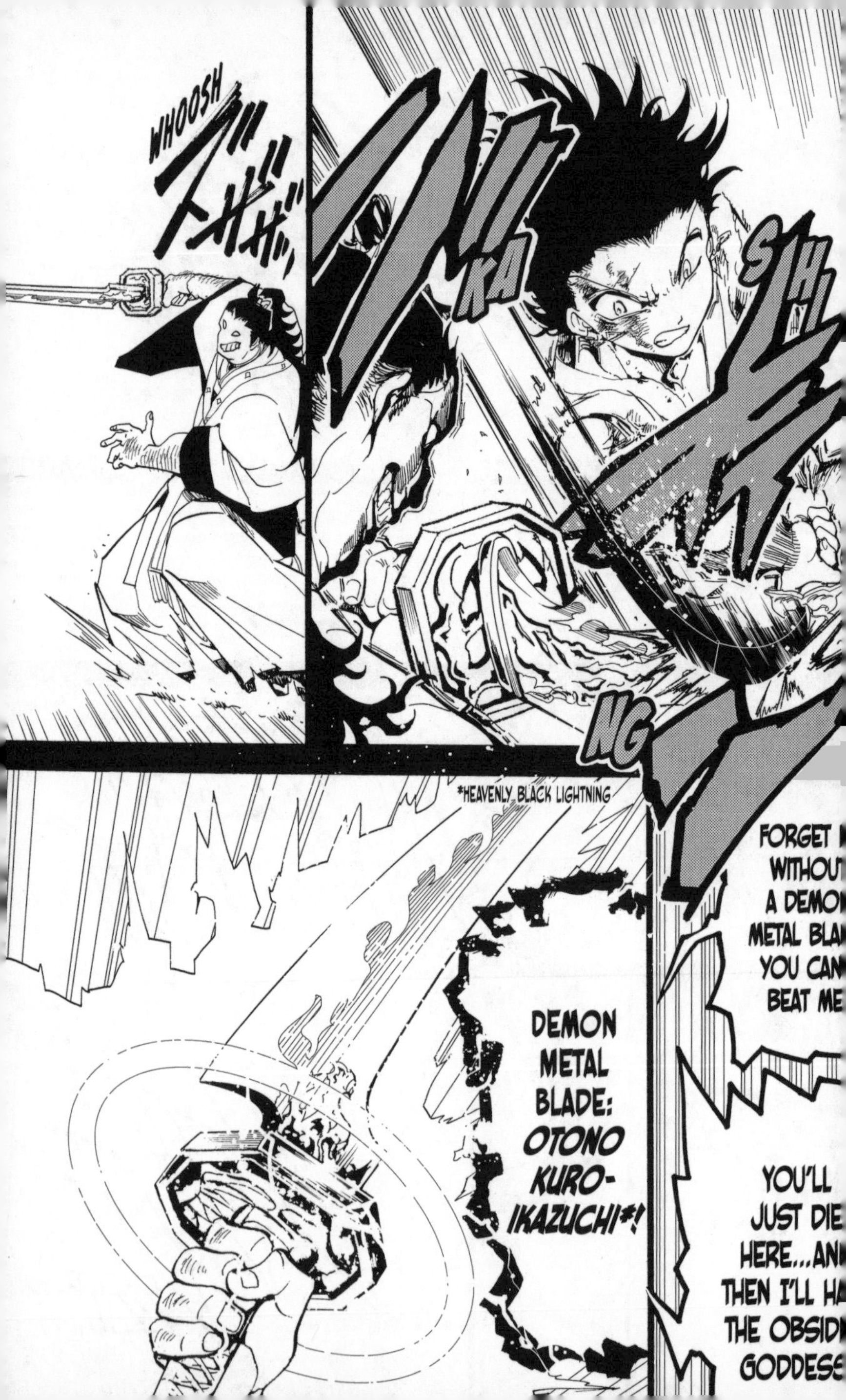
SHI
KA
NG
WHOOSH
FORGET
WITHOU
A DEMO
METAL BLA
YOU CAN
BEAT ME
YOU'LL
JUST DIE
HERE...AN
THEN I'LL HA
THE OBSID
GODDESE
DEMON METAL BLADE: OTONO KURO-IKAZUCHI*!
*HEAVENLY BLACK LIGHTNING

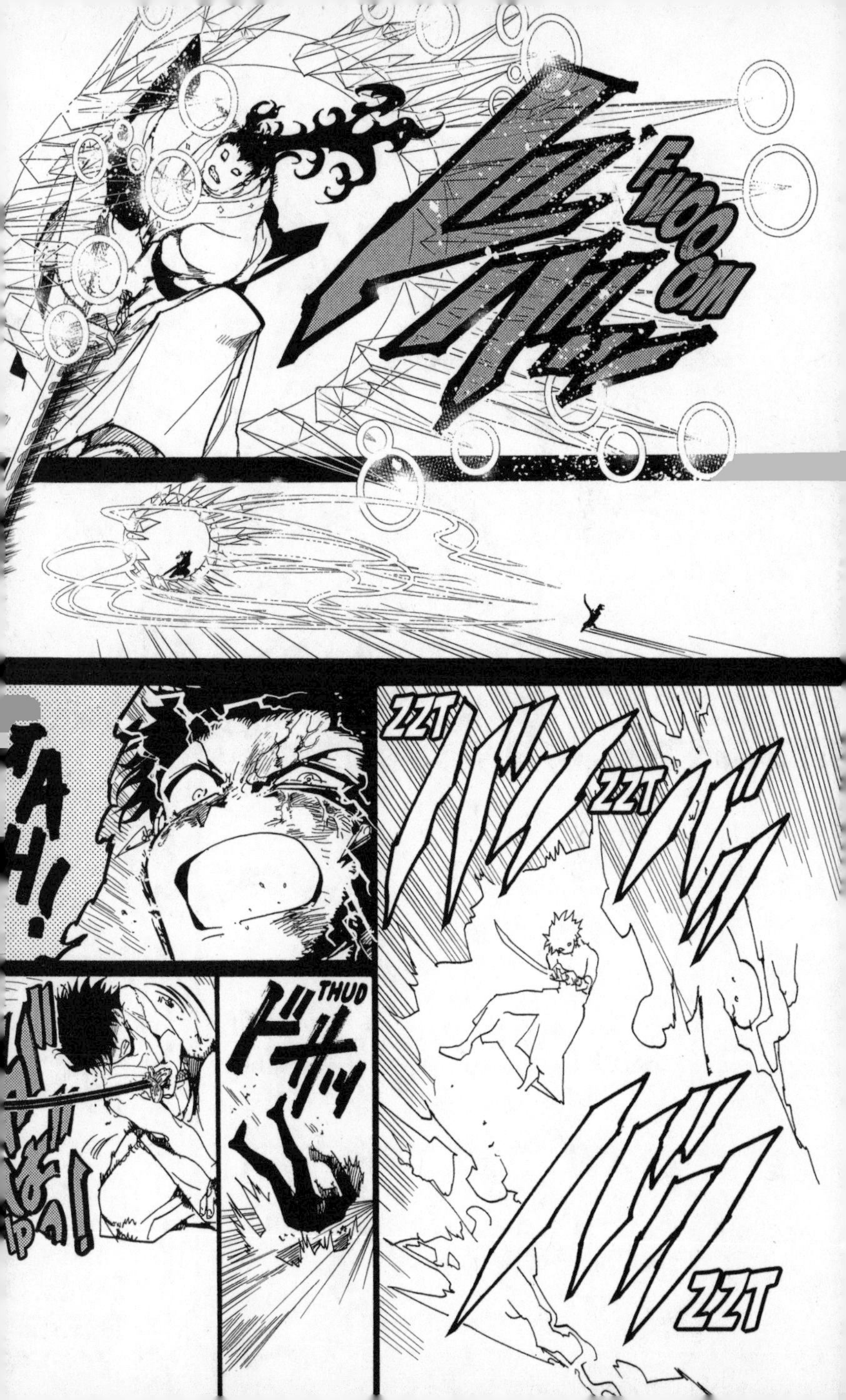
FWOOSH
ZZT
ZZT
ZZT
AH!!
THUD

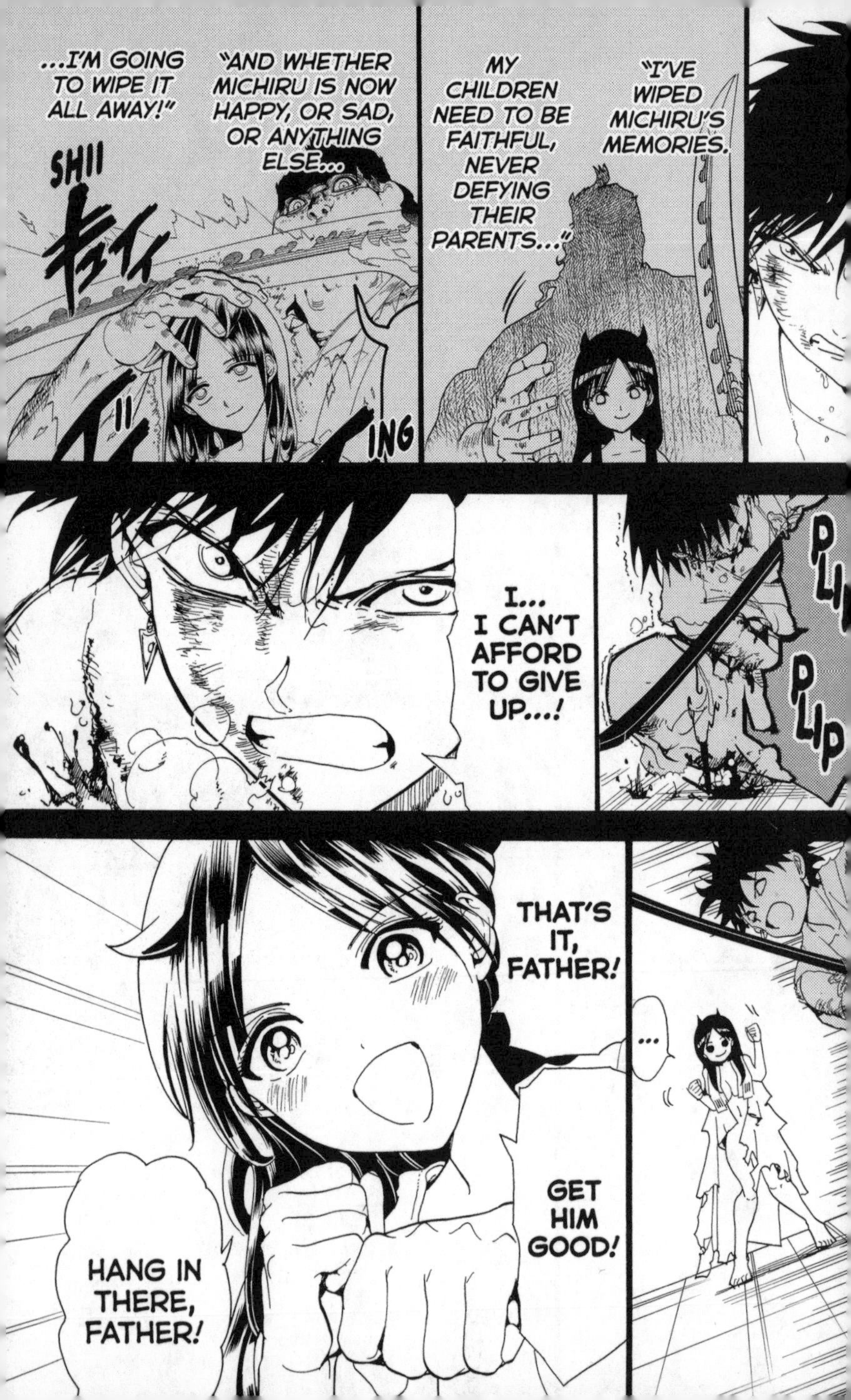

"I'VE WIPED MICHIRU'S MEMORIES.
MY CHILDREN NEED TO BE FAITHFUL, NEVER DEFYING THEIR PARENTS..."
"AND WHETHER MICHIRU IS NOW HAPPY, OR SAD, OR ANYTHING ELSE...
...I'M GOING TO WIPE IT ALL AWAY!"
SHII
キュイイ
ING
PLIP PLIP
I... I CAN'T AFFORD TO GIVE UP...!
...
THAT'S IT, FATHER!
GET HIM GOOD!
HANG IN THERE, FATHER!

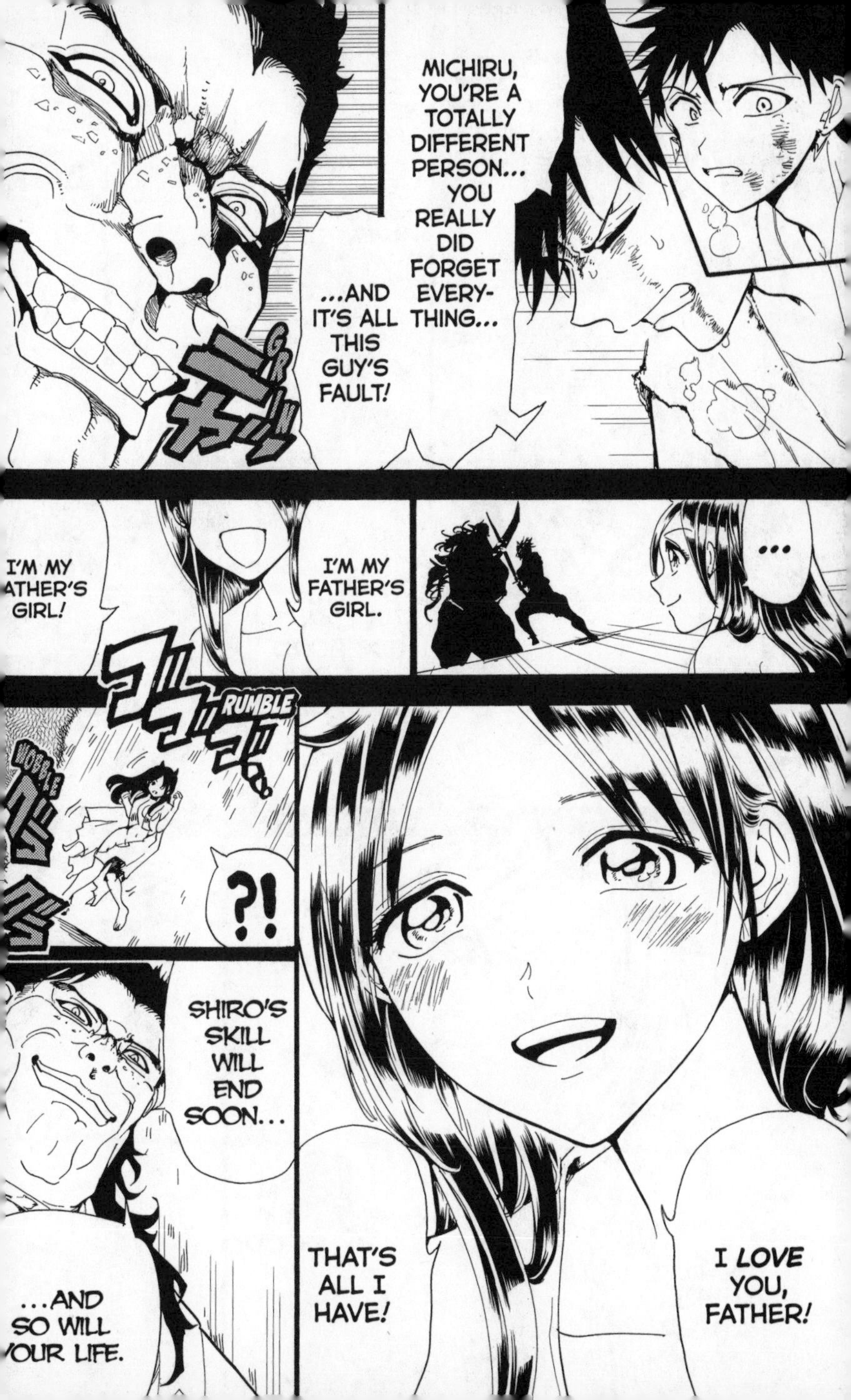
MICHIRU, YOU'RE A TOTALLY DIFFERENT PERSON... YOU REALLY DID FORGET EVERYTHING...
...AND IT'S ALL THIS GUY'S FAULT!
GRIN
...
I'M MY FATHER'S GIRL.
I'M MY ATHER'S GIRL!
I LOVE YOU, FATHER!
THAT'S ALL I HAVE!
RUMBLE
WOBBLE
?!
SHIRO'S SKILL WILL END SOON...
...AND SO WILL OUR LIFE.

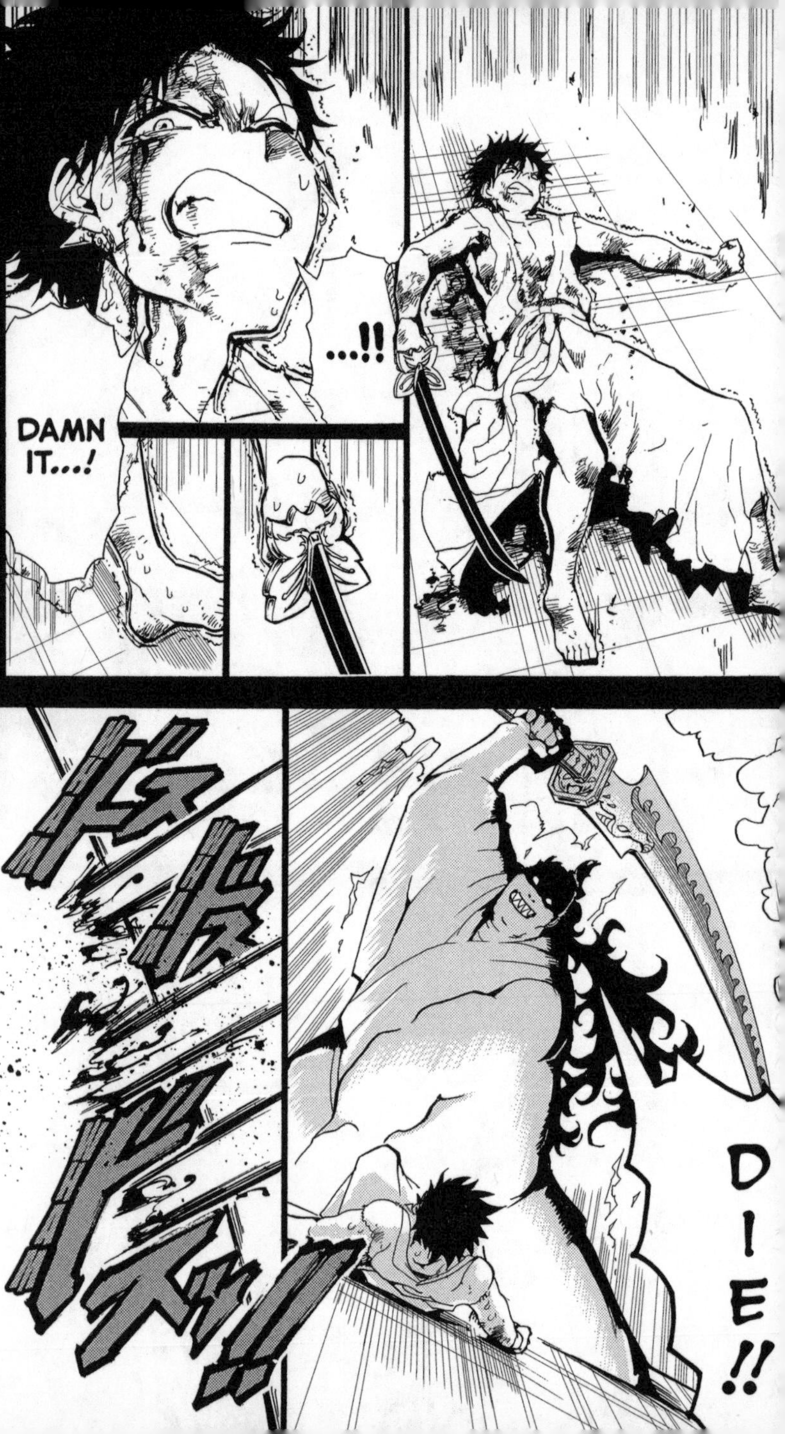
...!!
DAMN IT...!
DIE!!

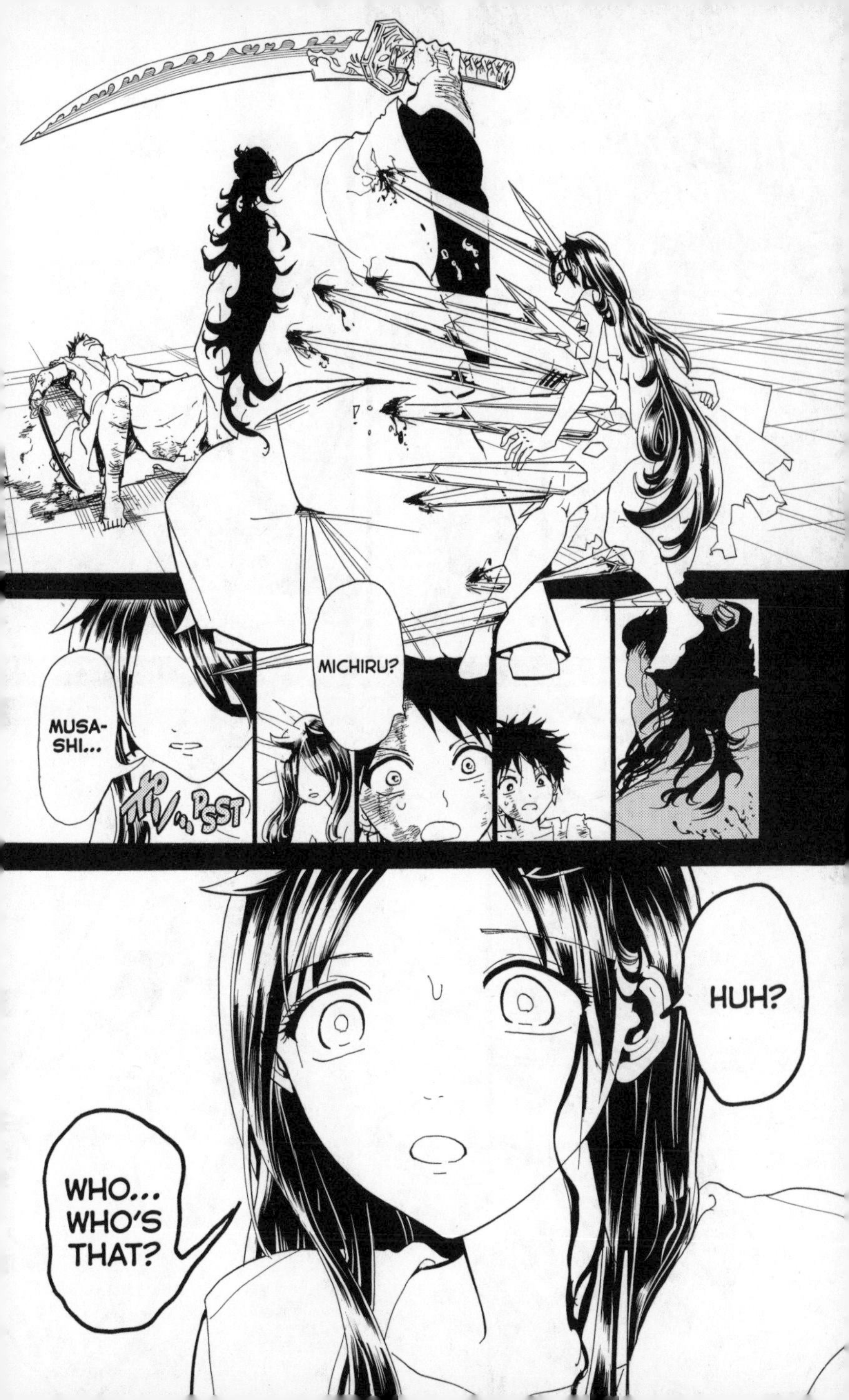
MICHIRU?
MUSA-SHI...
PSST
HUH?
WHO... WHO'S THAT?

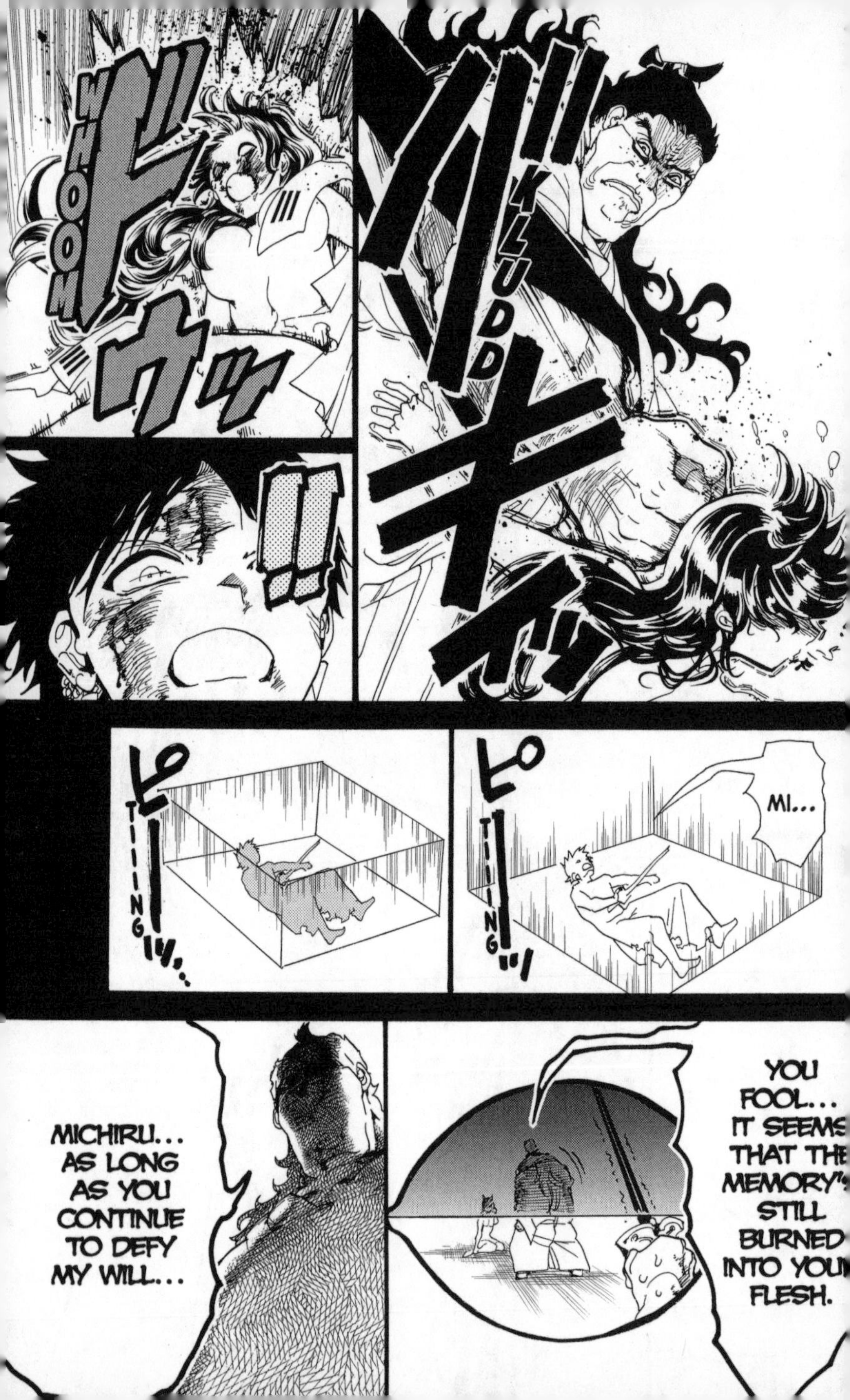
KLUDD
WHOOOM
!!
TIIIING
MI...
TIIIING
YOU FOOL... IT SEEMS THAT THE MEMORY'S STILL BURNED INTO YOUR FLESH.
MICHIRU... AS LONG AS YOU CONTINUE TO DEFY MY WILL...

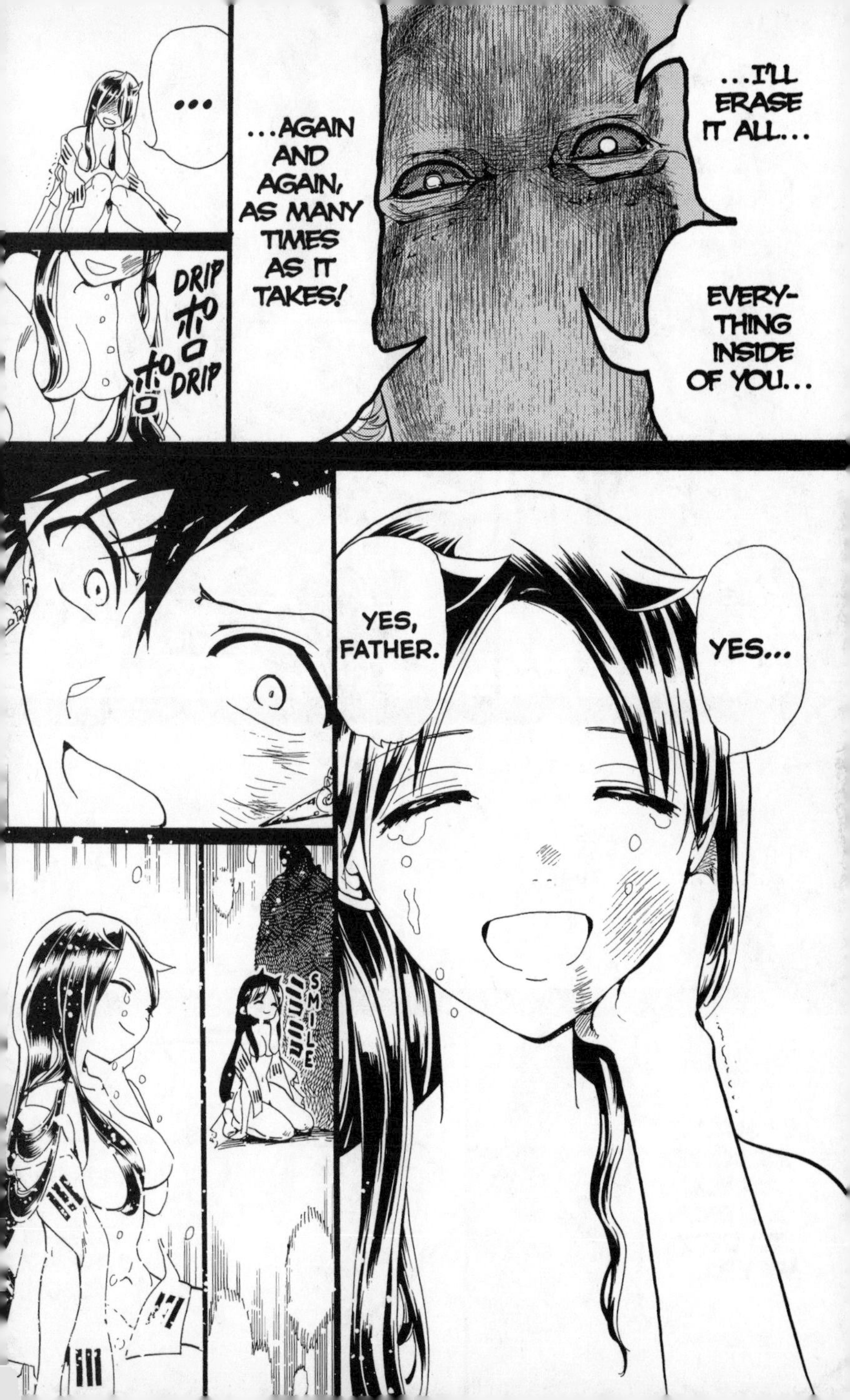
...I'LL ERASE IT ALL...
EVERY-THING INSIDE OF YOU...
...AGAIN AND AGAIN, AS MANY TIMES AS IT TAKES!
...
DRIP
ポロ
DRIP
ポロ
YES...
YES, FATHER.
SMILE

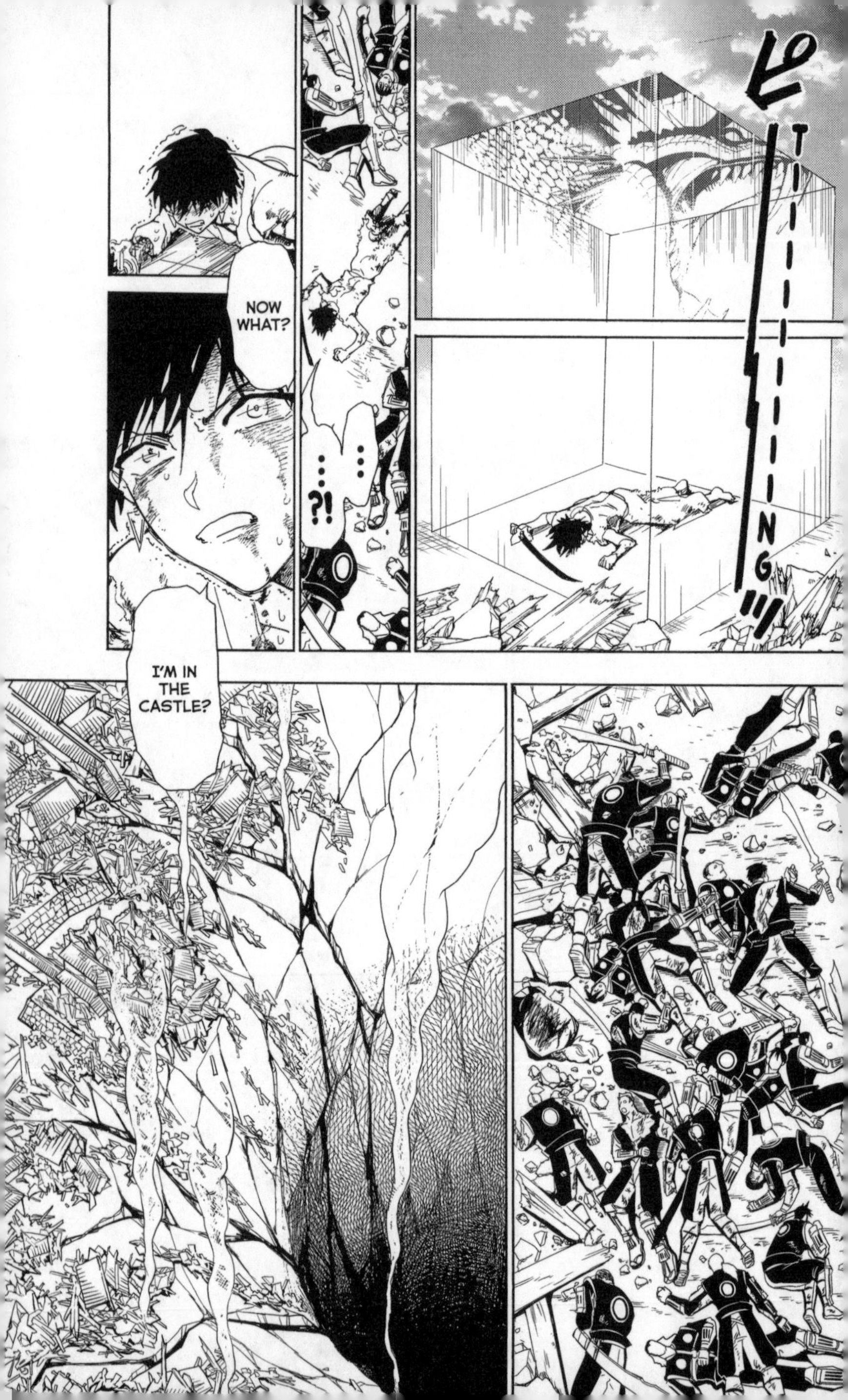
ピ
TIIIIIIIIING!!!
...
...?!
NOW WHAT?
I'M IN THE CASTLE?

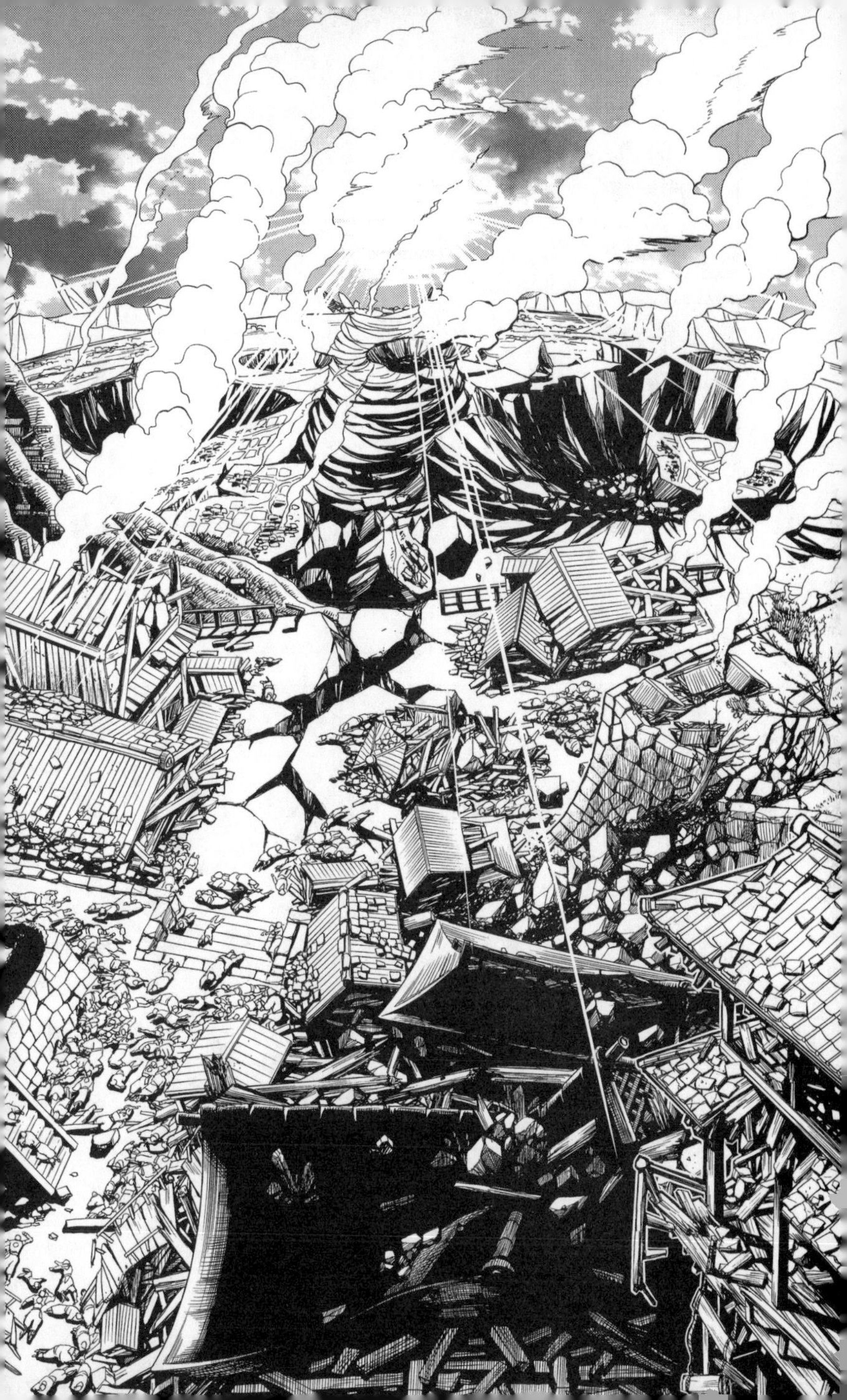

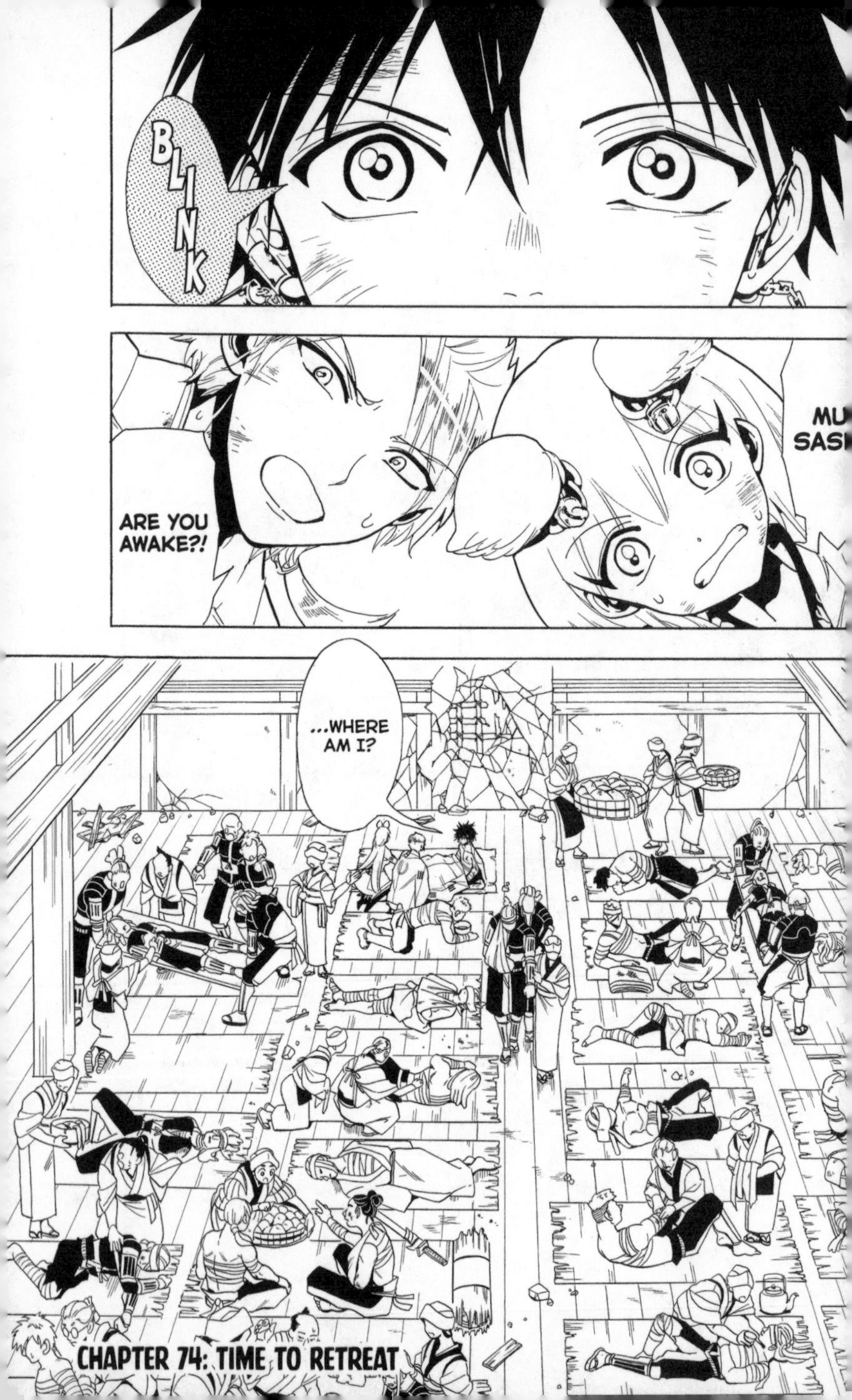
BLINK
MU SAS
ARE YOU AWAKE?!
...WHERE AM I?
CHAPTER 74: TIME TO RETREAT

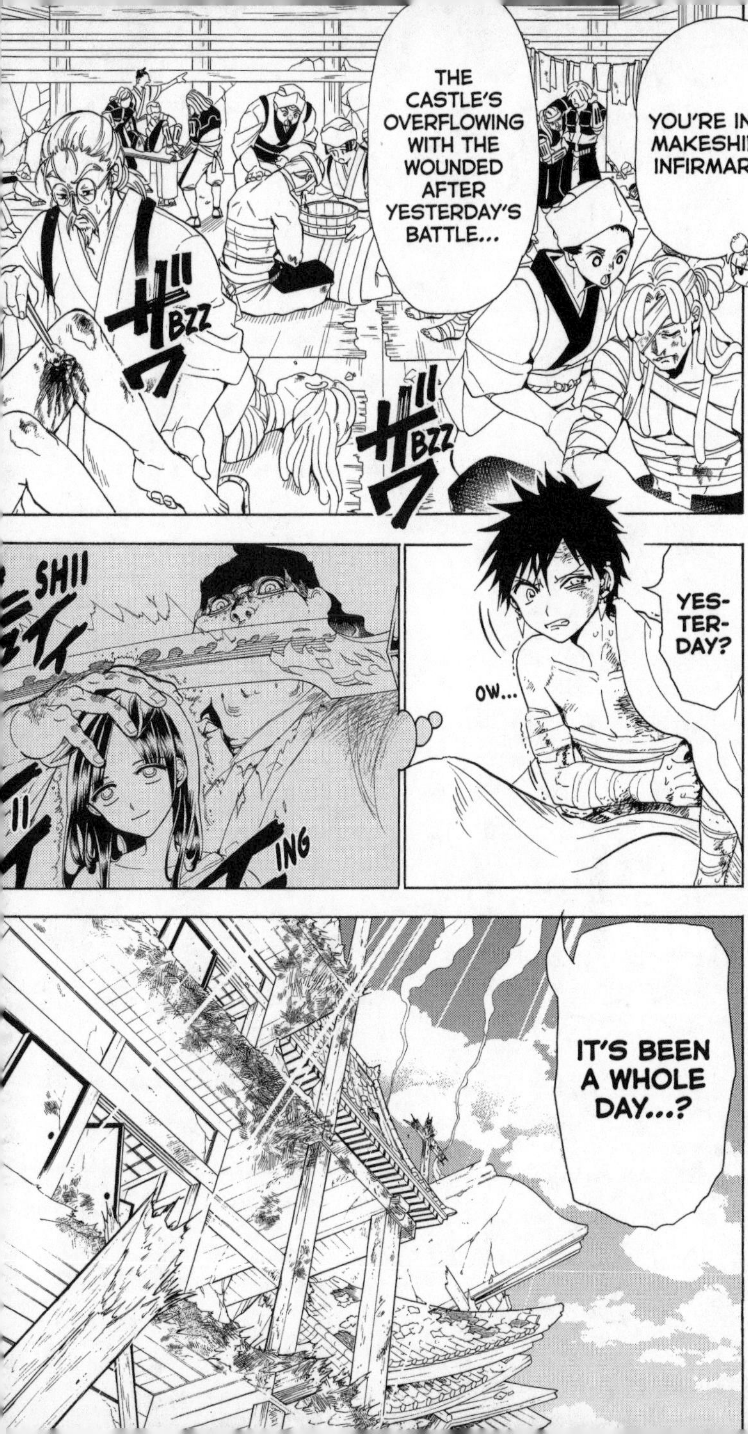
YOU'RE IN A MAKESHIFT INFIRMARY.
THE CASTLE'S OVERFLOWING WITH THE WOUNDED AFTER YESTERDAY'S BATTLE...
BZZ
BZZ
YES-TER-DAY?
OW...
SHII
ING
IT'S BEEN A WHOLE DAY...?

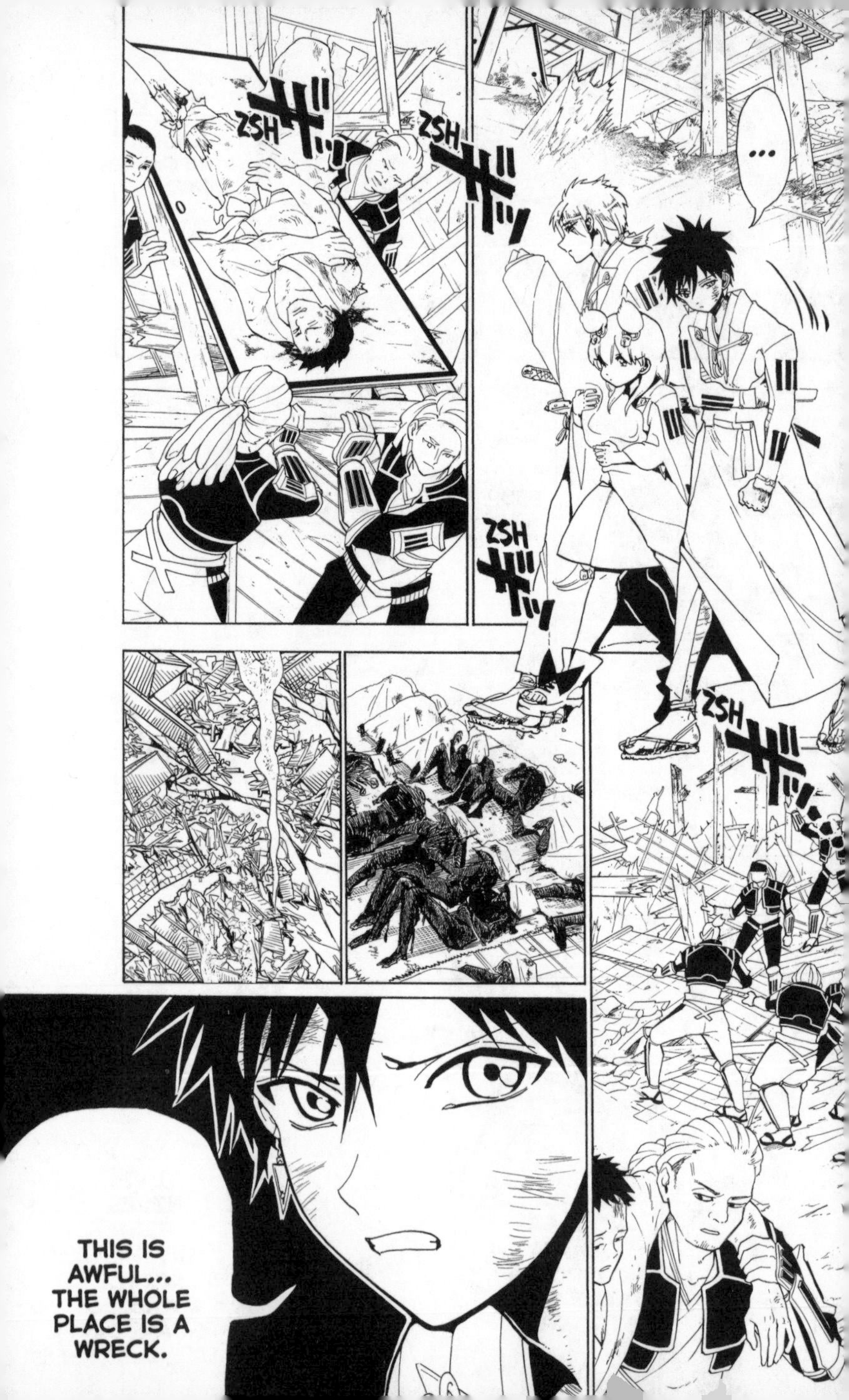
...
ZSH
ZSH
ZSH
ZSH
THIS IS AWFUL... THE WHOLE PLACE IS A WRECK.

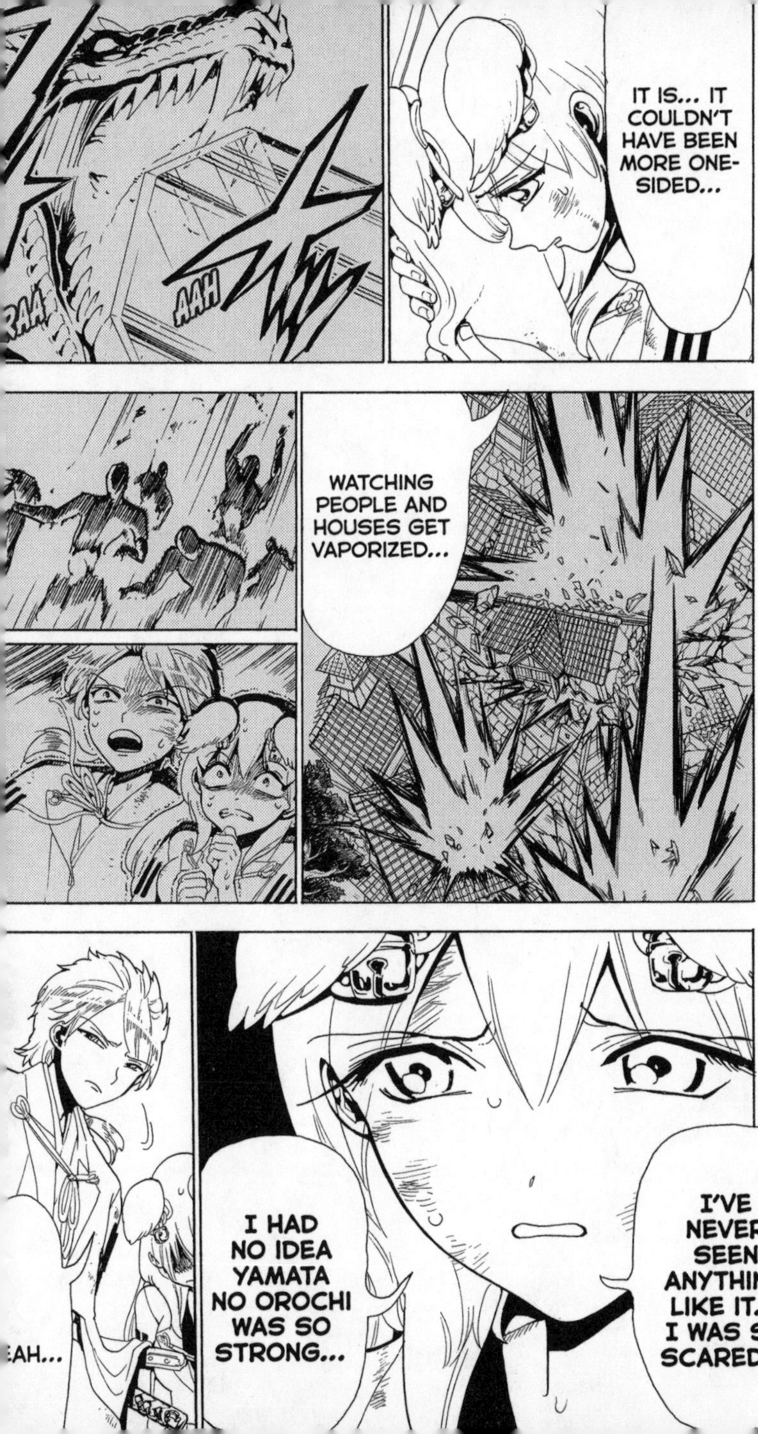
IT IS... IT COULDN'T HAVE BEEN MORE ONE-SIDED...
AAH
RAA
WATCHING PEOPLE AND HOUSES GET VAPORIZED...
I'VE NEVER SEEN ANYTHING LIKE IT... I WAS SO SCARED...
I HAD NO IDEA YAMATA NO OROCHI WAS SO STRONG...
EAH...

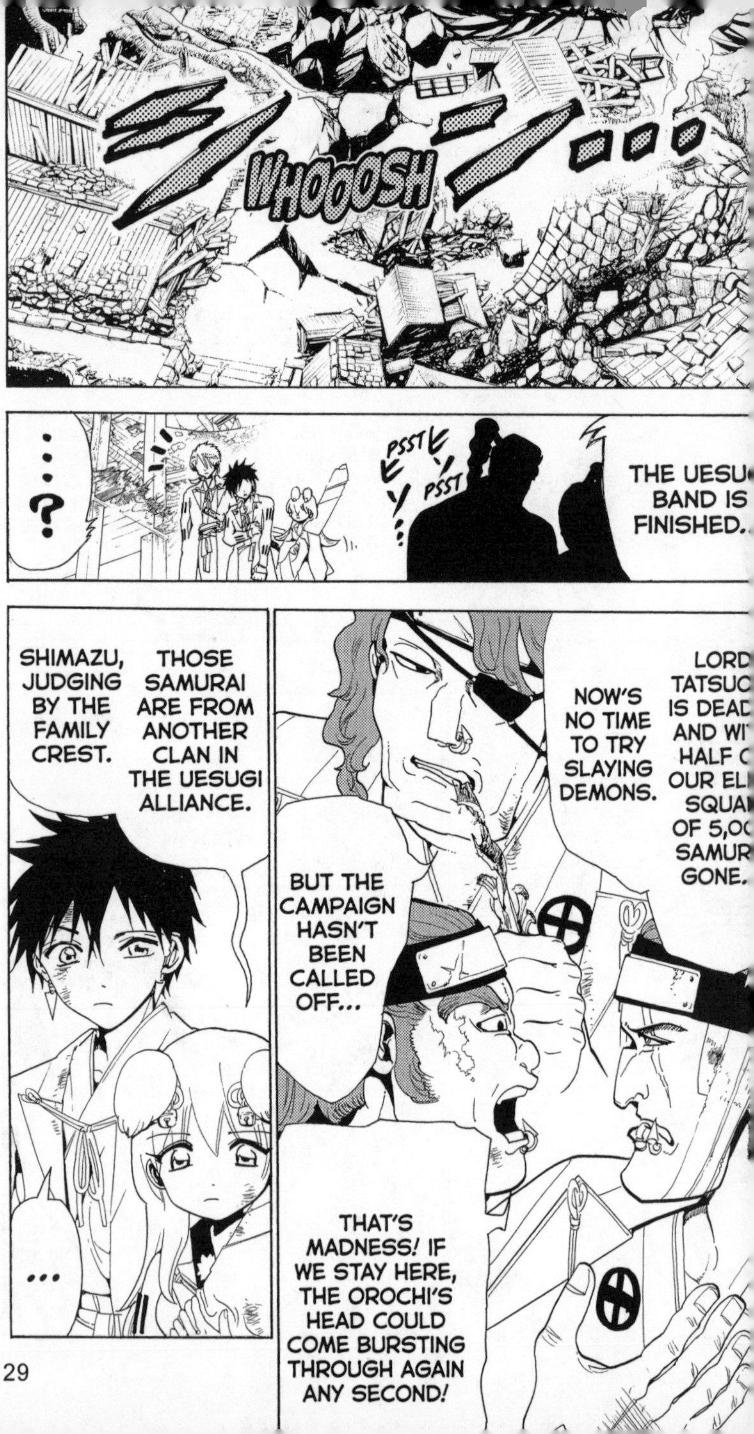
WHOOOSH
PSST PSST
THE UESU BAND IS FINISHED..
...?
LORD TATSU IS DEAD AND WI HALF OUR EL SQUA OF 5,0 SAMUR GONE.
NOW'S NO TIME TO TRY SLAYING DEMONS.
BUT THE CAMPAIGN HASN'T BEEN CALLED OFF...
THAT'S MADNESS! IF WE STAY HERE, THE OROCHI'S HEAD COULD COME BURSTING THROUGH AGAIN ANY SECOND!
THOSE SAMURAI ARE FROM ANOTHER CLAN IN THE UESUGI ALLIANCE.
SHIMAZU, JUDGING BY THE FAMILY CREST.
...

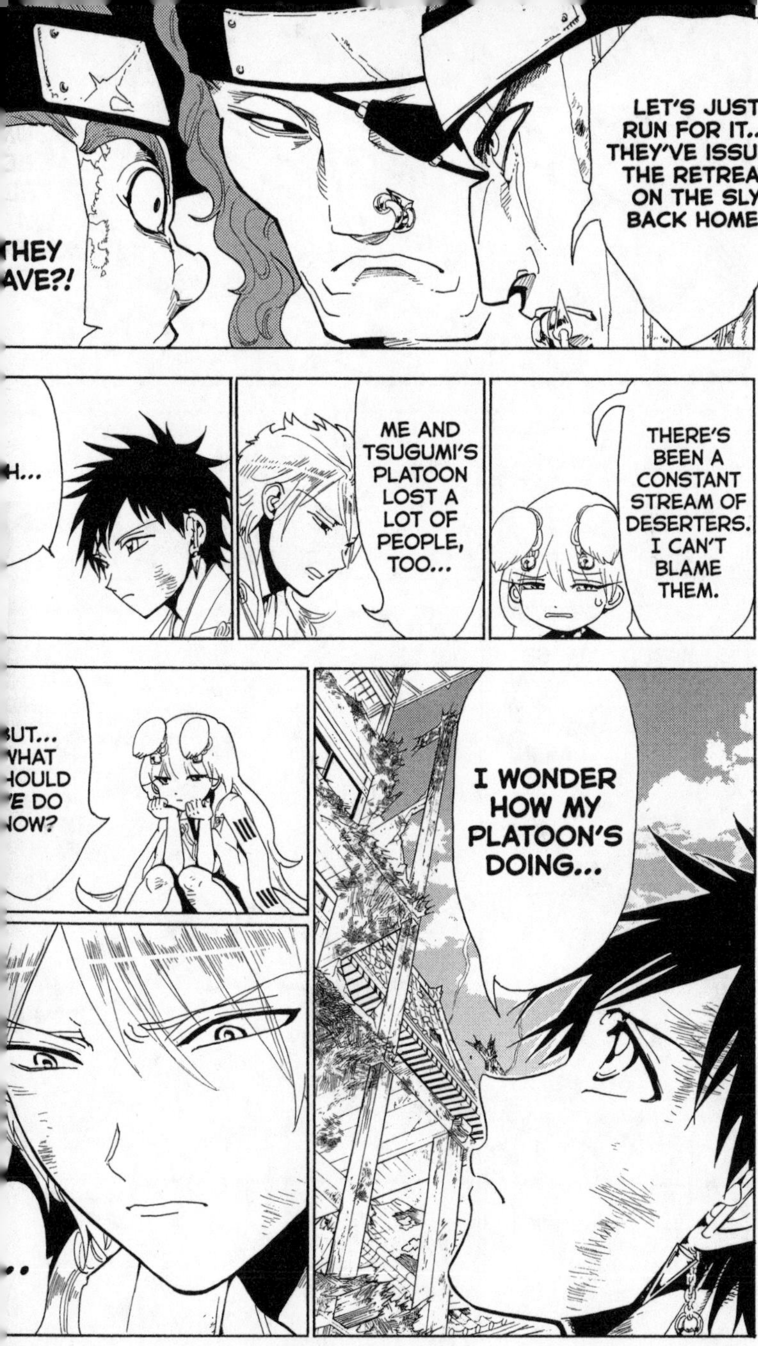
LET'S JUST RUN FOR IT... THEY'VE ISSUED THE RETREAT ON THE SLY BACK HOME.
THEY AVE?!
THERE'S BEEN A CONSTANT STREAM OF DESERTERS. I CAN'T BLAME THEM.
ME AND TSUGUMI'S PLATOON LOST A LOT OF PEOPLE, TOO...
H...
I WONDER HOW MY PLATOON'S DOING...
UT... WHAT HOULD E DO OW?
..

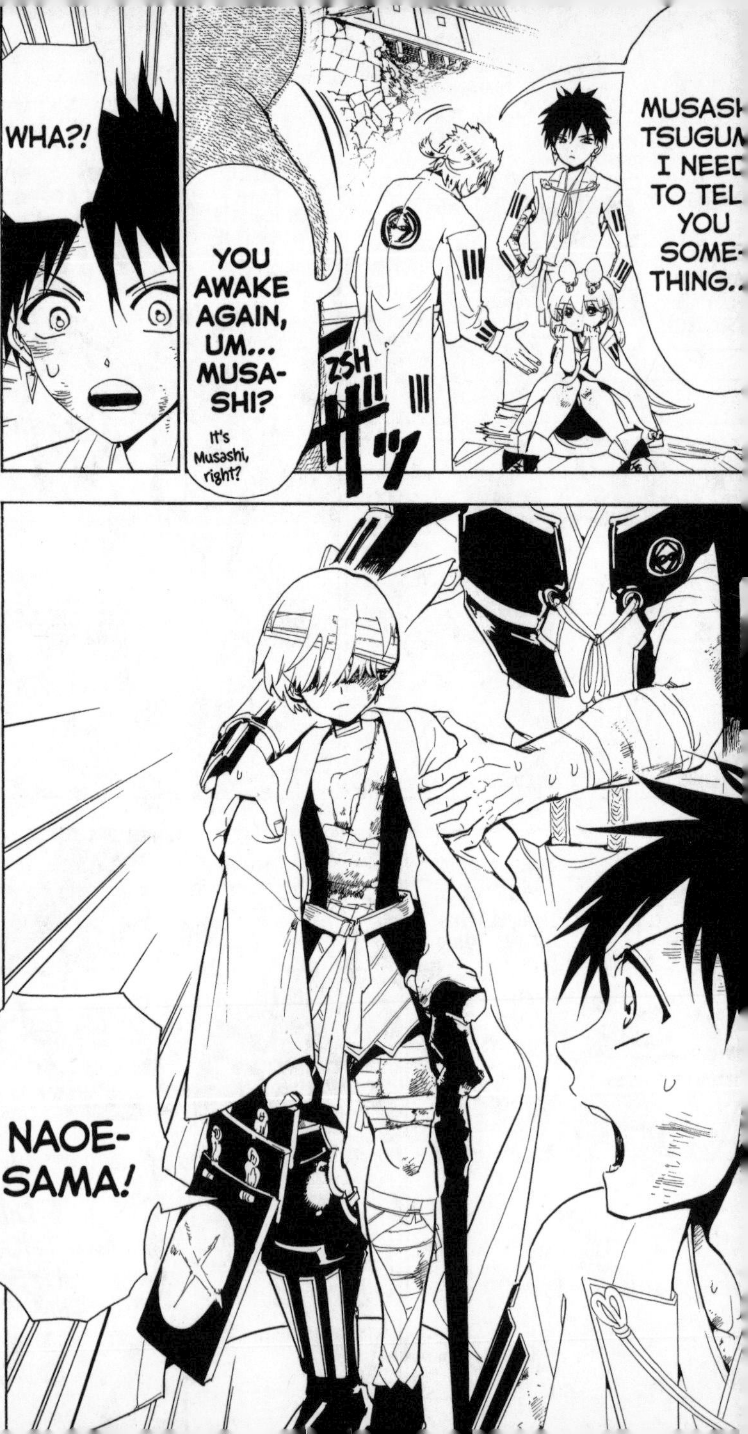
MUSASH TSUGUM I NEED TO TEL YOU SOME- THING..
YOU AWAKE AGAIN, UM... MUSA- SHI?
It's Musashi, right?
ZSH
WHA?!
NAOE- SAMA!

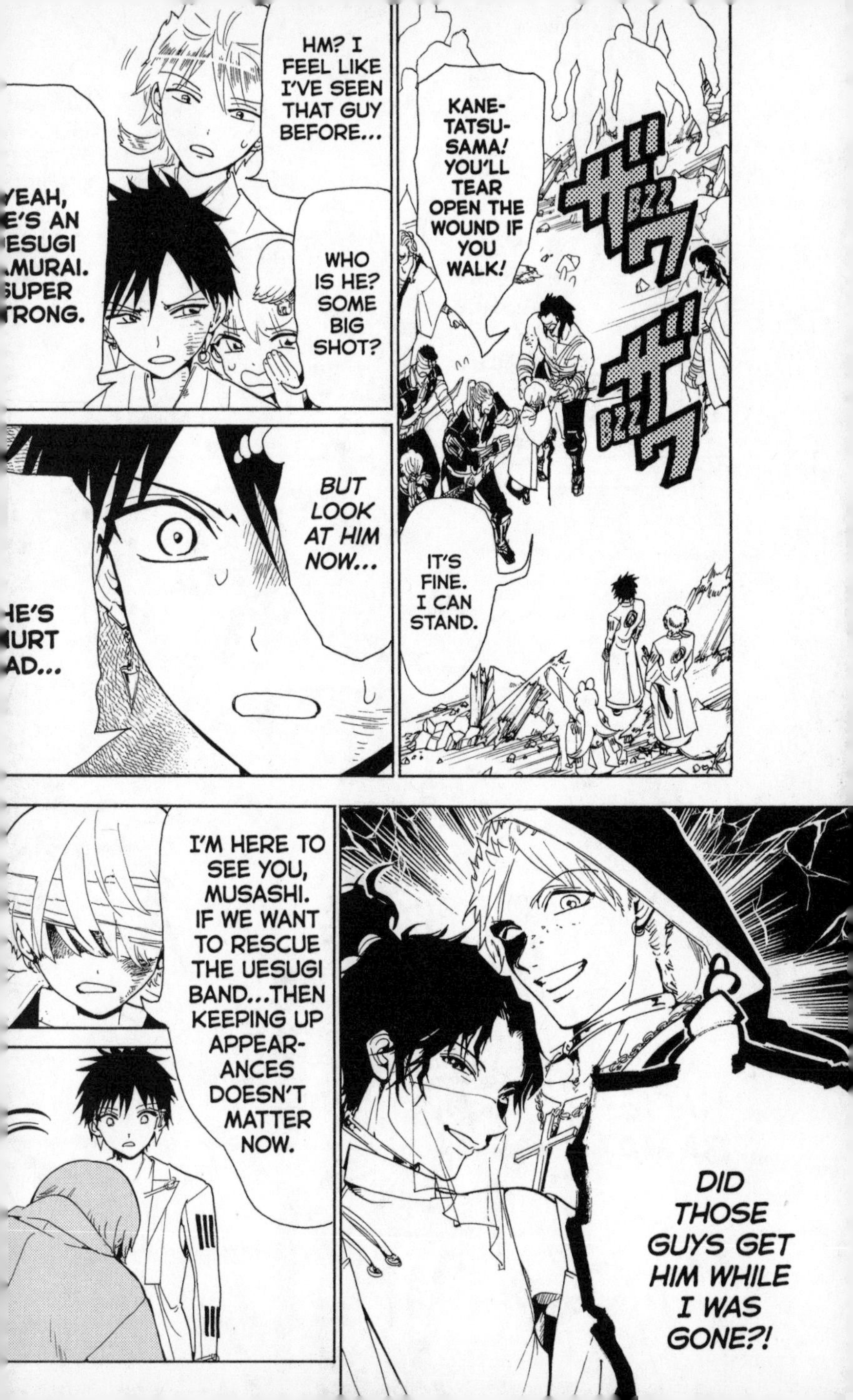
KANE-TATSU-SAMA! YOU'LL TEAR OPEN THE WOUND IF YOU WALK!
ザワ BZZ
ザワ BZZ
IT'S FINE. I CAN STAND.
HM? I FEEL LIKE I'VE SEEN THAT GUY BEFORE...
WHO IS HE? SOME BIG SHOT?
YEAH, E'S AN ESUGI AMURAI. SUPER TRONG.
BUT LOOK AT HIM NOW...
HE'S URT AD...
DID THOSE GUYS GET HIM WHILE I WAS GONE?!
I'M HERE TO SEE YOU, MUSASHI. IF WE WANT TO RESCUE THE UESUGI BAND...THEN KEEPING UP APPEARANCES DOESN'T MATTER NOW.

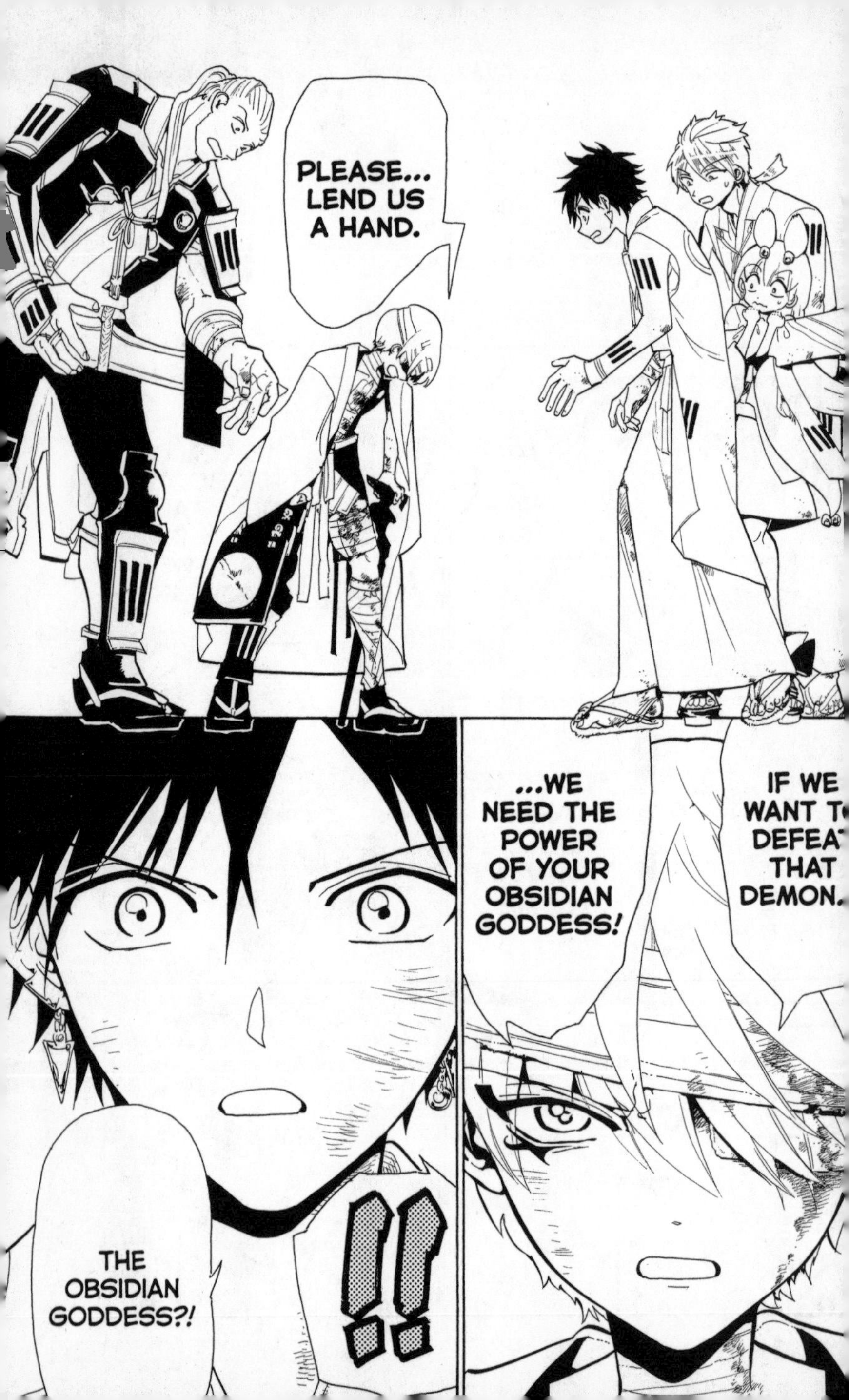
PLEASE... LEND US A HAND.
IF WE WANT T DEFEA THAT DEMON.
...WE NEED THE POWER OF YOUR OBSIDIAN GODDESS!
THE OBSIDIAN GODDESS?!
!!

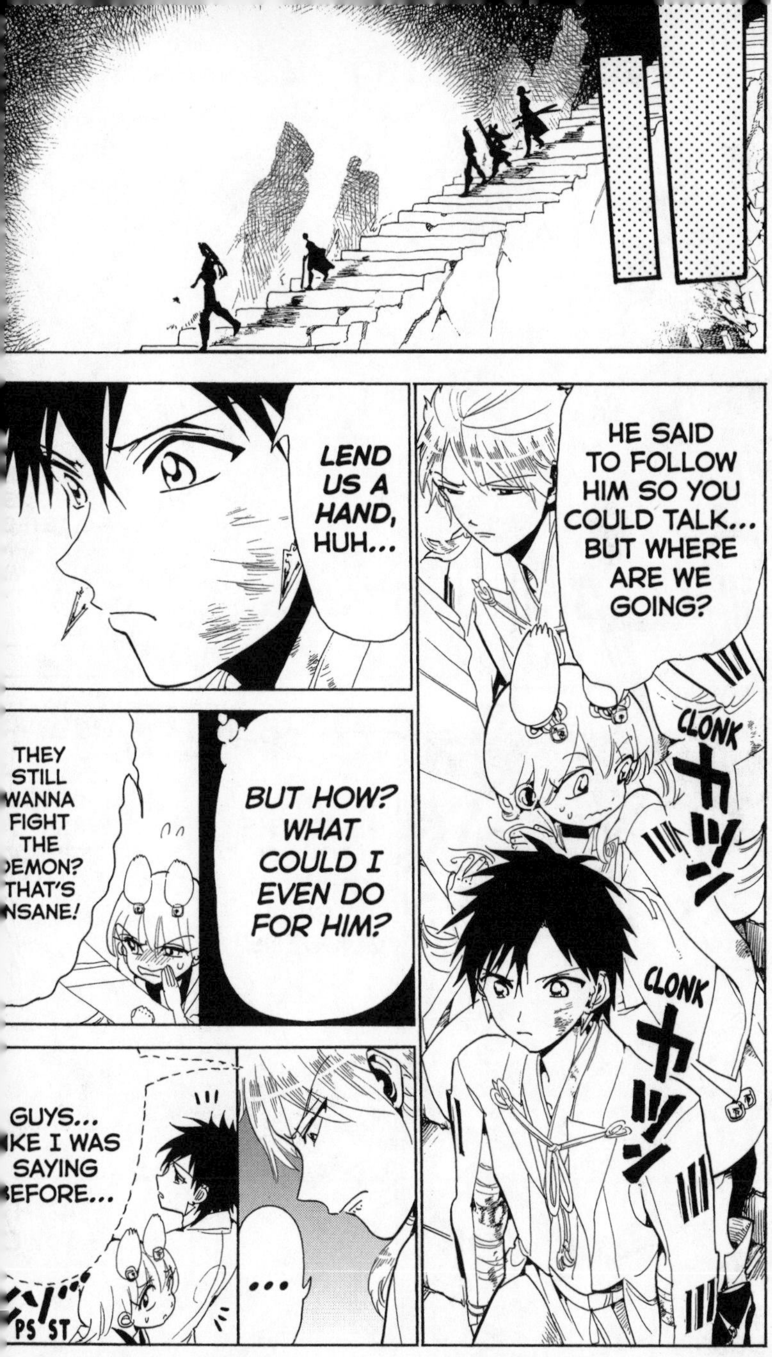
HE SAID TO FOLLOW HIM SO YOU COULD TALK... BUT WHERE ARE WE GOING?
CLONK
CLONK
LEND US A HAND, HUH...
BUT HOW? WHAT COULD I EVEN DO FOR HIM?
THEY STILL WANNA FIGHT THE EMON? THAT'S NSANE!
...
GUYS... KE I WAS SAYING EFORE...
PSST

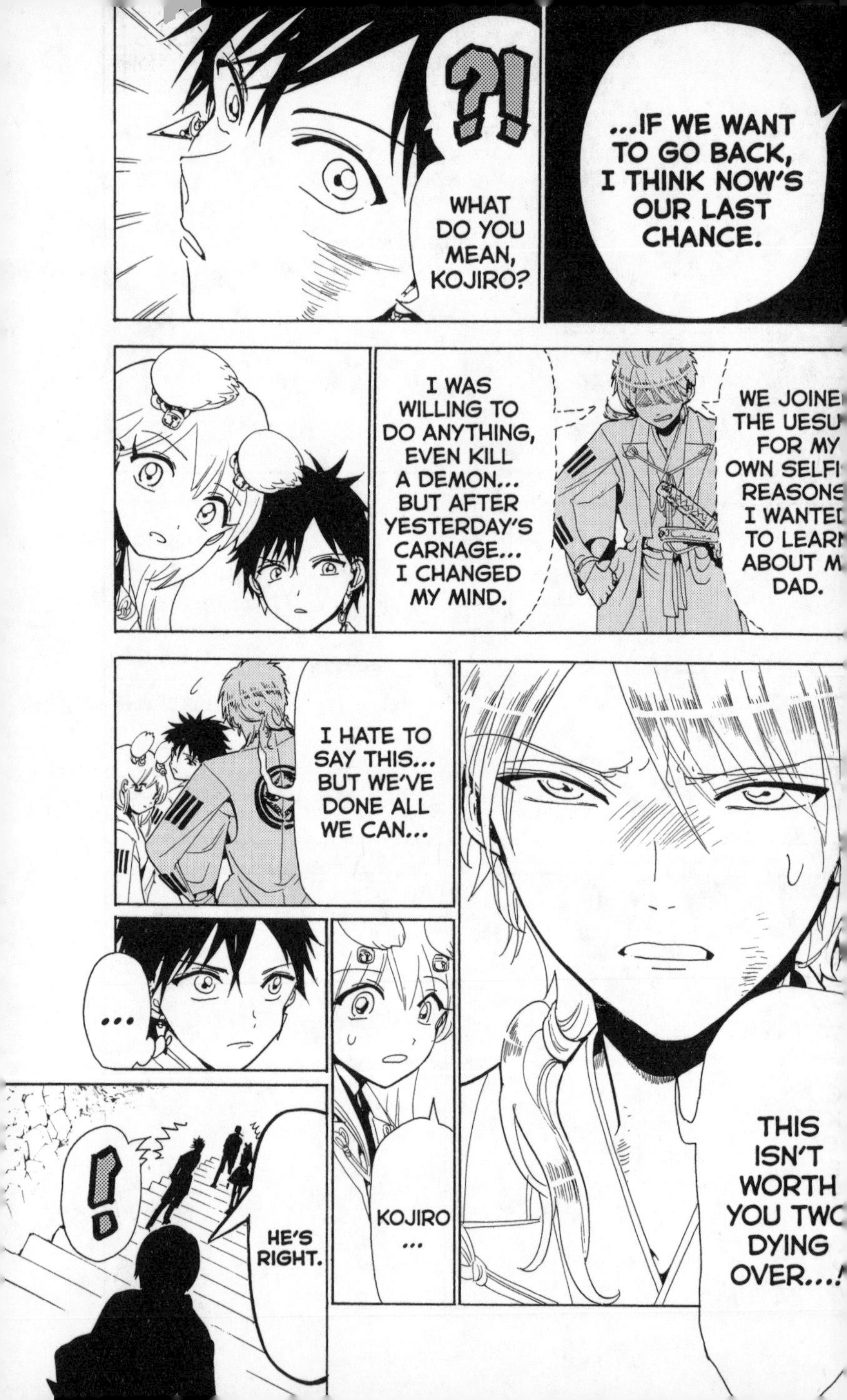
...IF WE WANT TO GO BACK, I THINK NOW'S OUR LAST CHANCE.
?!
WHAT DO YOU MEAN, KOJIRO?
WE JOINE THE UESU FOR MY OWN SELFI REASONS I WANTE TO LEAR ABOUT M DAD.
I WAS WILLING TO DO ANYTHING, EVEN KILL A DEMON... BUT AFTER YESTERDAY'S CARNAGE... I CHANGED MY MIND.
THIS ISN'T WORTH YOU TW DYING OVER...!
I HATE TO SAY THIS... BUT WE'VE DONE ALL WE CAN...
KOJIRO ...
...
!
HE'S RIGHT.

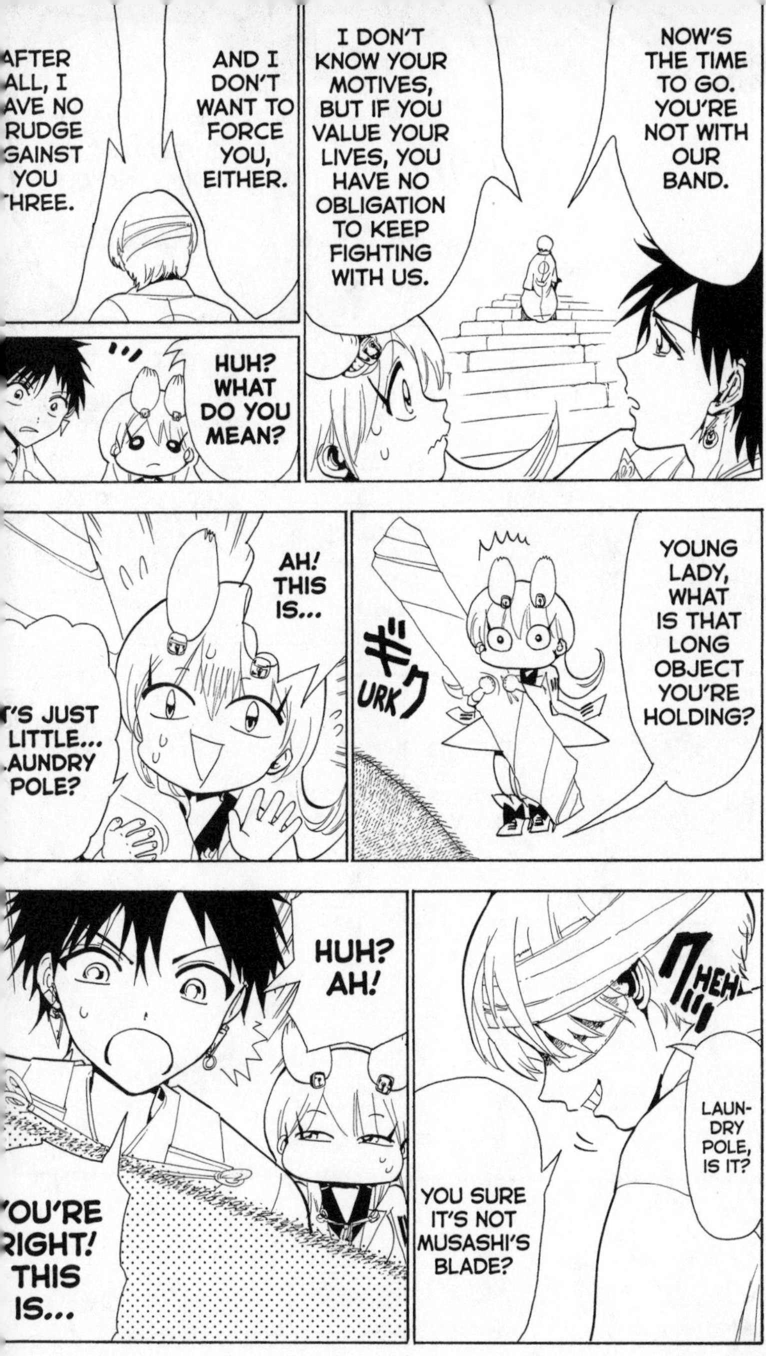
NOW'S THE TIME TO GO. YOU'RE NOT WITH OUR BAND.
I DON'T KNOW YOUR MOTIVES, BUT IF YOU VALUE YOUR LIVES, YOU HAVE NO OBLIGATION TO KEEP FIGHTING WITH US.
AND I DON'T WANT TO FORCE YOU, EITHER.
AFTER ALL, I AVE NO RUDGE GAINST YOU THREE.
HUH? WHAT DO YOU MEAN?
YOUNG LADY, WHAT IS THAT LONG OBJECT YOU'RE HOLDING?
ギク URK
AH! THIS IS...
'S JUST LITTLE... AUNDRY POLE?
HEH
LAUN-DRY POLE, IS IT?
YOU SURE IT'S NOT MUSASHI'S BLADE?
HUH? AH!
OU'RE RIGHT! THIS IS...

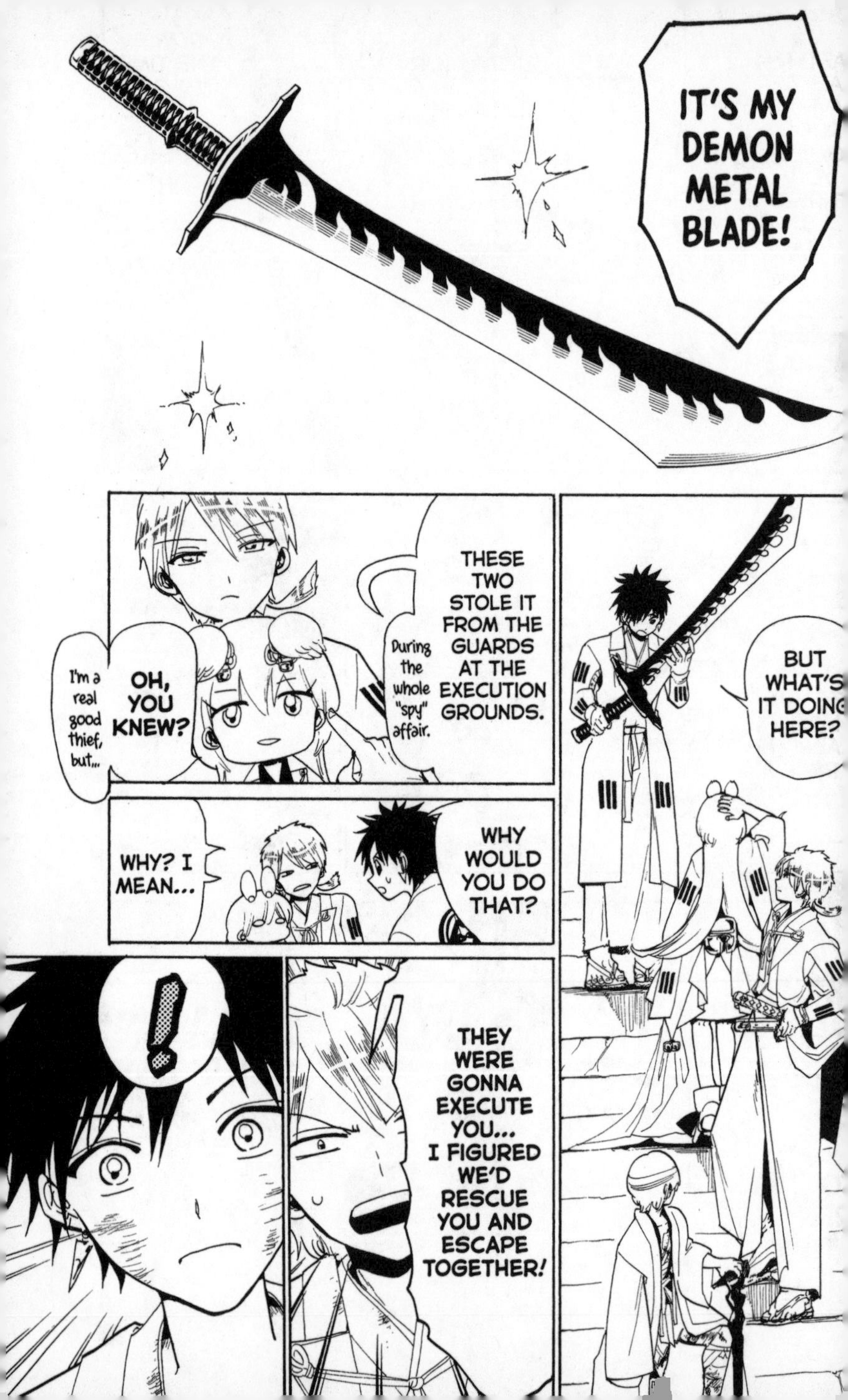
IT'S MY DEMON METAL BLADE!
BUT WHAT'S IT DOING HERE?
THESE TWO STOLE IT FROM THE GUARDS AT THE EXECUTION GROUNDS.
During the whole "spy" affair.
OH, YOU KNEW?
I'm a real good thief, but...
WHY WOULD YOU DO THAT?
WHY? I MEAN...
THEY WERE GONNA EXECUTE YOU... I FIGURED WE'D RESCUE YOU AND ESCAPE TOGETHER!
!

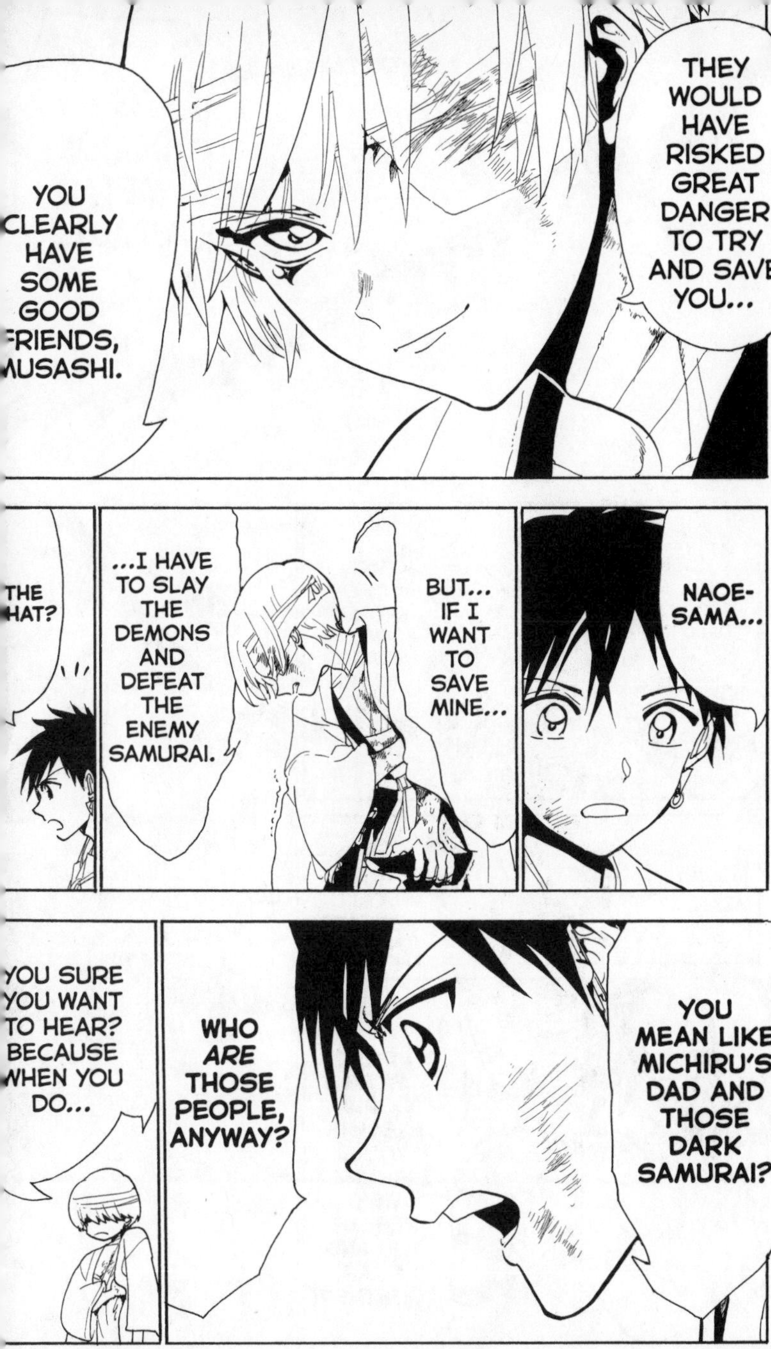
THEY WOULD HAVE RISKED GREAT DANGER TO TRY AND SAVE YOU...
YOU CLEARLY HAVE SOME GOOD FRIENDS, MUSASHI.
NAOE-SAMA...
BUT... IF I WANT TO SAVE MINE...
...I HAVE TO SLAY THE DEMONS AND DEFEAT THE ENEMY SAMURAI.
THE HAT?
YOU MEAN LIKE MICHIRU'S DAD AND THOSE DARK SAMURAI?
WHO *ARE* THOSE PEOPLE, ANYWAY?
YOU SURE YOU WANT TO HEAR? BECAUSE WHEN YOU DO...

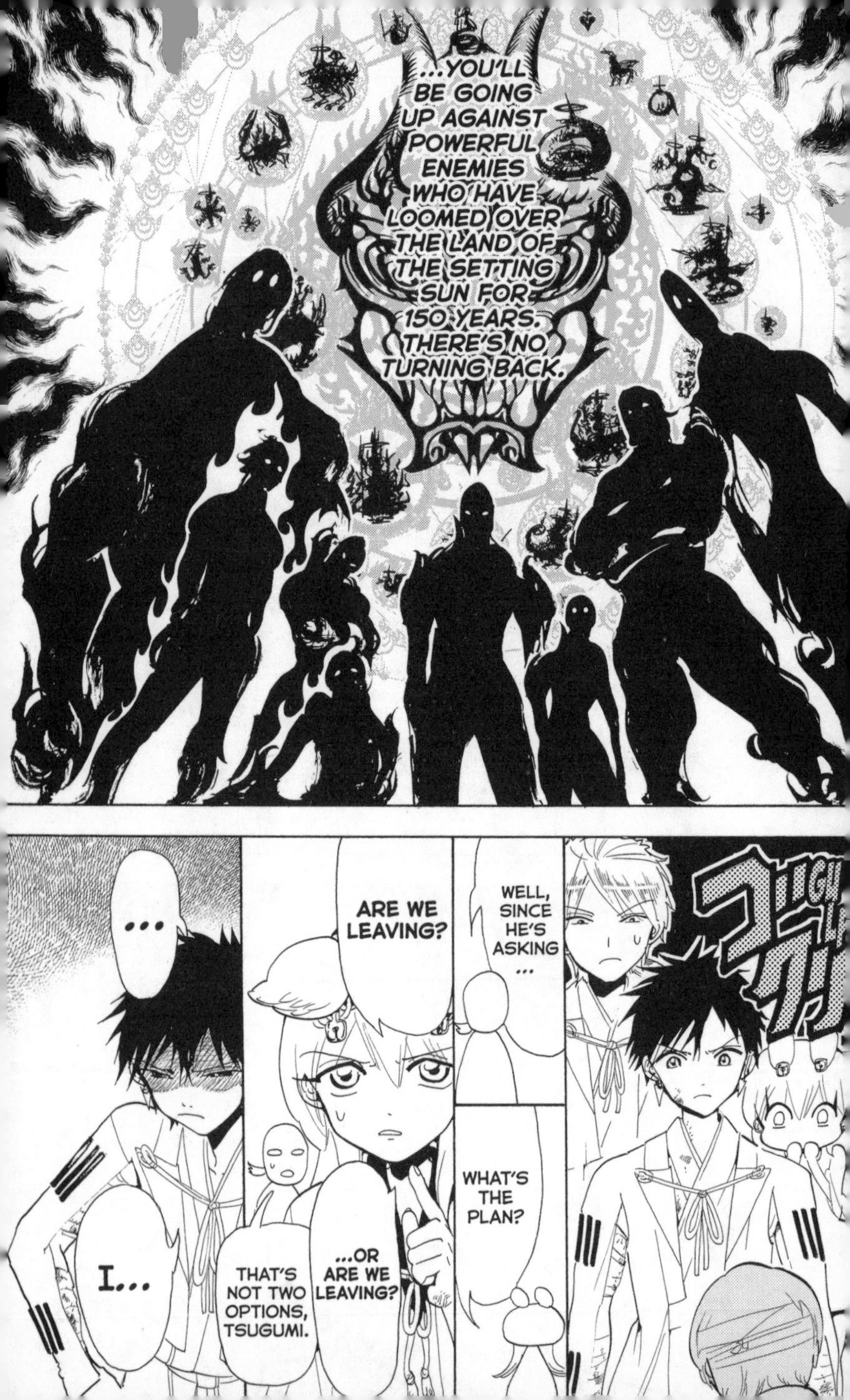
...YOU'LL BE GOING UP AGAINST POWERFUL ENEMIES WHO HAVE LOOMED OVER THE LAND OF THE SETTING SUN FOR 150 YEARS. THERE'S NO TURNING BACK.
WELL, SINCE HE'S ASKING...
WHAT'S THE PLAN?
ARE WE LEAVING?
...OR ARE WE LEAVING?
THAT'S NOT TWO OPTIONS, TSUGUMI.
...
I...

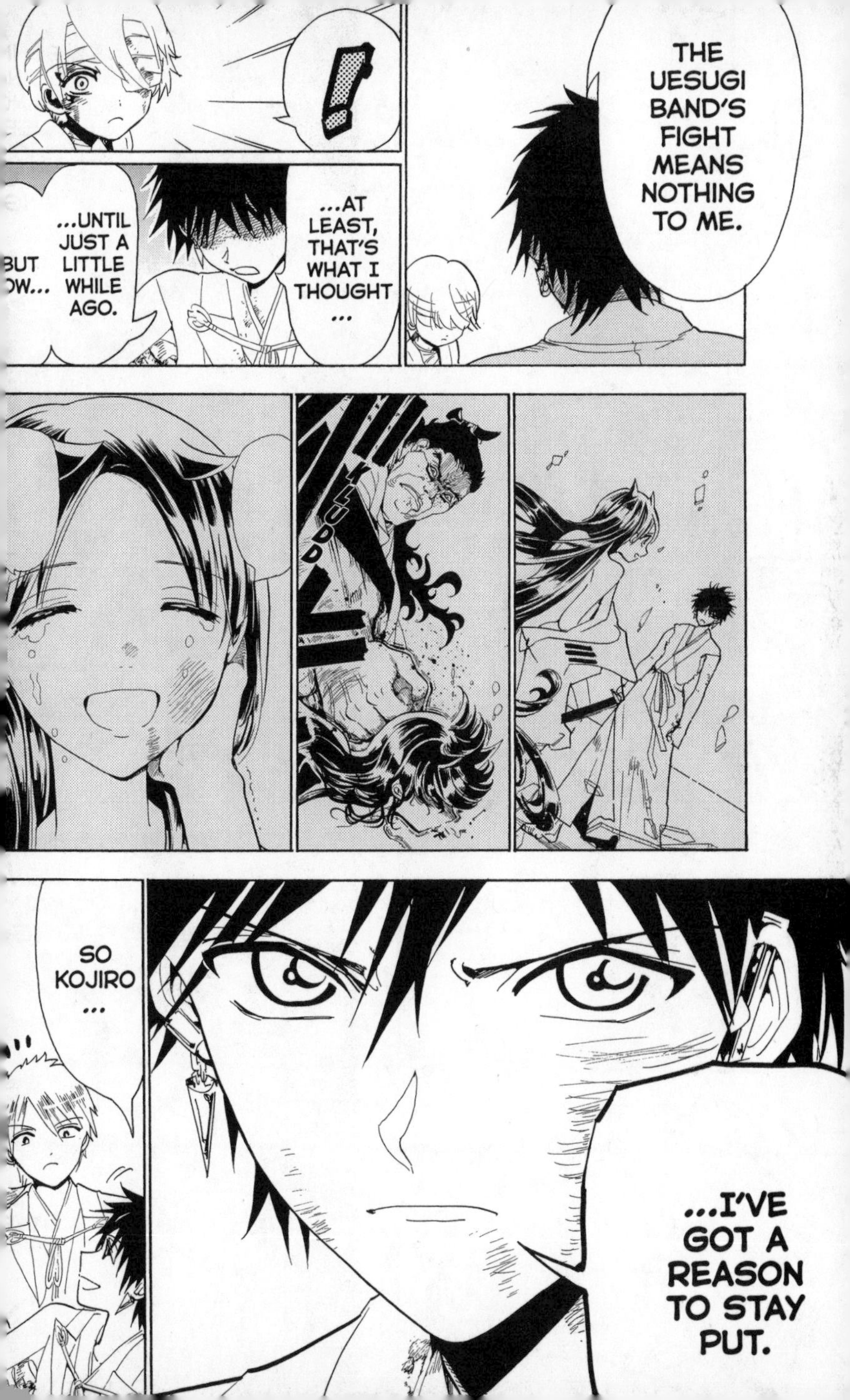
THE UESUGI BAND'S FIGHT MEANS NOTHING TO ME.
!
...AT LEAST, THAT'S WHAT I THOUGHT...
...UNTIL JUST A LITTLE WHILE AGO.
BUT OW...
KLUDD
...I'VE GOT A REASON TO STAY PUT.
SO KOJIRO...

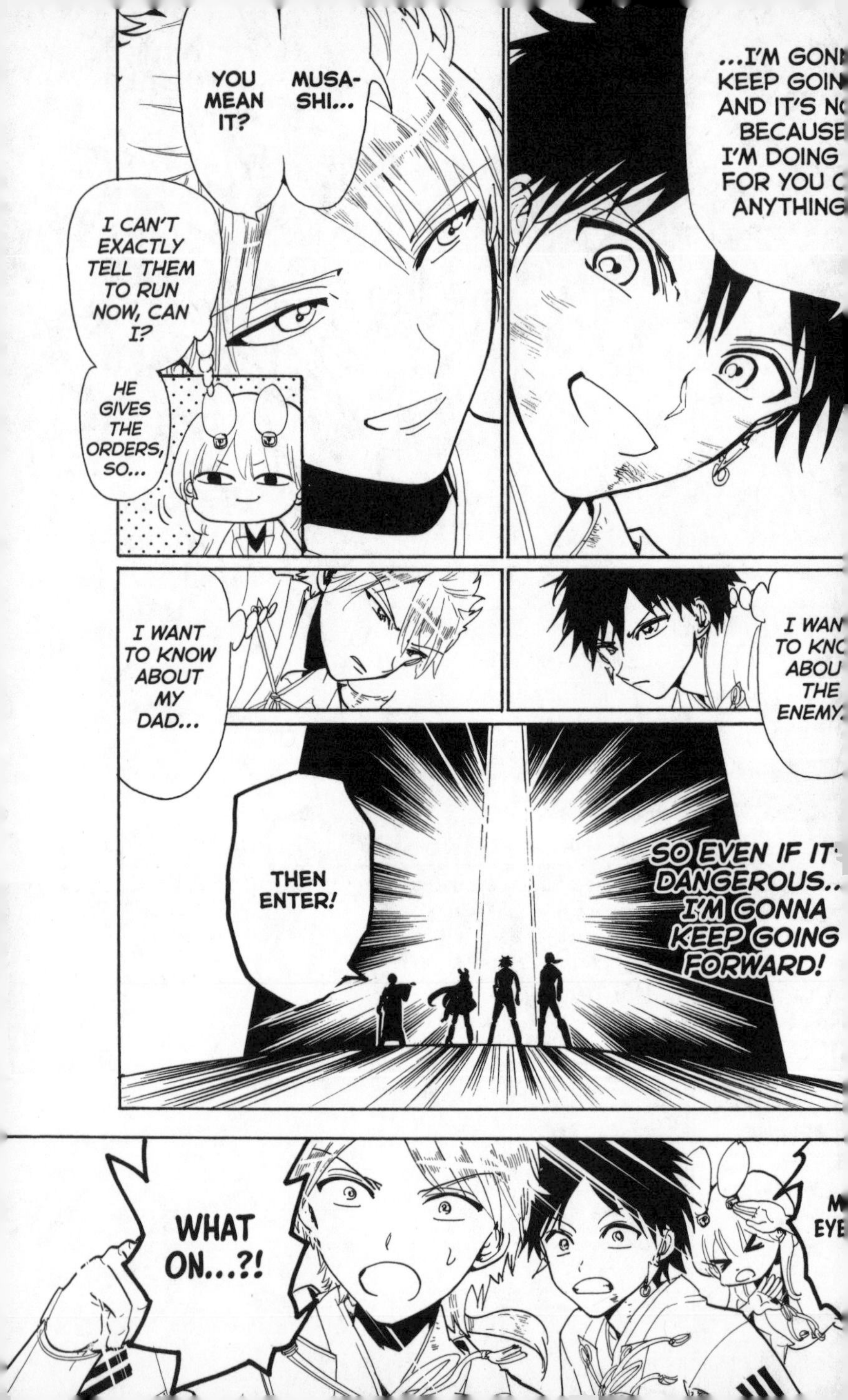
...I'M GON KEEP GOIN AND IT'S N BECAUSE I'M DOING FOR YOU ANYTHING
MUSA-SHI...
YOU MEAN IT?
I CAN'T EXACTLY TELL THEM TO RUN NOW, CAN I?
HE GIVES THE ORDERS, SO...
I WAN TO KNO ABOU THE ENEMY.
I WANT TO KNOW ABOUT MY DAD...
SO EVEN IF IT DANGEROUS.. I'M GONNA KEEP GOING FORWARD!
THEN ENTER!
M EYE
WHAT ON...?!

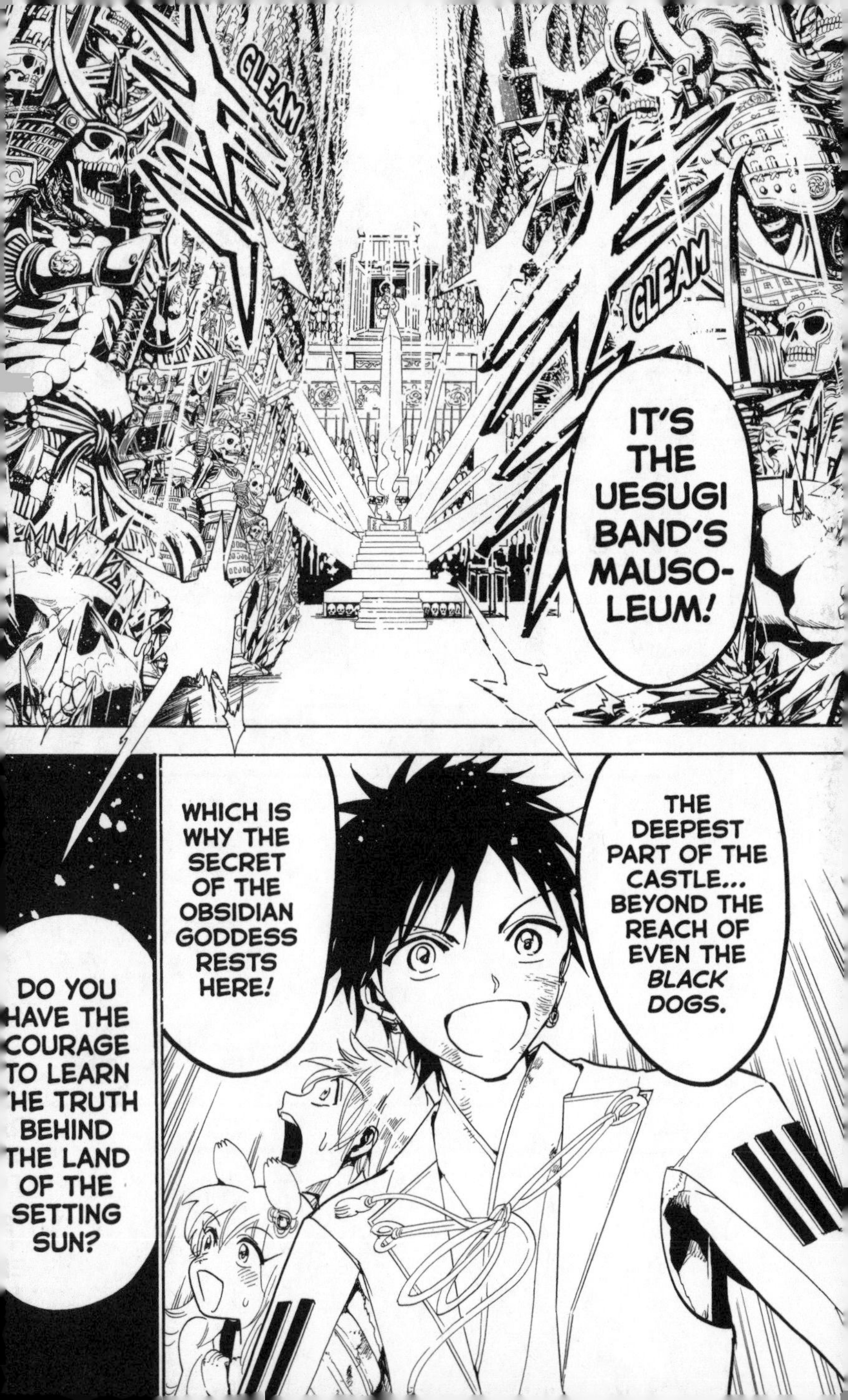
GLEAM
IT'S THE UESUGI BAND'S MAUSO-LEUM!
GLEAM
THE DEEPEST PART OF THE CASTLE... BEYOND THE REACH OF EVEN THE *BLACK DOGS*.
WHICH IS WHY THE SECRET OF THE OBSIDIAN GODDESS RESTS HERE!
DO YOU HAVE THE COURAGE TO LEARN HE TRUTH BEHIND THE LAND OF THE SETTING SUN?

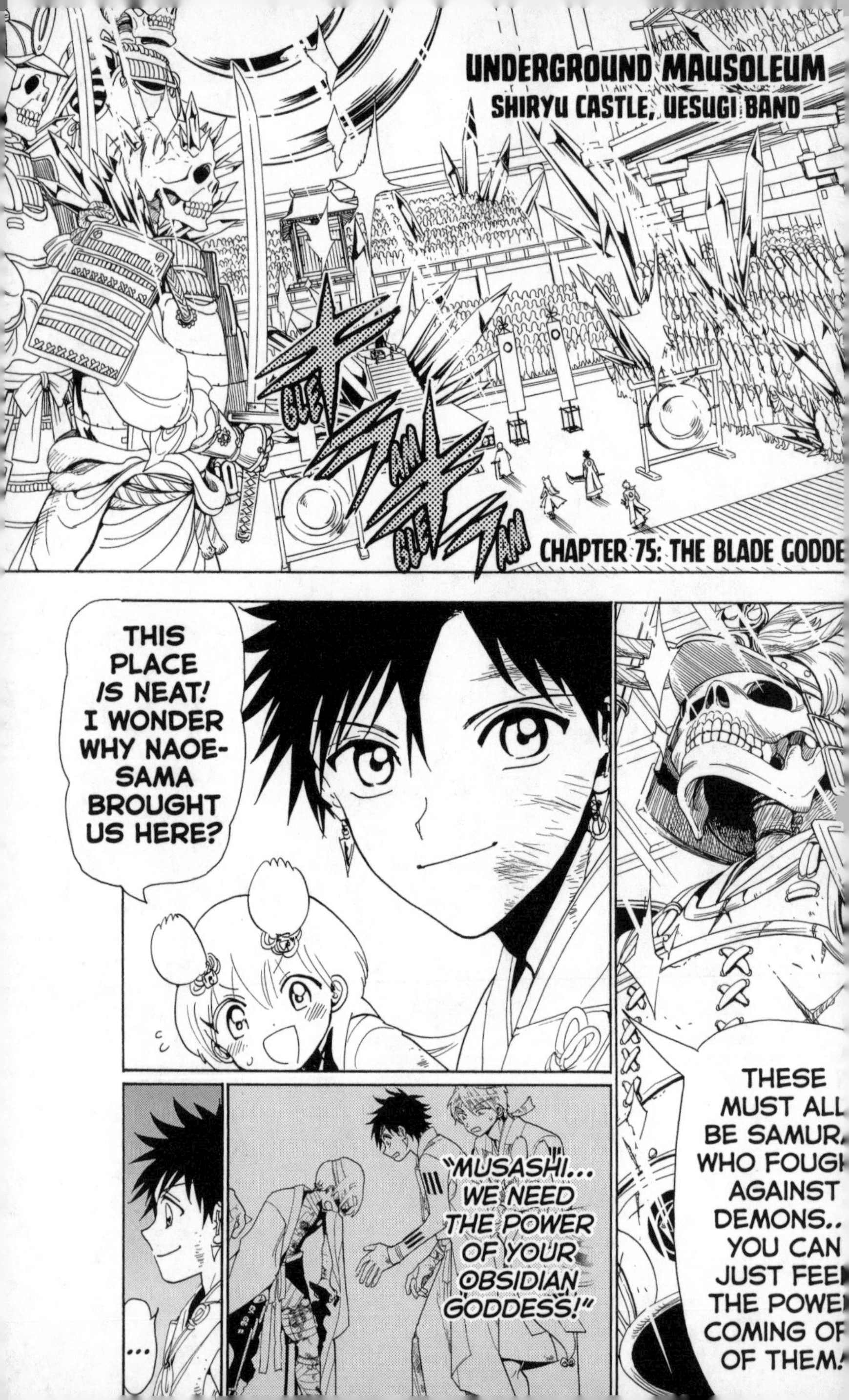
UNDERGROUND MAUSOLEUM
SHIRYU CASTLE, UESUGI BAND
CHAPTER 75: THE BLADE GODDE
THESE MUST ALL BE SAMUR WHO FOUGH AGAINST DEMONS.. YOU CAN JUST FEE THE POWE COMING OF OF THEM!
THIS PLACE IS NEAT! I WONDER WHY NAOE-SAMA BROUGHT US HERE?
"MUSASHI... WE NEED THE POWER OF YOUR OBSIDIAN GODDESS!"
...

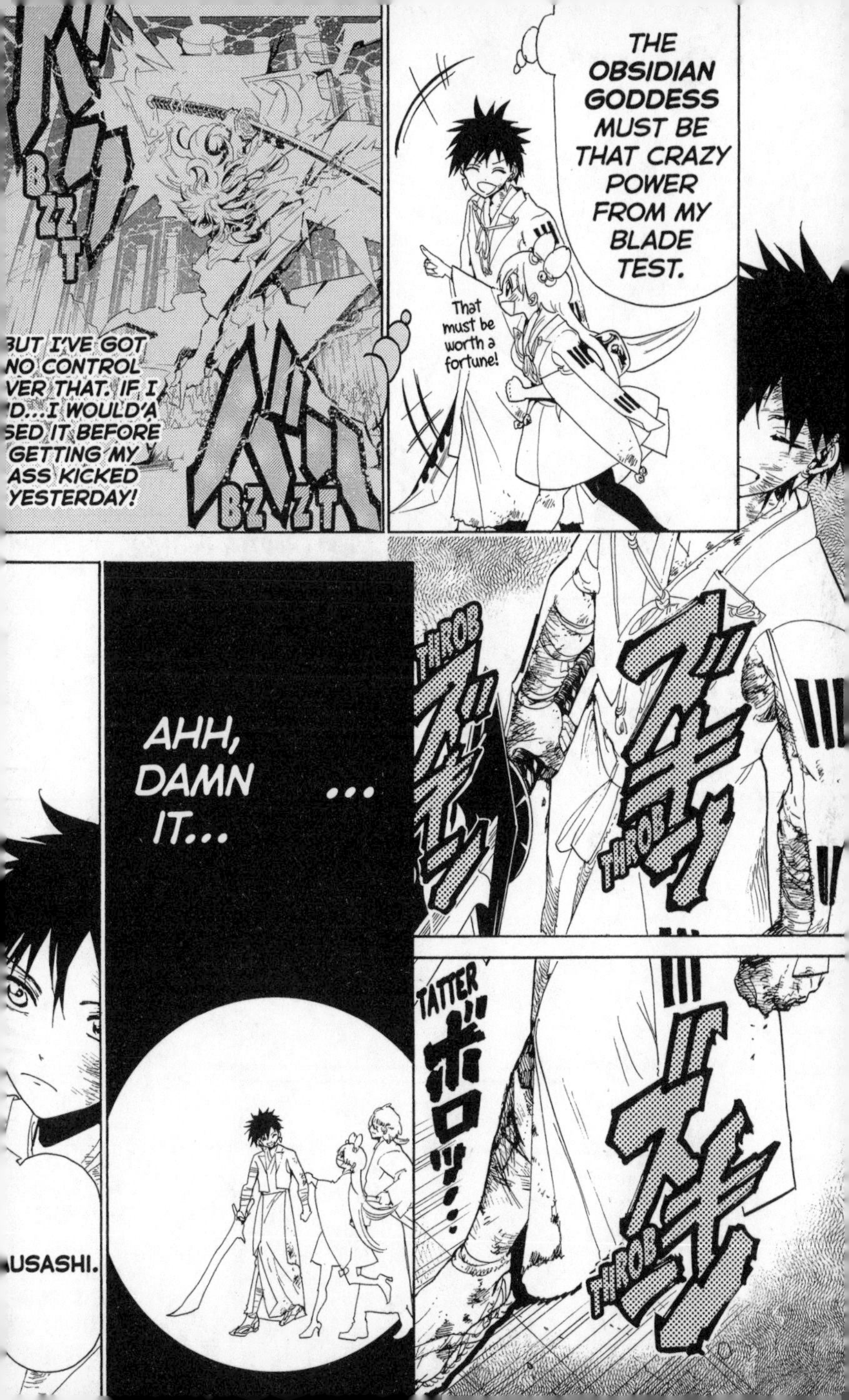

THE OBSIDIAN GODDESS MUST BE THAT CRAZY POWER FROM MY BLADE TEST.
That must be worth a fortune!
BZZT
BUT I'VE GOT NO CONTROL VER THAT. IF I D...I WOULD'A SED IT BEFORE GETTING MY ASS KICKED YESTERDAY!
BZZT
THROB
THROB
TATTER
THROB
AHH, DAMN IT...
...
USASHI.

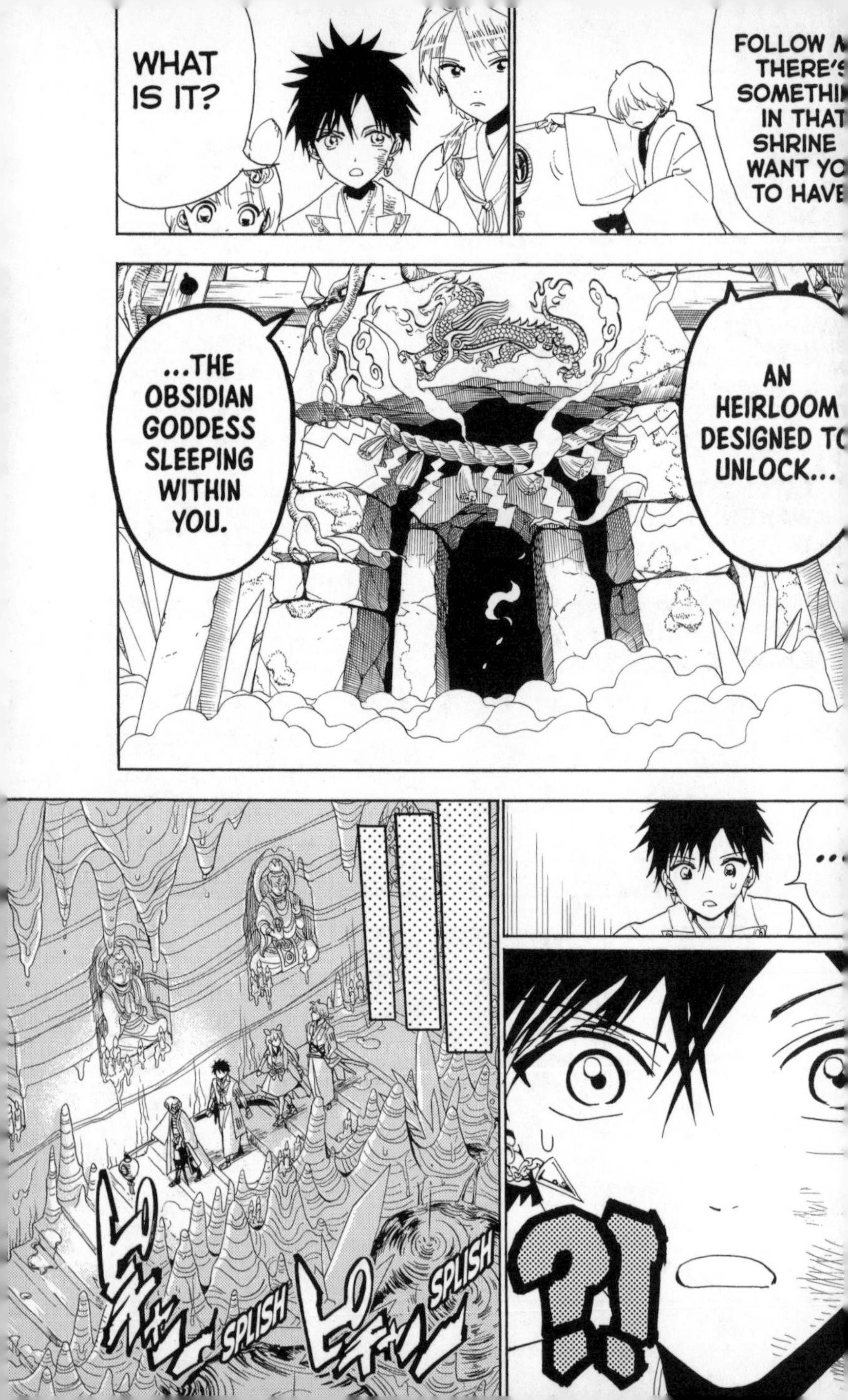
FOLLOW M
THERE'S
SOMETHI
IN THAT
SHRINE
WANT YO
TO HAVE
WHAT IS IT?
AN HEIRLOOM DESIGNED TO UNLOCK...
...THE OBSIDIAN GODDESS SLEEPING WITHIN YOU.
...
?!
SPLISH
SPLISH

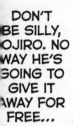
DON'T BE SILLY, KOJIRO. NO WAY HE'S GOING TO GIVE IT AWAY FOR FREE...

WHAT'S HE UP TO? WHY WOULD HE JUST *GIVE* MUSASHI SOMETHING THAT'LL MAKE HIM STRONGER?

I WANT TO AWAKEN THE POWER WITHIN MUSASHI SO HE CAN HELP US DEFEAT YAMATA NO OROCHI.

YOU'RE RIGHT.

...

WHY?

...WHY ARE THE UESUGI SO OBSESSED WITH SLAYING THAT DEMON? YOU'RE ALL BARELY KEEPING IT TOGETHER AS IT IS...

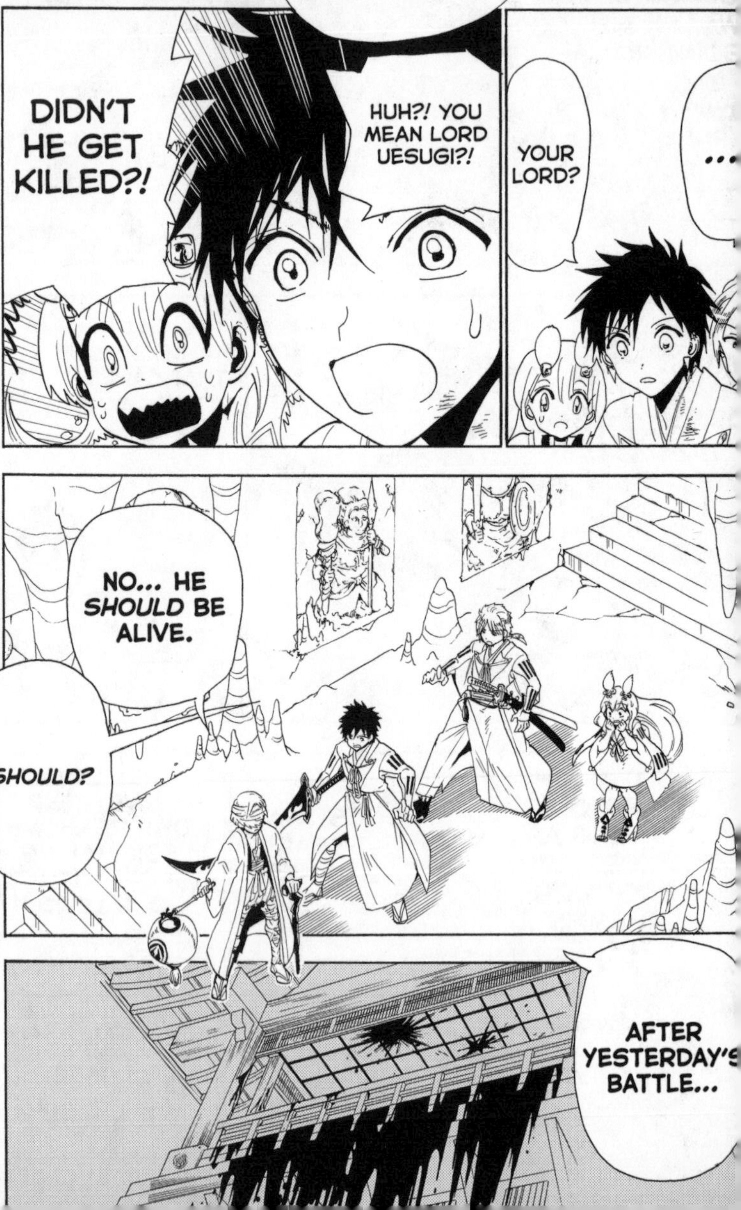
...
YOUR LORD?
HUH?! YOU MEAN LORD UESUGI?!
DIDN'T HE GET KILLED?!
NO... HE *SHOULD* BE ALIVE.
SHOULD?
AFTER YESTERDAY'S BATTLE...

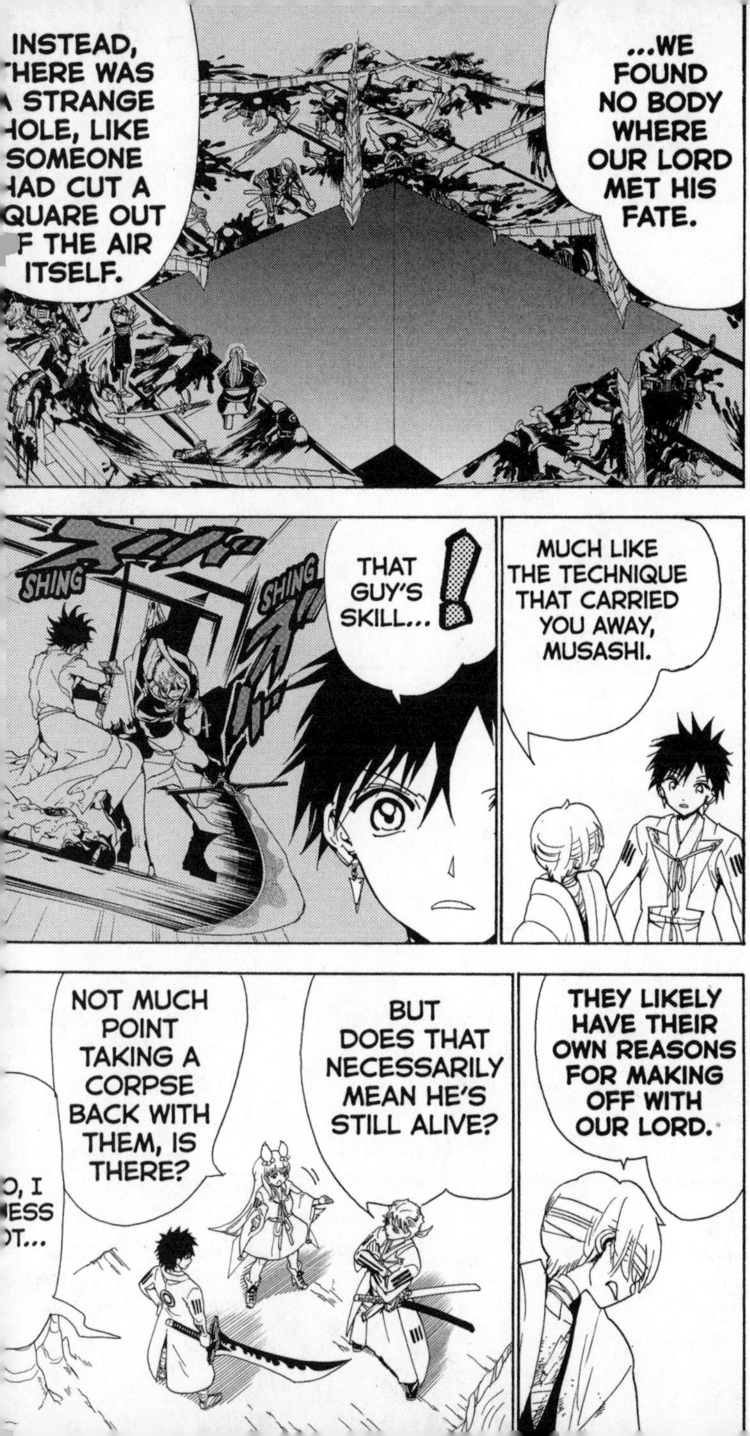
...WE FOUND NO BODY WHERE OUR LORD MET HIS FATE.
INSTEAD, HERE WAS STRANGE IOLE, LIKE SOMEONE IAD CUT A QUARE OUT F THE AIR ITSELF.
MUCH LIKE THE TECHNIQUE THAT CARRIED YOU AWAY, MUSASHI.
THAT GUY'S SKILL...!
SHING
SHING
THEY LIKELY HAVE THEIR OWN REASONS FOR MAKING OFF WITH OUR LORD.
BUT DOES THAT NECESSARILY MEAN HE'S STILL ALIVE?
NOT MUCH POINT TAKING A CORPSE BACK WITH THEM, IS THERE?
O, I ESS OT...

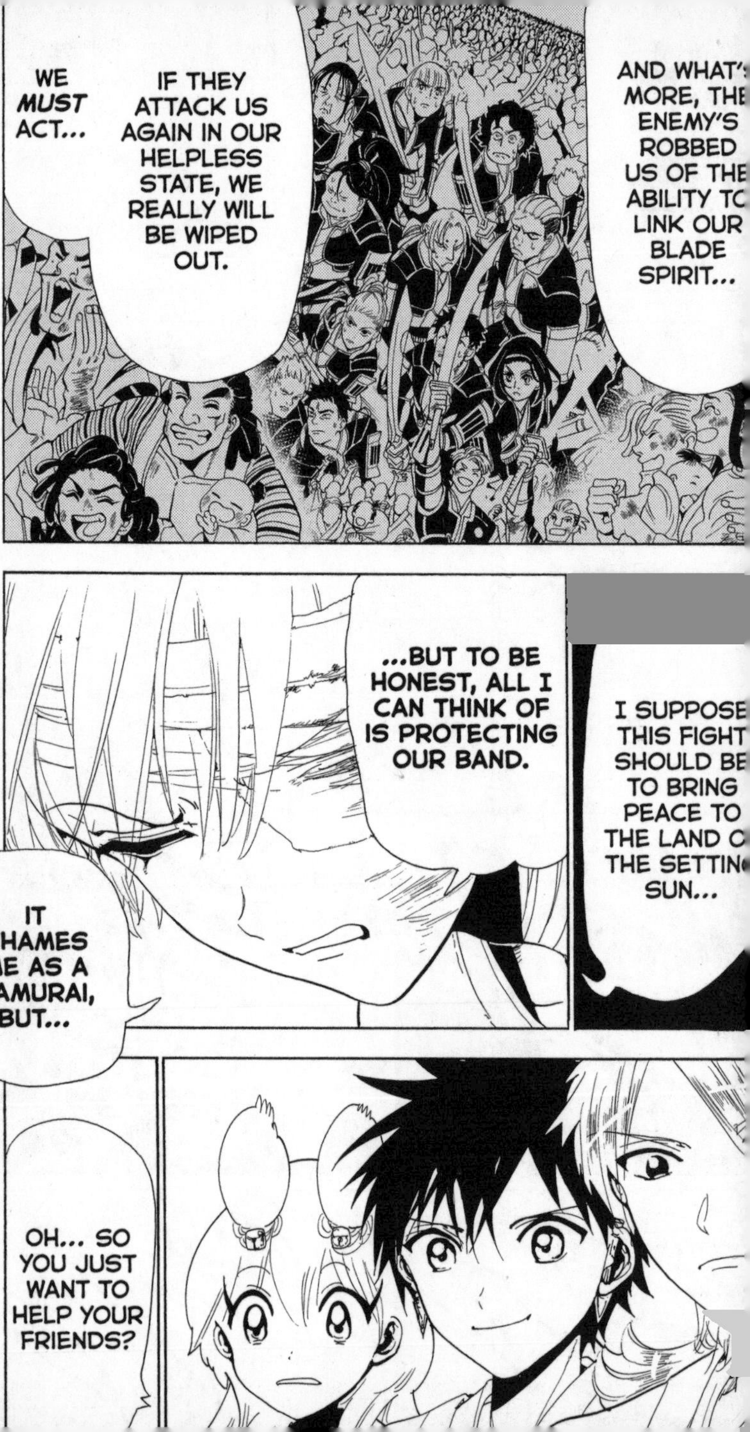
AND WHAT'S MORE, THE ENEMY'S ROBBED US OF THE ABILITY TO LINK OUR BLADE SPIRIT...
IF THEY ATTACK US AGAIN IN OUR HELPLESS STATE, WE REALLY WILL BE WIPED OUT.
WE *MUST* ACT...
I SUPPOSE THIS FIGHT SHOULD BE TO BRING PEACE TO THE LAND OF THE SETTING SUN...
...BUT TO BE HONEST, ALL I CAN THINK OF IS PROTECTING OUR BAND.
IT SHAMES ME AS A SAMURAI, BUT...
OH... SO YOU JUST WANT TO HELP YOUR FRIENDS?

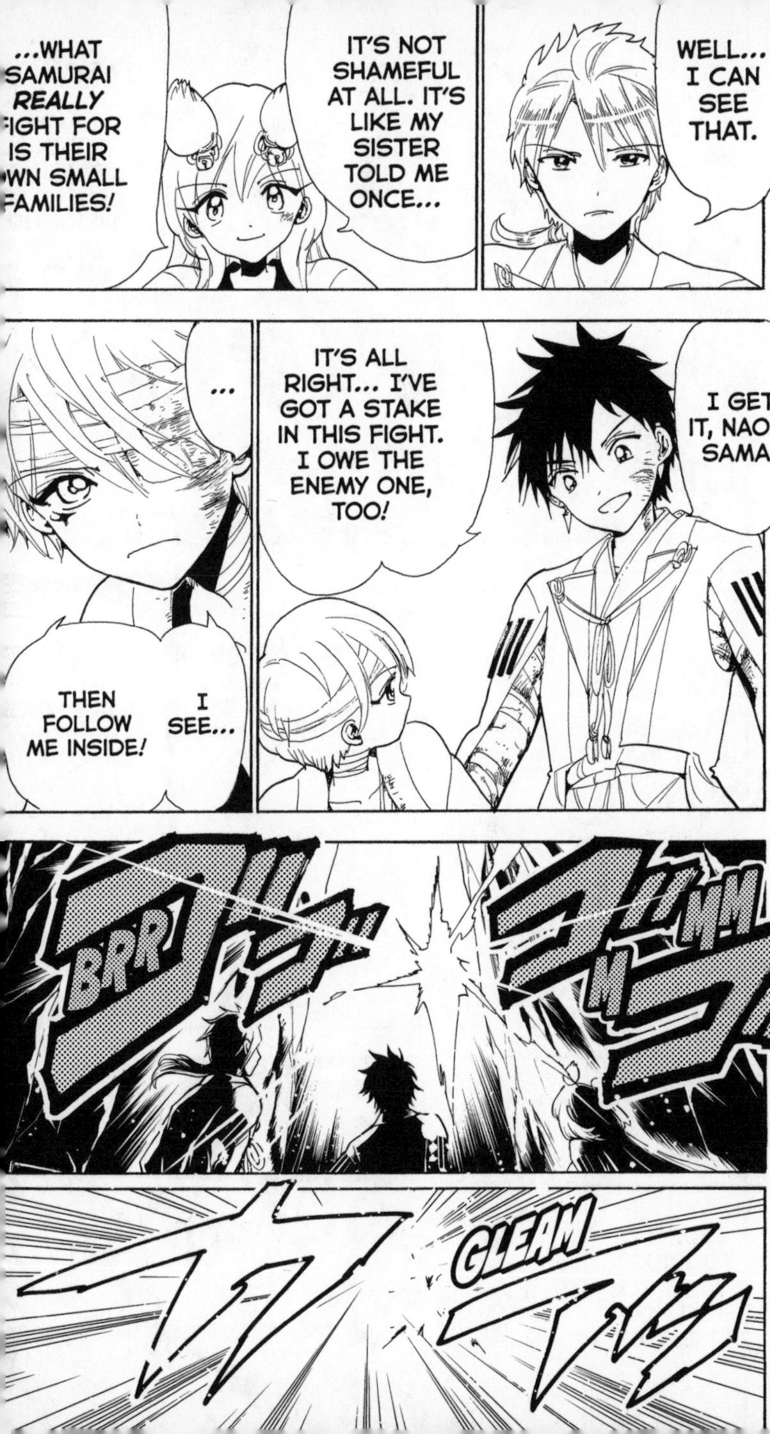
WELL... I CAN SEE THAT.
IT'S NOT SHAMEFUL AT ALL. IT'S LIKE MY SISTER TOLD ME ONCE...
...WHAT SAMURAI *REALLY* FIGHT FOR IS THEIR OWN SMALL FAMILIES!
I GET IT, NAOE-SAMA!
IT'S ALL RIGHT... I'VE GOT A STAKE IN THIS FIGHT. I OWE THE ENEMY ONE, TOO!
...
I SEE...
THEN FOLLOW ME INSIDE!
BRR
MMM
GLEAM

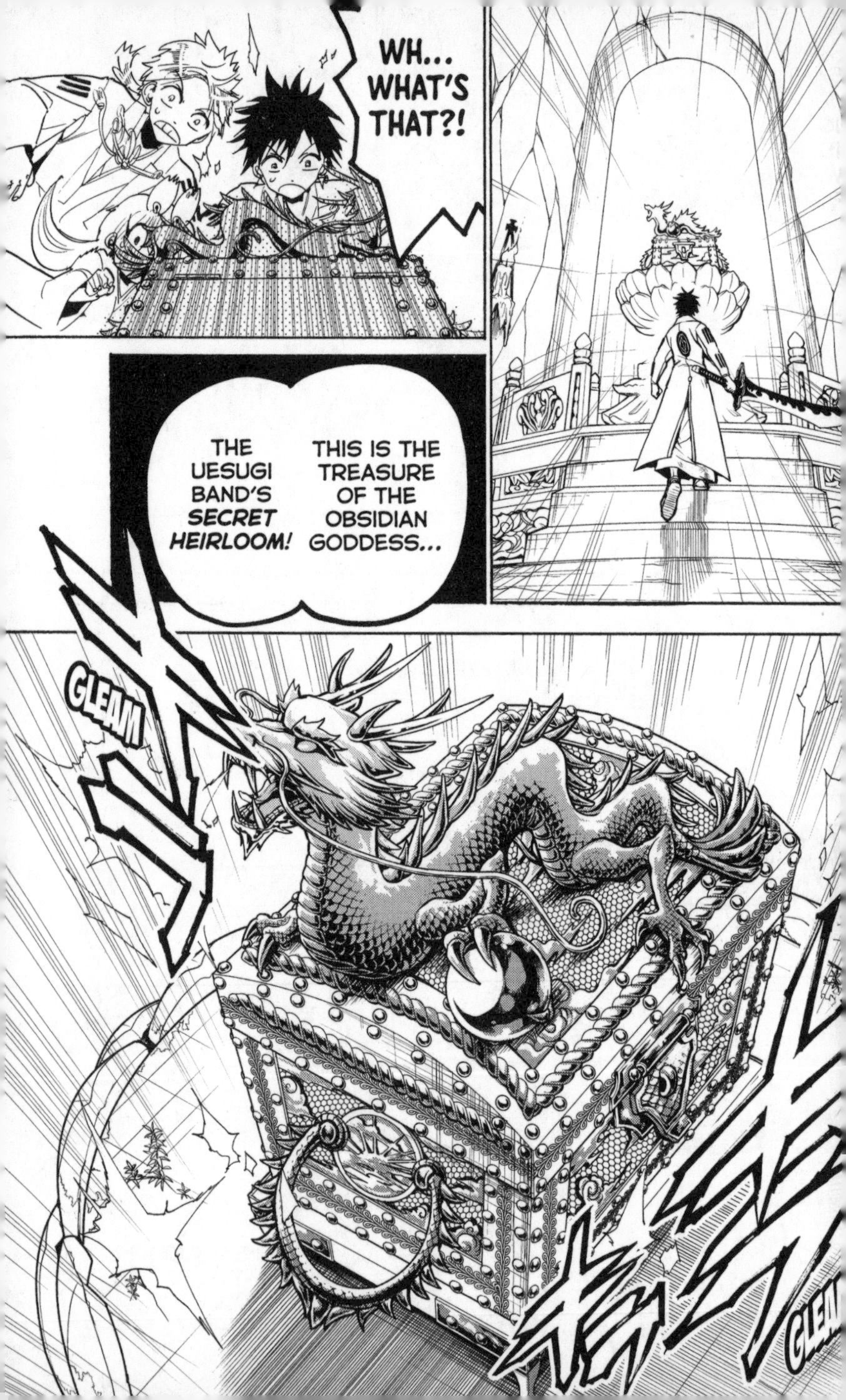
WH... WHAT'S THAT?!
THIS IS THE TREASURE OF THE OBSIDIAN GODDESS...
THE UESUGI BAND'S *SECRET HEIRLOOM!*
GLEAM

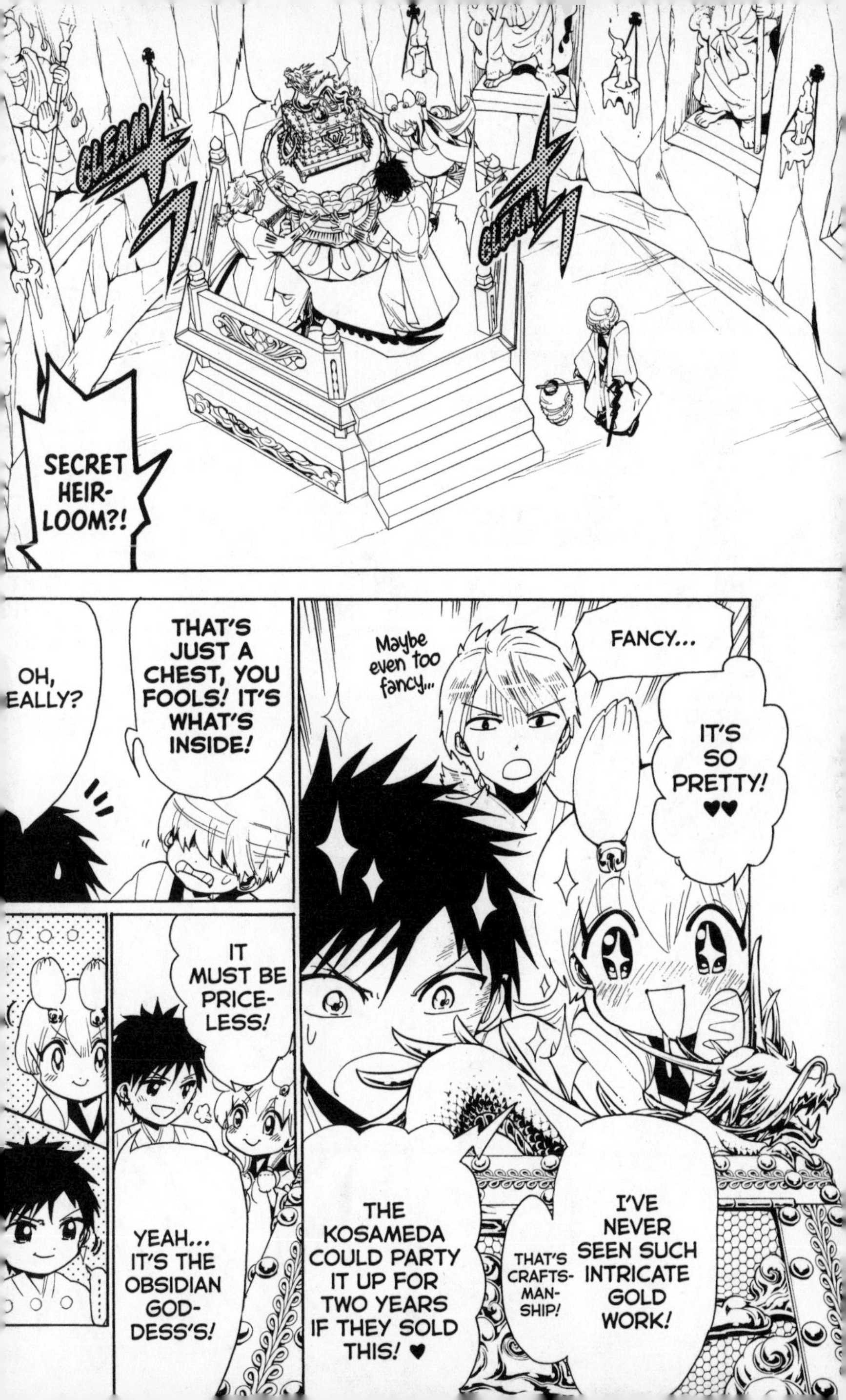

GLEAM
GLEAM
SECRET HEIR-LOOM?!
FANCY...
IT'S SO PRETTY! ♥♥
Maybe even too fancy...
I'VE NEVER SEEN SUCH INTRICATE GOLD WORK!
THAT'S CRAFTS-MAN-SHIP!
THE KOSAMEDA COULD PARTY IT UP FOR TWO YEARS IF THEY SOLD THIS! ♥
THAT'S JUST A CHEST, YOU FOOLS! IT'S WHAT'S INSIDE!
OH, EALLY?
IT MUST BE PRICE-LESS!
YEAH... IT'S THE OBSIDIAN GOD-DESS'S!

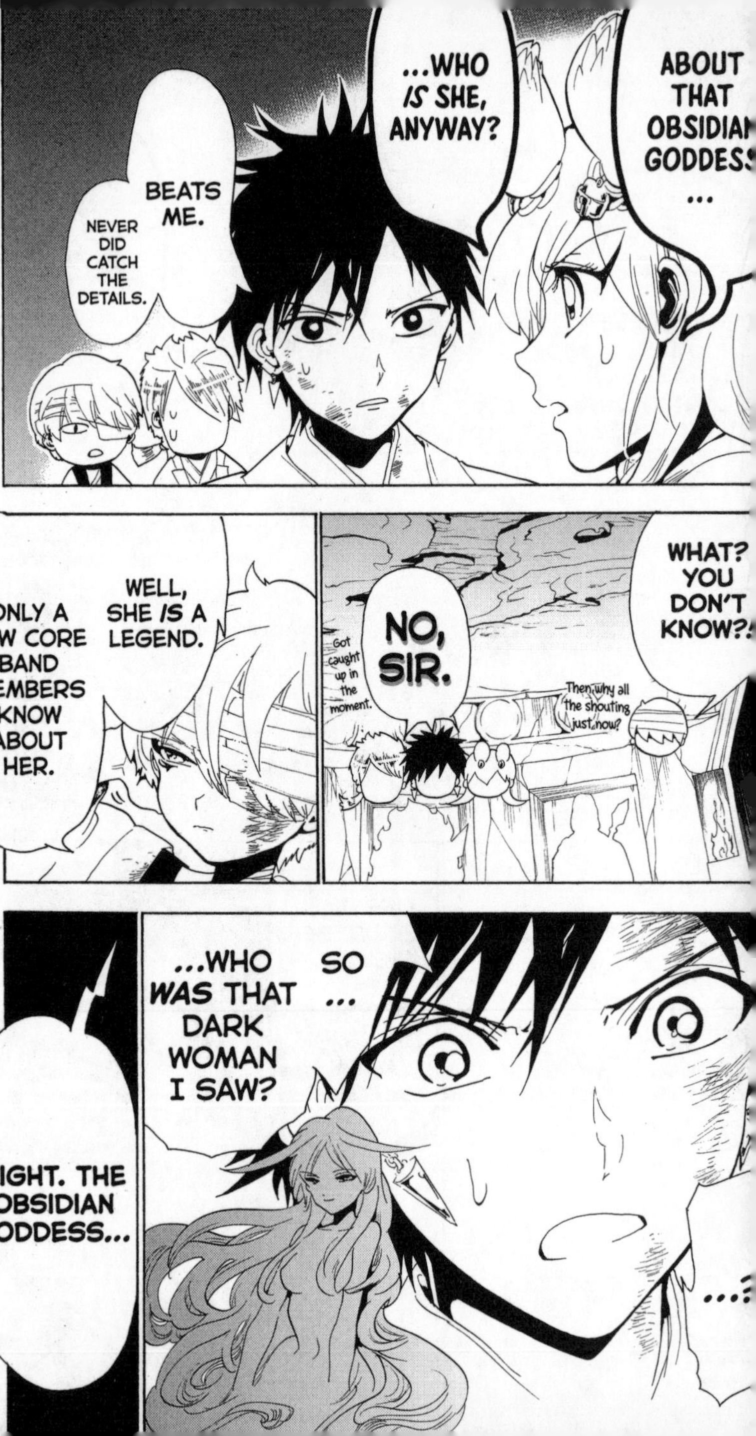
ABOUT THAT OBSIDIAN GODDESS...
...WHO IS SHE, ANYWAY?
BEATS ME.
NEVER DID CATCH THE DETAILS.
WHAT? YOU DON'T KNOW?!
NO, SIR.
Then why all the shouting just now?
Got caught up in the moment.
WELL, SHE IS A LEGEND.
ONLY A FEW CORE BAND MEMBERS KNOW ABOUT HER.
SO ...
...WHO WAS THAT DARK WOMAN I SAW?
RIGHT. THE OBSIDIAN GODDESS...

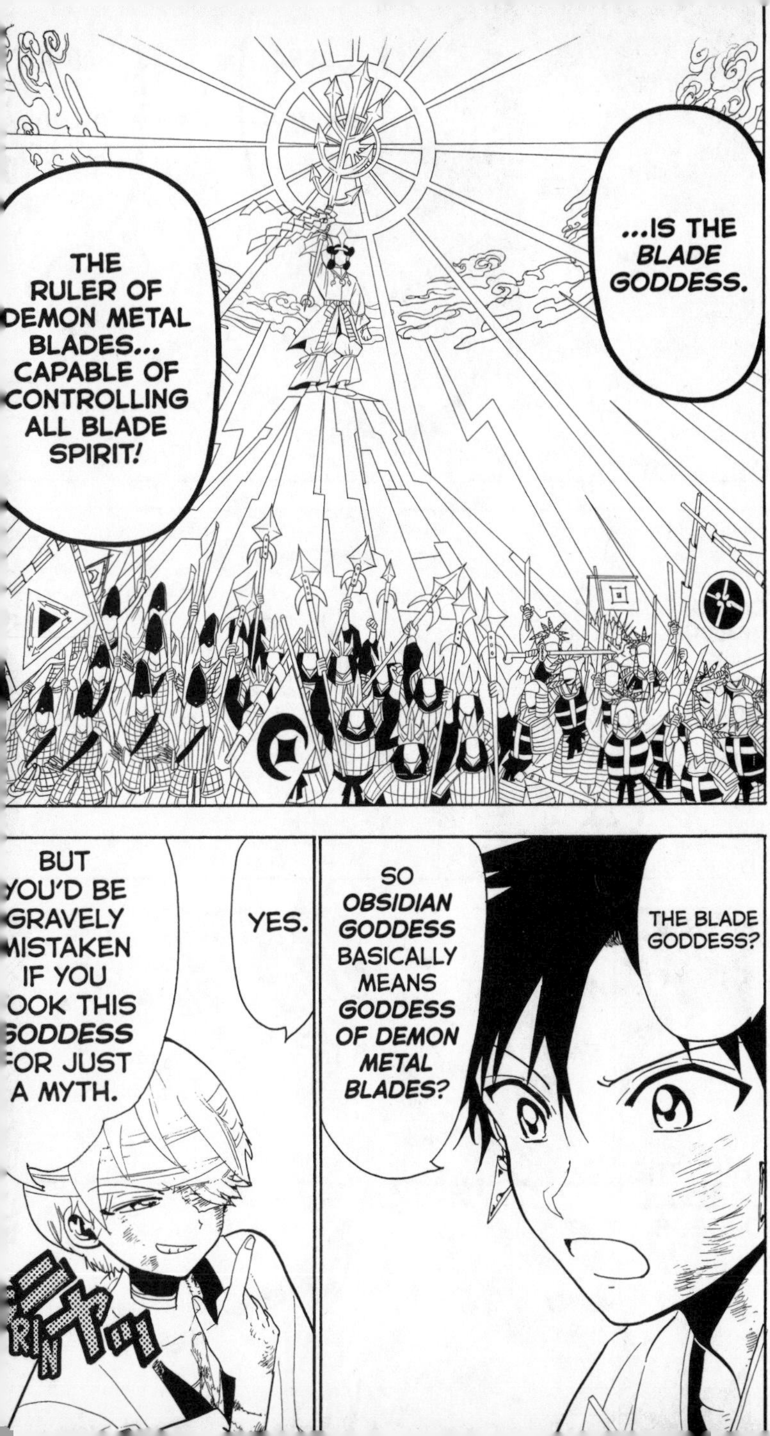
THE RULER OF DEMON METAL BLADES... CAPABLE OF CONTROLLING ALL BLADE SPIRIT!
...IS THE BLADE GODDESS.
THE BLADE GODDESS?
SO OBSIDIAN GODDESS BASICALLY MEANS GODDESS OF DEMON METAL BLADES?
YES.
BUT YOU'D BE GRAVELY MISTAKEN IF YOU TOOK THIS GODDESS FOR JUST A MYTH.
ニヤッ

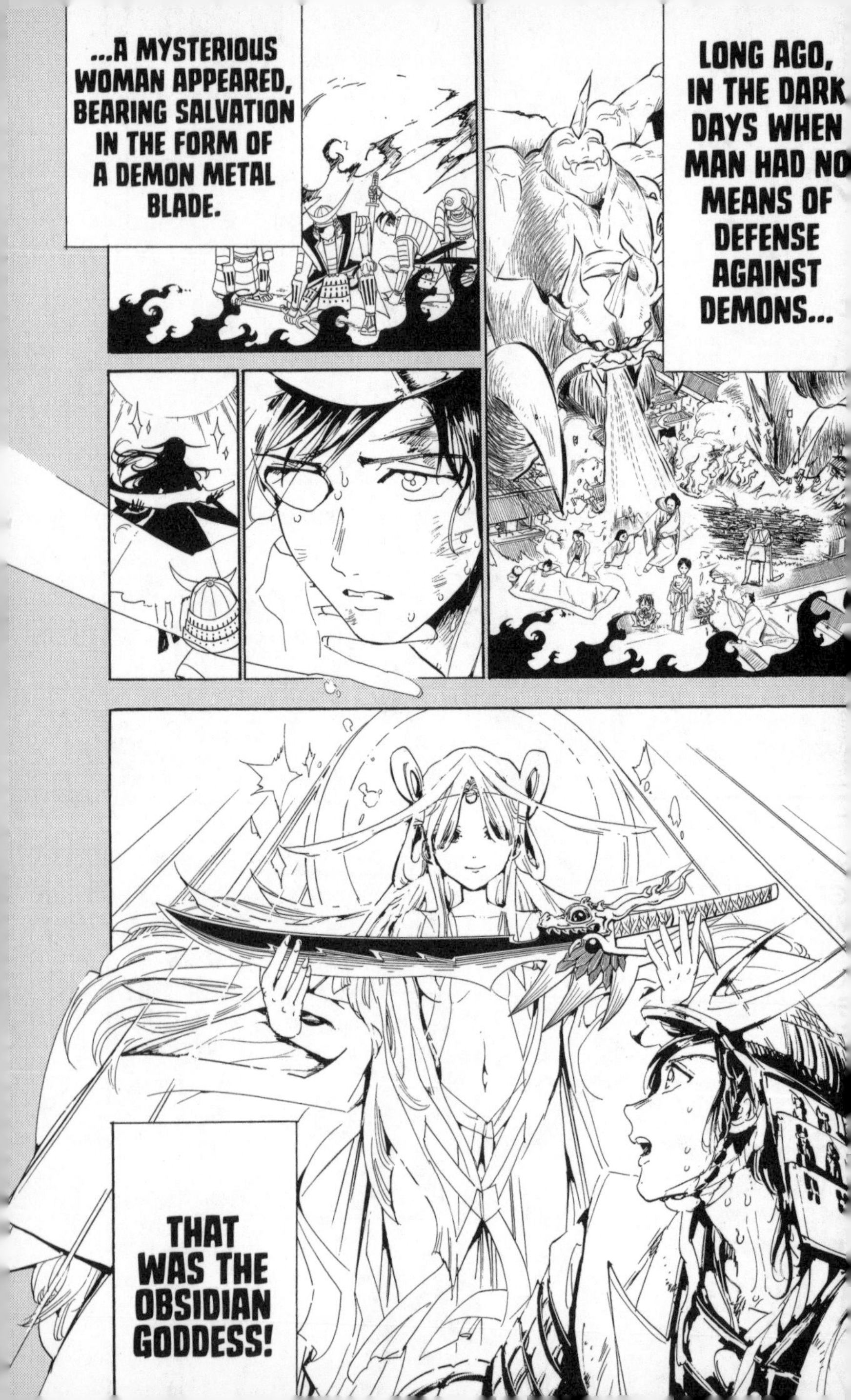
LONG AGO, IN THE DARK DAYS WHEN MAN HAD NO MEANS OF DEFENSE AGAINST DEMONS...
...A MYSTERIOUS WOMAN APPEARED, BEARING SALVATION IN THE FORM OF A DEMON METAL BLADE.
THAT WAS THE OBSIDIAN GODDESS!

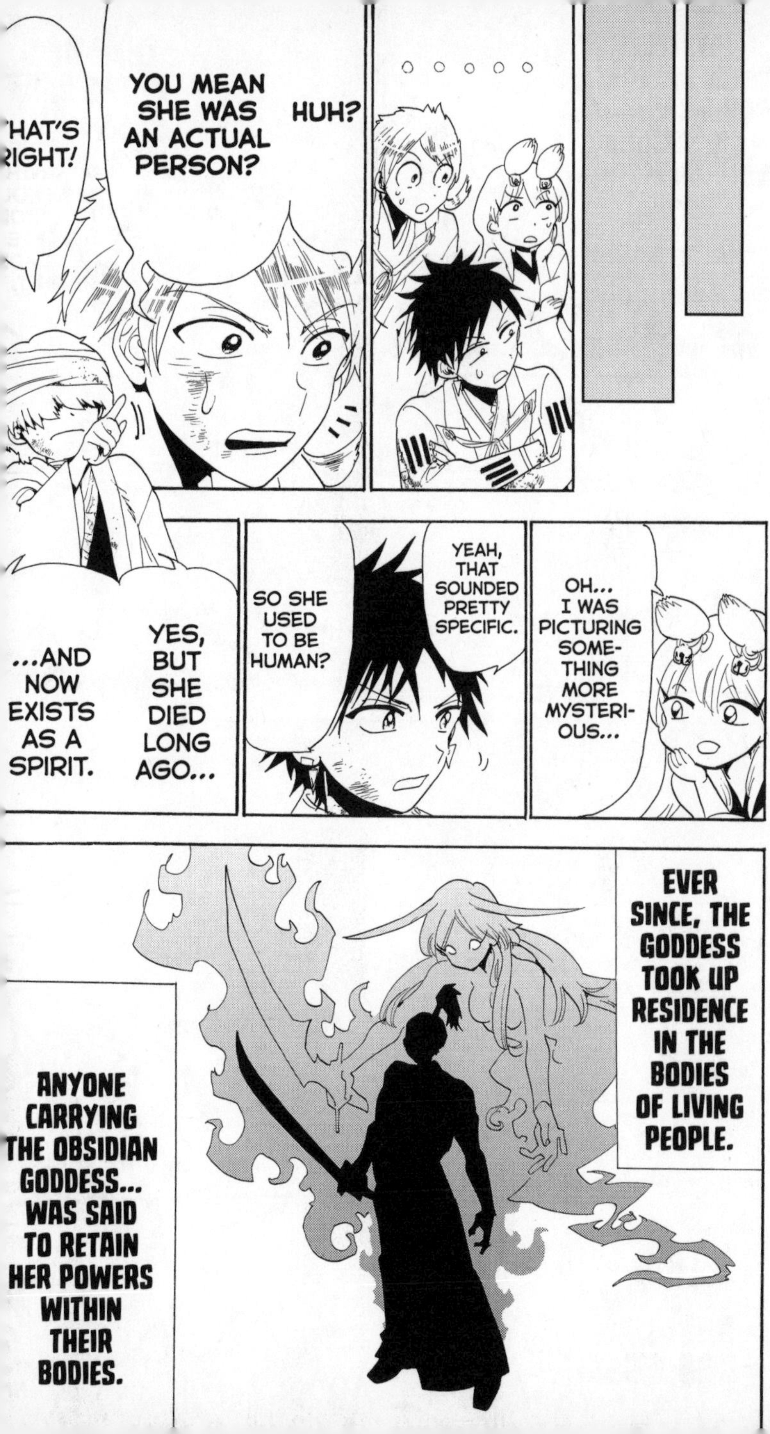
.....
HUH?
YOU MEAN SHE WAS AN ACTUAL PERSON?
HAT'S RIGHT!
OH... I WAS PICTURING SOME-THING MORE MYSTERI-OUS...
YEAH, THAT SOUNDED PRETTY SPECIFIC.
SO SHE USED TO BE HUMAN?
YES, BUT SHE DIED LONG AGO...
...AND NOW EXISTS AS A SPIRIT.
EVER SINCE, THE GODDESS TOOK UP RESIDENCE IN THE BODIES OF LIVING PEOPLE.
ANYONE CARRYING THE OBSIDIAN GODDESS... WAS SAID TO RETAIN HER POWERS WITHIN THEIR BODIES.

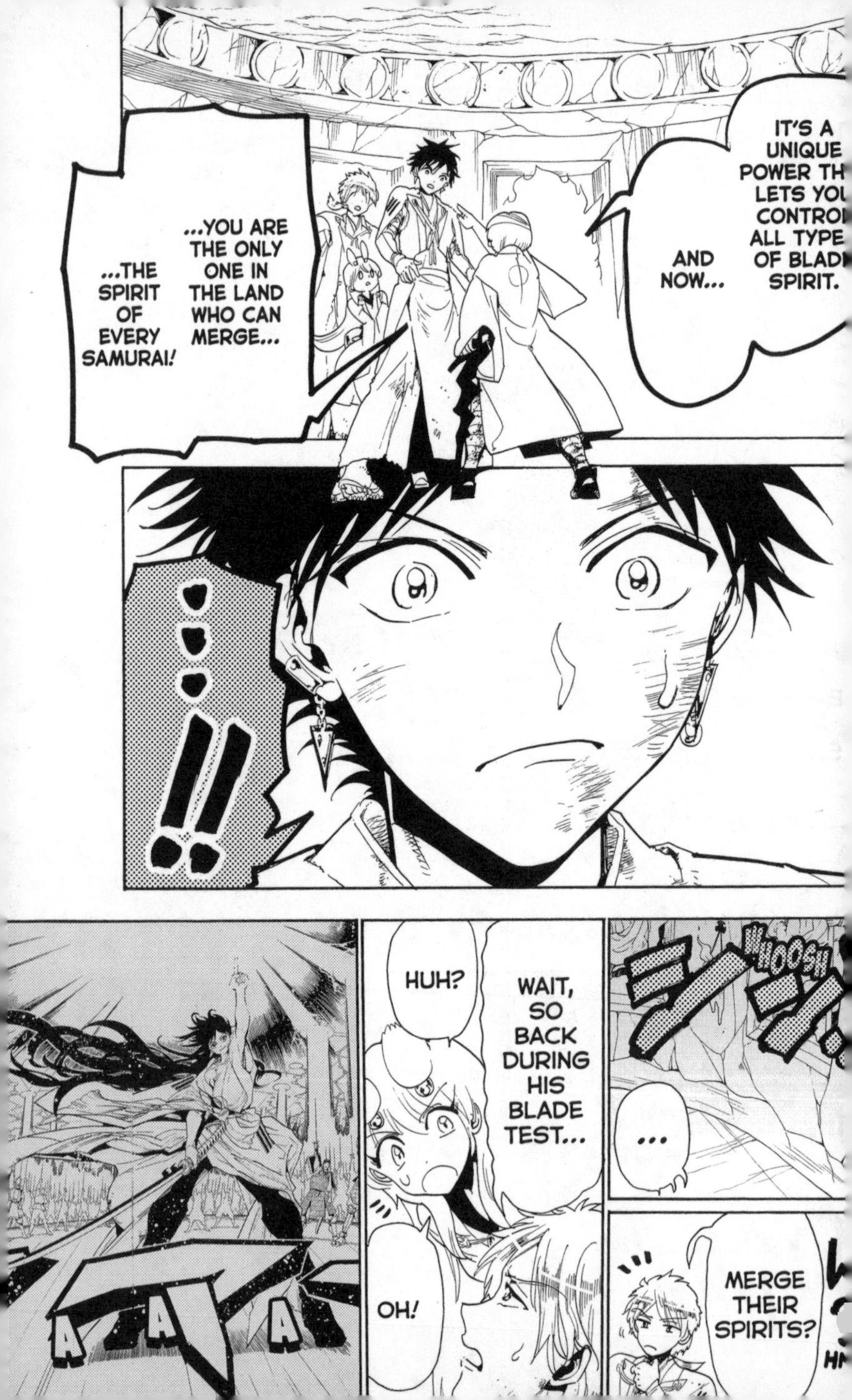
IT'S A UNIQUE POWER TH LETS YOU CONTROL ALL TYPE OF BLAD SPIRIT.
AND NOW...
...YOU ARE THE ONLY ONE IN THE LAND WHO CAN MERGE...
...THE SPIRIT OF EVERY SAMURAI!
...!!
WHOOSH
...
MERGE THEIR SPIRITS?
WAIT, SO BACK DURING HIS BLADE TEST...
HUH?
OH!
A A A

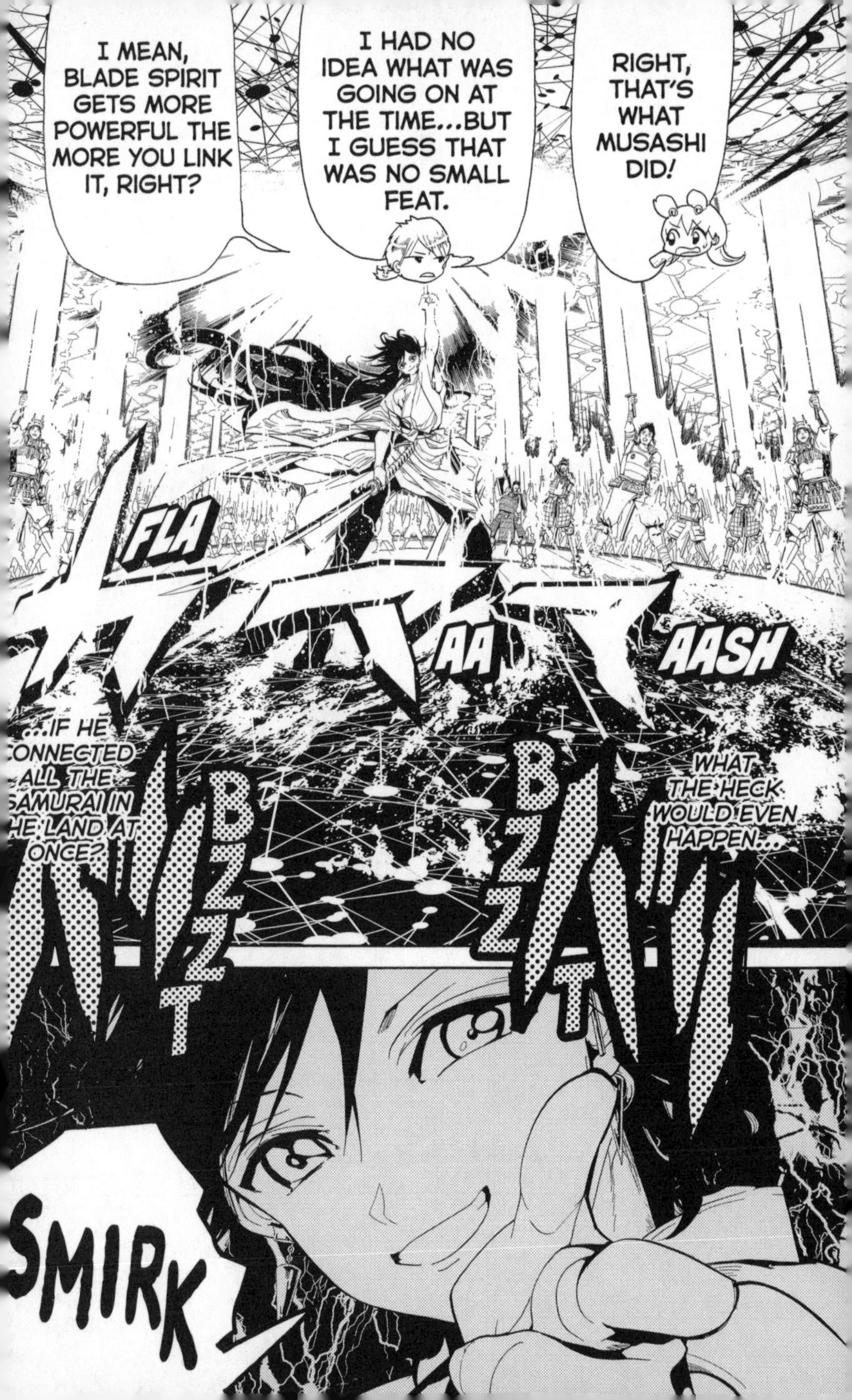
RIGHT, THAT'S WHAT MUSASHI DID!
I HAD NO IDEA WHAT WAS GOING ON AT THE TIME...BUT I GUESS THAT WAS NO SMALL FEAT.
I MEAN, BLADE SPIRIT GETS MORE POWERFUL THE MORE YOU LINK IT, RIGHT?
FLA
AA
AASH
WHAT THE HECK WOULD EVEN HAPPEN...
...IF HE CONNECTED ALL THE SAMURAI IN THE LAND AT ONCE?
BZZT
BZZT
SMIRK

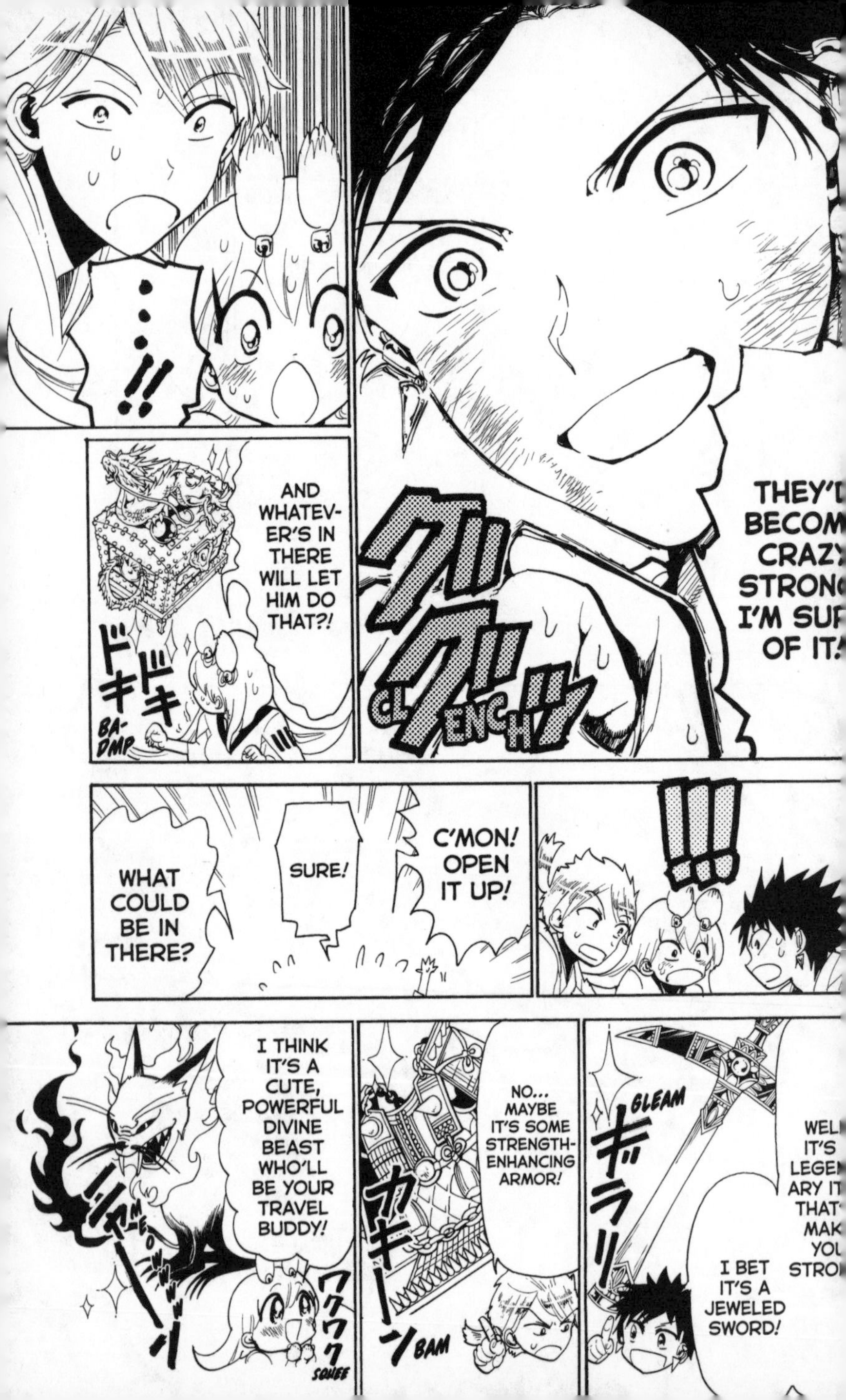

THEY'D BECOM CRAZY STRONG I'M SUR OF IT!
CLENCH
...!!
AND WHATEVER'S IN THERE WILL LET HIM DO THAT?!
BA-DMP
!!!
C'MON! OPEN IT UP!
SURE!
WHAT COULD BE IN THERE?
WEL IT'S LEGEN ARY IT THAT MAK YOU STRO
GLEAM
I BET IT'S A JEWELED SWORD!
NO... MAYBE IT'S SOME STRENGTH-ENHANCING ARMOR!
BAM
I THINK IT'S A CUTE, POWERFUL DIVINE BEAST WHO'LL BE YOUR TRAVEL BUDDY!
MEOWWW
SQUEE

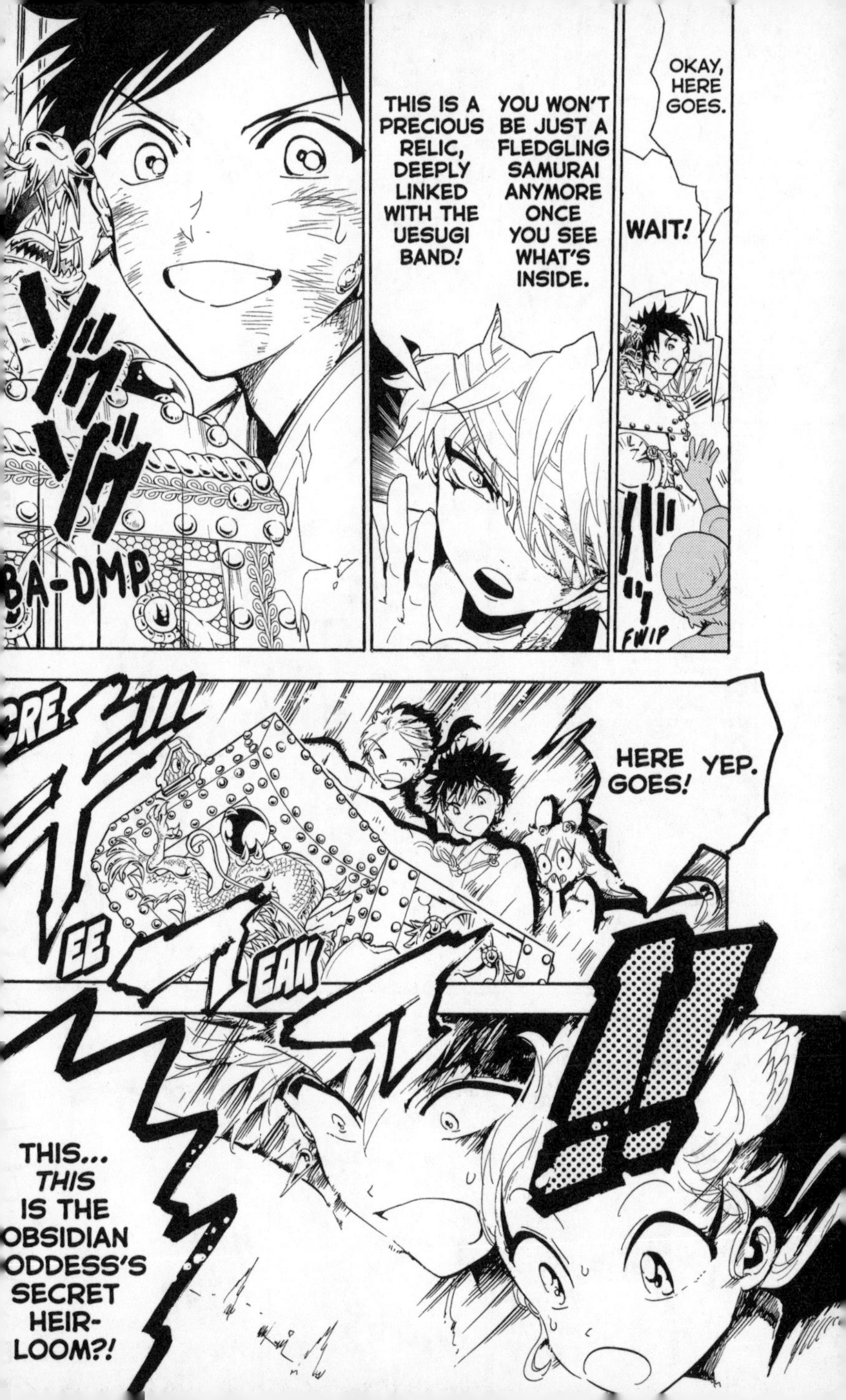
OKAY, HERE GOES.
WAIT!
FWIP
YOU WON'T BE JUST A FLEDGLING SAMURAI ANYMORE ONCE YOU SEE WHAT'S INSIDE.
THIS IS A PRECIOUS RELIC, DEEPLY LINKED WITH THE UESUGI BAND!
BA-DMP
YEP.
HERE GOES!
CRE
EE
EAK
THIS... THIS IS THE OBSIDIAN ODDESS'S SECRET HEIR-LOOM?!

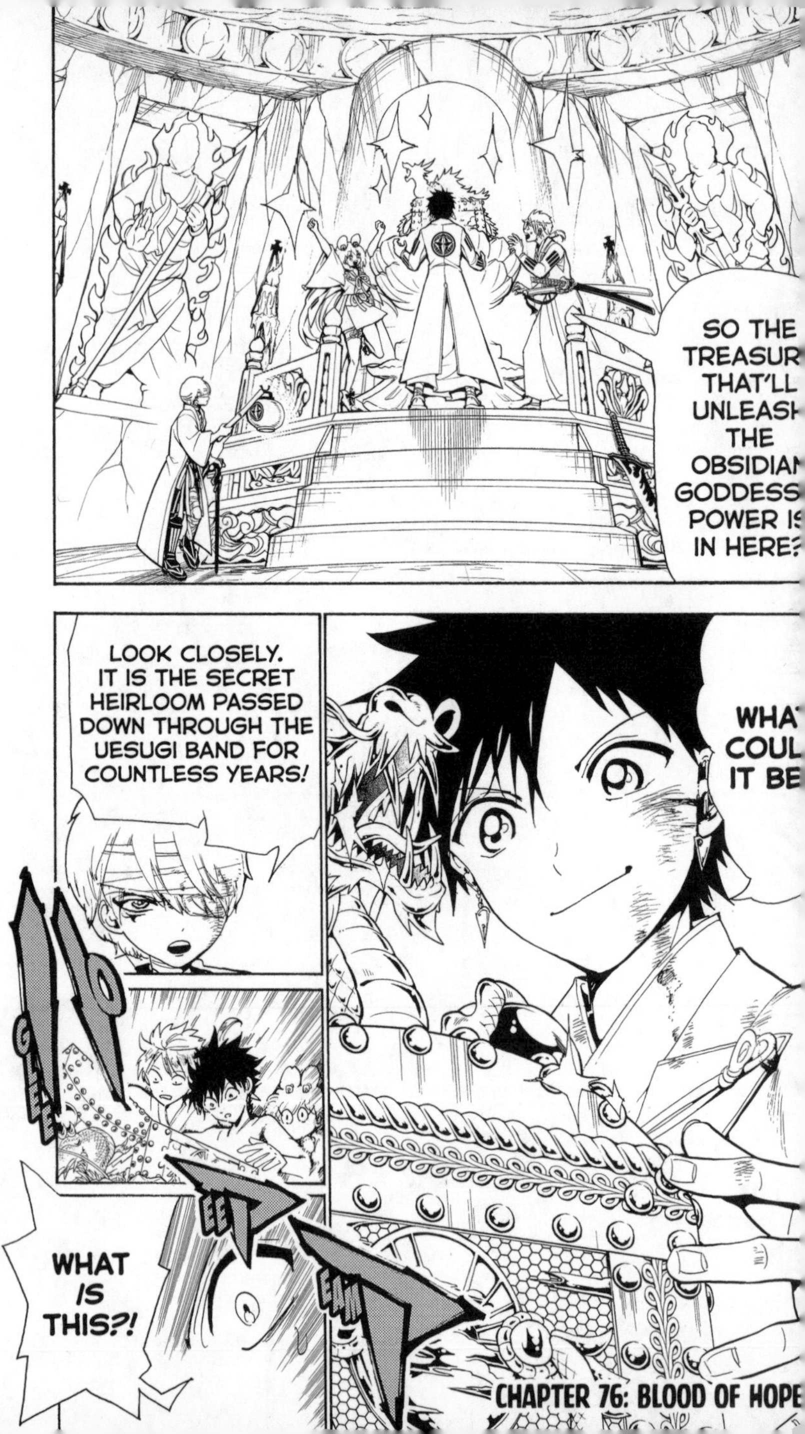
SO THE TREASUR THAT'LL UNLEASH THE OBSIDIAN GODDESS POWER IS IN HERE?
WHA COUL IT BE
LOOK CLOSELY. IT IS THE SECRET HEIRLOOM PASSED DOWN THROUGH THE UESUGI BAND FOR COUNTLESS YEARS!
WHAT IS THIS?!
CHAPTER 76: BLOOD OF HOPE

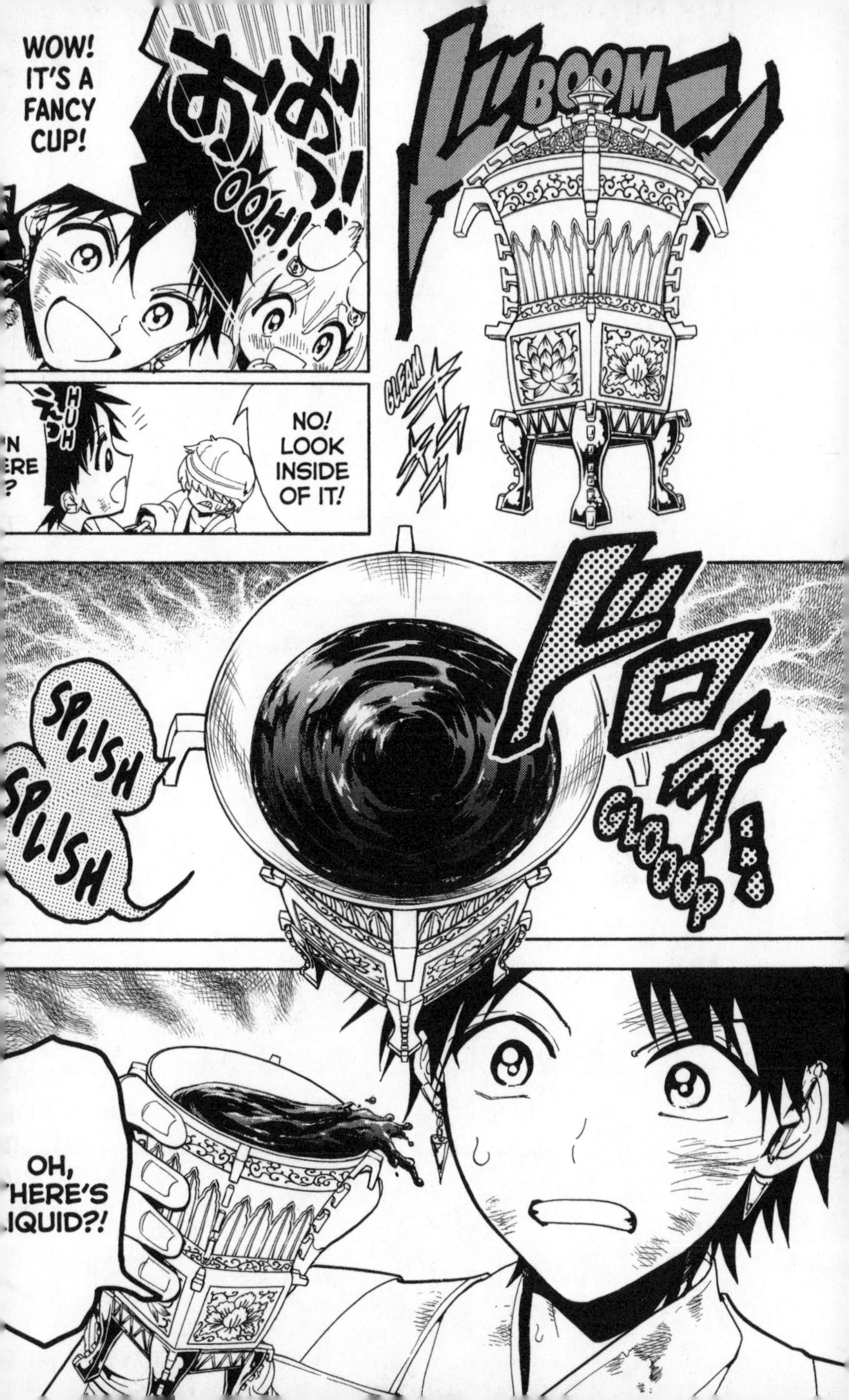
BOOM
GLEAM
WOW! IT'S A FANCY CUP!
OOH!
NO! LOOK INSIDE OF IT!
HUH
GLOOOP
SPLISH SPLISH SPLISH
OH, HERE'S IQUID?!

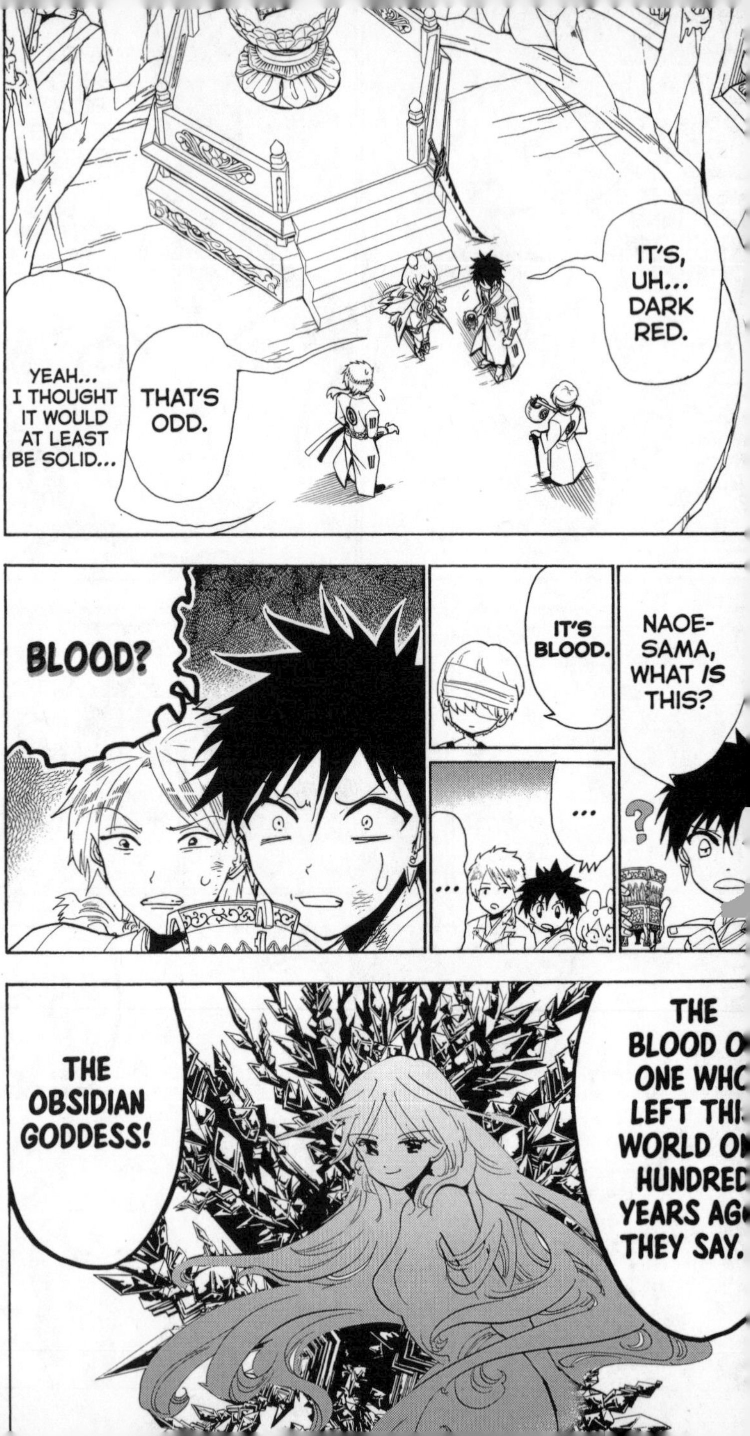
IT'S, UH... DARK RED.
THAT'S ODD.
YEAH... I THOUGHT IT WOULD AT LEAST BE SOLID...
NAOE-SAMA, WHAT *IS* THIS?
IT'S BLOOD.
...
...
BLOOD?
THE BLOOD O ONE WHO LEFT THI WORLD O HUNDRED YEARS AG THEY SAY.
THE OBSIDIAN GODDESS!

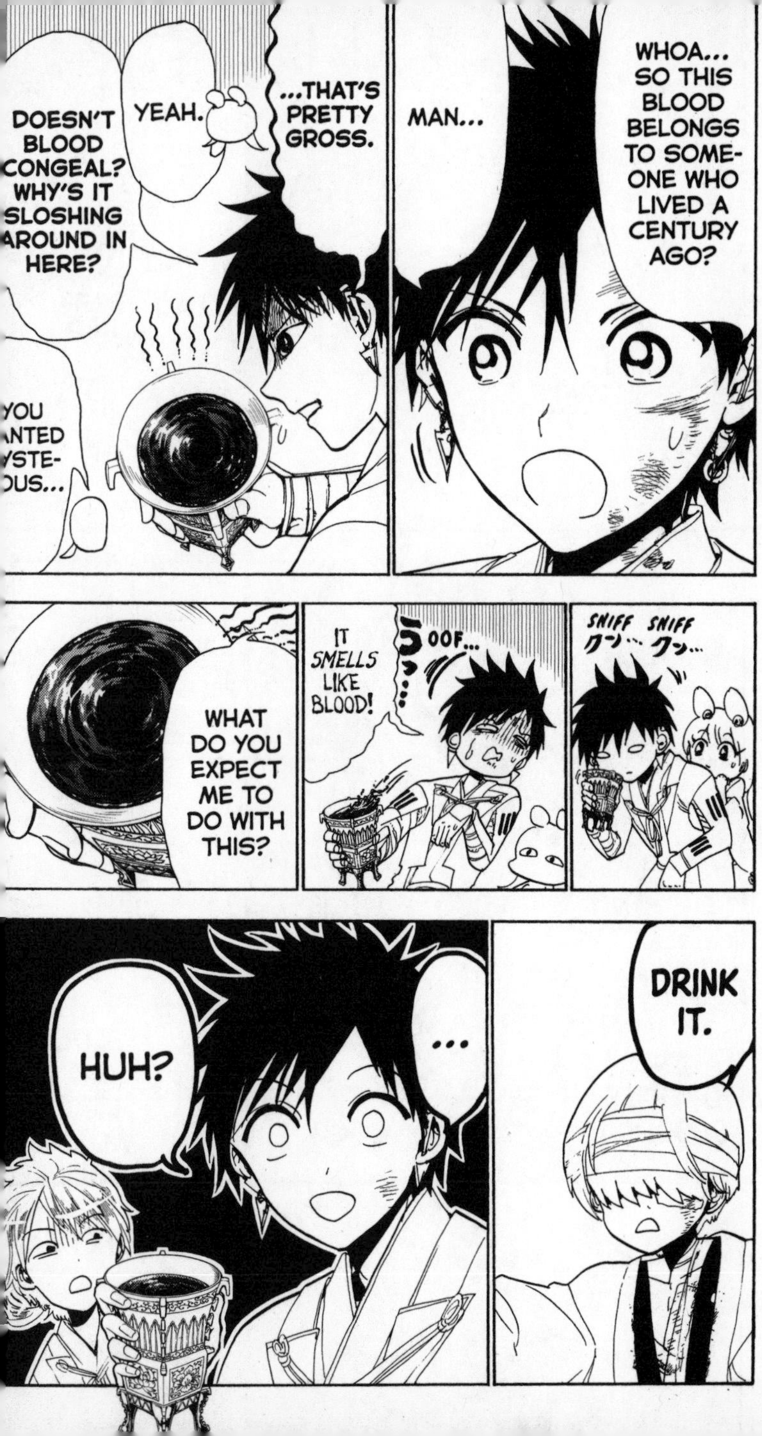
WHOA... SO THIS BLOOD BELONGS TO SOME-ONE WHO LIVED A CENTURY AGO?
MAN...
...THAT'S PRETTY GROSS.
YEAH.
DOESN'T BLOOD CONGEAL? WHY'S IT SLOSHING AROUND IN HERE?
YOU ANTED YSTE- OUS...
SNIFF SNIFF
クン… クン…
OOF...
う…
IT SMELLS LIKE BLOOD!
WHAT DO YOU EXPECT ME TO DO WITH THIS?
DRINK IT.
...
HUH?

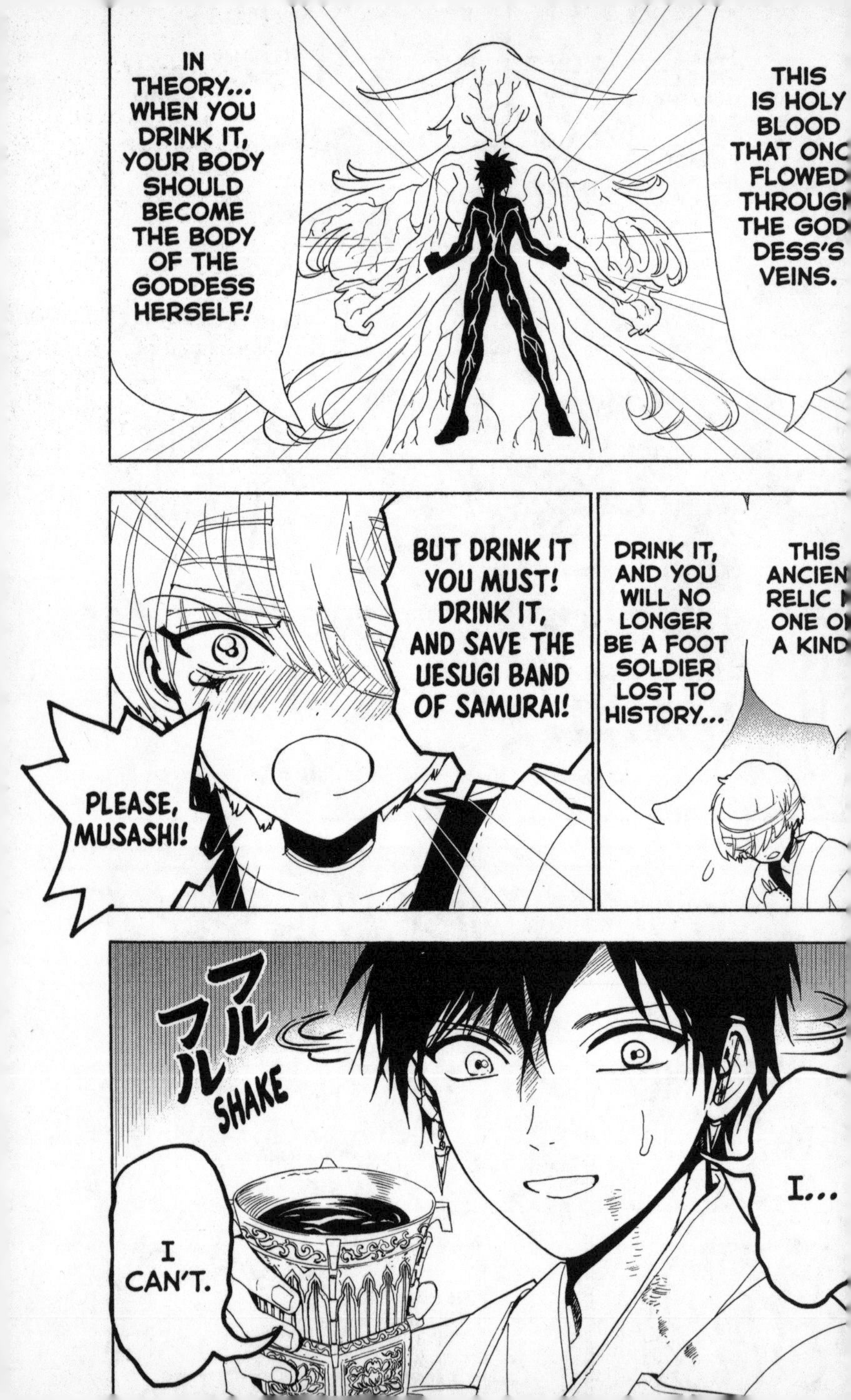
THIS IS HOLY BLOOD THAT ONC FLOWED THROUG THE GOD DESS'S VEINS.
IN THEORY... WHEN YOU DRINK IT, YOUR BODY SHOULD BECOME THE BODY OF THE GODDESS HERSELF!
THIS ANCIEN RELIC ONE O A KIND
DRINK IT, AND YOU WILL NO LONGER BE A FOOT SOLDIER LOST TO HISTORY...
BUT DRINK IT YOU MUST! DRINK IT, AND SAVE THE UESUGI BAND OF SAMURAI!
PLEASE, MUSASHI!
I...
フルフル
SHAKE
I CAN'T.

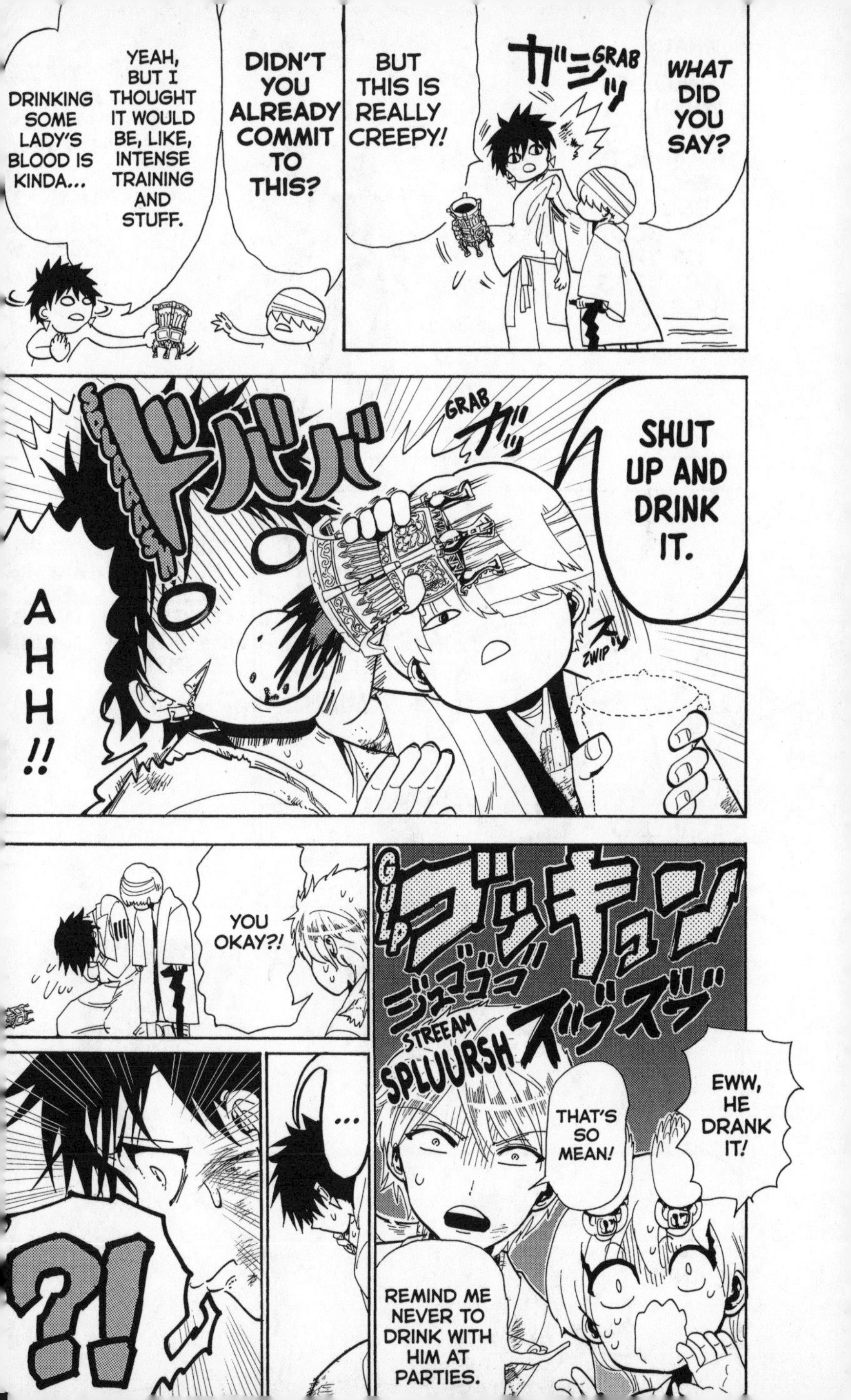
GRAB
WHAT DID YOU SAY?
BUT THIS IS REALLY CREEPY!
DIDN'T YOU ALREADY COMMIT TO THIS?
YEAH, BUT I THOUGHT IT WOULD BE, LIKE, INTENSE TRAINING AND STUFF.
DRINKING SOME LADY'S BLOOD IS KINDA...
SHUT UP AND DRINK IT.
GRAB
ZWIP
AHH!!
STREEAM
SPLUURSH
EWW, HE DRANK IT!
THAT'S SO MEAN!
REMIND ME NEVER TO DRINK WITH HIM AT PARTIES.
YOU OKAY?!
...
?!

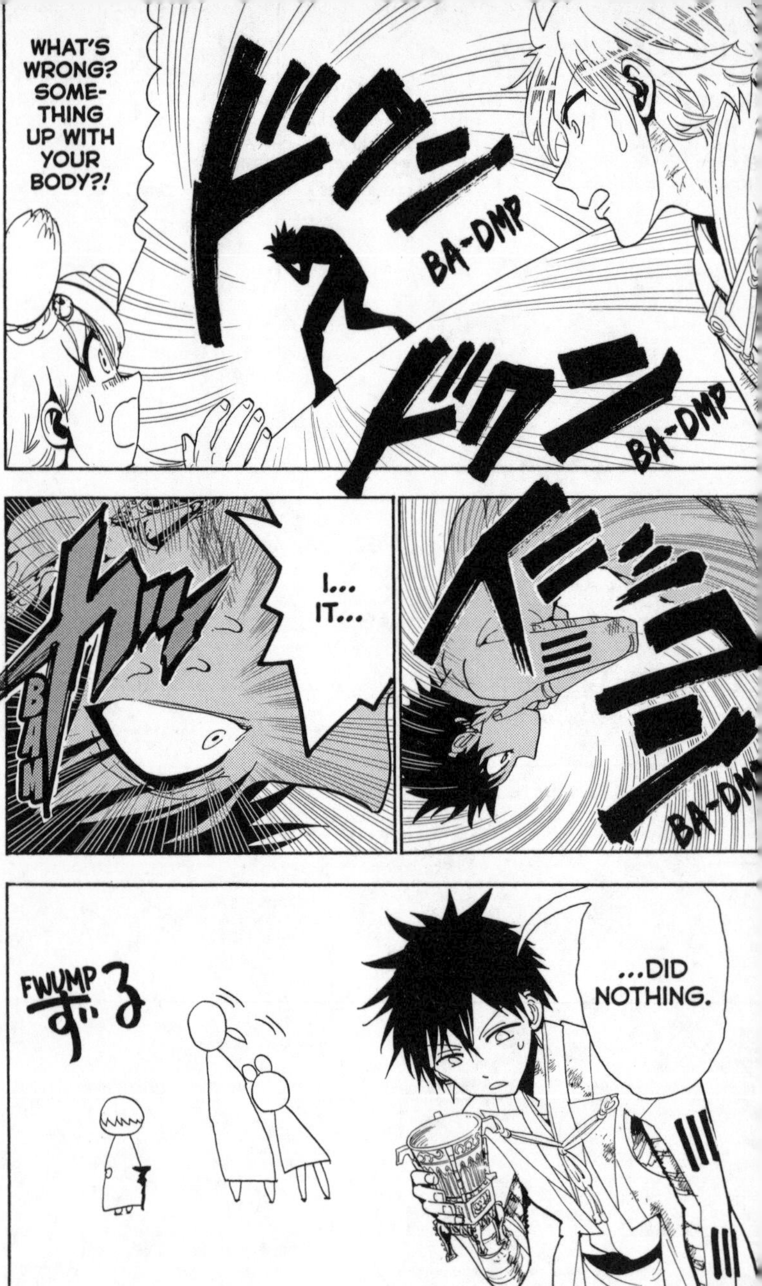
BA-DMP
WHAT'S WRONG? SOME-THING UP WITH YOUR BODY?!
BA-DMP
BA-DM
I... IT...
BAM
...DID NOTHING.
FWUMP

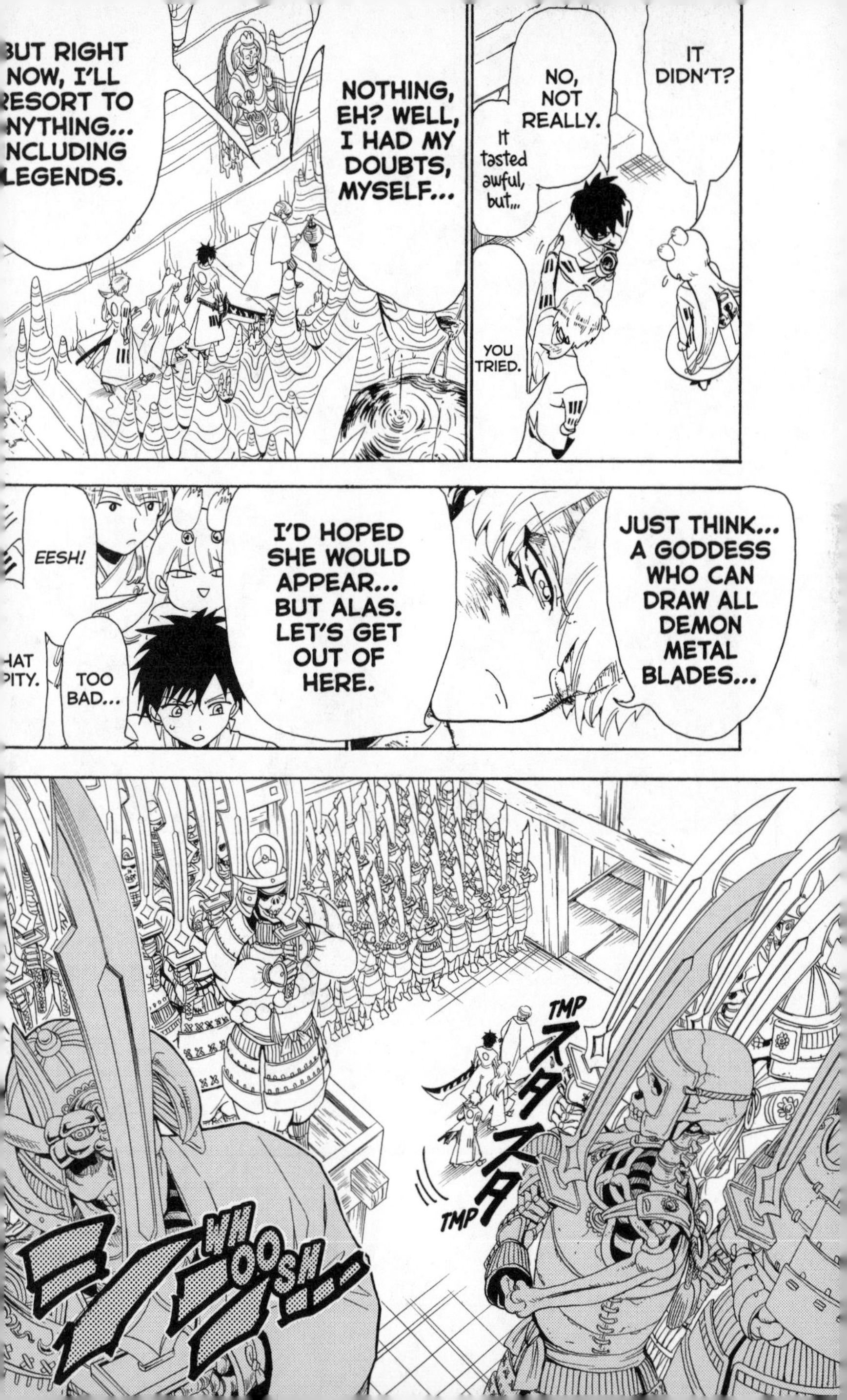
IT DIDN'T?
NO, NOT REALLY.
It tasted awful, but...
YOU TRIED.
NOTHING, EH? WELL, I HAD MY DOUBTS, MYSELF...
BUT RIGHT NOW, I'LL RESORT TO NYTHING... NCLUDING LEGENDS.
JUST THINK... A GODDESS WHO CAN DRAW ALL DEMON METAL BLADES...
I'D HOPED SHE WOULD APPEAR... BUT ALAS. LET'S GET OUT OF HERE.
EESH!
TOO BAD...
HAT PITY.
TMP
TMP
WHOOSH!

DID THAT COME FROM INSIDE?

HUH?

OR MAYBE NOT?

FWIP

CRASH

LET'S GO, MUSASHI.

OKAY.

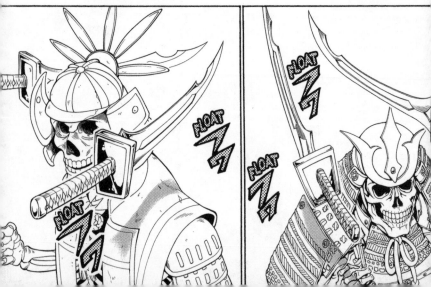

FLOAT

FLOAT

FLOAT

FLOAT

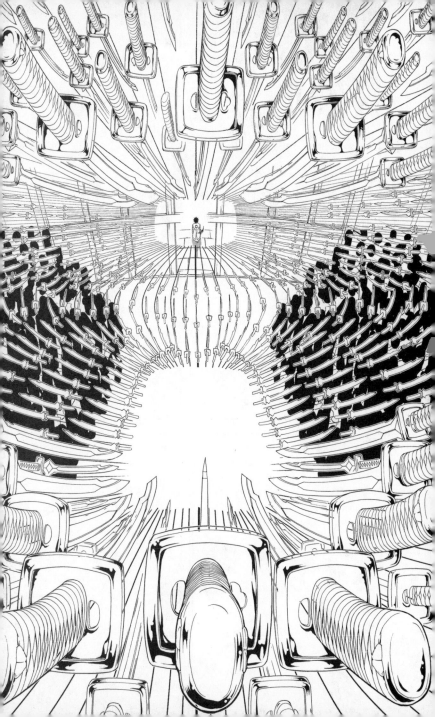

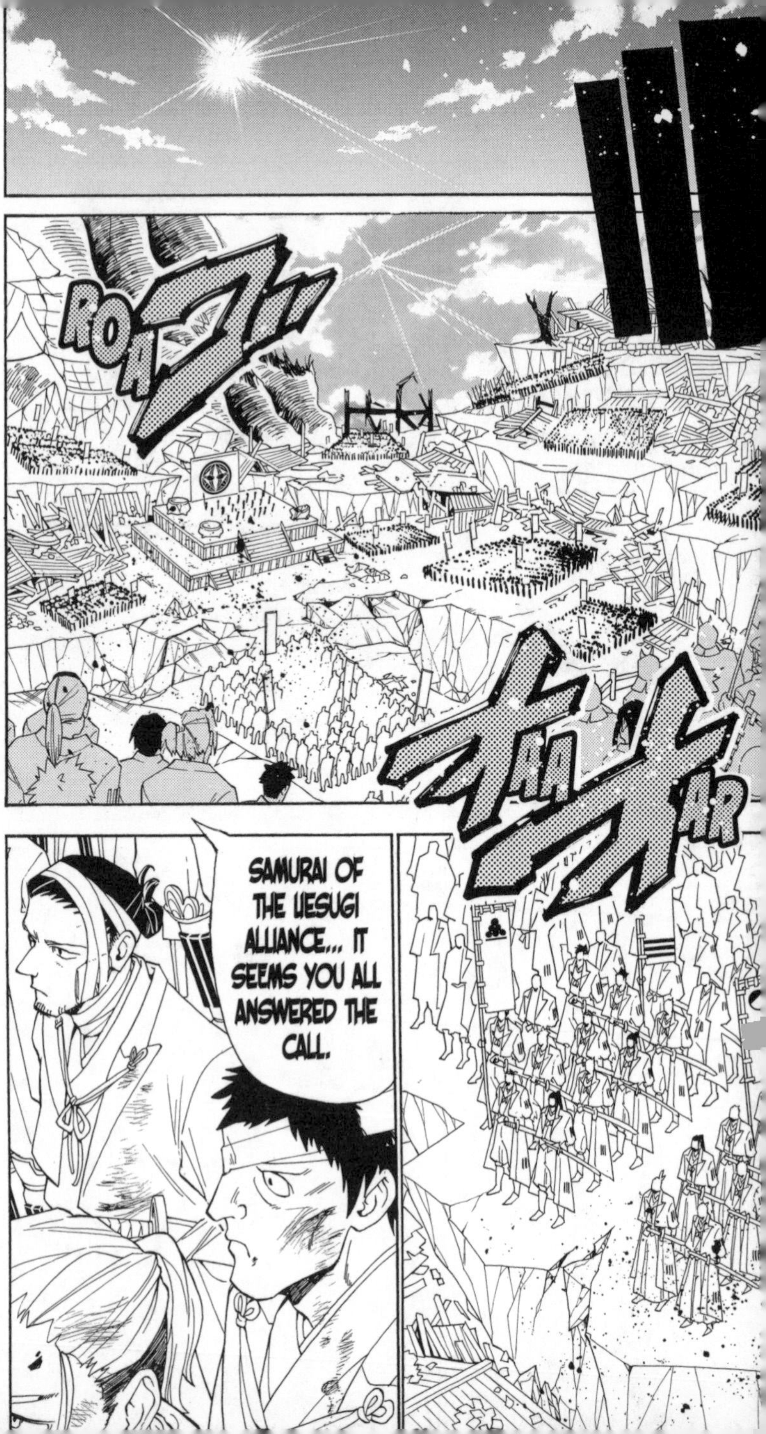
ROAR
WAAAR
SAMURAI OF THE UESUGI ALLIANCE... IT SEEMS YOU ALL ANSWERED THE CALL.

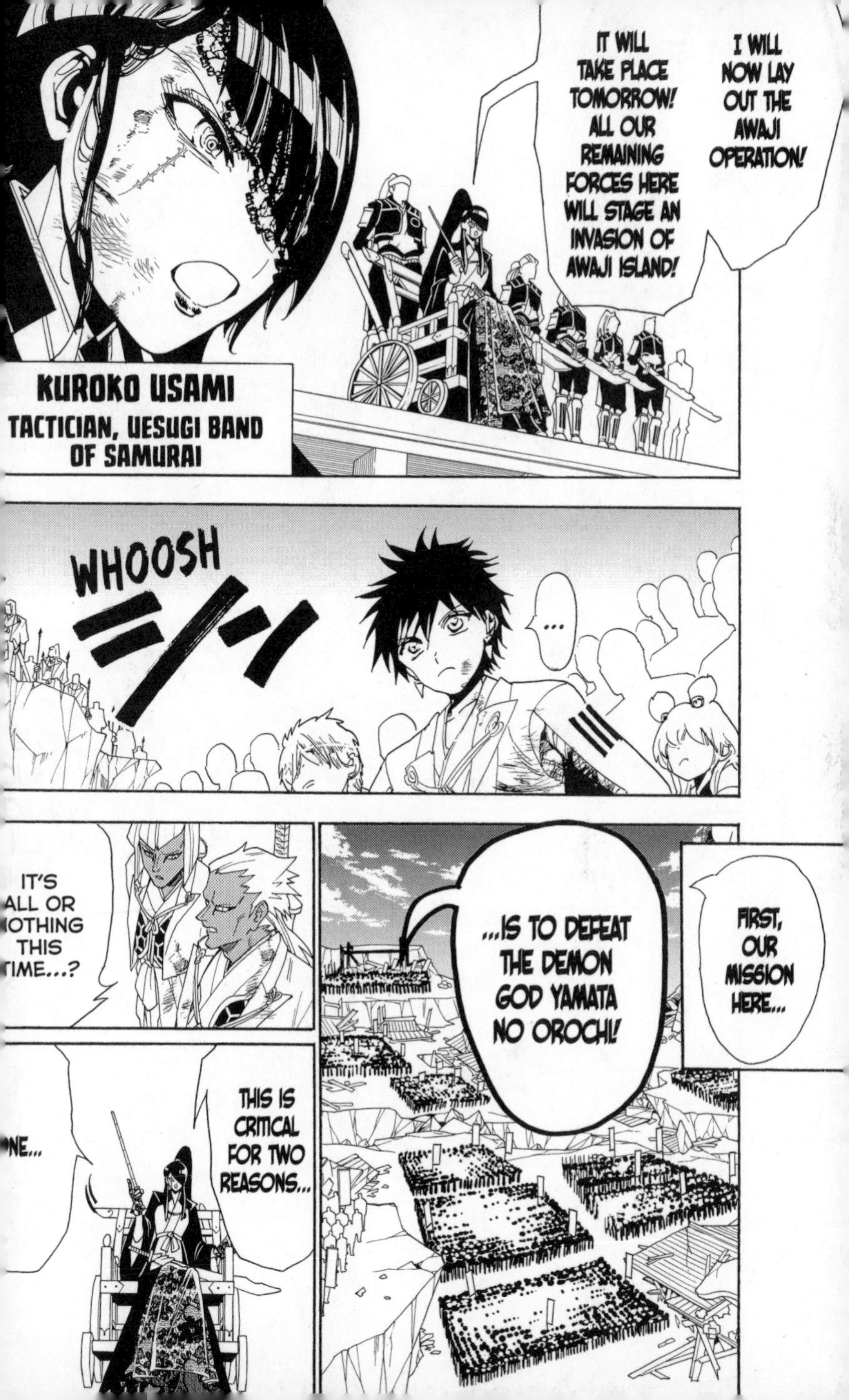
I WILL NOW LAY OUT THE AWAJI OPERATION!
IT WILL TAKE PLACE TOMORROW! ALL OUR REMAINING FORCES HERE WILL STAGE AN INVASION OF AWAJI ISLAND!
KUROKO USAMI
TACTICIAN, UESUGI BAND OF SAMURAI
WHOOSH
...
FIRST, OUR MISSION HERE...
...IS TO DEFEAT THE DEMON GOD YAMATA NO OROCHI!
IT'S ALL OR OTHING THIS IME...?
THIS IS CRITICAL FOR TWO REASONS...
NE...

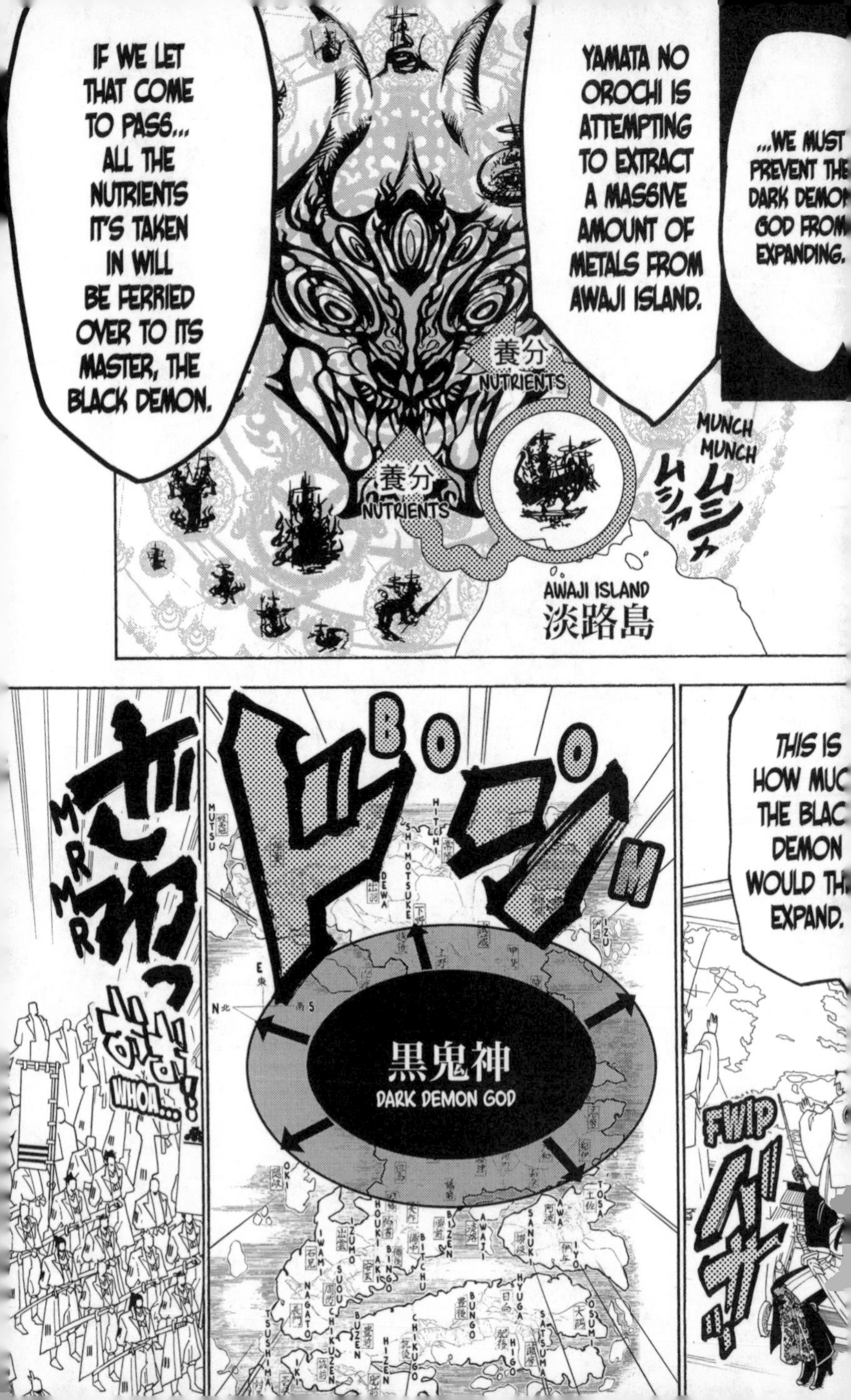

...WE MUST PREVENT THE DARK DEMO GOD FROM EXPANDING.
YAMATA NO OROCHI IS ATTEMPTING TO EXTRACT A MASSIVE AMOUNT OF METALS FROM AWAJI ISLAND.
IF WE LET THAT COME TO PASS... ALL THE NUTRIENTS IT'S TAKEN IN WILL BE FERRIED OVER TO ITS MASTER, THE BLACK DEMON.
養分 NUTRIENTS
養分 NUTRIENTS
MUNCH MUNCH ムシャムシャ
AWAJI ISLAND 淡路島
THIS IS HOW MUC THE BLAC DEMON WOULD TH EXPAND.
FWIP
BOOOM
黒鬼神 DARK DEMON GOD
E 東
N 北
西 S
MUTSU
HITACHI
SHIMOTSUKE 下野
DEWA
IZU
OKI
HOUKI
IZUMO
IWAMI
NAGATO
SUOU
AKI
BINGO
BITCHU
BIZEN
AWAJI
SANUKI
AWA
TOSA
IYO
BUZEN
CHIKUZEN
CHIKUGO
HIZEN
BUNGO
HYUGA
HIGO
SATSUMA
OSUMI
TSUSHIMA
IKI
MRMR ざわっ
WHOA... おおっ

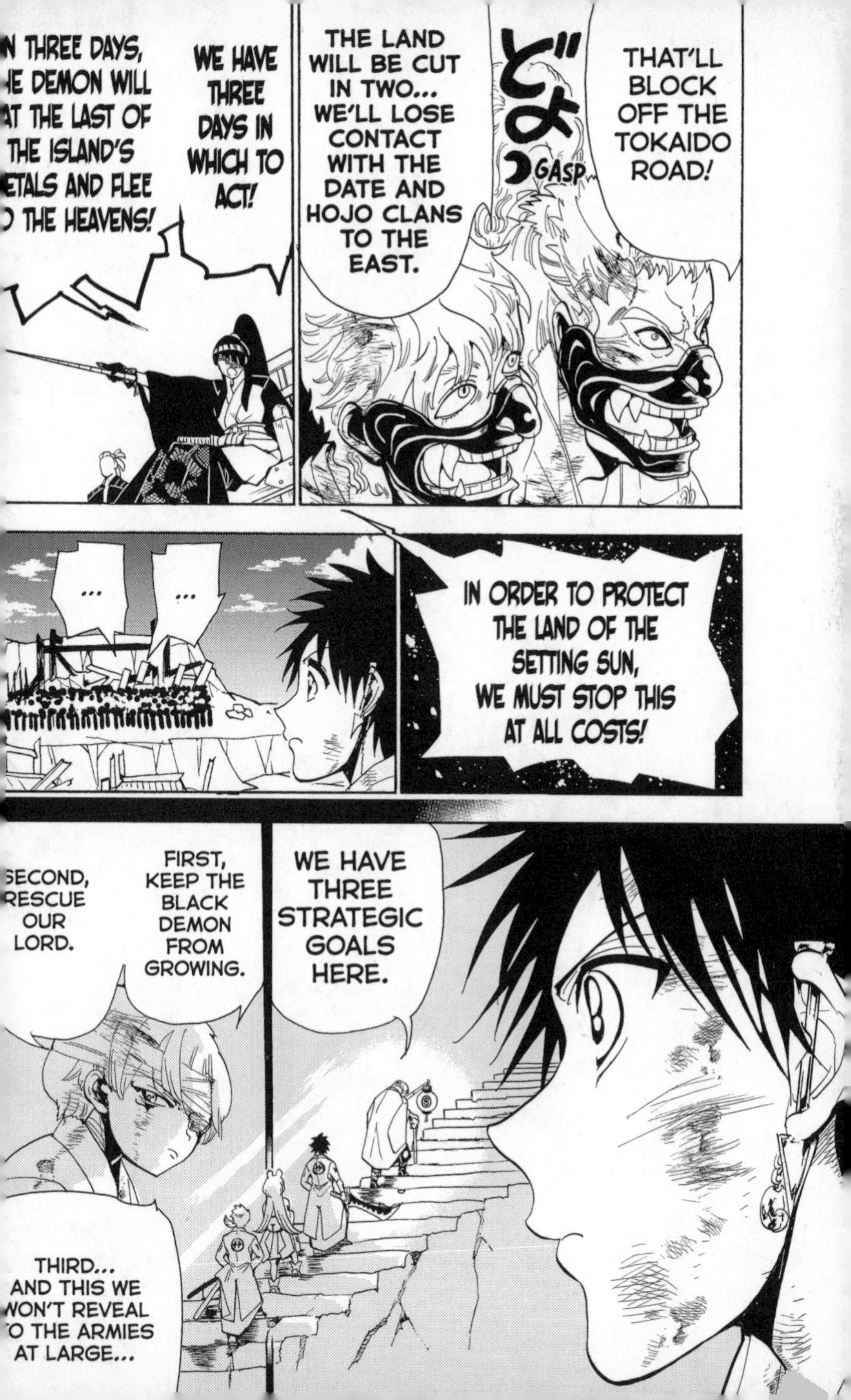
THAT'LL BLOCK OFF THE TOKAIDO ROAD!
どよ
GASP
THE LAND WILL BE CUT IN TWO... WE'LL LOSE CONTACT WITH THE DATE AND HOJO CLANS TO THE EAST.
WE HAVE THREE DAYS IN WHICH TO ACT!
N THREE DAYS, HE DEMON WILL AT THE LAST OF THE ISLAND'S ETALS AND FLEE THE HEAVENS!
IN ORDER TO PROTECT THE LAND OF THE SETTING SUN, WE MUST STOP THIS AT ALL COSTS!
...
...
WE HAVE THREE STRATEGIC GOALS HERE.
FIRST, KEEP THE BLACK DEMON FROM GROWING.
SECOND, RESCUE OUR LORD.
THIRD... AND THIS WE WON'T REVEAL TO THE ARMIES AT LARGE...

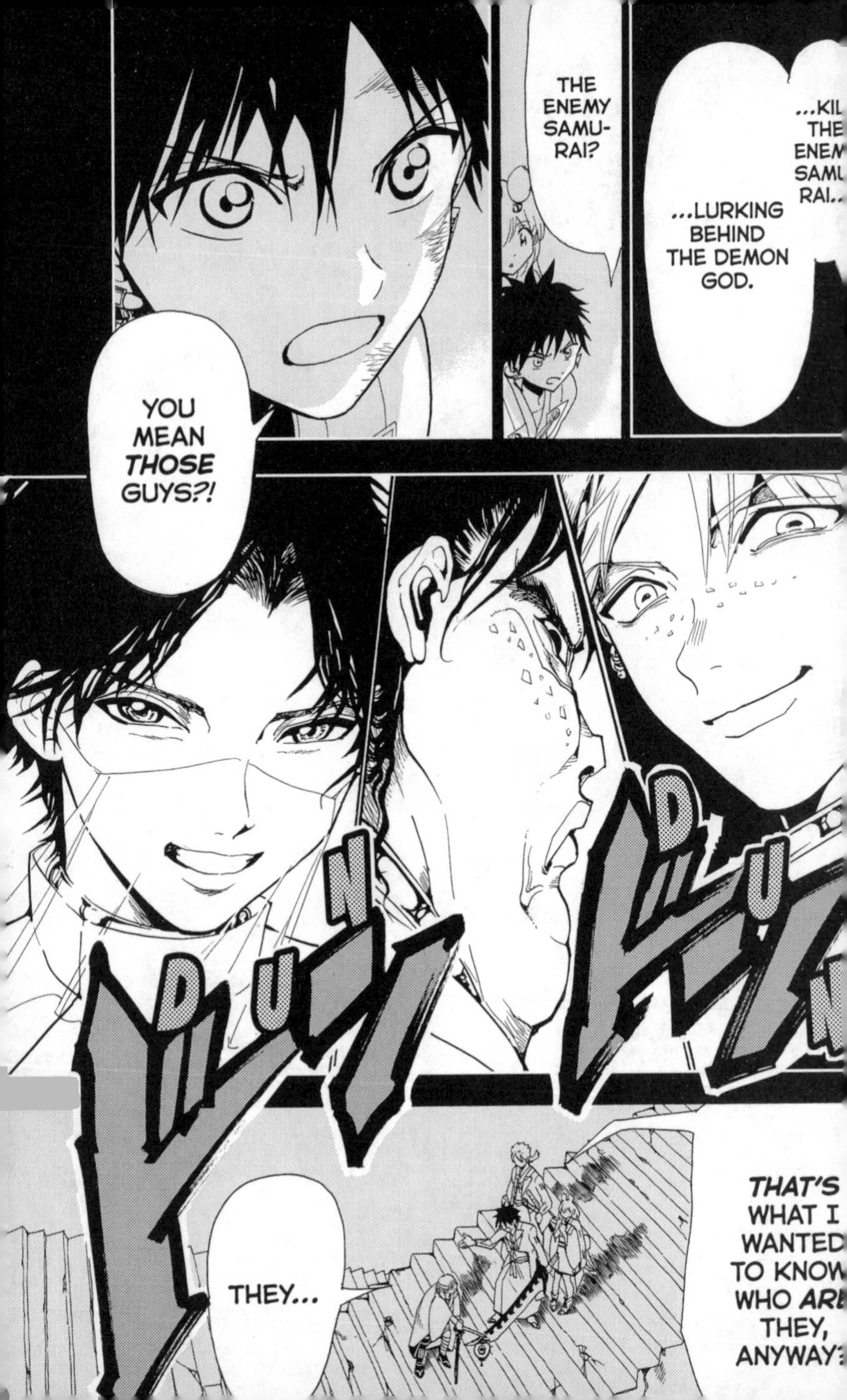
...KIL THE ENEM SAMU RAI...
...LURKING BEHIND THE DEMON GOD.
THE ENEMY SAMU-RAI?
YOU MEAN *THOSE* GUYS?!
DUN
DUN
THAT'S WHAT I WANTED TO KNOW WHO *ARE* THEY, ANYWAY?
THEY...

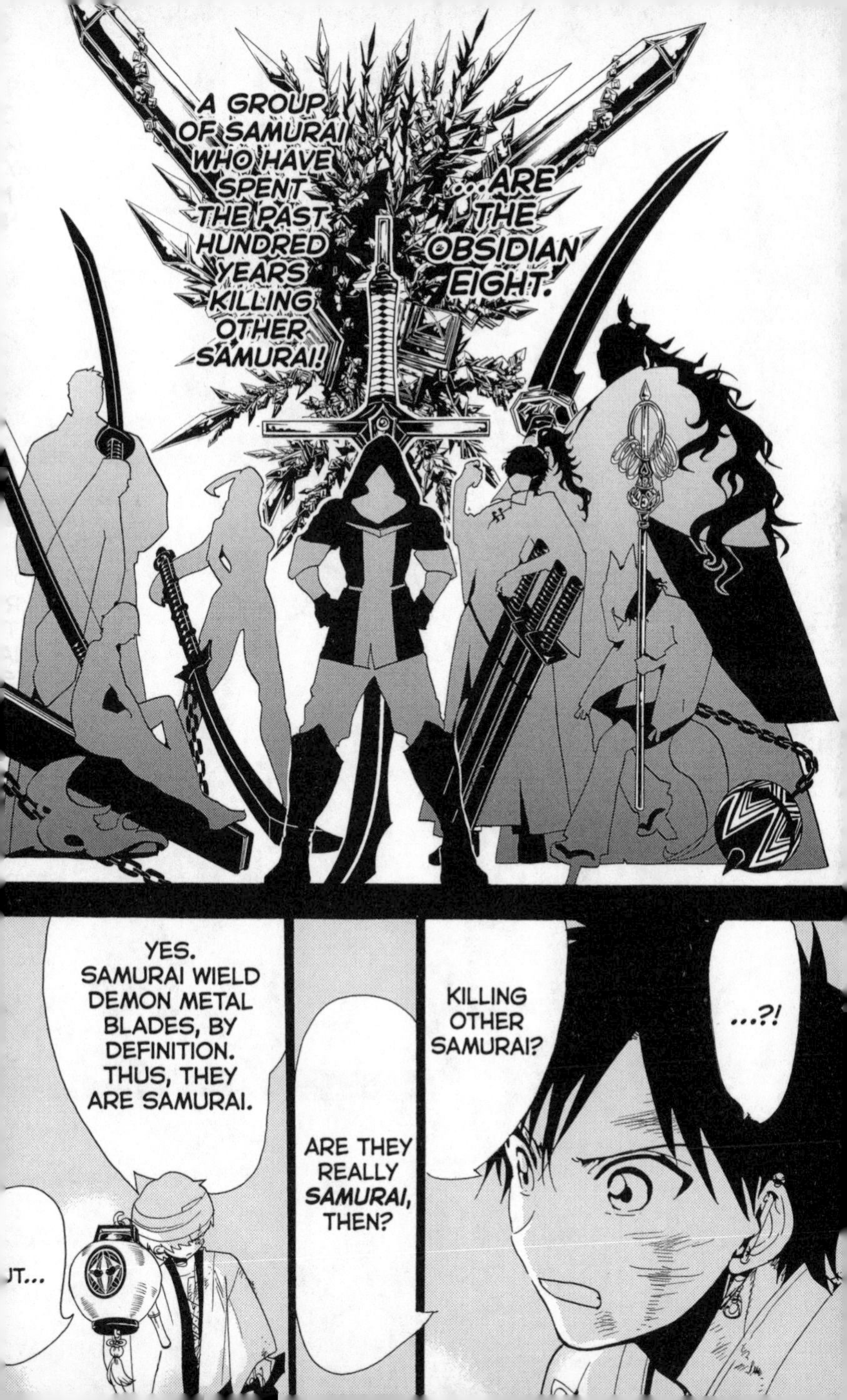
A GROUP OF SAMURAI WHO HAVE SPENT THE PAST HUNDRED YEARS KILLING OTHER SAMURAI!
...ARE THE OBSIDIAN EIGHT.
...?!
KILLING OTHER SAMURAI?
ARE THEY REALLY SAMURAI, THEN?
YES. SAMURAI WIELD DEMON METAL BLADES, BY DEFINITION. THUS, THEY ARE SAMURAI.
UT...

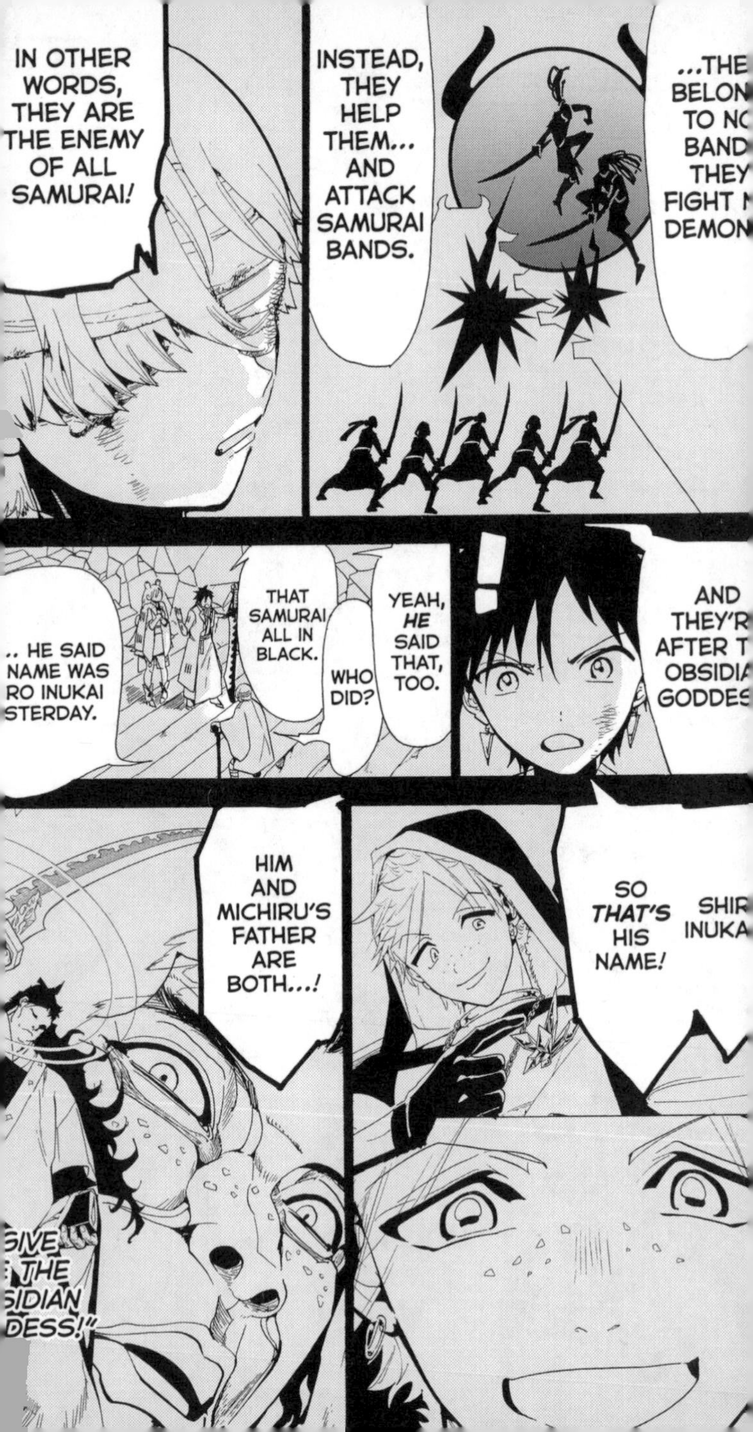
...THE BELON TO NO BAND THEY FIGHT DEMON
INSTEAD, THEY HELP THEM... AND ATTACK SAMURAI BANDS.
IN OTHER WORDS, THEY ARE THE ENEMY OF ALL SAMURAI!
!
AND THEY'R AFTER T OBSIDIA GODDES
YEAH, *HE* SAID THAT, TOO.
WHO DID?
THAT SAMURAI ALL IN BLACK.
.. HE SAID NAME WAS RO INUKAI STERDAY.
SHIR INUKA
SO *THAT'S* HIS NAME!
HIM AND MICHIRU'S FATHER ARE BOTH...!
GIVE E THE SIDIAN DESS!"

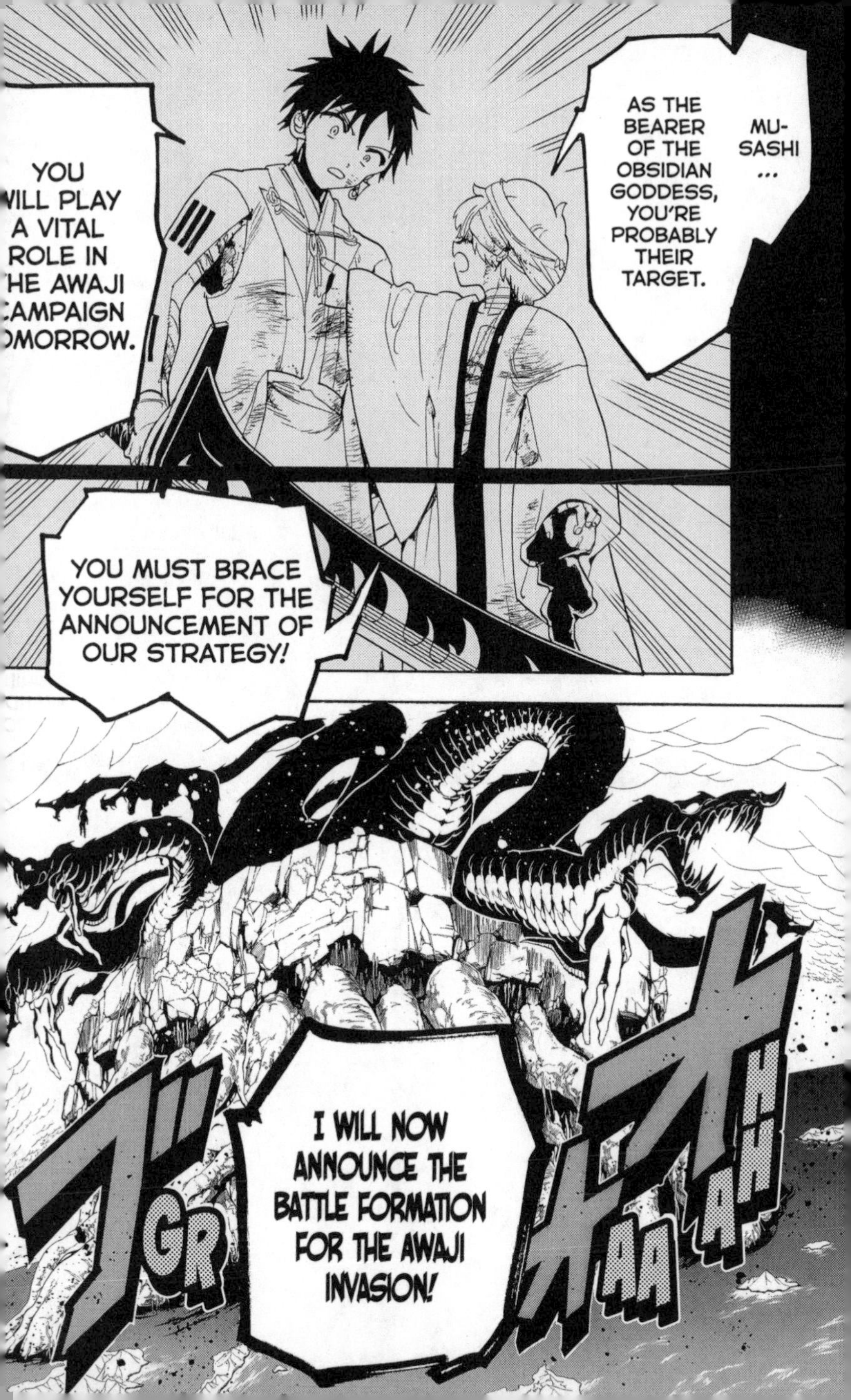
MU-SASHI...
AS THE BEARER OF THE OBSIDIAN GODDESS, YOU'RE PROBABLY THEIR TARGET.
YOU WILL PLAY A VITAL ROLE IN HE AWAJI CAMPAIGN OMORROW.
YOU MUST BRACE YOURSELF FOR THE ANNOUNCEMENT OF OUR STRATEGY!
I WILL NOW ANNOUNCE THE BATTLE FORMATION FOR THE AWAJI INVASION!
GR
AAAHH!!

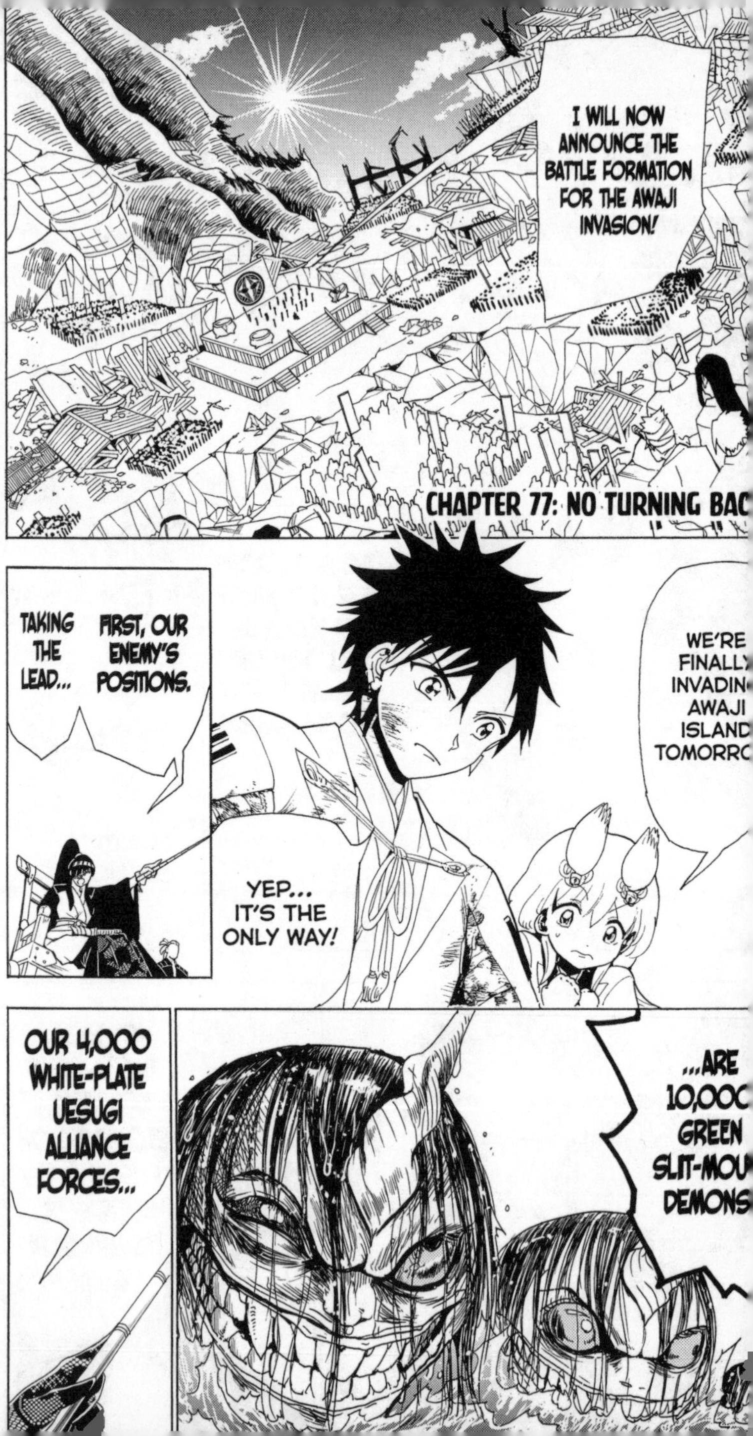
I WILL NOW ANNOUNCE THE BATTLE FORMATION FOR THE AWAJI INVASION!
CHAPTER 77: NO TURNING BAC
WE'RE FINALLY INVADIN AWAJI ISLAND TOMORRO
YEP... IT'S THE ONLY WAY!
FIRST, OUR ENEMY'S POSITIONS.
TAKING THE LEAD...
...ARE 10,000 GREEN SLIT-MOU DEMONS
OUR 4,000 WHITE-PLATE UESUGI ALLIANCE FORCES...

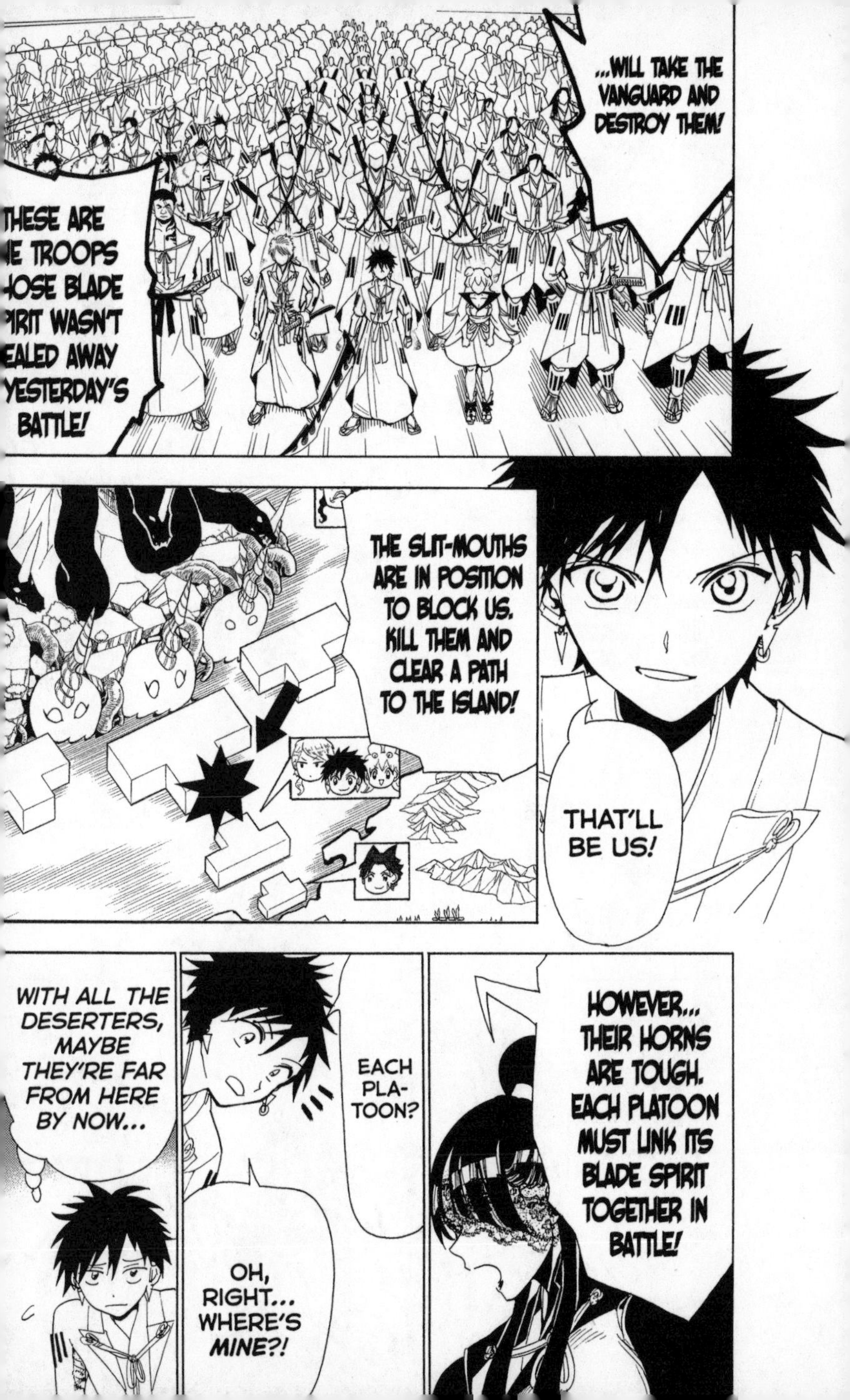
...WILL TAKE THE VANGUARD AND DESTROY THEM!
THESE ARE
E TROOPS
HOSE BLADE
IRIT WASN'T
EALED AWAY
YESTERDAY'S BATTLE!
THE SLIT-MOUTHS ARE IN POSITION TO BLOCK US. KILL THEM AND CLEAR A PATH TO THE ISLAND!
THAT'LL BE US!
HOWEVER... THEIR HORNS ARE TOUGH. EACH PLATOON MUST LINK ITS BLADE SPIRIT TOGETHER IN BATTLE!
EACH PLA-TOON?
OH, RIGHT... WHERE'S MINE?!
WITH ALL THE DESERTERS, MAYBE THEY'RE FAR FROM HERE BY NOW...

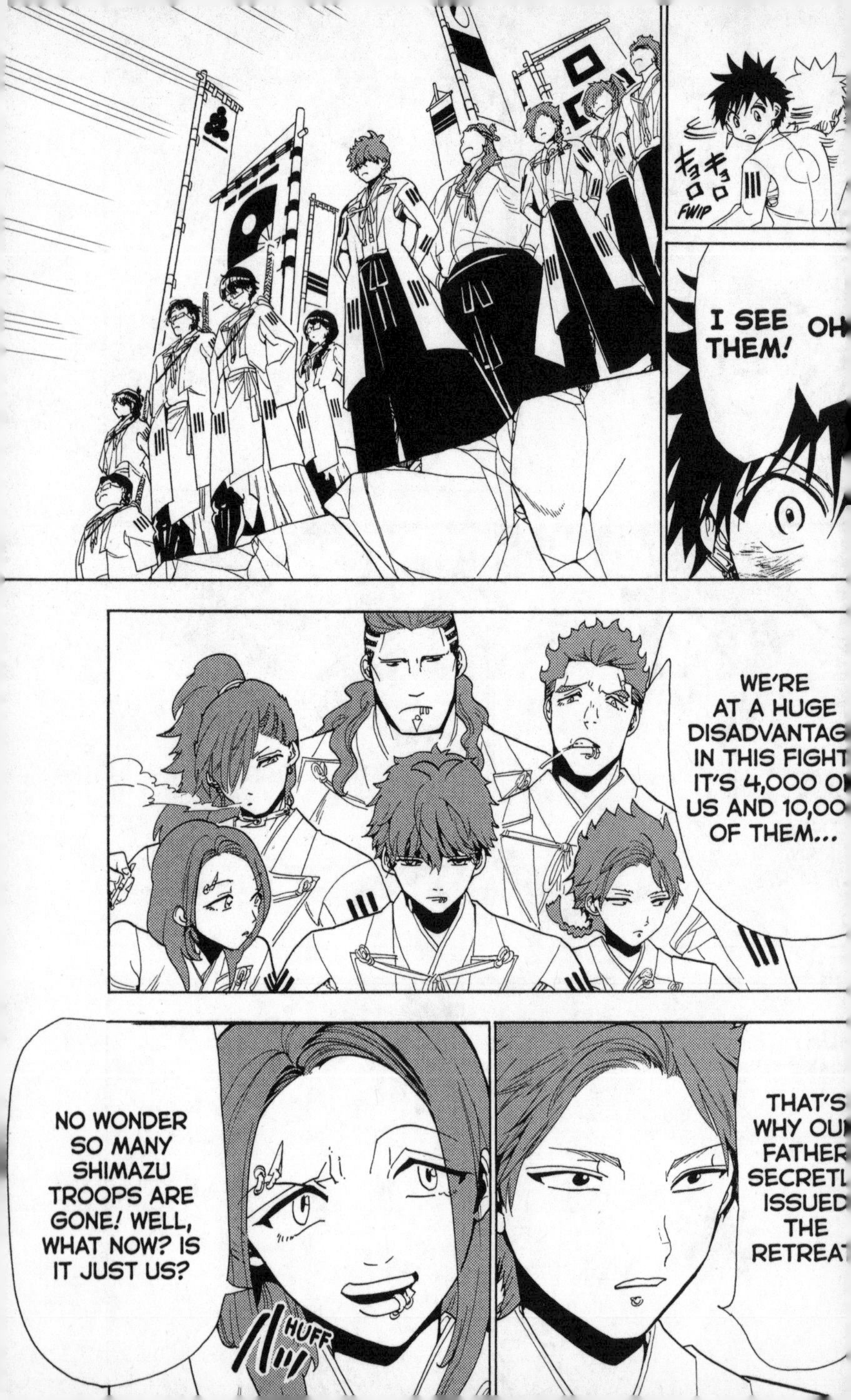
キョロキョロ
FWIP
OH
I SEE THEM!
WE'RE AT A HUGE DISADVANTAG IN THIS FIGHT IT'S 4,000 O US AND 10,00 OF THEM...
THAT'S WHY OU FATHER SECRETL ISSUED THE RETREA
NO WONDER SO MANY SHIMAZU TROOPS ARE GONE! WELL, WHAT NOW? IS IT JUST US?
HUFF

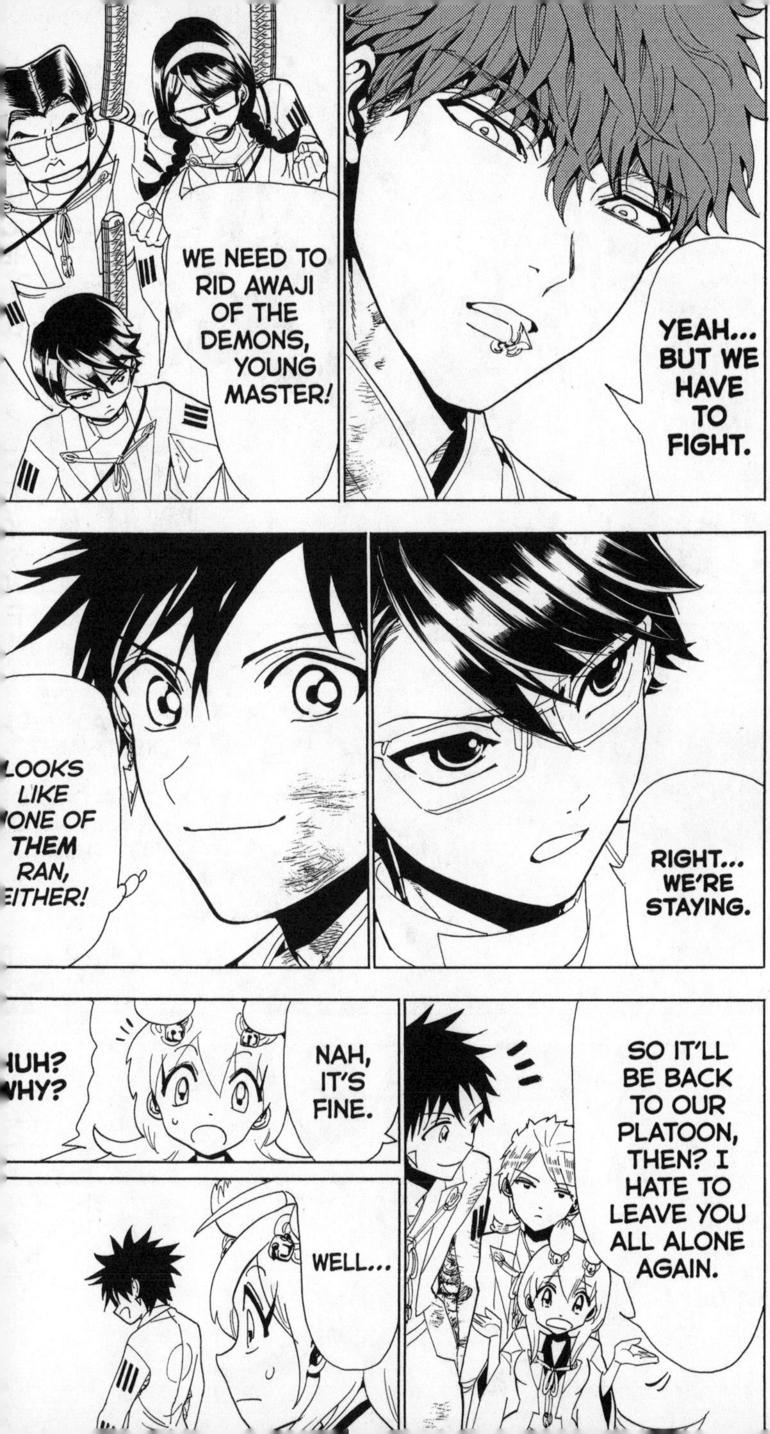
YEAH... BUT WE HAVE TO FIGHT.
WE NEED TO RID AWAJI OF THE DEMONS, YOUNG MASTER!
RIGHT... WE'RE STAYING.
LOOKS LIKE NONE OF THEM RAN, EITHER!
SO IT'LL BE BACK TO OUR PLATOON, THEN? I HATE TO LEAVE YOU ALL ALONE AGAIN.
NAH, IT'S FINE.
HUH? WHY?
WELL...

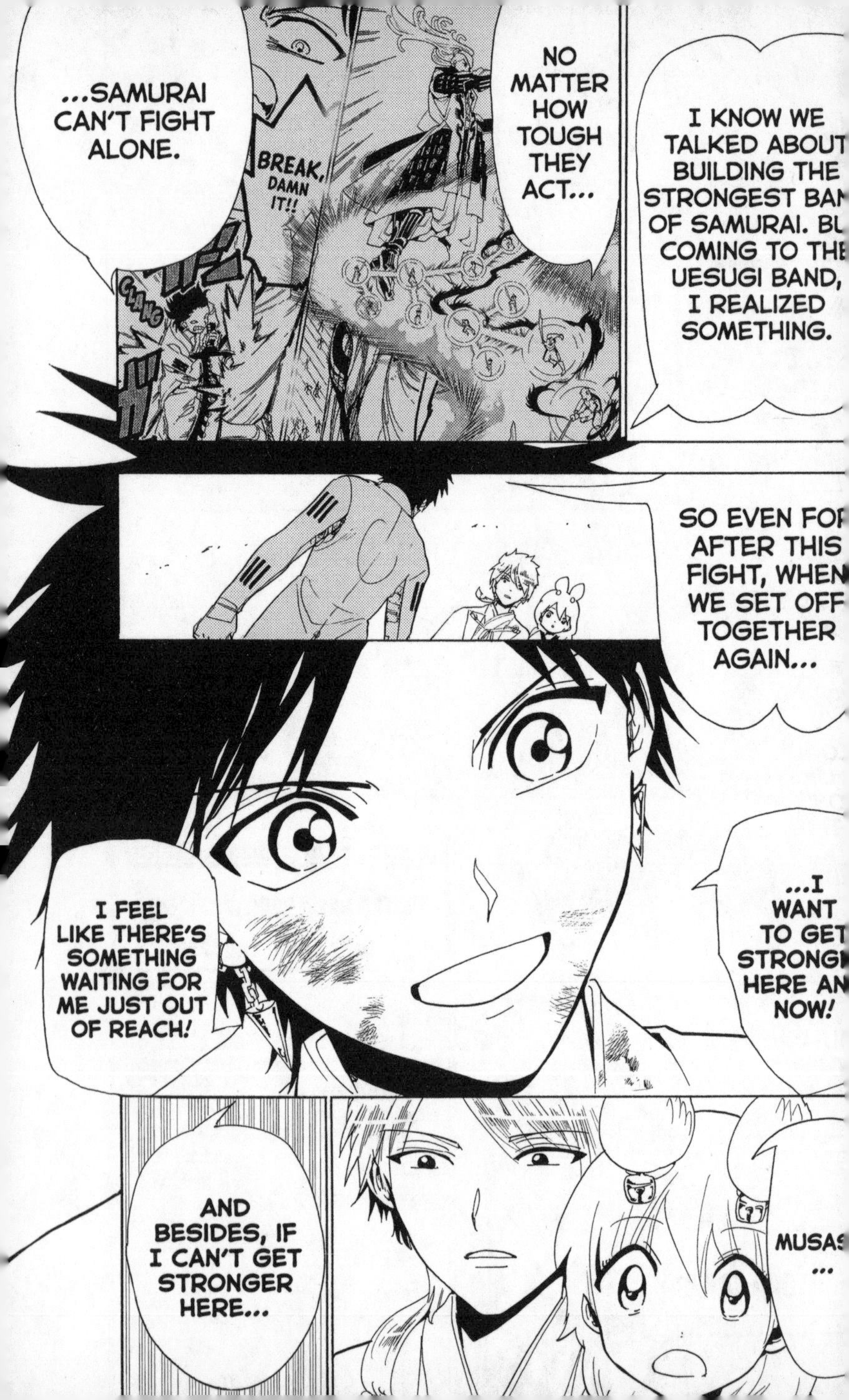
I KNOW WE TALKED ABOUT BUILDING THE STRONGEST BAN OF SAMURAI. BU COMING TO THE UESUGI BAND, I REALIZED SOMETHING.
NO MATTER HOW TOUGH THEY ACT...
BREAK, DAMN IT!!
...SAMURAI CAN'T FIGHT ALONE.
CLANG
SO EVEN FO AFTER THIS FIGHT, WHEN WE SET OFF TOGETHER AGAIN...
...I WANT TO GET STRONG HERE AN NOW!
I FEEL LIKE THERE'S SOMETHING WAITING FOR ME JUST OUT OF REACH!
MUSAS ...
AND BESIDES, IF I CAN'T GET STRONGER HERE...

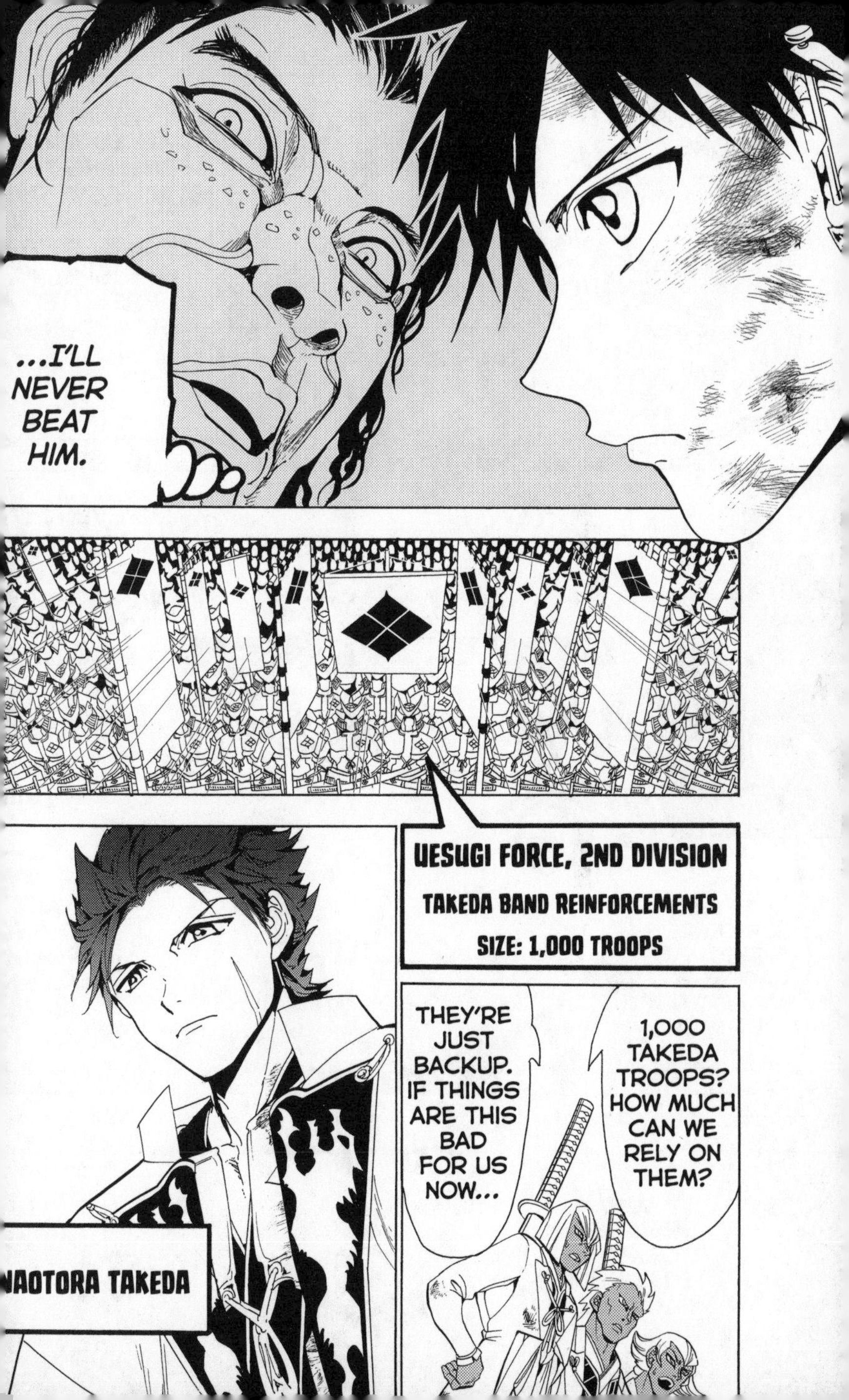
...I'LL NEVER BEAT HIM.
UESUGI FORCE, 2ND DIVISION
TAKEDA BAND REINFORCEMENTS
SIZE: 1,000 TROOPS
1,000 TAKEDA TROOPS? HOW MUCH CAN WE RELY ON THEM?
THEY'RE JUST BACKUP. IF THINGS ARE THIS BAD FOR US NOW...
NAOTORA TAKEDA

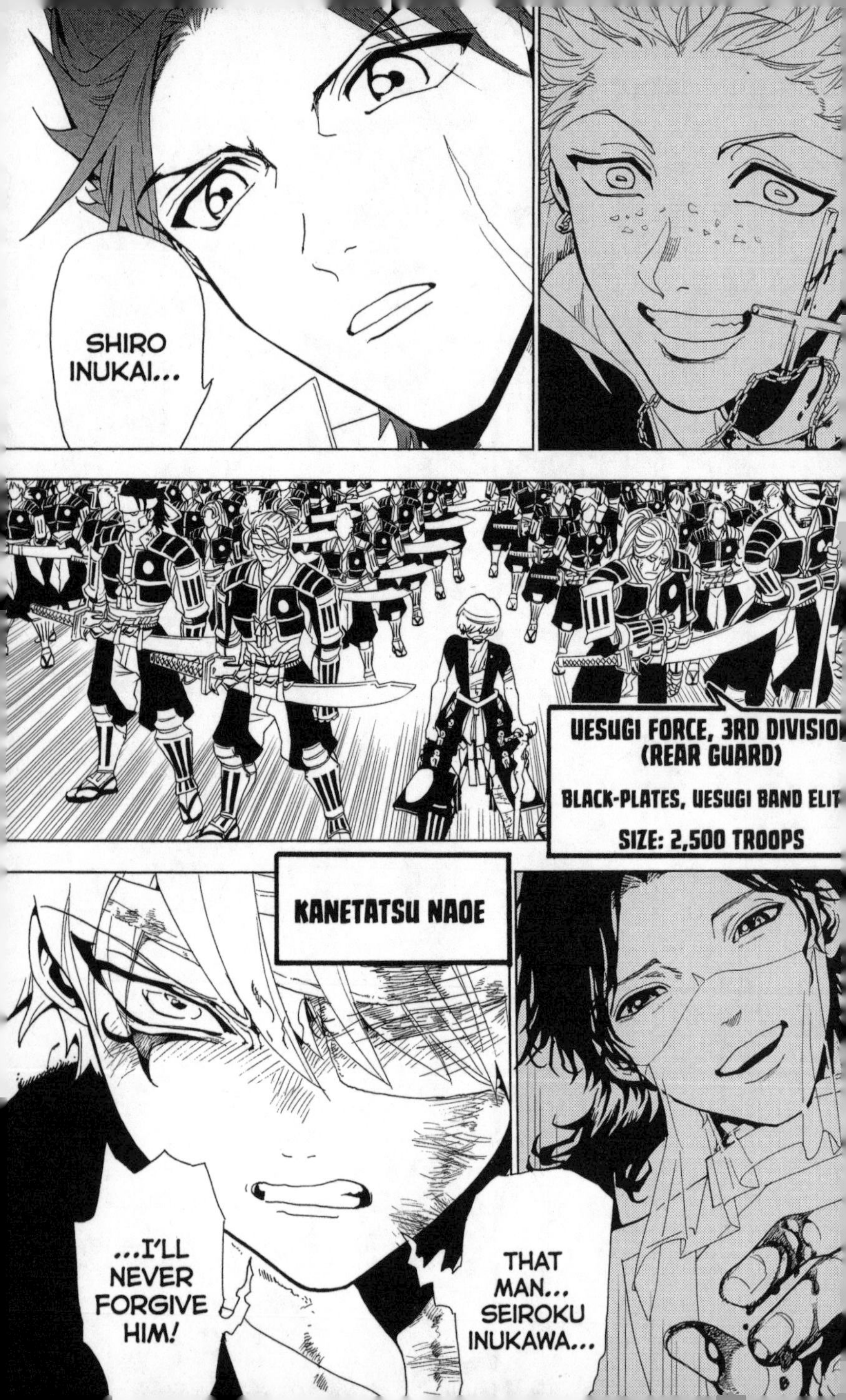
SHIRO INUKAI...
UESUGI FORCE, 3RD DIVISIO
(REAR GUARD)
BLACK-PLATES, UESUGI BAND ELIT
SIZE: 2,500 TROOPS
THAT MAN... SEIROKU INUKAWA...
KANETATSU NAOE
...I'LL NEVER FORGIVE HIM!

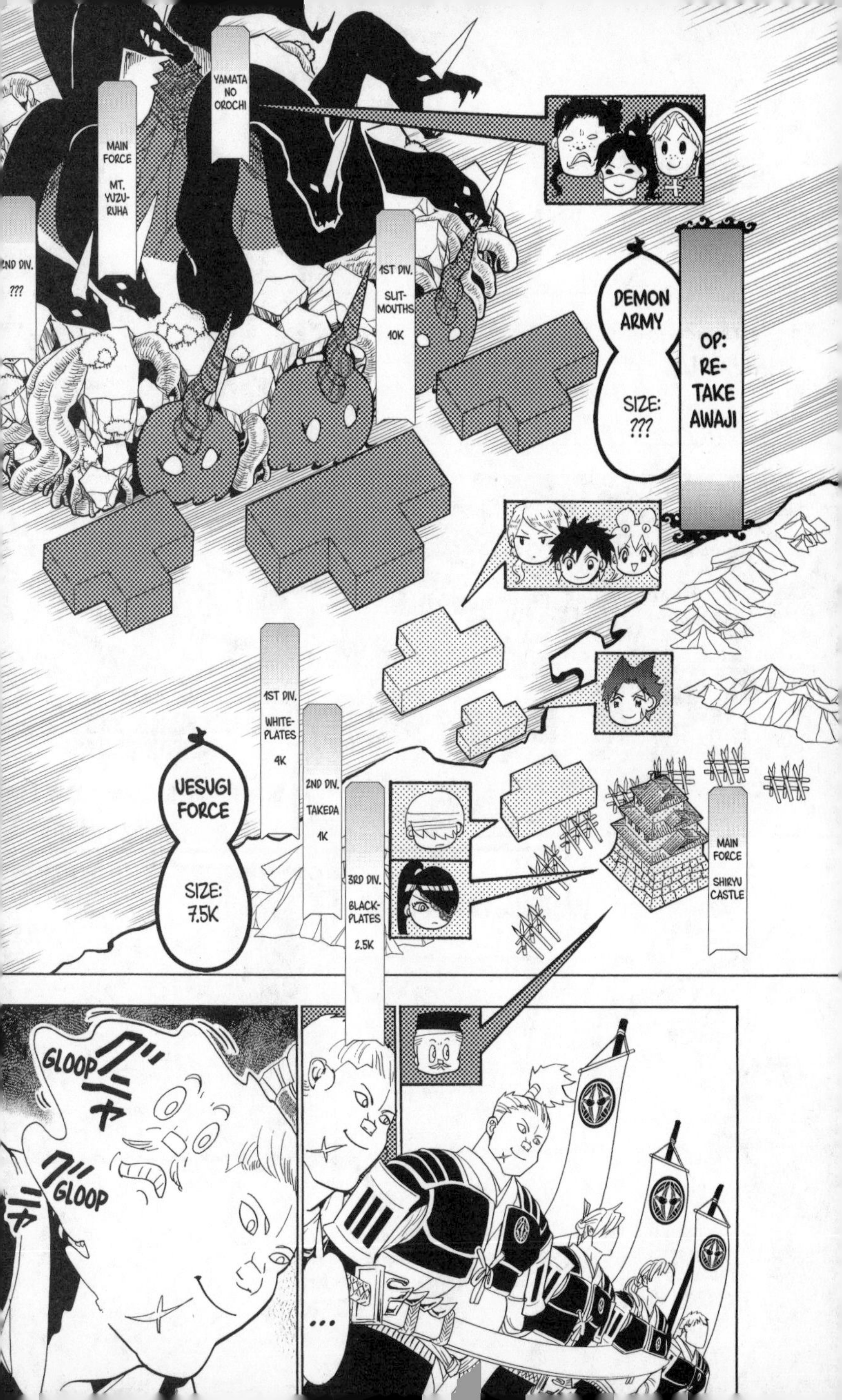
OP: RE-TAKE AWAJI
DEMON ARMY
SIZE: ???
YAMATA NO OROCHI
MAIN FORCE
MT. YUZU-RUHA
1ST DIV.
SLIT-MOUTHS
10K
2ND DIV.
???
MAIN FORCE
SHIRYU CASTLE
3RD DIV.
BLACK-PLATES
2.5K
2ND DIV.
TAKEDA
1K
1ST DIV.
WHITE-PLATES
4K
UESUGI FORCE
SIZE: 7.5K
...
GLOOP
GLOOP

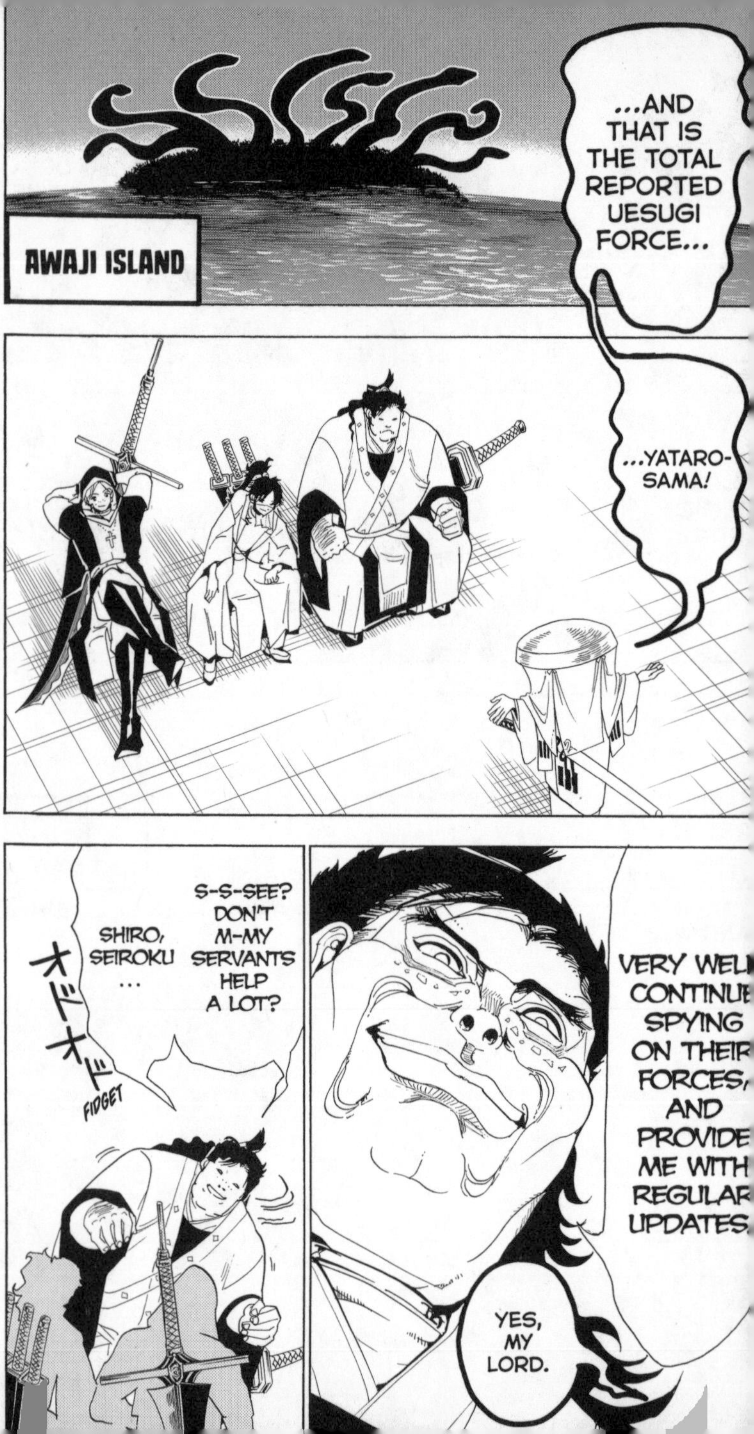
...AND THAT IS THE TOTAL REPORTED UESUGI FORCE...
AWAJI ISLAND
...YATARO-SAMA!
VERY WEL CONTINU SPYING ON THEI FORCES, AND PROVIDE ME WITH REGULA UPDATES.
YES, MY LORD.
S-S-SEE? DON'T M-MY SERVANTS HELP A LOT?
SHIRO, SEIROKU ...
オドオド
FIDGET

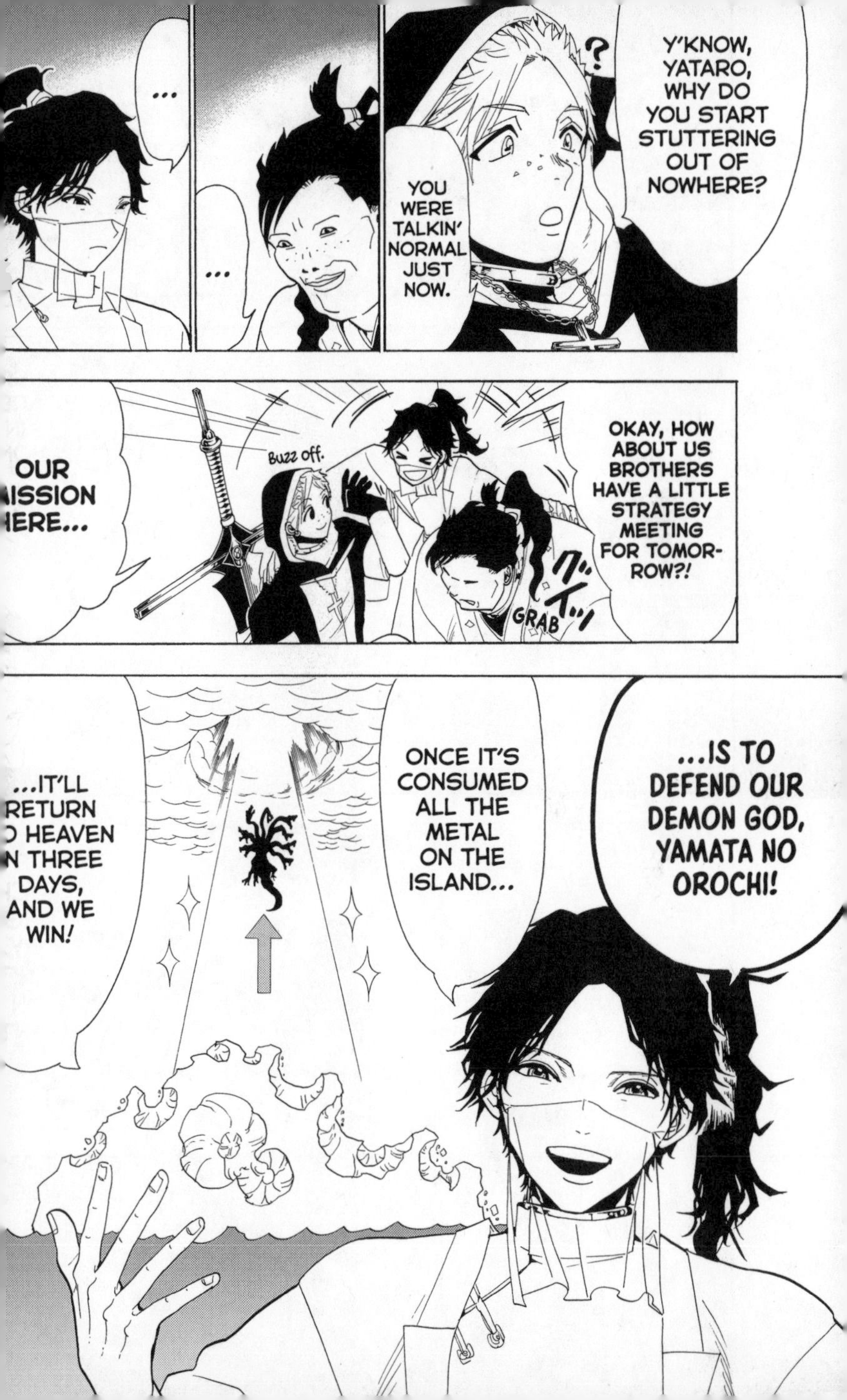
Y'KNOW, YATARO, WHY DO YOU START STUTTERING OUT OF NOWHERE?
YOU WERE TALKIN' NORMAL JUST NOW.
...
...
OKAY, HOW ABOUT US BROTHERS HAVE A LITTLE STRATEGY MEETING FOR TOMORROW?!
GRAB
Buzz off.
OUR ISSION HERE...
...IS TO DEFEND OUR DEMON GOD, YAMATA NO OROCHI!
ONCE IT'S CONSUMED ALL THE METAL ON THE ISLAND...
...IT'LL RETURN O HEAVEN N THREE DAYS, AND WE WIN!

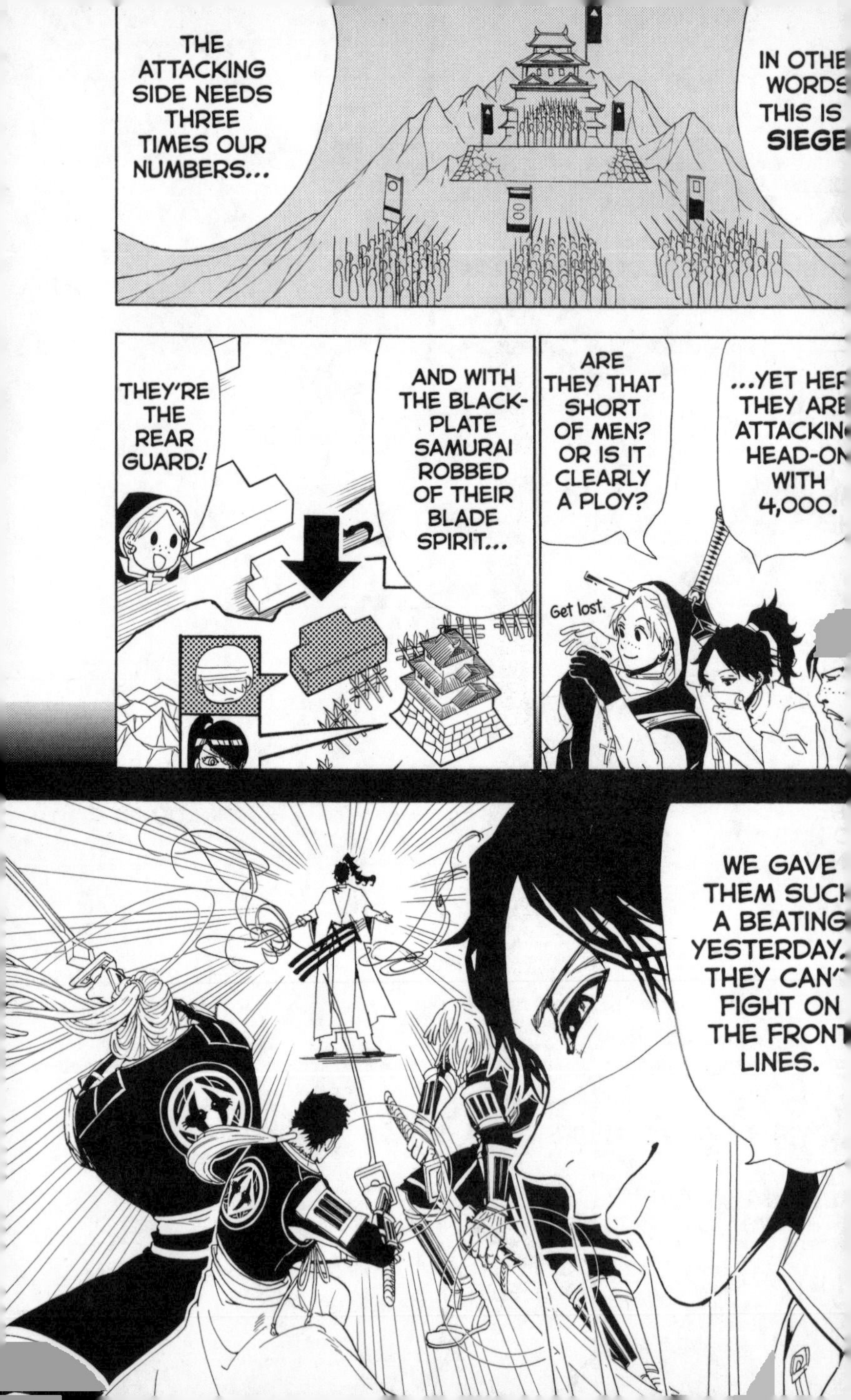
IN OTHE WORDS THIS IS SIEGE
THE ATTACKING SIDE NEEDS THREE TIMES OUR NUMBERS...
...YET HER THEY ARE ATTACKIN HEAD-ON WITH 4,000.
ARE THEY THAT SHORT OF MEN? OR IS IT CLEARLY A PLOY?
Get lost.
AND WITH THE BLACK-PLATE SAMURAI ROBBED OF THEIR BLADE SPIRIT...
THEY'RE THE REAR GUARD!
WE GAVE THEM SUC A BEATING YESTERDAY. THEY CAN' FIGHT ON THE FRONT LINES.

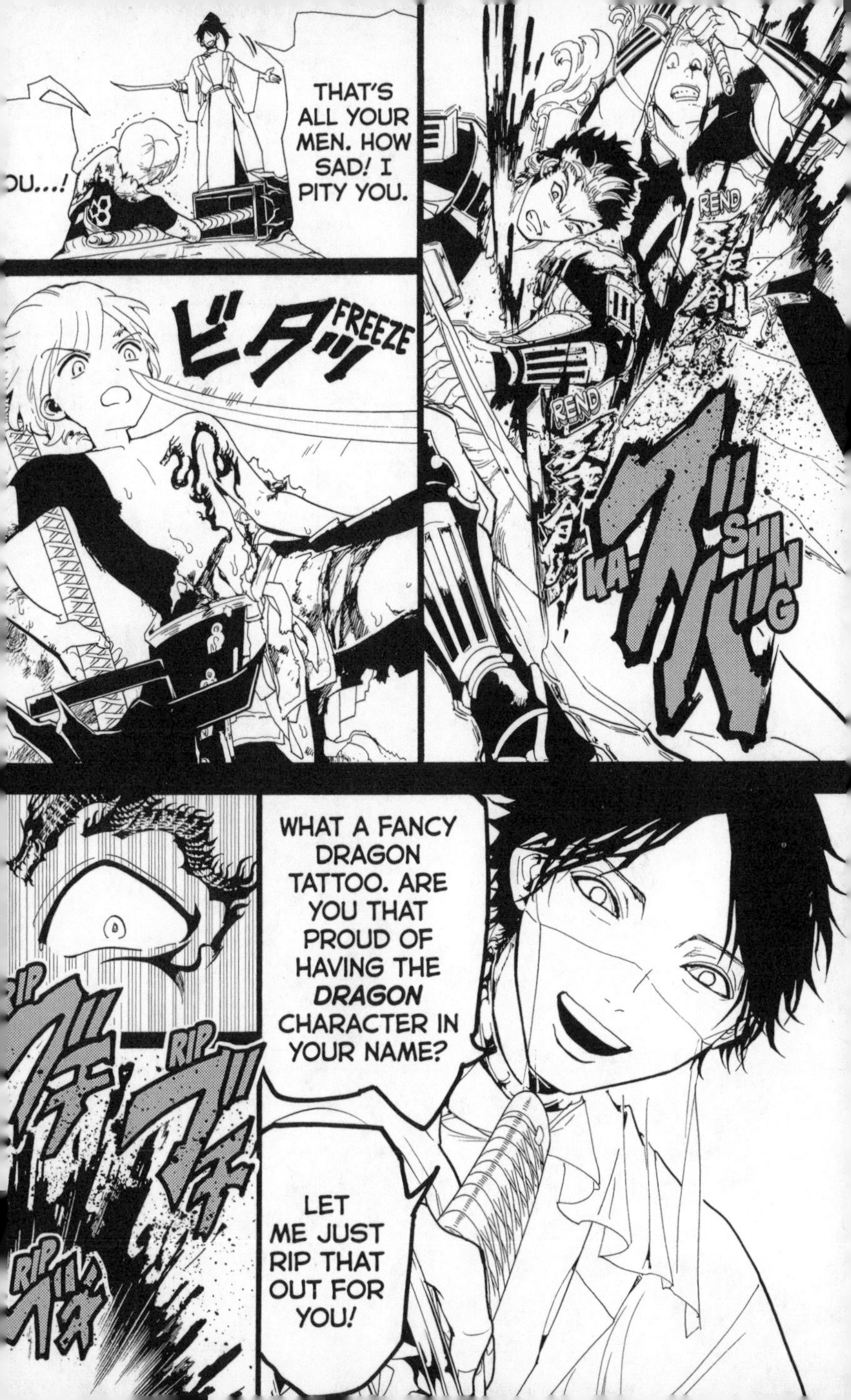
REND
REND
KA-SHIING
THAT'S ALL YOUR MEN. HOW SAD! I PITY YOU.
OU...!
FREEZE
WHAT A FANCY DRAGON TATTOO. ARE YOU THAT PROUD OF HAVING THE *DRAGON* CHARACTER IN YOUR NAME?
LET ME JUST RIP THAT OUT FOR YOU!
RIP
RIP
RIP

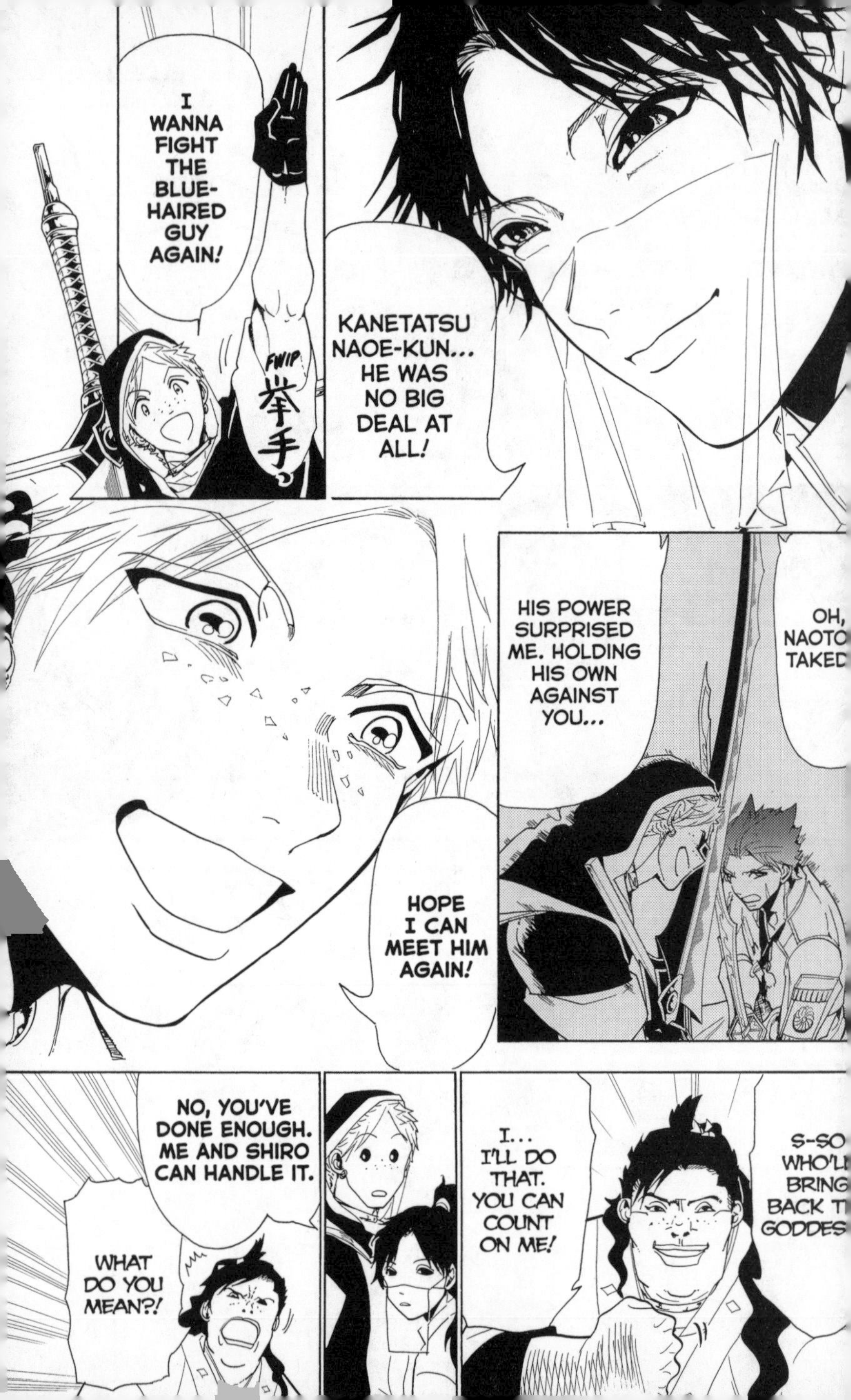
KANETATSU NAOE-KUN... HE WAS NO BIG DEAL AT ALL!
I WANNA FIGHT THE BLUE-HAIRED GUY AGAIN!
FWIP
挙手
OH, NAOTO TAKED
HIS POWER SURPRISED ME. HOLDING HIS OWN AGAINST YOU...
HOPE I CAN MEET HIM AGAIN!
S-SO WHO'L BRING BACK T GODDES
I... I'LL DO THAT. YOU CAN COUNT ON ME!
NO, YOU'VE DONE ENOUGH. ME AND SHIRO CAN HANDLE IT.
WHAT DO YOU MEAN?!

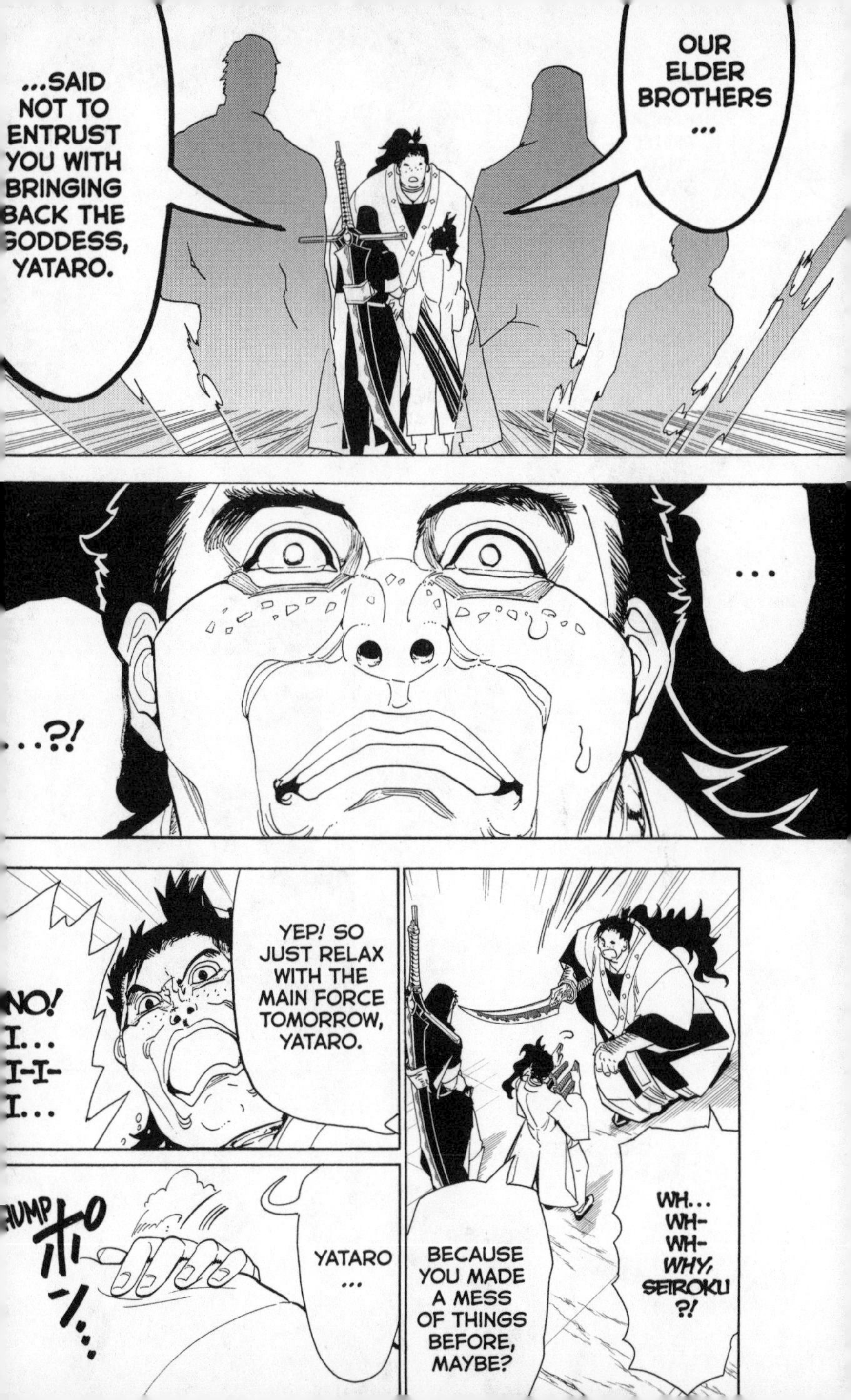
OUR ELDER BROTHERS ...
...SAID NOT TO ENTRUST YOU WITH BRINGING BACK THE GODDESS, YATARO.
...
...?!
WH... WH- WH- WHY, SEIROKU ?!
YEP! SO JUST RELAX WITH THE MAIN FORCE TOMORROW, YATARO.
NO! I... I-I- I...
BECAUSE YOU MADE A MESS OF THINGS BEFORE, MAYBE?
YATARO ...
THUMP
ポン...

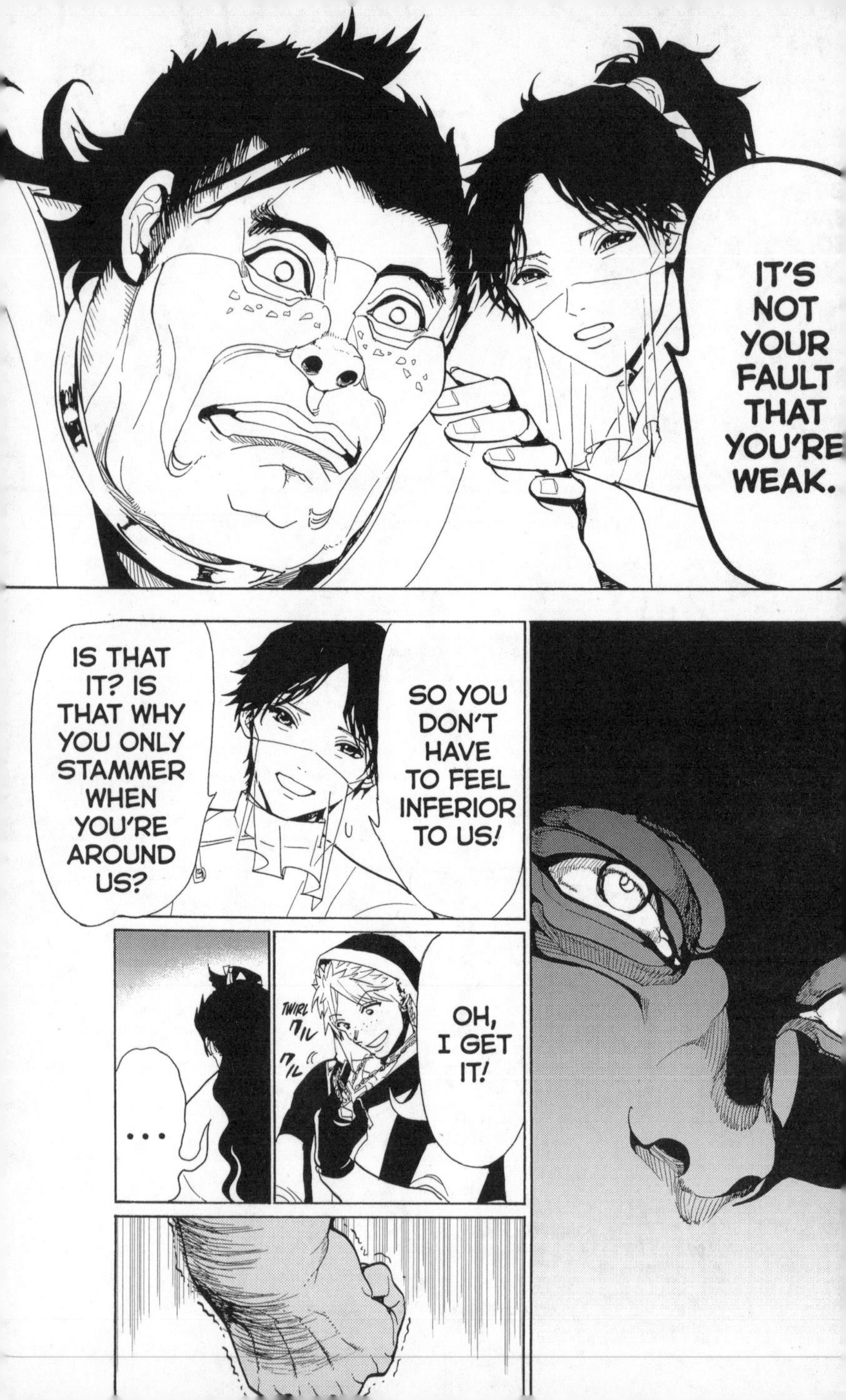
IT'S NOT YOUR FAULT THAT YOU'RE WEAK.
SO YOU DON'T HAVE TO FEEL INFERIOR TO US!
IS THAT IT? IS THAT WHY YOU ONLY STAMMER WHEN YOU'RE AROUND US?
OH, I GET IT!
TWIRL
...

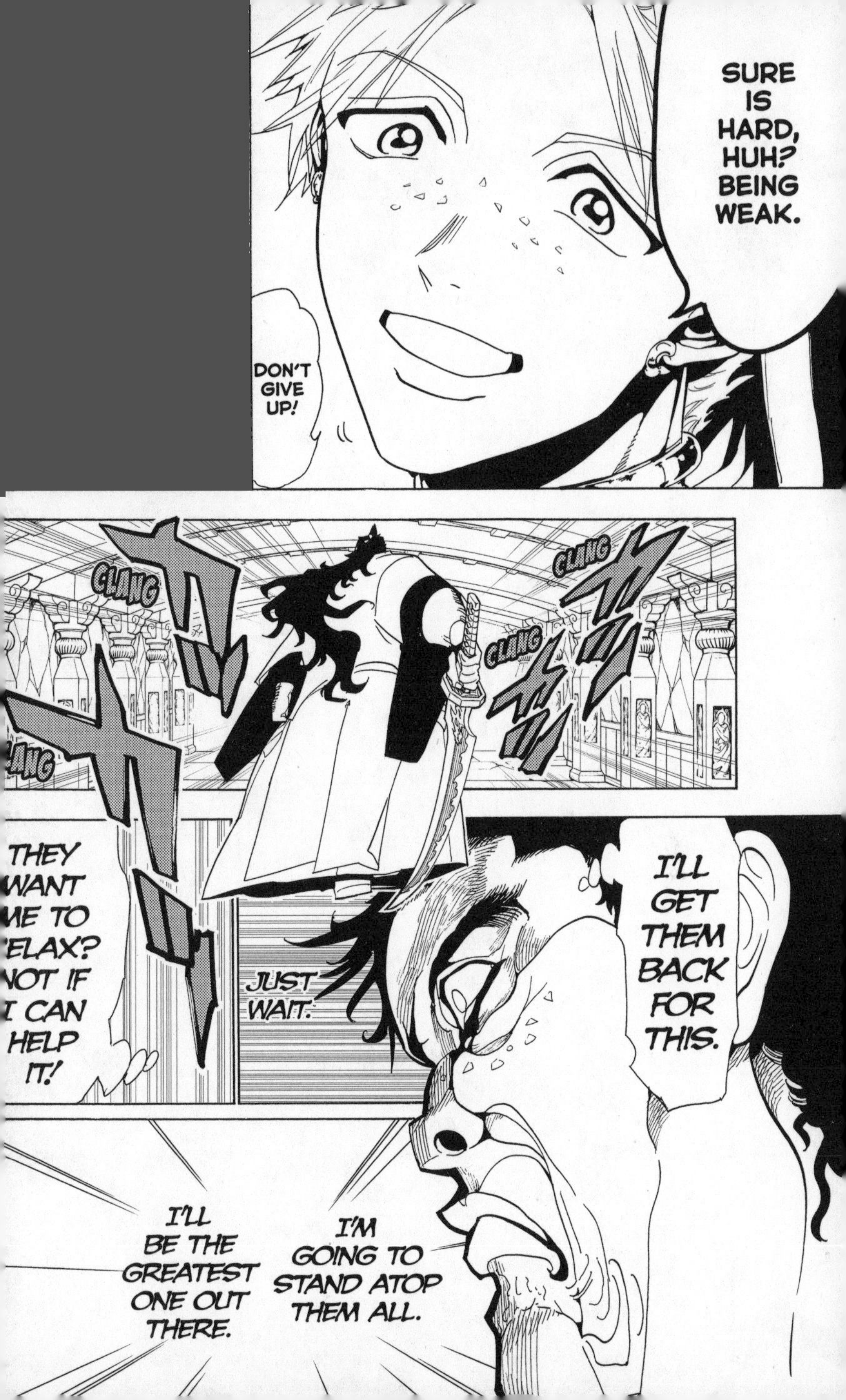
SURE IS HARD, HUH? BEING WEAK.
DON'T GIVE UP!
CLANG
CLANG
CLANG
CLANG
I'LL GET THEM BACK FOR THIS.
JUST WAIT.
THEY WANT ME TO RELAX? NOT IF I CAN HELP IT!
I'M GOING TO STAND ATOP THEM ALL.
I'LL BE THE GREATEST ONE OUT THERE.

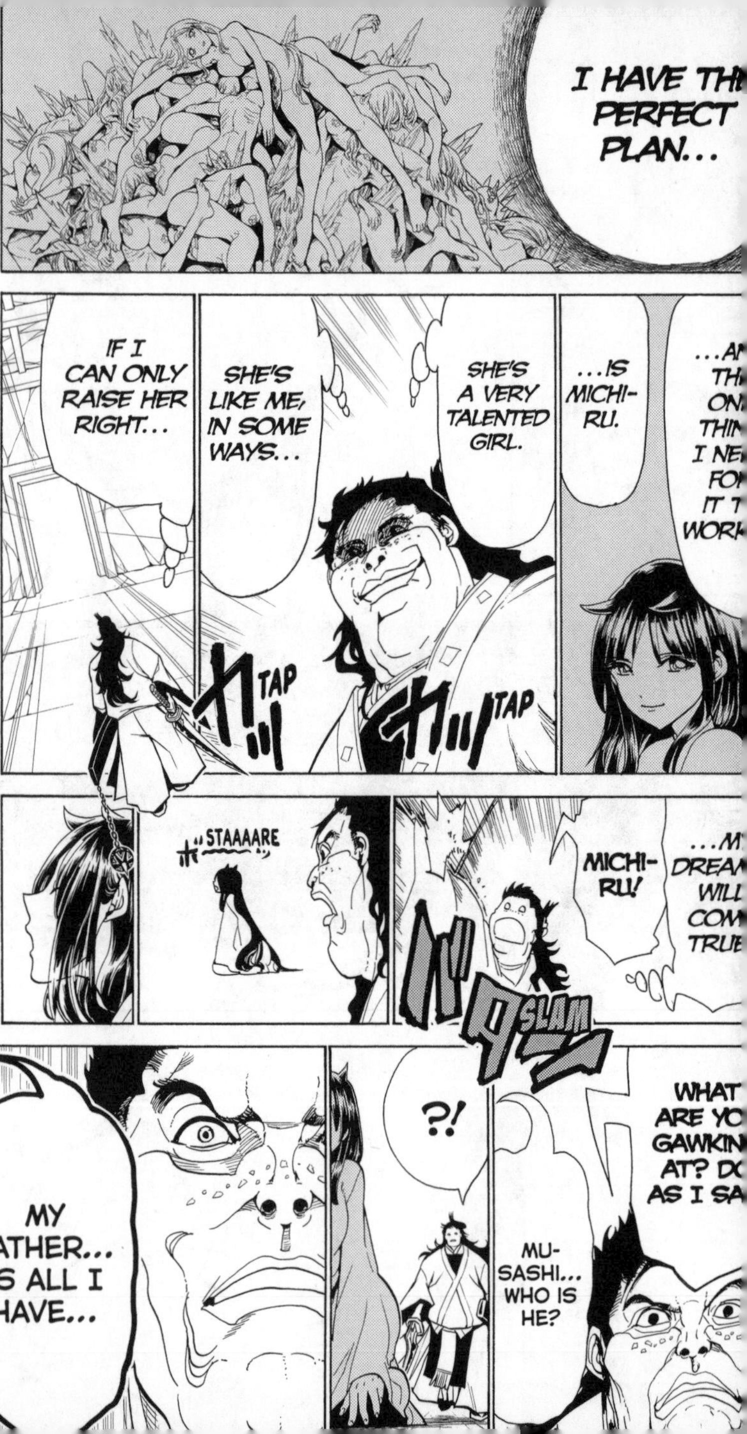

I HAVE TH PERFECT PLAN…
…AN TH ON THIN I NE FO IT T WORK
…IS MICHI-RU.
SHE'S A VERY TALENTED GIRL.
TAP
SHE'S LIKE ME, IN SOME WAYS…
TAP
IF I CAN ONLY RAISE HER RIGHT…
…M DREA WILL COM TRUE
MICHI-RU!
SLAM
STAAAARE
WHAT ARE YO GAWKIN AT? DO AS I SA
MU-SASHI… WHO IS HE?
?!
MY FATHER… IS ALL I HAVE…

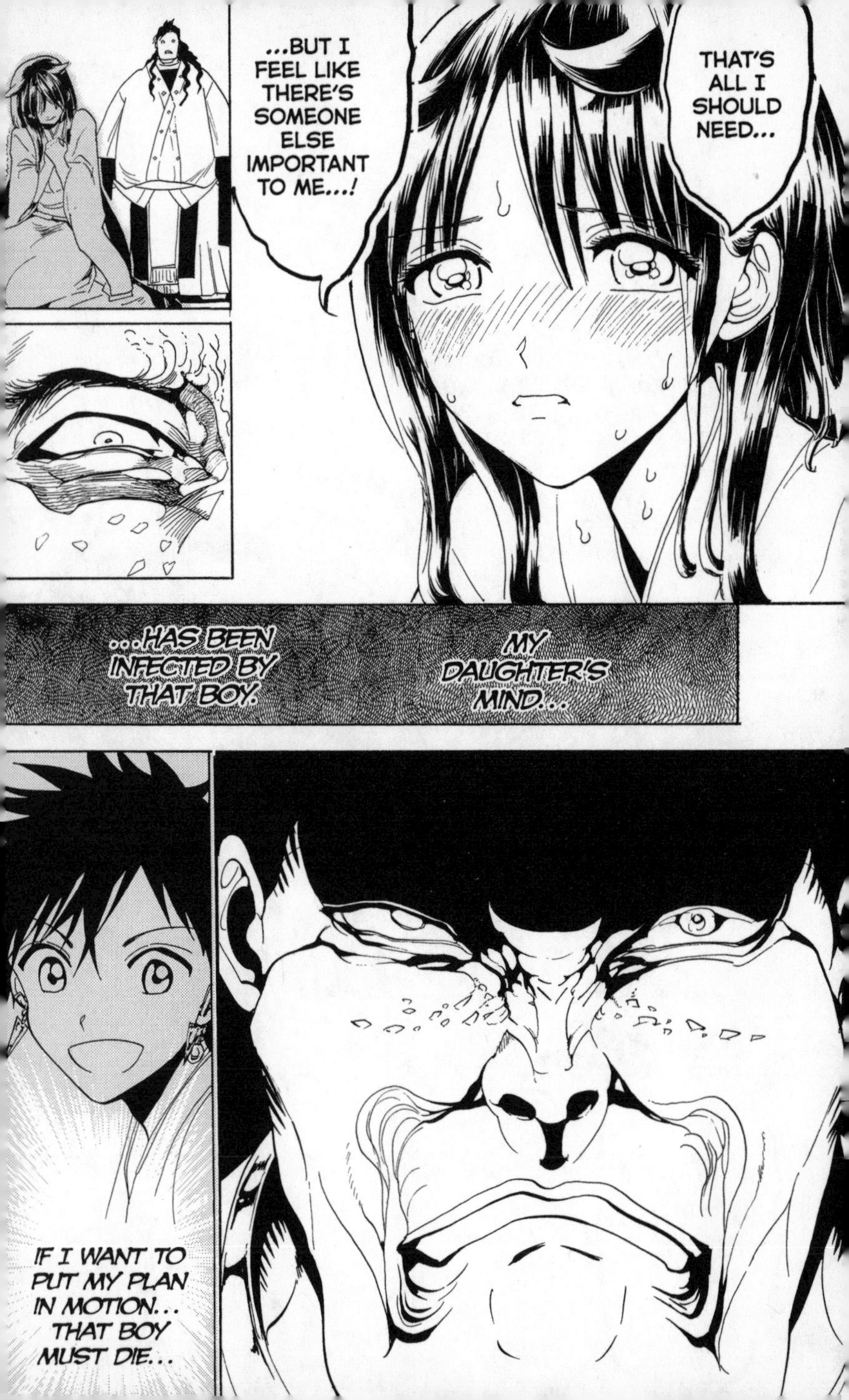
THAT'S ALL I SHOULD NEED...
...BUT I FEEL LIKE THERE'S SOMEONE ELSE IMPORTANT TO ME...!
MY DAUGHTER'S MIND...
...HAS BEEN INFECTED BY THAT BOY.
IF I WANT TO PUT MY PLAN IN MOTION... THAT BOY MUST DIE...

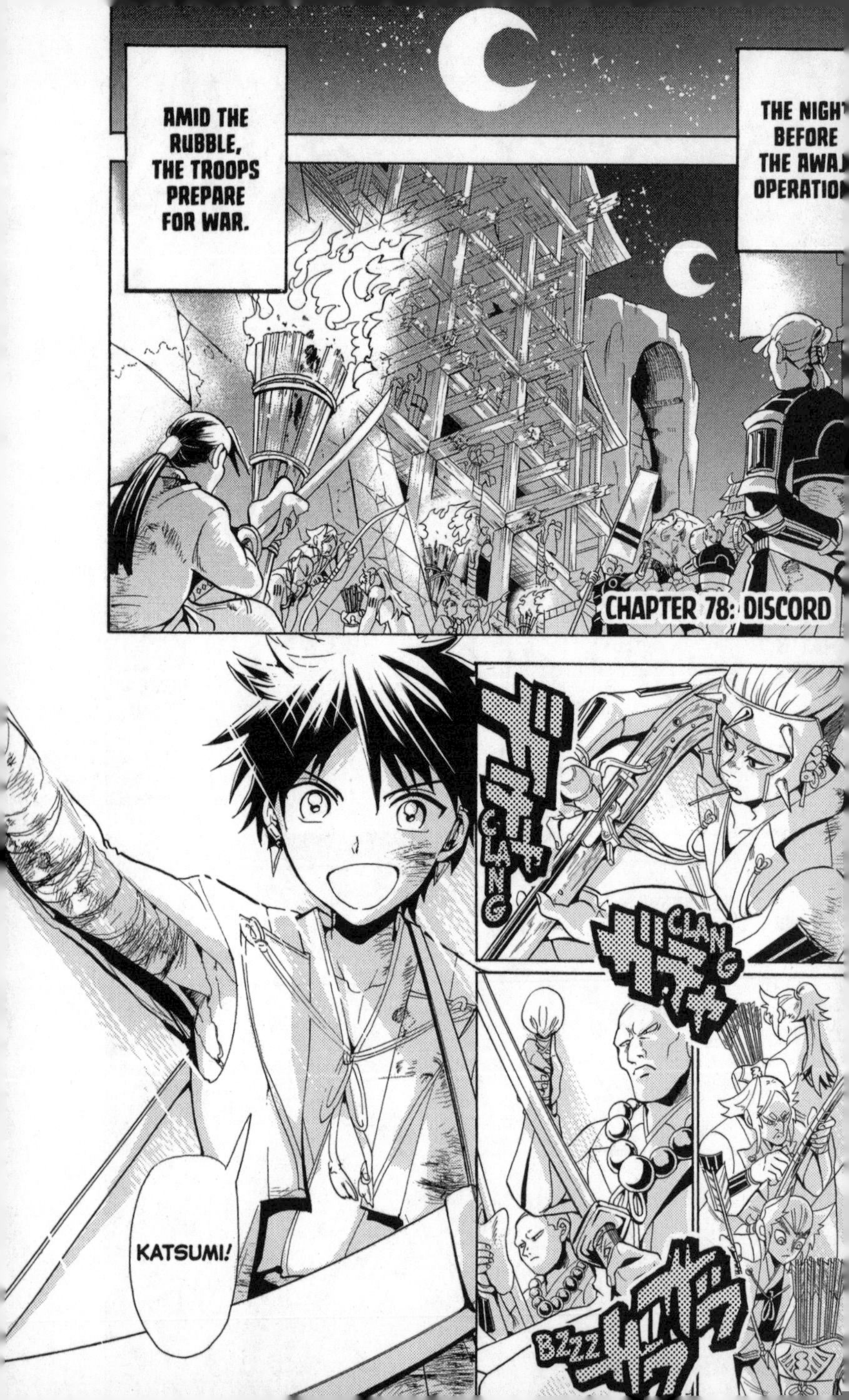
THE NIGHT BEFORE THE AWAJ OPERATIO
AMID THE RUBBLE, THE TROOPS PREPARE FOR WAR.
CHAPTER 78: DISCORD
CLANG
CLANG
BZZZ
KATSUMI!

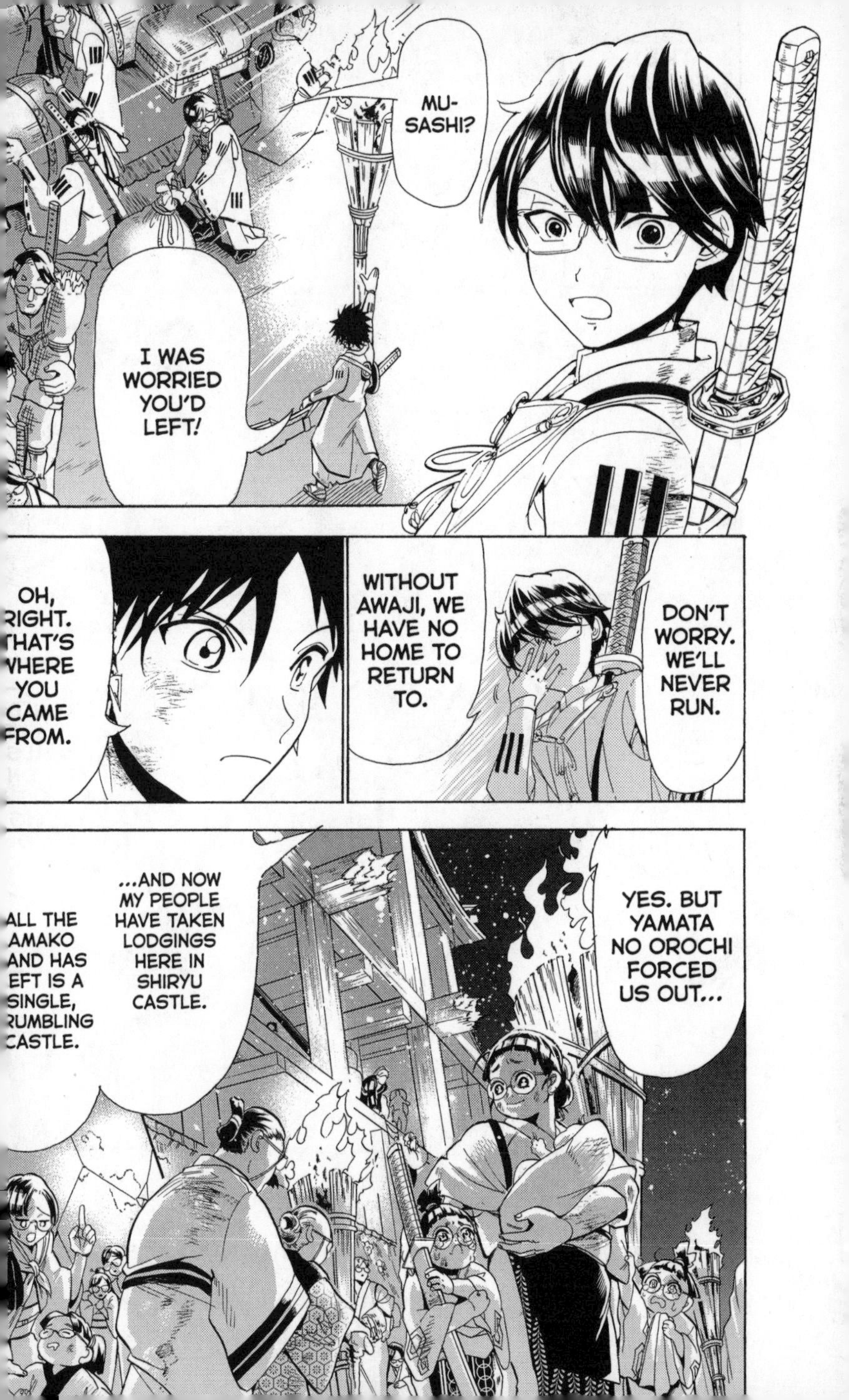
MU-SASHI?
I WAS WORRIED YOU'D LEFT!
DON'T WORRY. WE'LL NEVER RUN.
WITHOUT AWAJI, WE HAVE NO HOME TO RETURN TO.
OH, IGHT. HAT'S HERE YOU CAME ROM.
YES. BUT YAMATA NO OROCHI FORCED US OUT...
...AND NOW MY PEOPLE HAVE TAKEN LODGINGS HERE IN SHIRYU CASTLE.
ALL THE AMAKO AND HAS EFT IS A SINGLE, UMBLING ASTLE.

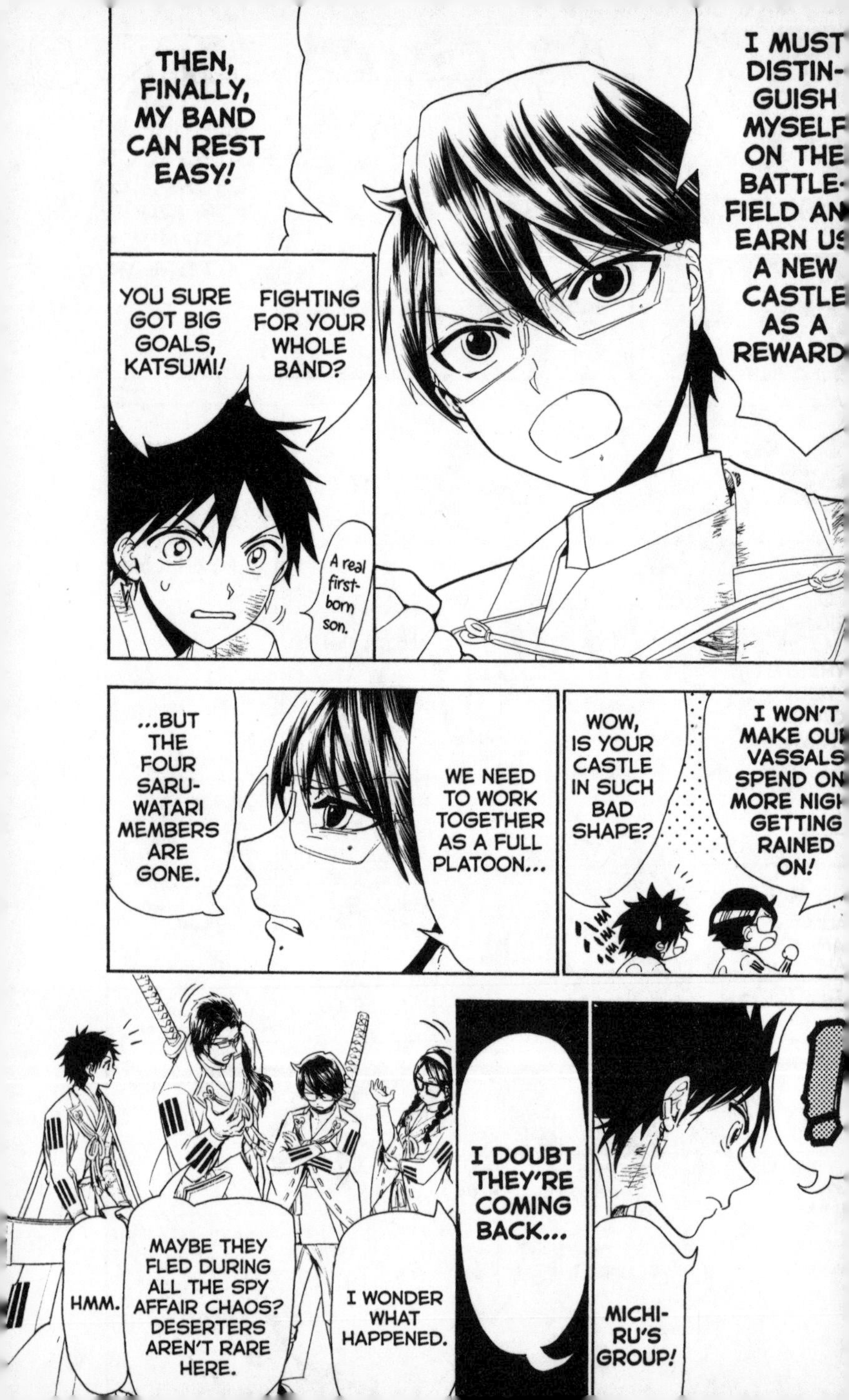
I MUST DISTIN-GUISH MYSELF ON THE BATTLE-FIELD AN EARN US A NEW CASTLE AS A REWARD
THEN, FINALLY, MY BAND CAN REST EASY!
FIGHTING FOR YOUR WHOLE BAND?
YOU SURE GOT BIG GOALS, KATSUMI!
A real first-born son.
I WON'T MAKE OU VASSALS SPEND ON MORE NIG GETTING RAINED ON!
WOW, IS YOUR CASTLE IN SUCH BAD SHAPE?
HA HA HA
WE NEED TO WORK TOGETHER AS A FULL PLATOON...
...BUT THE FOUR SARU-WATARI MEMBERS ARE GONE.
!
MICHI-RU'S GROUP!
I DOUBT THEY'RE COMING BACK...
I WONDER WHAT HAPPENED.
MAYBE THEY FLED DURING ALL THE SPY AFFAIR CHAOS? DESERTERS AREN'T RARE HERE.
HMM.

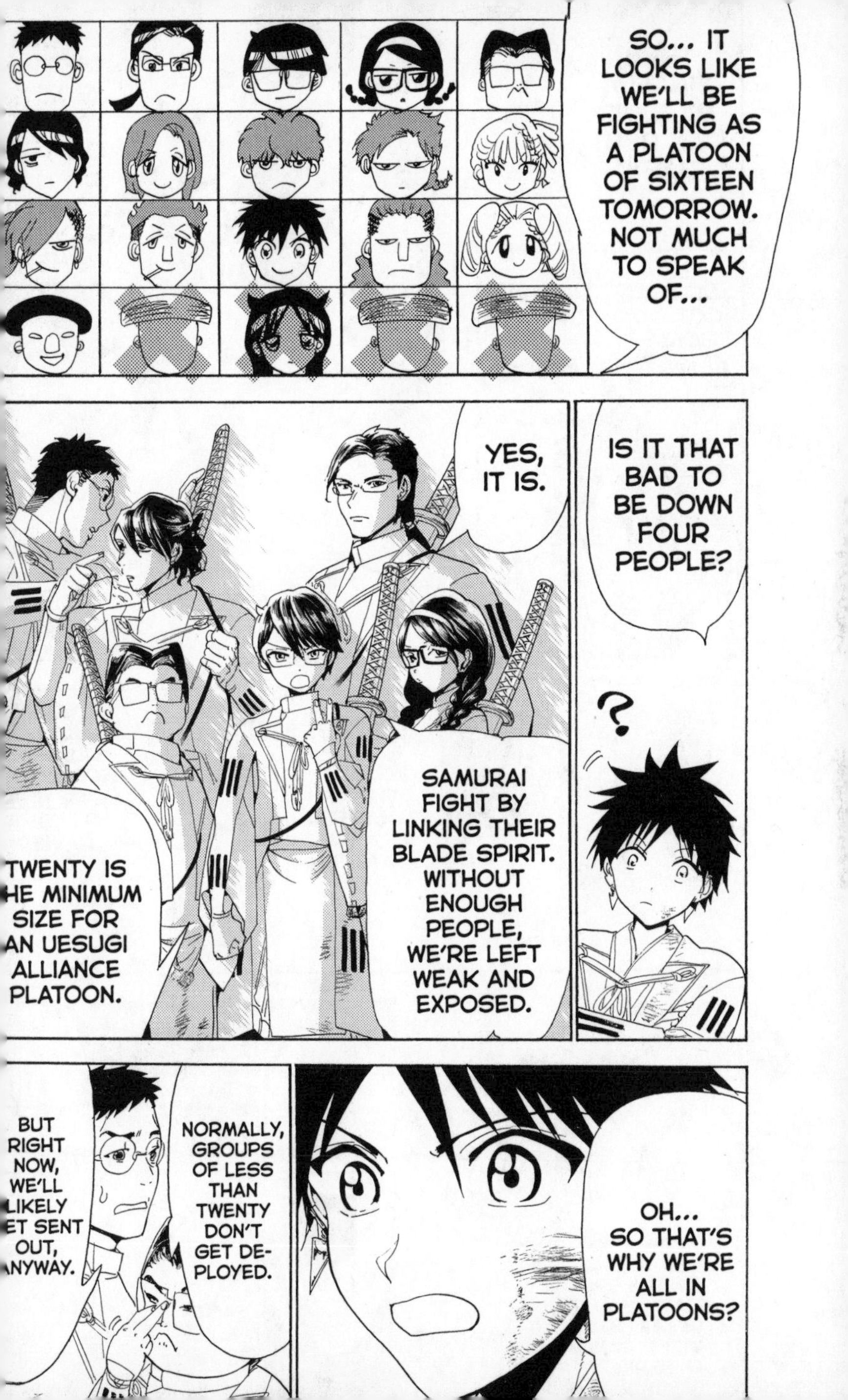
SO... IT LOOKS LIKE WE'LL BE FIGHTING AS A PLATOON OF SIXTEEN TOMORROW. NOT MUCH TO SPEAK OF...
IS IT THAT BAD TO BE DOWN FOUR PEOPLE?
YES, IT IS.
SAMURAI FIGHT BY LINKING THEIR BLADE SPIRIT. WITHOUT ENOUGH PEOPLE, WE'RE LEFT WEAK AND EXPOSED.
TWENTY IS HE MINIMUM SIZE FOR AN UESUGI ALLIANCE PLATOON.
OH... SO THAT'S WHY WE'RE ALL IN PLATOONS?
NORMALLY, GROUPS OF LESS THAN TWENTY DON'T GET DE-PLOYED.
BUT RIGHT NOW, WE'LL LIKELY ET SENT OUT, NYWAY.

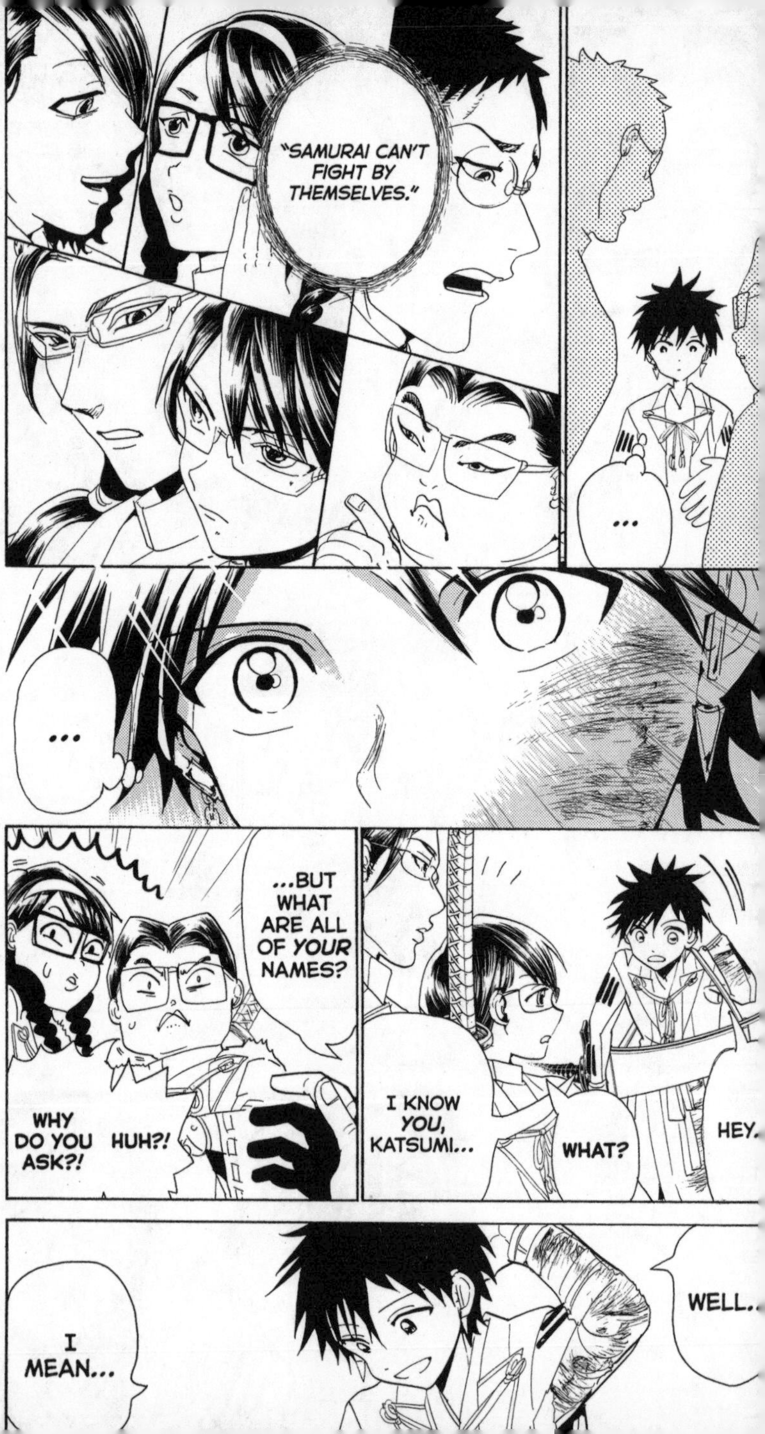
...
"SAMURAI CAN'T FIGHT BY THEMSELVES."
...
HEY.
WHAT?
I KNOW *YOU*, KATSUMI...
...BUT WHAT ARE ALL OF *YOUR* NAMES?
HUH?!
WHY DO YOU ASK?!
WELL...
I MEAN...

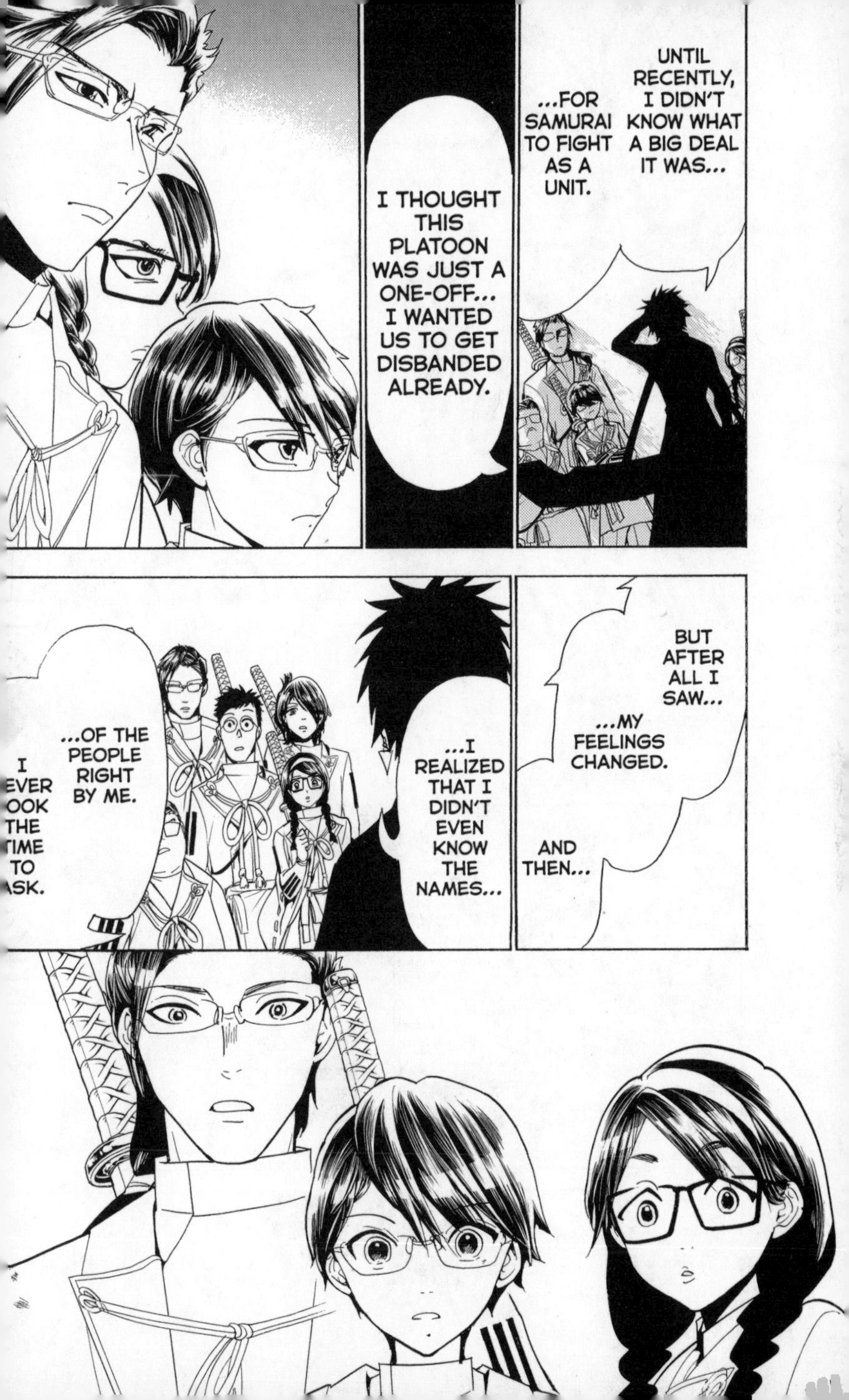
UNTIL RECENTLY, I DIDN'T KNOW WHAT A BIG DEAL IT WAS...
...FOR SAMURAI TO FIGHT AS A UNIT.
I THOUGHT THIS PLATOON WAS JUST A ONE-OFF... I WANTED US TO GET DISBANDED ALREADY.
BUT AFTER ALL I SAW...
...MY FEELINGS CHANGED.
AND THEN...
...I REALIZED THAT I DIDN'T EVEN KNOW THE NAMES...
...OF THE PEOPLE RIGHT BY ME.
I EVER OOK THE IME TO SK.

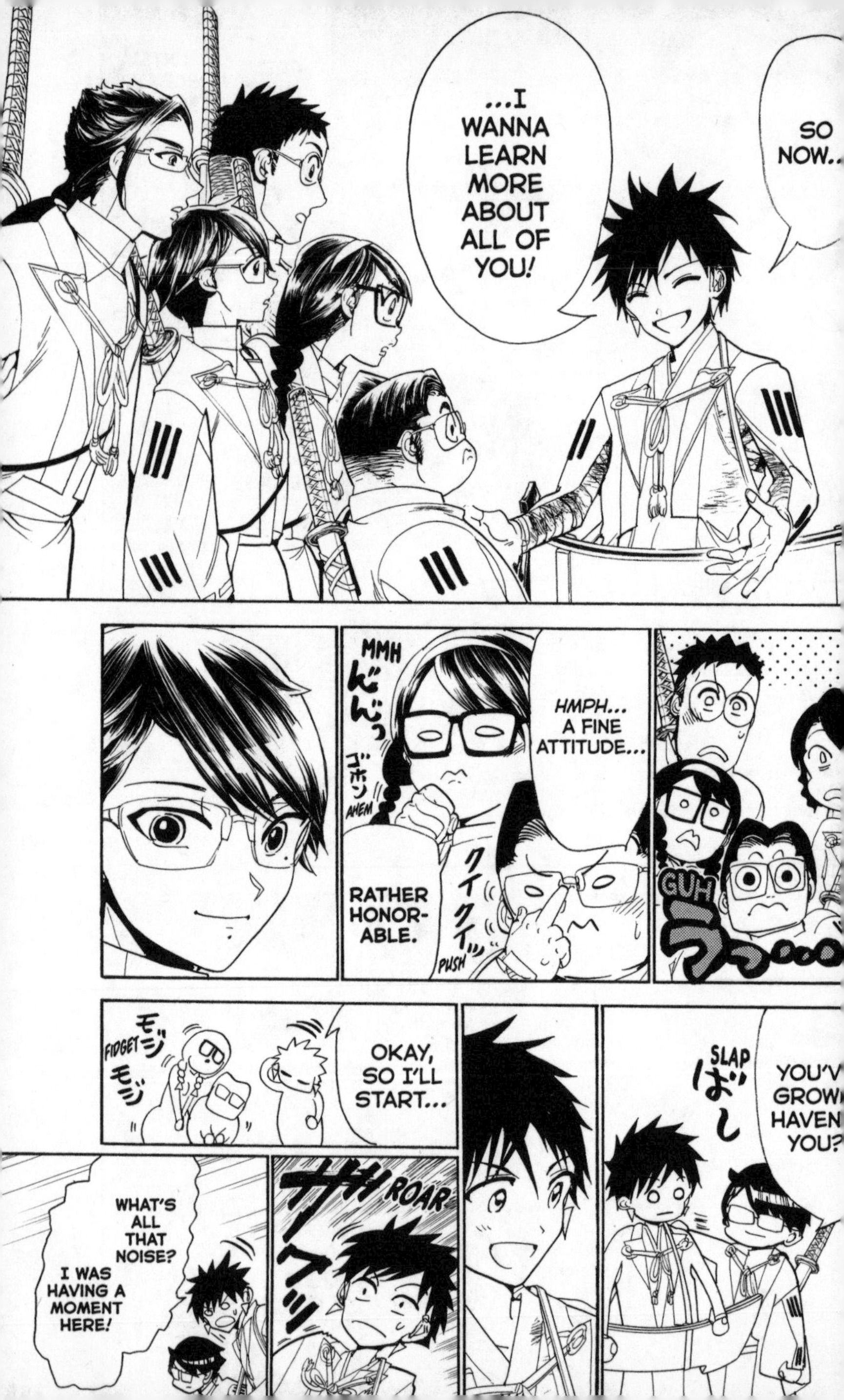
SO NOW...
...I WANNA LEARN MORE ABOUT ALL OF YOU!
GUH
うっ…
HMPH... A FINE ATTITUDE...
MMH
んじっ
ゴホン
AHEM
RATHER HONOR-ABLE.
クイクイ
PUSH
SLAP
ばし
YOU'V GROW HAVEN YOU?
OKAY, SO I'LL START...
FIDGET
モジ
モジ
ROAR
WHAT'S ALL THAT NOISE?
I WAS HAVING A MOMENT HERE!

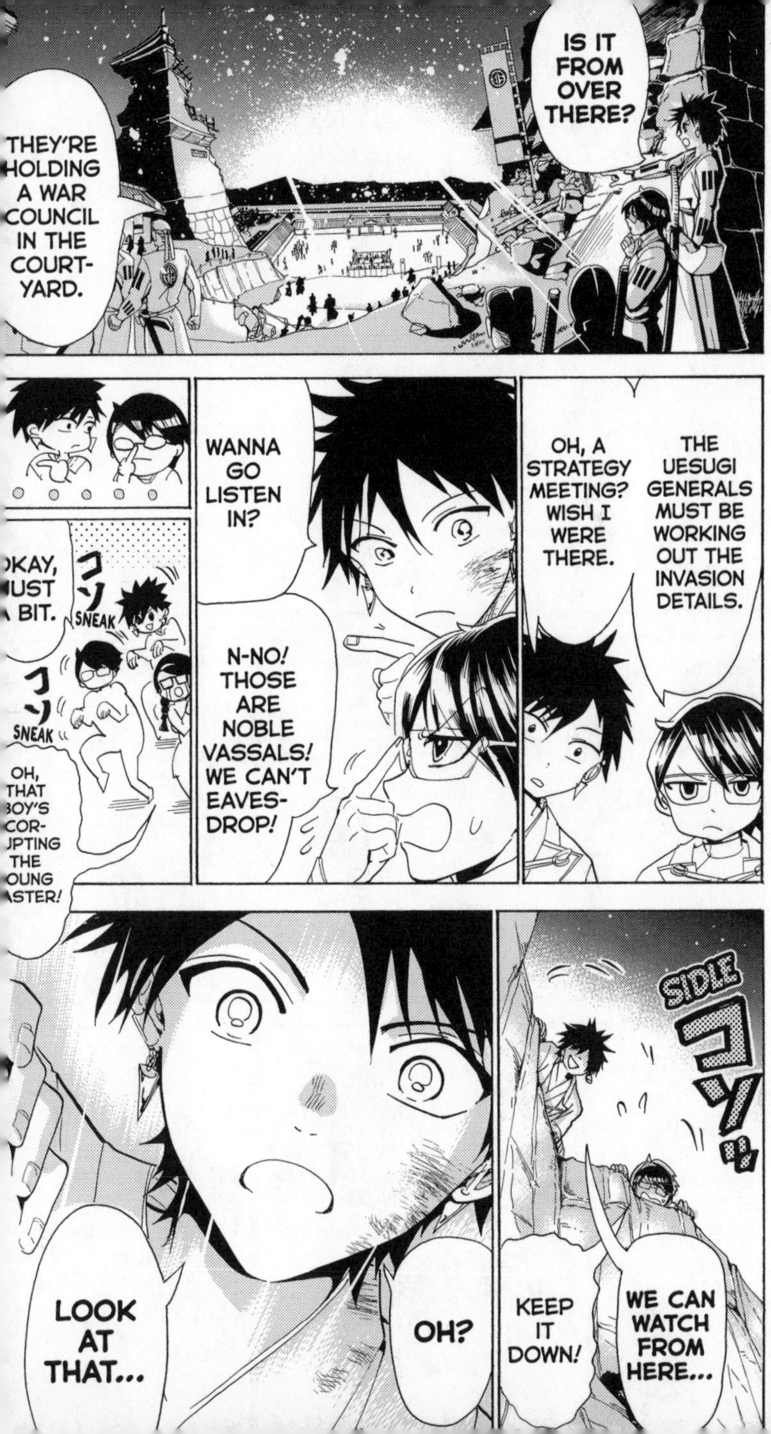
IS IT FROM OVER THERE?
THEY'RE HOLDING A WAR COUNCIL IN THE COURT-YARD.
THE UESUGI GENERALS MUST BE WORKING OUT THE INVASION DETAILS.
OH, A STRATEGY MEETING? WISH I WERE THERE.
WANNA GO LISTEN IN?
N-NO! THOSE ARE NOBLE VASSALS! WE CAN'T EAVES-DROP!
KAY, UST BIT.
コソ
SNEAK
コソ
SNEAK
OH, THAT OY'S COR-UPTING THE OUNG ASTER!
SIDLE
コソッ
WE CAN WATCH FROM HERE...
KEEP IT DOWN!
OH?
LOOK AT THAT...

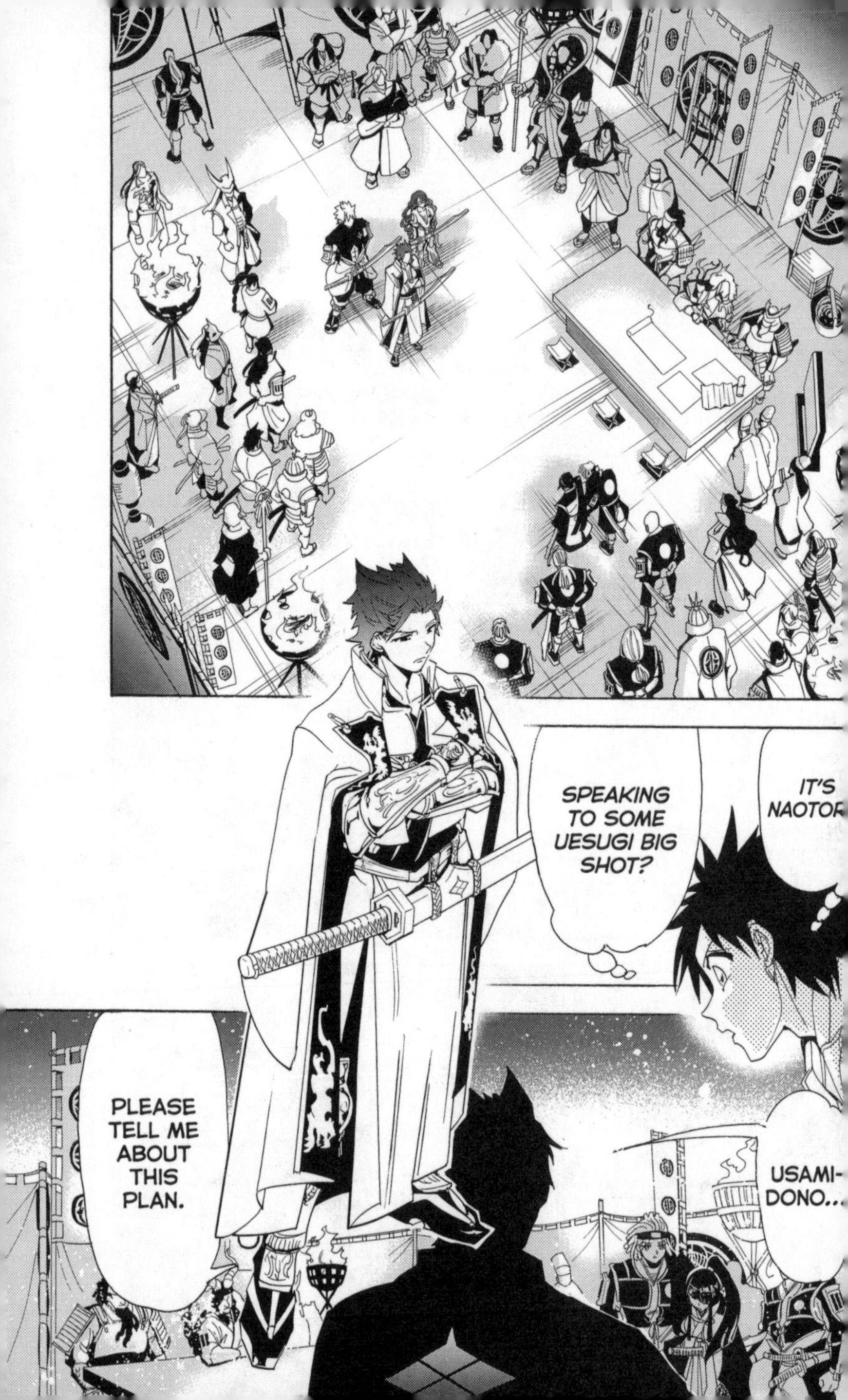
IT'S NAOTOR
SPEAKING TO SOME UESUGI BIG SHOT?
USAMI-DONO...
PLEASE TELL ME ABOUT THIS PLAN.

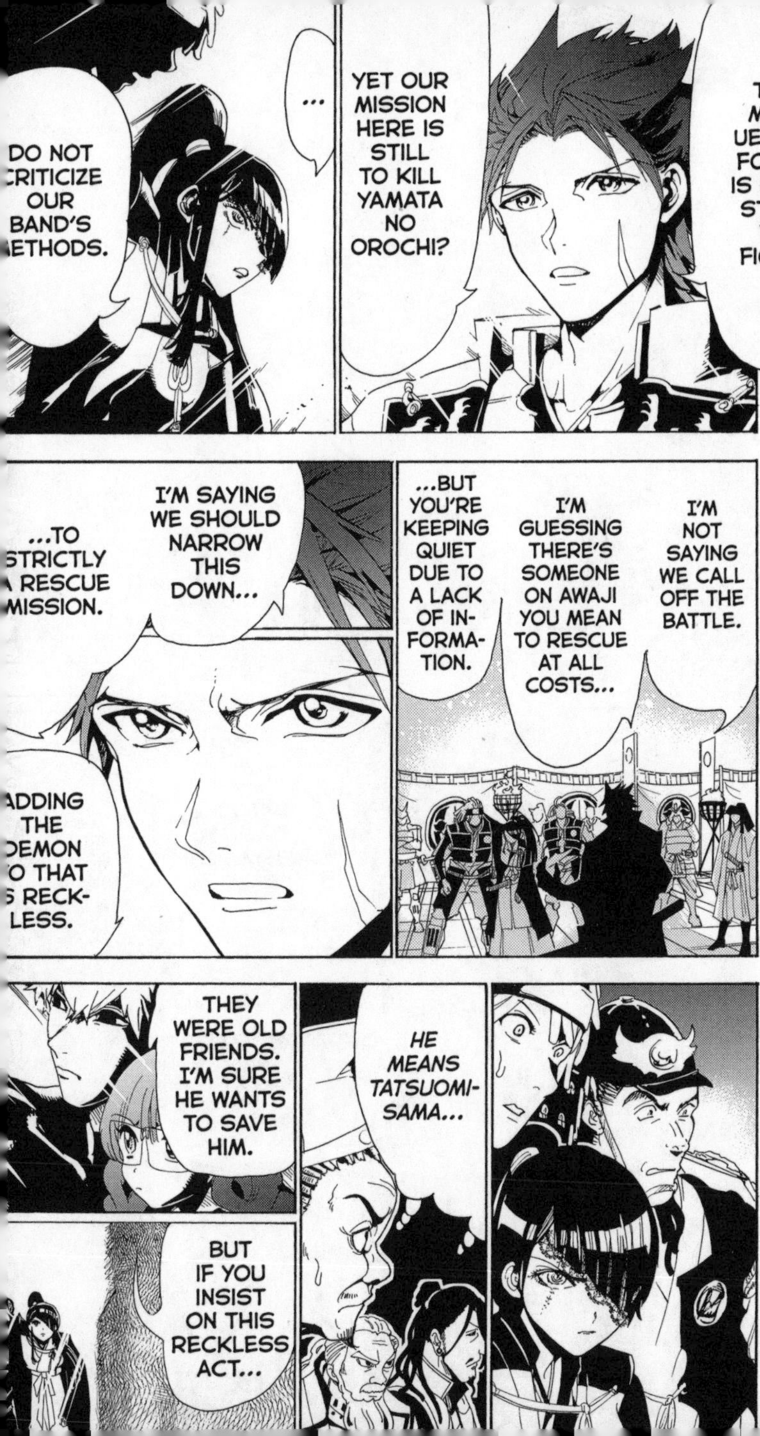
THE MAIN UESUGI FORCE IS IN NO STATE TO FIGHT.
YET OUR MISSION HERE IS STILL TO KILL YAMATA NO OROCHI?
...
DO NOT RITICIZE OUR BAND'S ETHODS.
I'M NOT SAYING WE CALL OFF THE BATTLE.
I'M GUESSING THERE'S SOMEONE ON AWAJI YOU MEAN TO RESCUE AT ALL COSTS...
...BUT YOU'RE KEEPING QUIET DUE TO A LACK OF INFORMATION.
I'M SAYING WE SHOULD NARROW THIS DOWN...
...TO STRICTLY RESCUE MISSION.
DDING THE EMON O THAT RECK-LESS.
HE MEANS TATSUOMI-SAMA...
THEY WERE OLD FRIENDS. I'M SURE HE WANTS TO SAVE HIM.
BUT IF YOU INSIST ON THIS RECKLESS ACT...

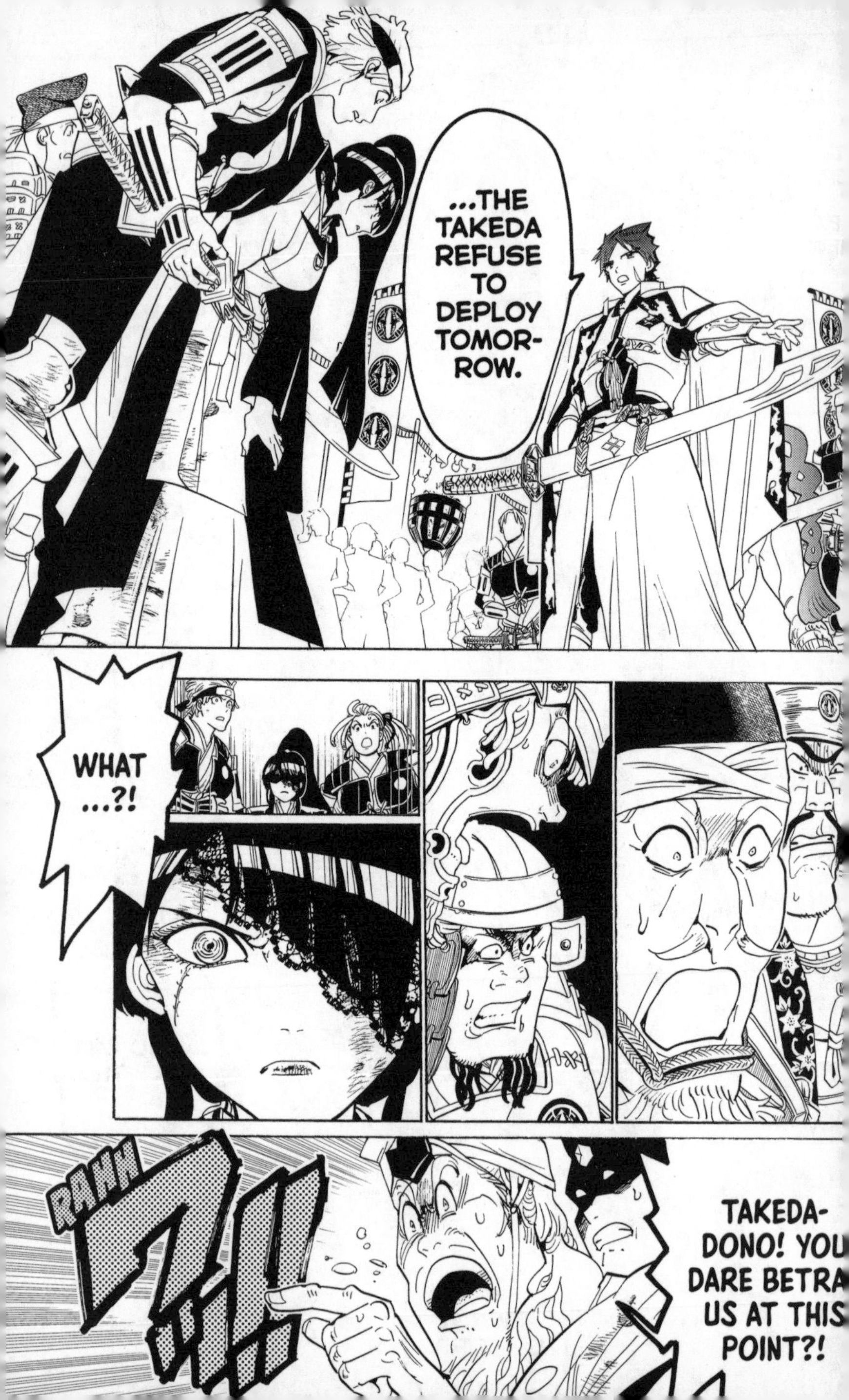
...THE TAKEDA REFUSE TO DEPLOY TOMORROW.
WHAT ...?!
TAKEDA-DONO! YOU DARE BETRA US AT THIS POINT?!
RAHH

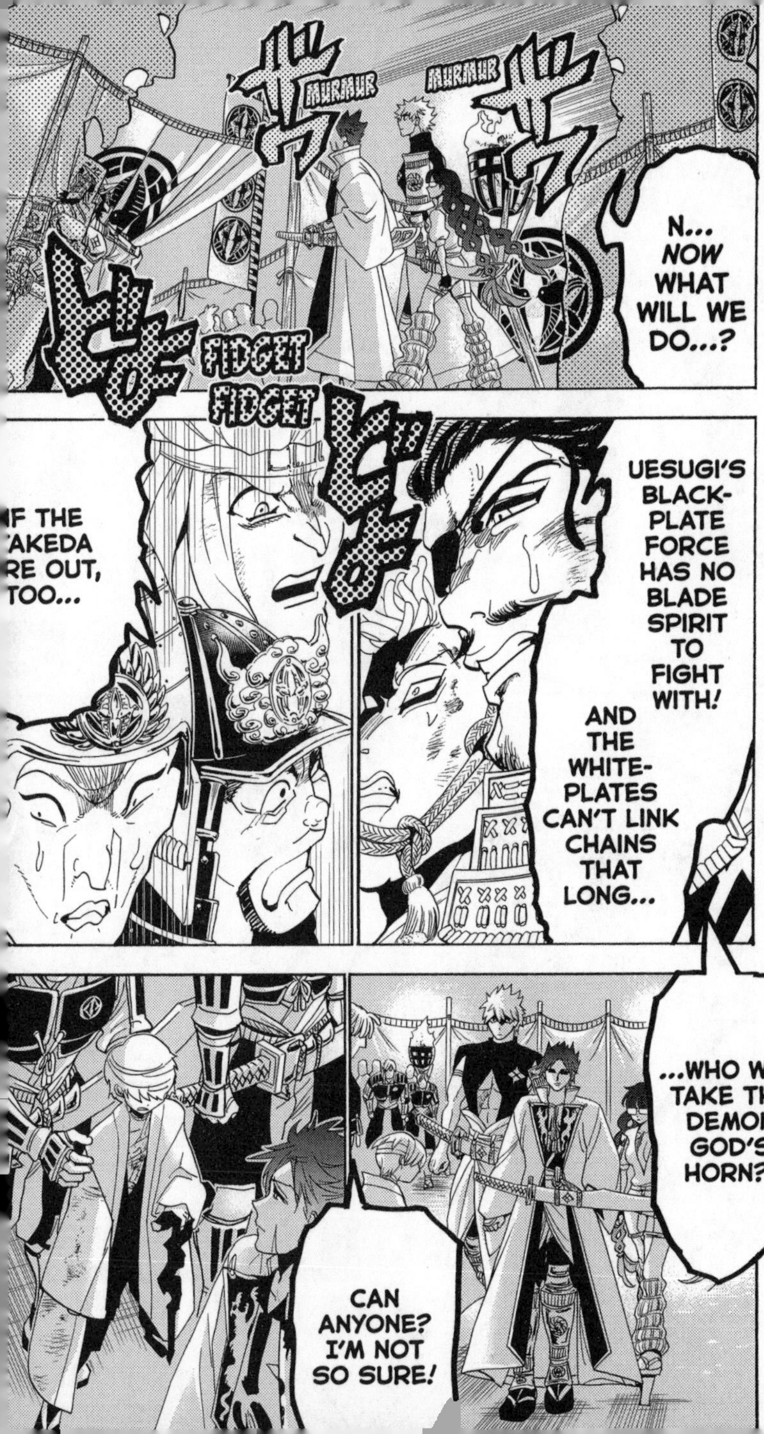
MURMUR
MURMUR
N... NOW WHAT WILL WE DO...?
FIDGET
FIDGET
UESUGI'S BLACK-PLATE FORCE HAS NO BLADE SPIRIT TO FIGHT WITH!
AND THE WHITE-PLATES CAN'T LINK CHAINS THAT LONG...
IF THE TAKEDA ARE OUT, TOO...
...WHO WILL TAKE THE DEMON GOD'S HORN?!
CAN ANYONE? I'M NOT SO SURE!

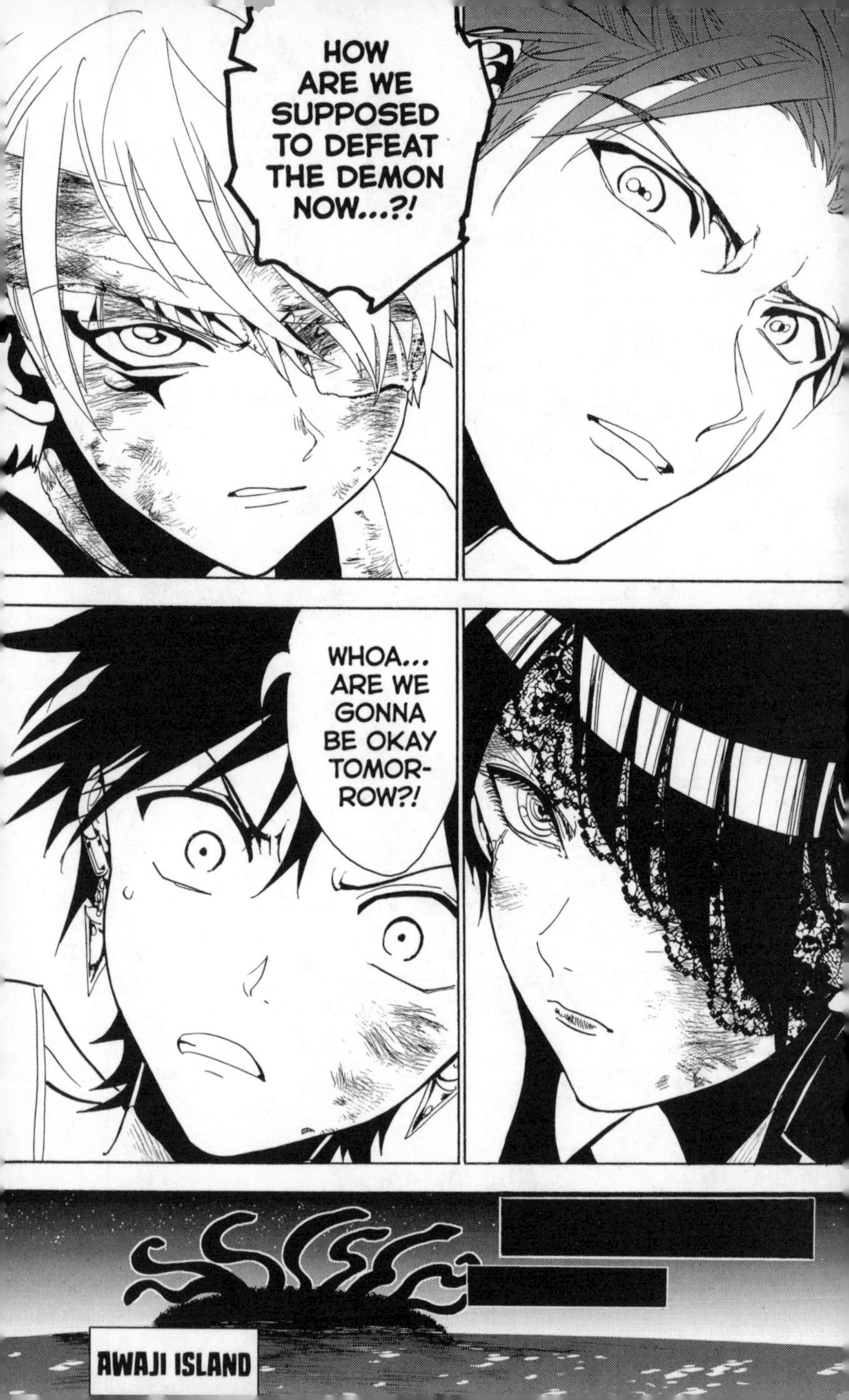
HOW ARE WE SUPPOSED TO DEFEAT THE DEMON NOW...?!
WHOA... ARE WE GONNA BE OKAY TOMORROW?!
[redacted]
[redacted]
AWAJI ISLAND

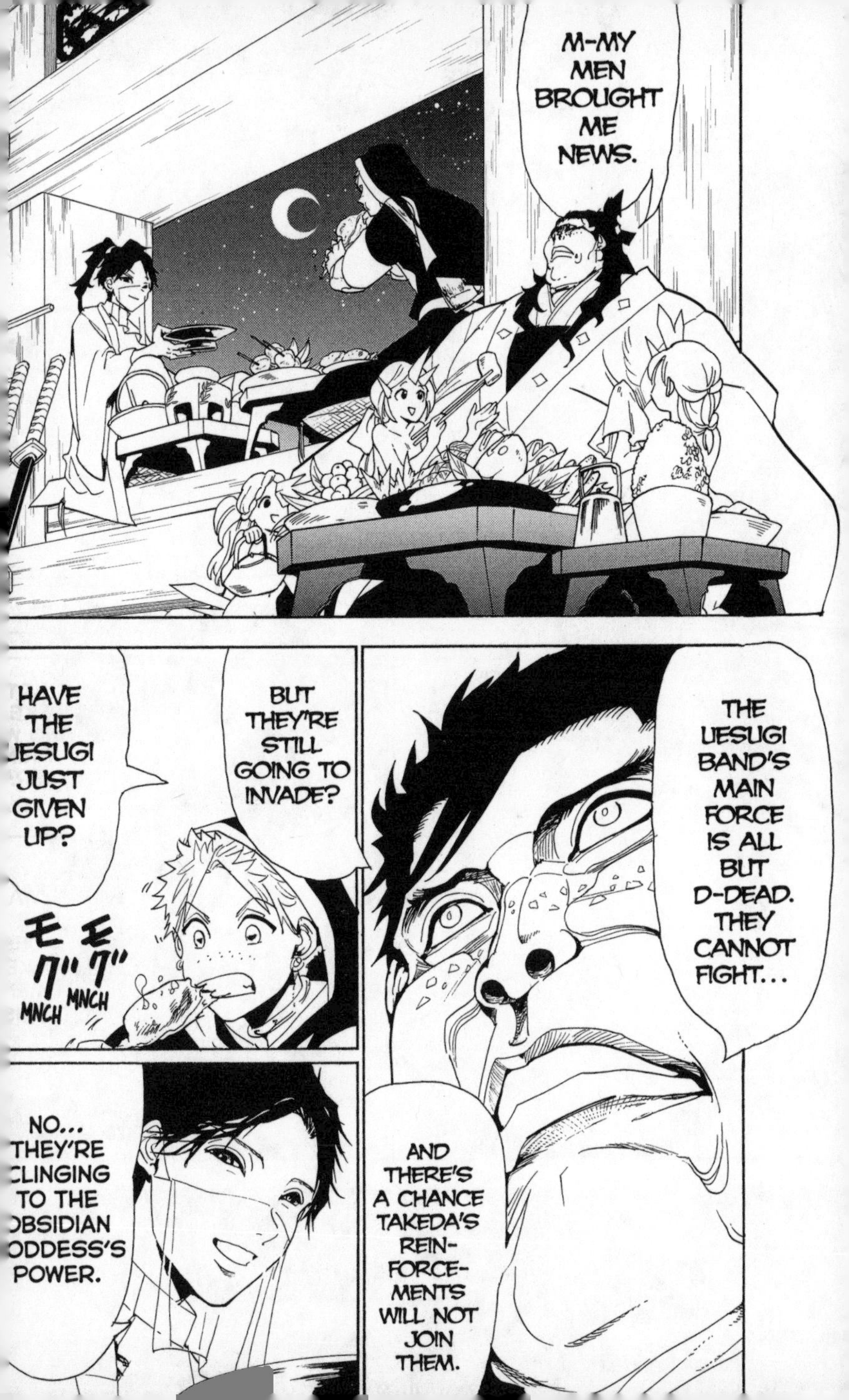
M-MY MEN BROUGHT ME NEWS.
THE UESUGI BAND'S MAIN FORCE IS ALL BUT D-DEAD. THEY CANNOT FIGHT...
AND THERE'S A CHANCE TAKEDA'S REIN-FORCE-MENTS WILL NOT JOIN THEM.
HAVE THE UESUGI JUST GIVEN UP?
BUT THEY'RE STILL GOING TO INVADE?
モグ モグ
MNCH MNCH
NO... THEY'RE CLINGING TO THE OBSIDIAN ODDESS'S POWER.

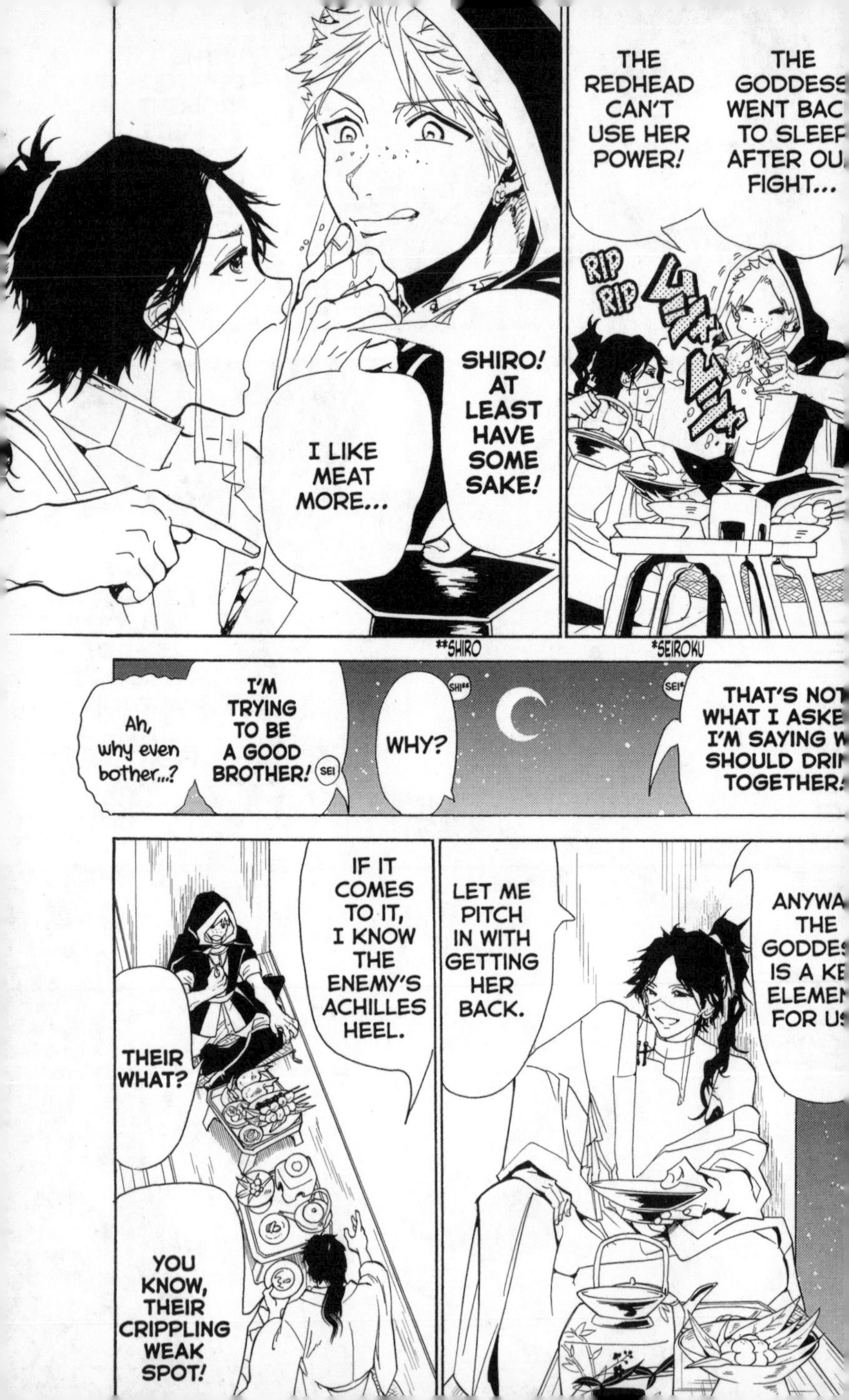
SEI* THE GODDESS WENT BAC TO SLEEF AFTER OU FIGHT...
THE REDHEAD CAN'T USE HER POWER!
RIP RIP
*SEIROKU
SHIRO! AT LEAST HAVE SOME SAKE!
I LIKE MEAT MORE...
**SHIRO
SEI* THAT'S NOT WHAT I ASKE I'M SAYING W SHOULD DRI TOGETHER!
SHI** WHY?
SEI I'M TRYING TO BE A GOOD BROTHER!
Ah, why even bother...?
ANYWA THE GODDES IS A KE ELEMEN FOR US
LET ME PITCH IN WITH GETTING HER BACK.
IF IT COMES TO IT, I KNOW THE ENEMY'S ACHILLES HEEL.
THEIR WHAT?
YOU KNOW, THEIR CRIPPLING WEAK SPOT!

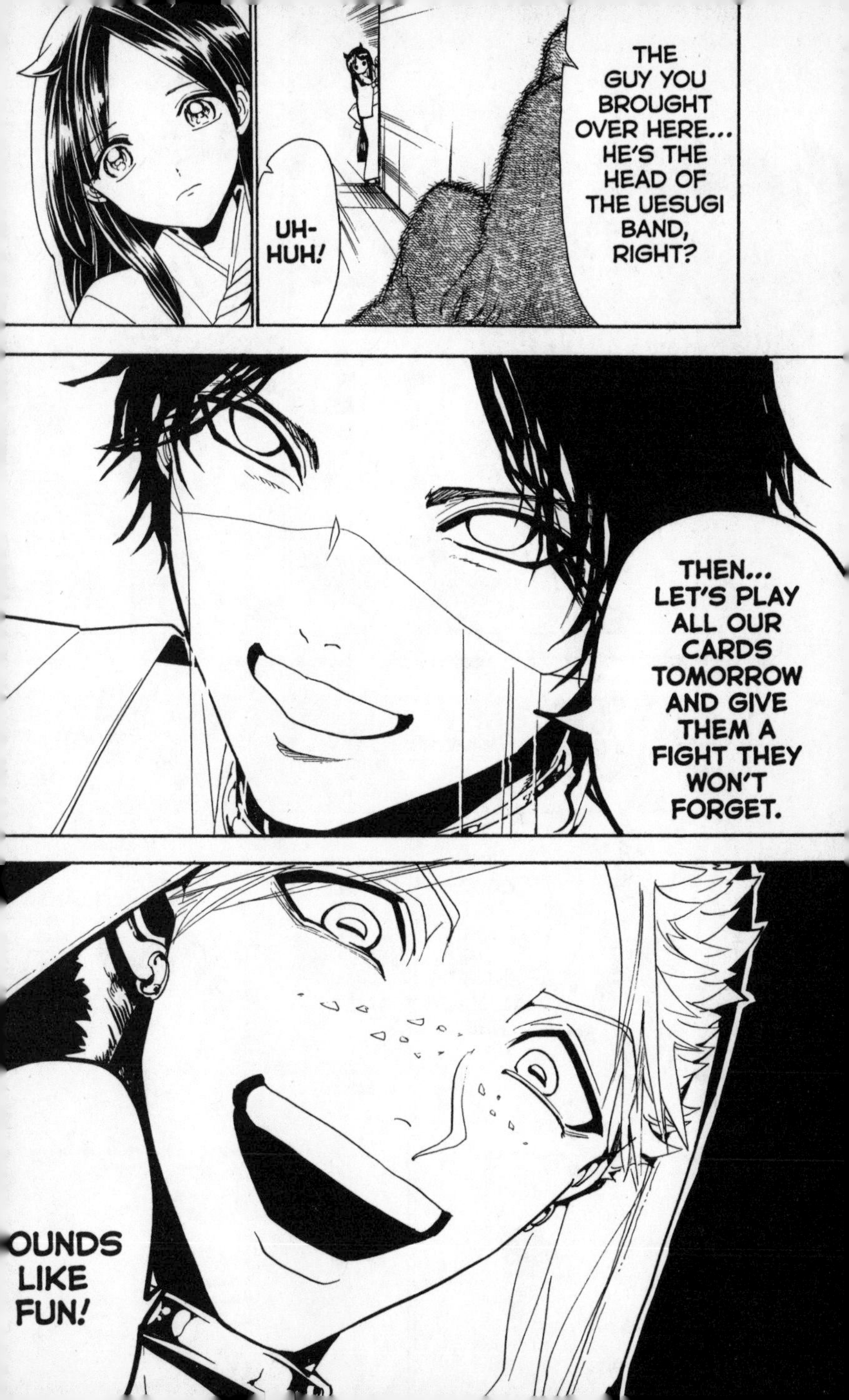
THE GUY YOU BROUGHT OVER HERE... HE'S THE HEAD OF THE UESUGI BAND, RIGHT?
UH-HUH!
THEN... LET'S PLAY ALL OUR CARDS TOMORROW AND GIVE THEM A FIGHT THEY WON'T FORGET.
OUNDS LIKE FUN!

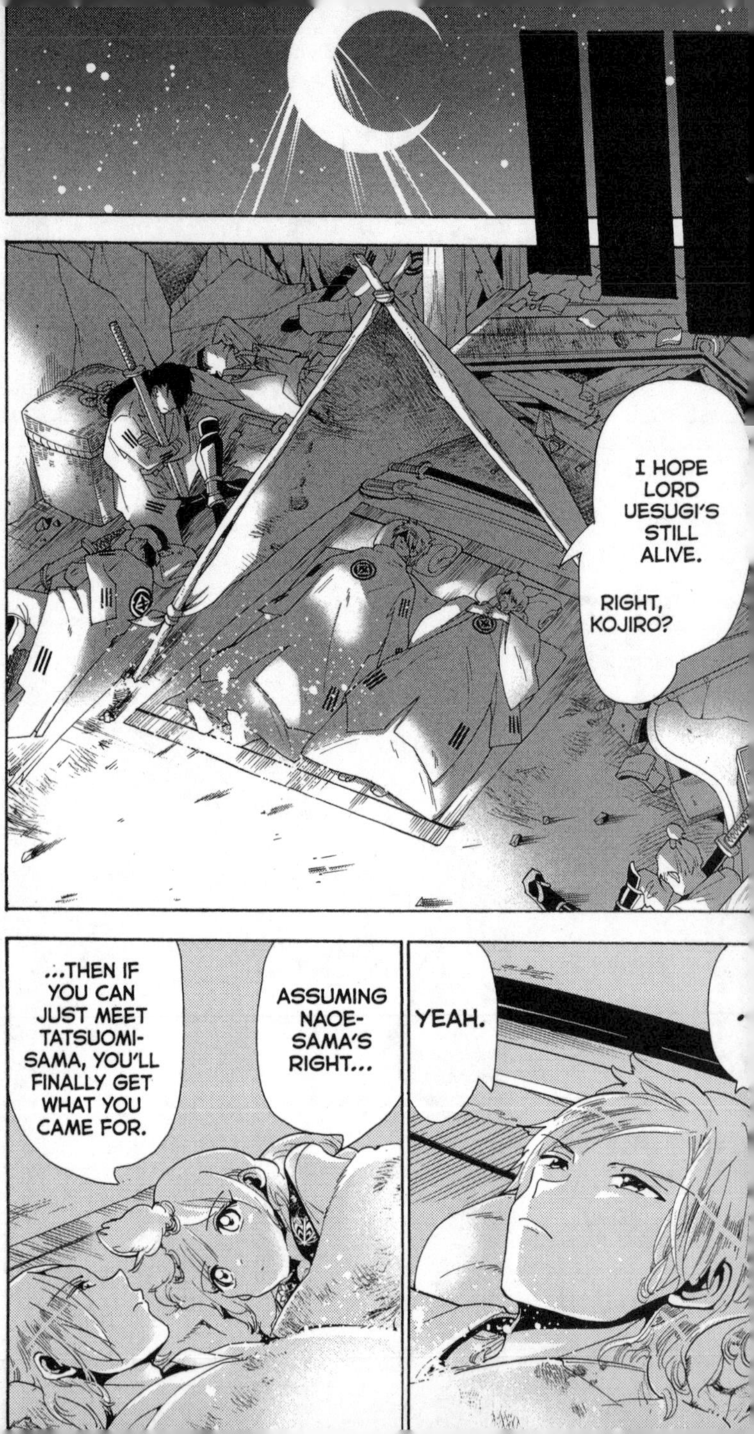
I HOPE LORD UESUGI'S STILL ALIVE.
RIGHT, KOJIRO?
YEAH.
ASSUMING NAOE-SAMA'S RIGHT...
...THEN IF YOU CAN JUST MEET TATSUOMI-SAMA, YOU'LL FINALLY GET WHAT YOU CAME FOR.

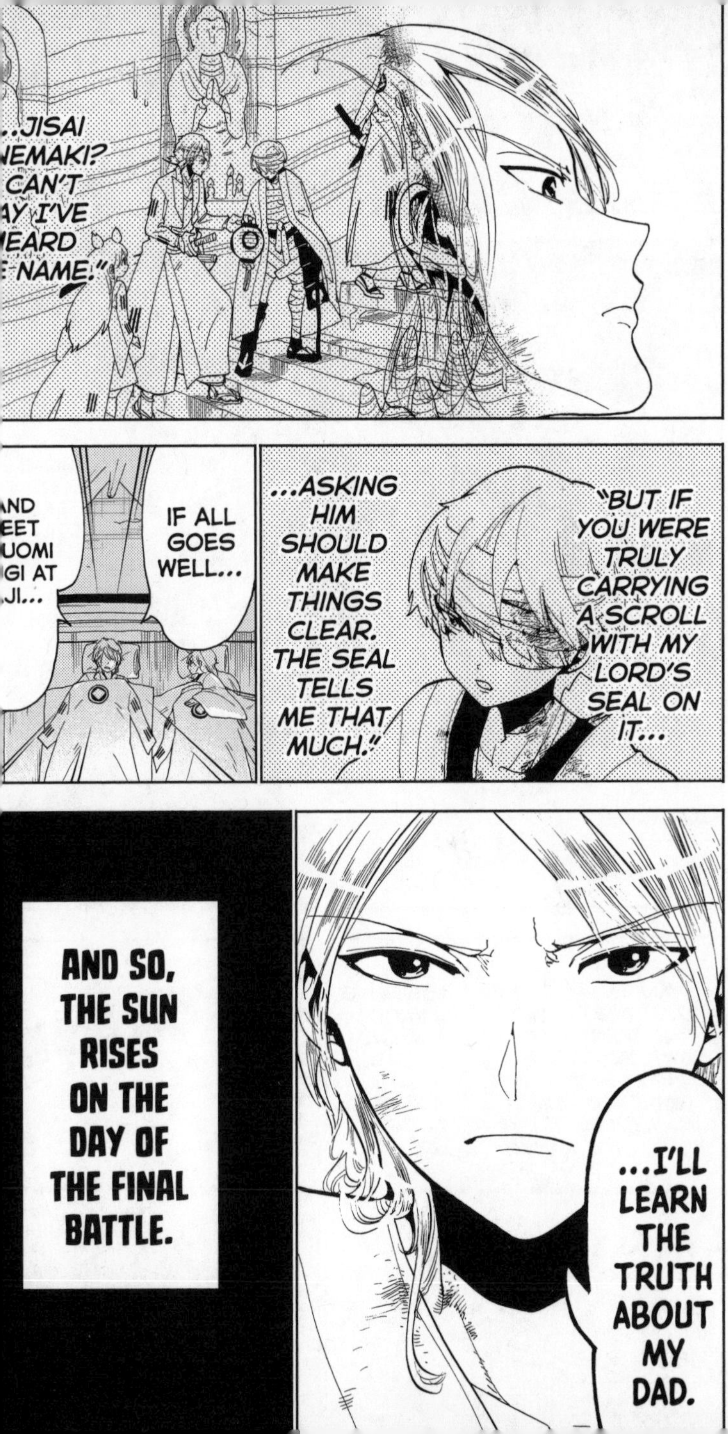
...JISAI NEMAKI? CAN'T AY I'VE EARD E NAME."
"BUT IF YOU WERE TRULY CARRYING A SCROLL WITH MY LORD'S SEAL ON IT...
...ASKING HIM SHOULD MAKE THINGS CLEAR. THE SEAL TELLS ME THAT MUCH."
IF ALL GOES WELL...
AND EET UOMI GI AT JI...
...I'LL LEARN THE TRUTH ABOUT MY DAD.
AND SO, THE SUN RISES ON THE DAY OF THE FINAL BATTLE.

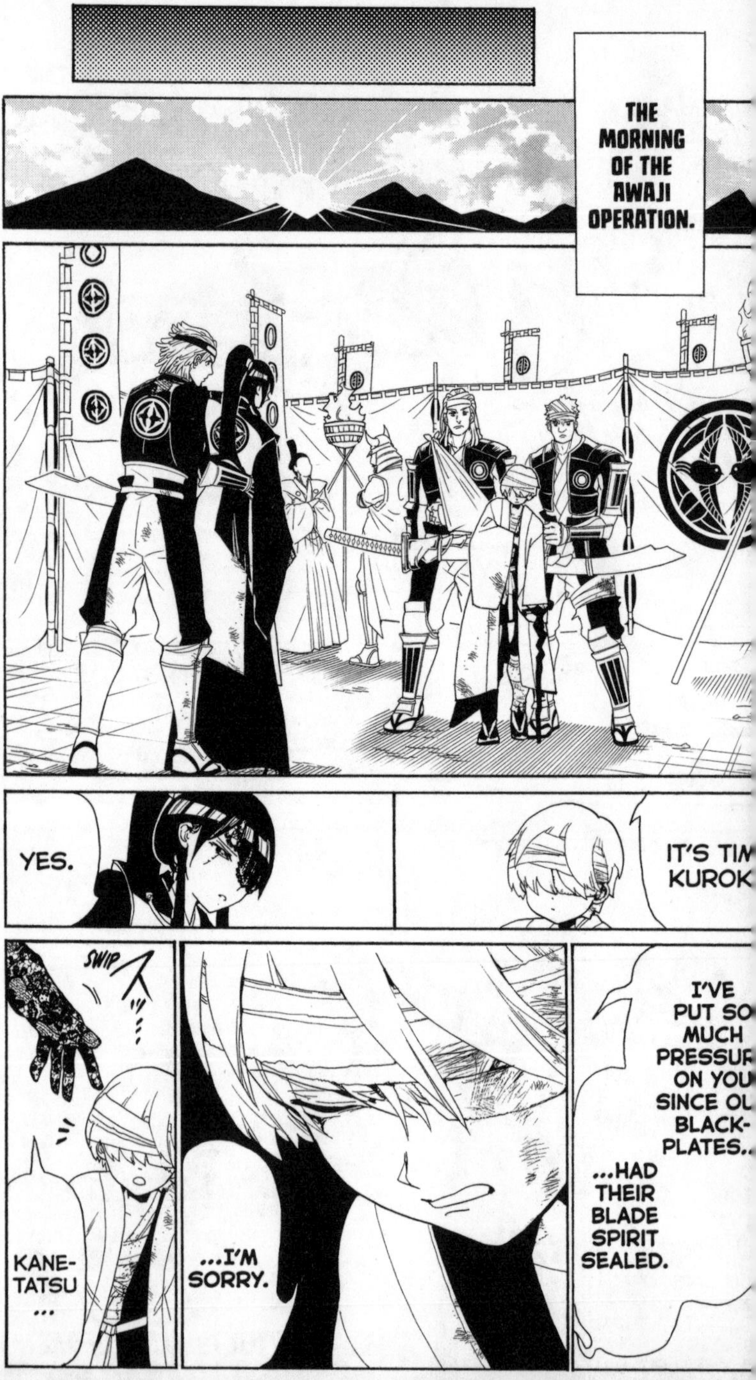
THE MORNING OF THE AWAJI OPERATION.
IT'S TIM
KUROK
YES.
I'VE PUT SO MUCH PRESSUR ON YOU SINCE OU BLACK-PLATES..
...HAD THEIR BLADE SPIRIT SEALED.
...I'M SORRY.
SWIP
KANE-TATSU ...

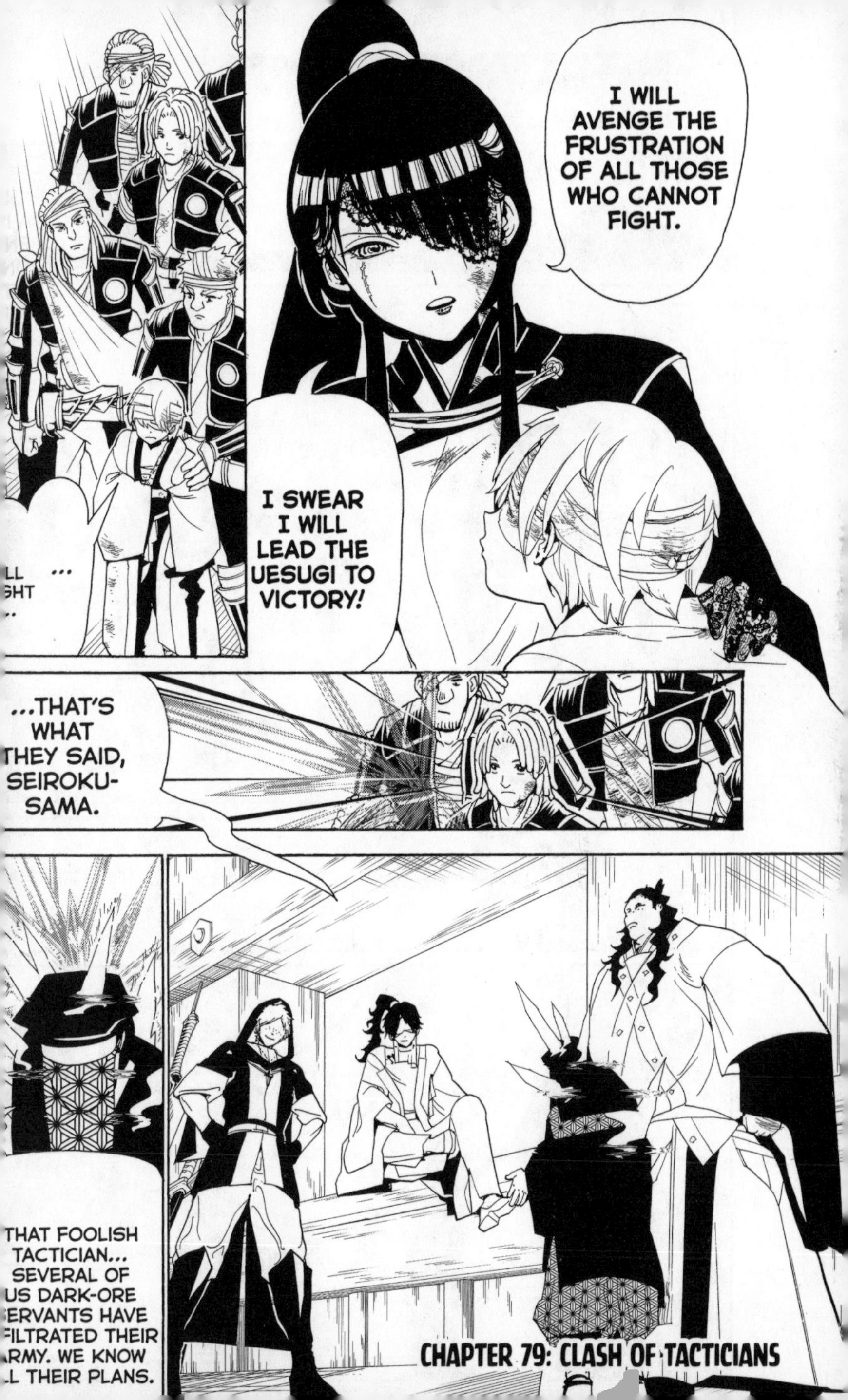
I WILL AVENGE THE FRUSTRATION OF ALL THOSE WHO CANNOT FIGHT.
I SWEAR I WILL LEAD THE UESUGI TO VICTORY!
...THAT'S WHAT THEY SAID, SEIROKU-SAMA.
CHAPTER 79: CLASH OF TACTICIANS
THAT FOOLISH TACTICIAN... SEVERAL OF US DARK-ORE ERVANTS HAVE FILTRATED THEIR RMY. WE KNOW L THEIR PLANS.

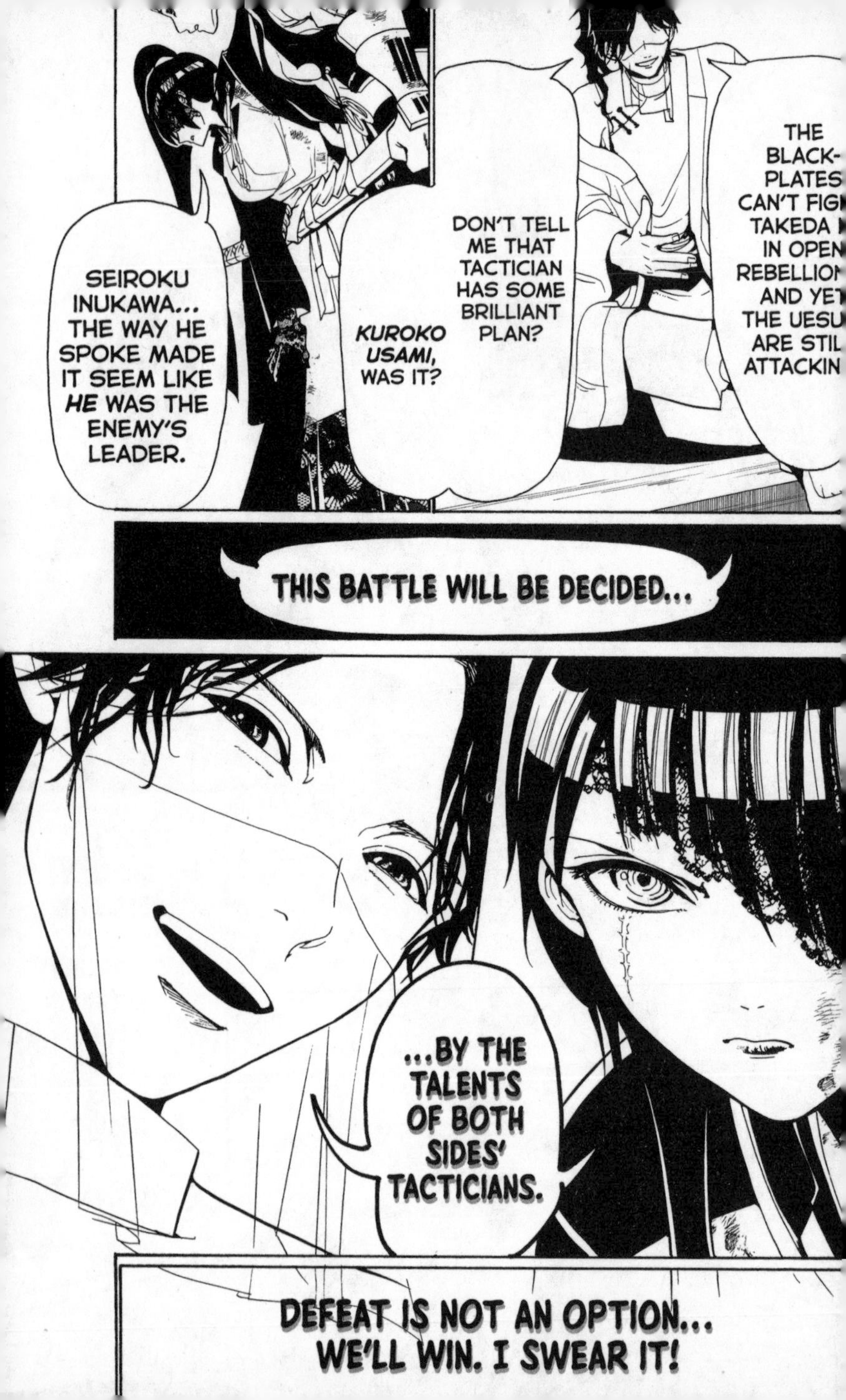
THE BLACK-PLATES CAN'T FIG TAKEDA IN OPEN REBELLIO AND YET THE UESU ARE STIL ATTACKIN
DON'T TELL ME THAT TACTICIAN HAS SOME BRILLIANT PLAN?
KUROKO USAMI, WAS IT?
SEIROKU INUKAWA... THE WAY HE SPOKE MADE IT SEEM LIKE *HE* WAS THE ENEMY'S LEADER.
THIS BATTLE WILL BE DECIDED...
...BY THE TALENTS OF BOTH SIDES' TACTICIANS.
DEFEAT IS NOT AN OPTION... WE'LL WIN. I SWEAR IT!

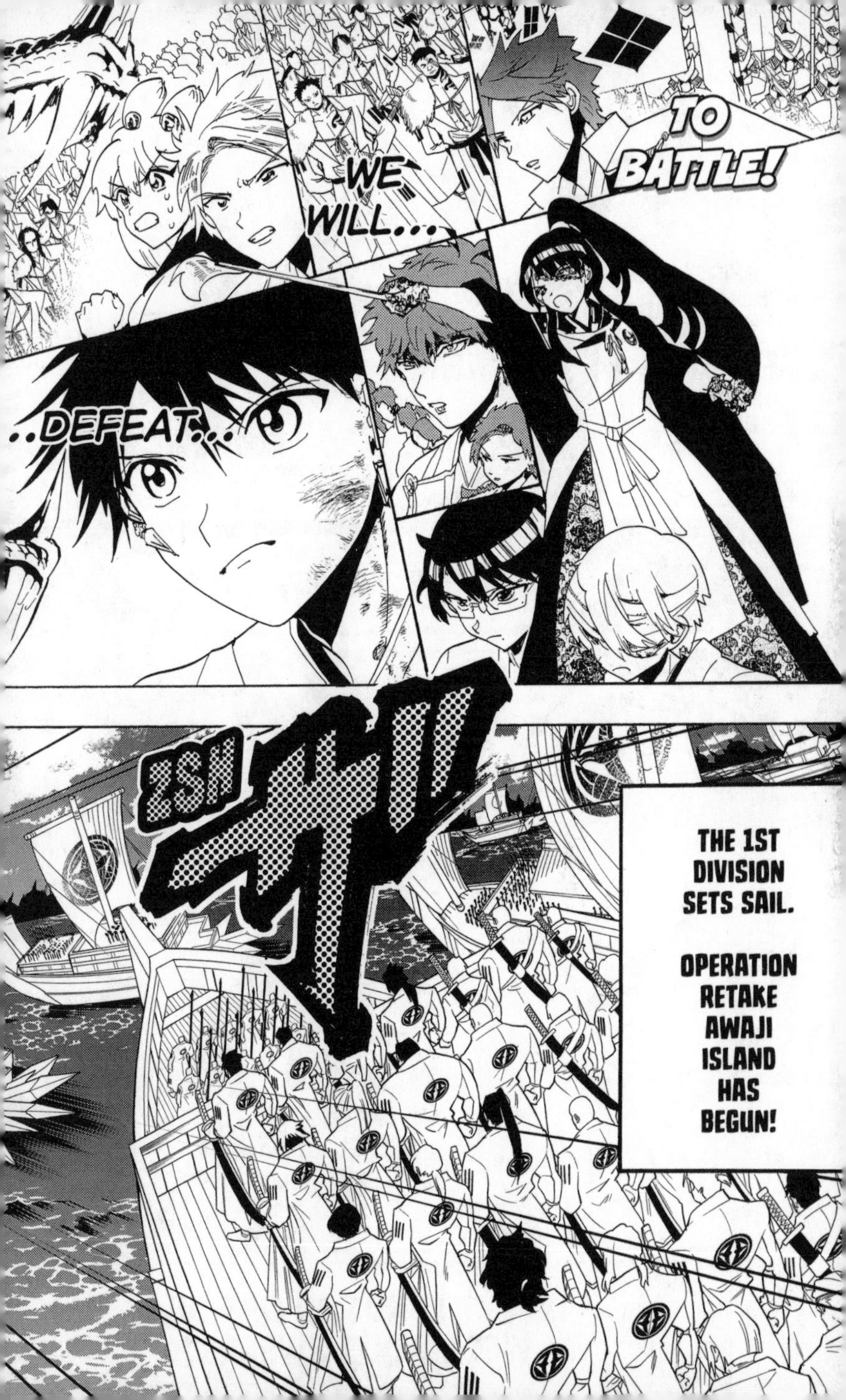
TO BATTLE!
WE WILL...
..DEFEAT...
ZSH
THE 1ST DIVISION SETS SAIL.
OPERATION RETAKE AWAJI ISLAND HAS BEGUN!

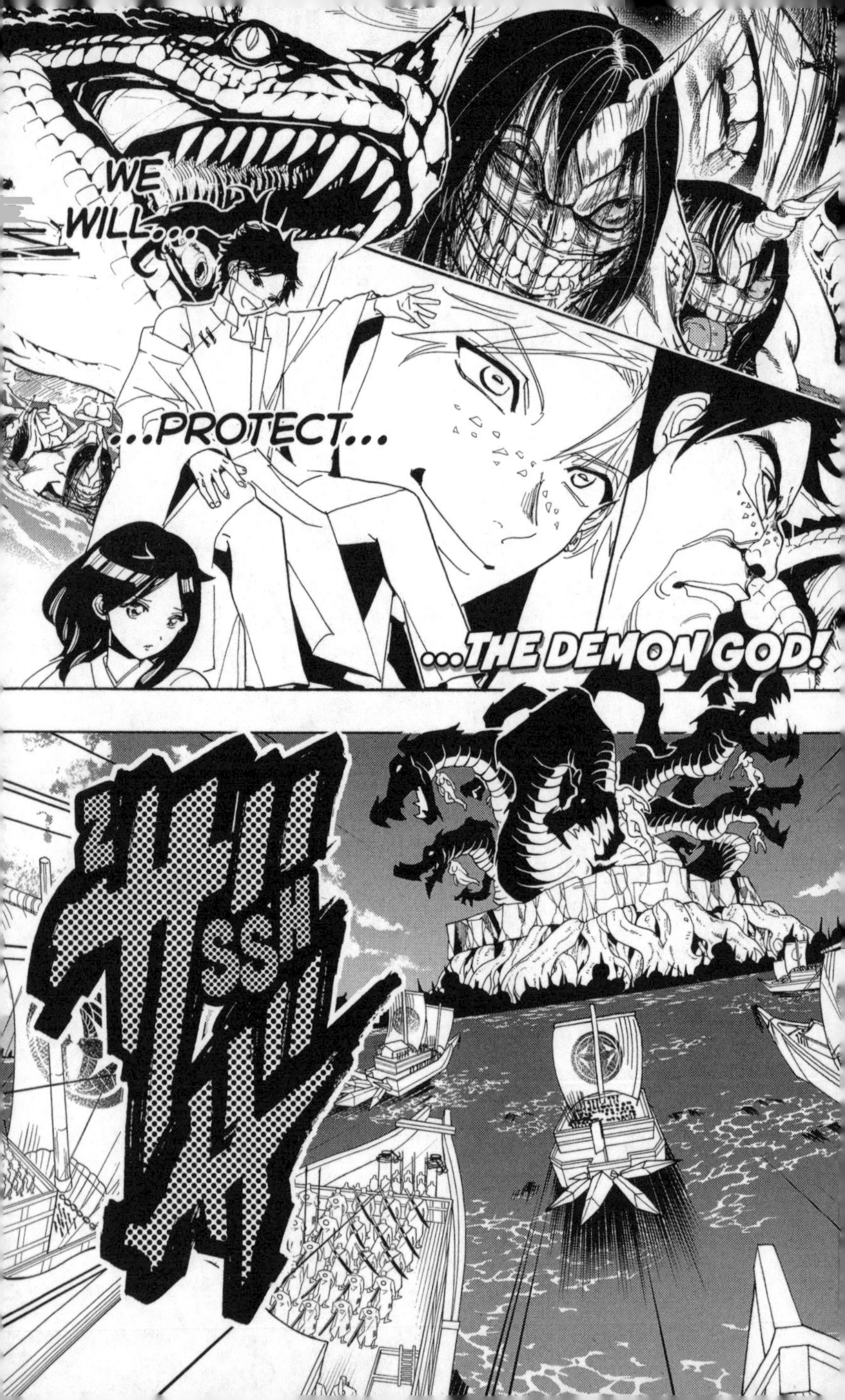
WE WILL...
...PROTECT...
...THE DEMON GOD!

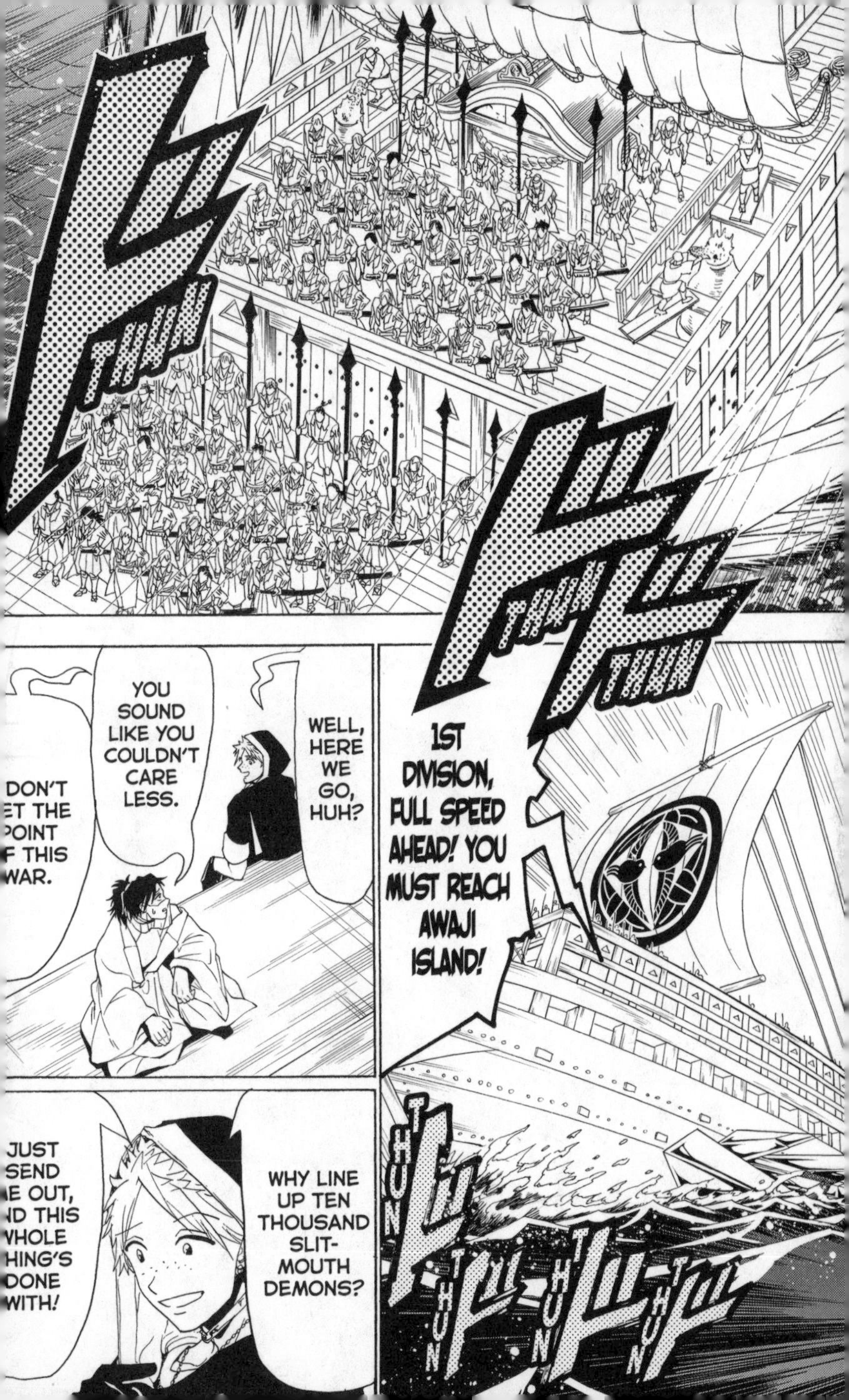
1ST DIVISION, FULL SPEED AHEAD! YOU MUST REACH AWAJI ISLAND!
THUN THUN THUN THUN
WELL, HERE WE GO, HUH?
YOU SOUND LIKE YOU COULDN'T CARE LESS.
DON'T ET THE POINT F THIS WAR.
WHY LINE UP TEN THOUSAND SLIT-MOUTH DEMONS?
JUST SEND E OUT, D THIS WHOLE HING'S DONE WITH!

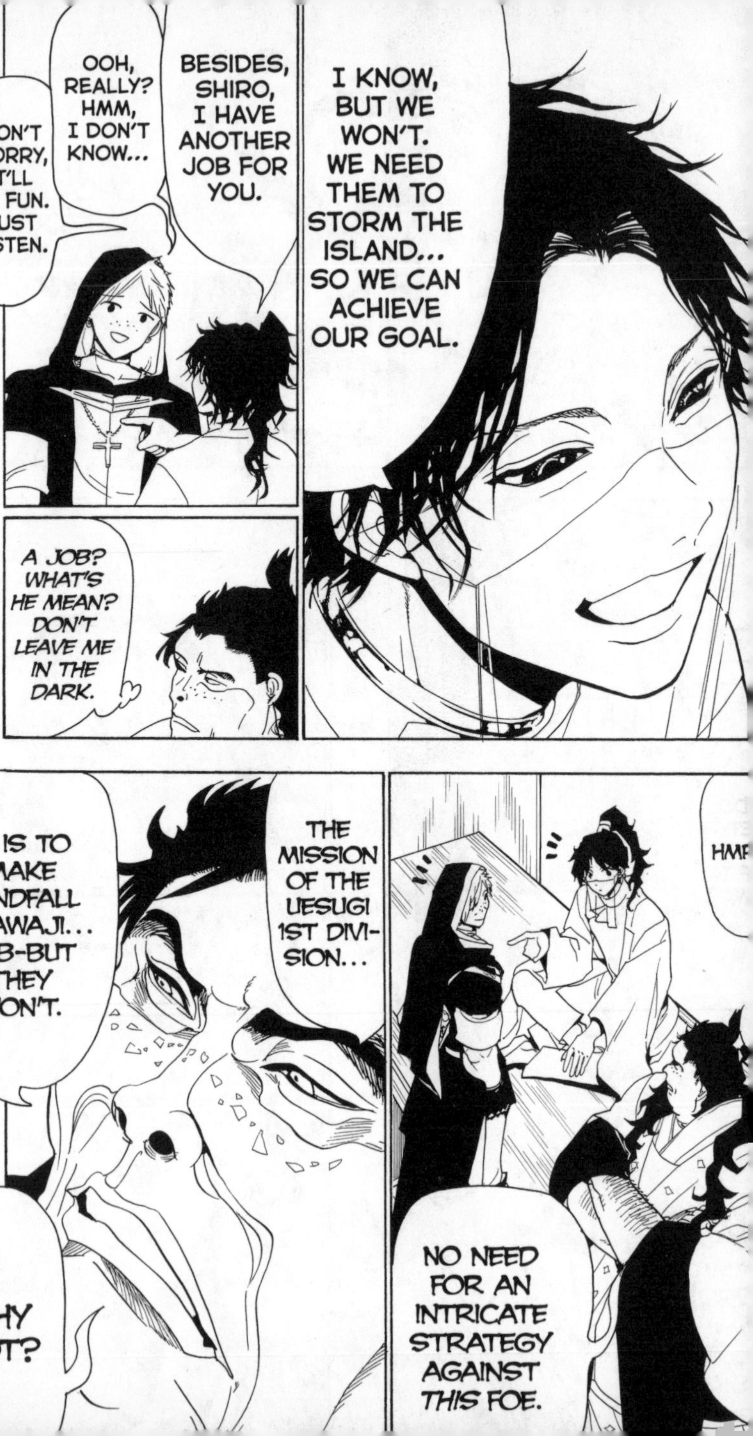
I KNOW, BUT WE WON'T. WE NEED THEM TO STORM THE ISLAND... SO WE CAN ACHIEVE OUR GOAL.
BESIDES, SHIRO, I HAVE ANOTHER JOB FOR YOU.
OOH, REALLY? HMM, I DON'T KNOW...
DON'T WORRY, IT'LL BE FUN. JUST LISTEN.
A JOB? WHAT'S HE MEAN? DON'T LEAVE ME IN THE DARK.
HMP
NO NEED FOR AN INTRICATE STRATEGY AGAINST *THIS* FOE.
THE MISSION OF THE UESUGI 1ST DIVISION...
...IS TO MAKE LANDFALL ON AWAJI... B-B-BUT THEY WON'T.
WHY NOT?

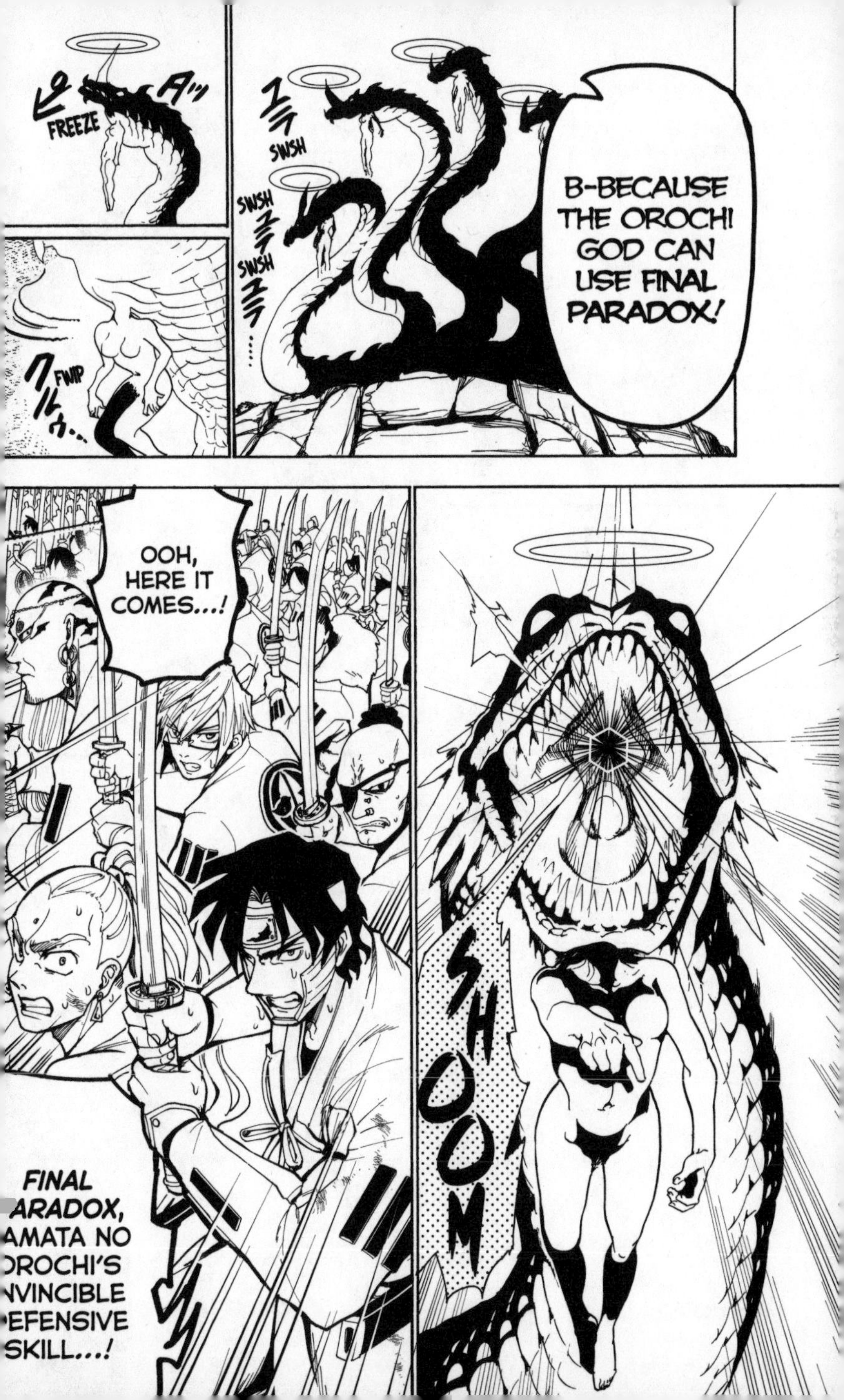
SWSH
SWSH
SWSH
B-BECAUSE THE OROCHI GOD CAN USE FINAL PARADOX!
FREEZE
FWIP
SHOOOM
OOH, HERE IT COMES...!
FINAL ARADOX, AMATA NO ROCHI'S NVINCIBLE EFENSIVE SKILL...!

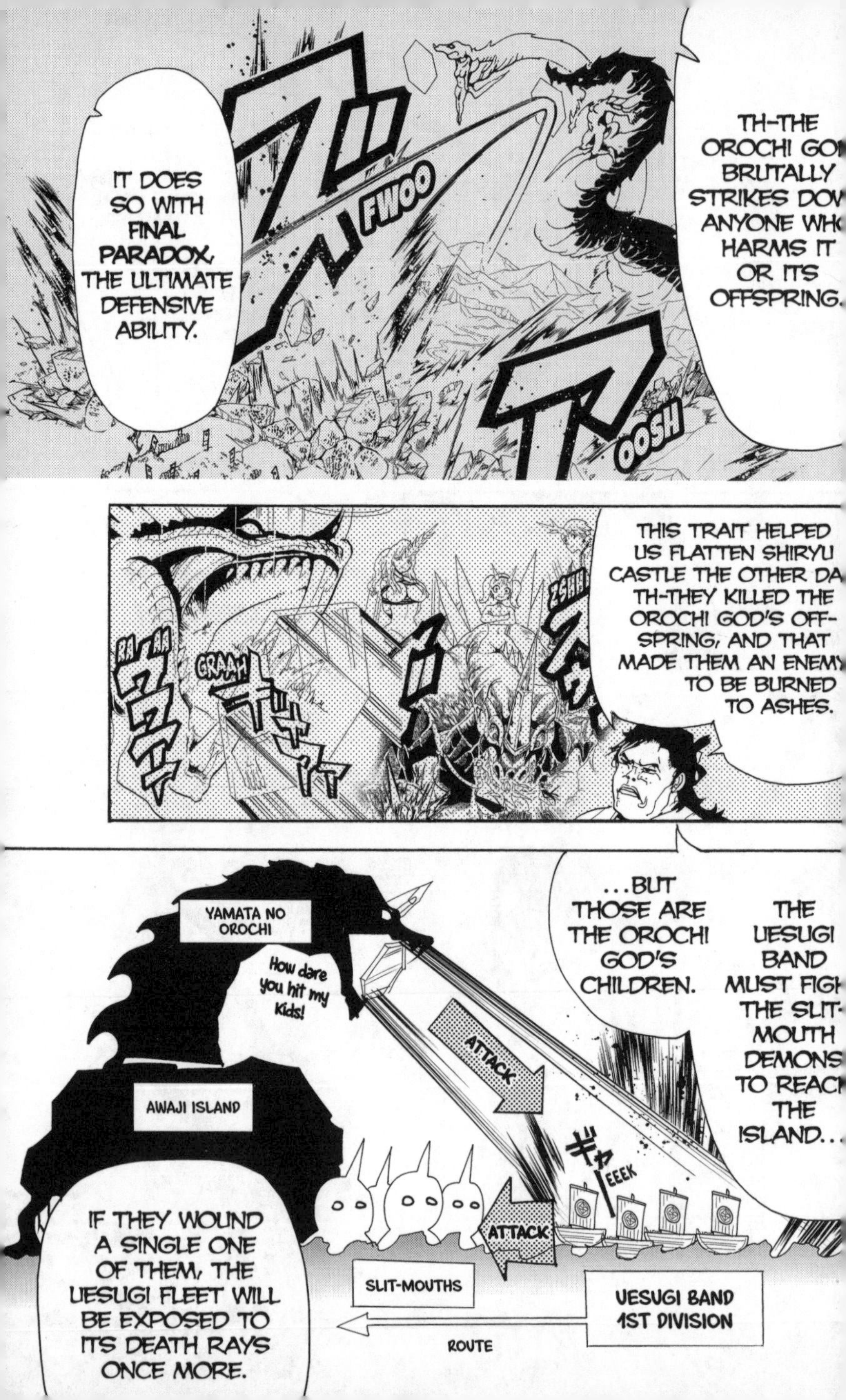
TH-THE OROCHI GO BRUTALLY STRIKES DOW ANYONE WH HARMS IT OR ITS OFFSPRING.
FWOO
OOSH
IT DOES SO WITH FINAL PARADOX, THE ULTIMATE DEFENSIVE ABILITY.
THIS TRAIT HELPED US FLATTEN SHIRYU CASTLE THE OTHER DA TH-THEY KILLED THE OROCHI GOD'S OFF-SPRING, AND THAT MADE THEM AN ENEM TO BE BURNED TO ASHES.
ZSHH
GRAAH
RAAA
THE UESUGI BAND MUST FIG THE SLIT-MOUTH DEMONS TO REAC THE ISLAND...
...BUT THOSE ARE THE OROCHI GOD'S CHILDREN.
YAMATA NO OROCHI
How dare you hit my kids!
ATTACK
AWAJI ISLAND
EEEK
ATTACK
SLIT-MOUTHS
UESUGI BAND 1ST DIVISION
ROUTE
IF THEY WOUND A SINGLE ONE OF THEM, THE UESUGI FLEET WILL BE EXPOSED TO ITS DEATH RAYS ONCE MORE.

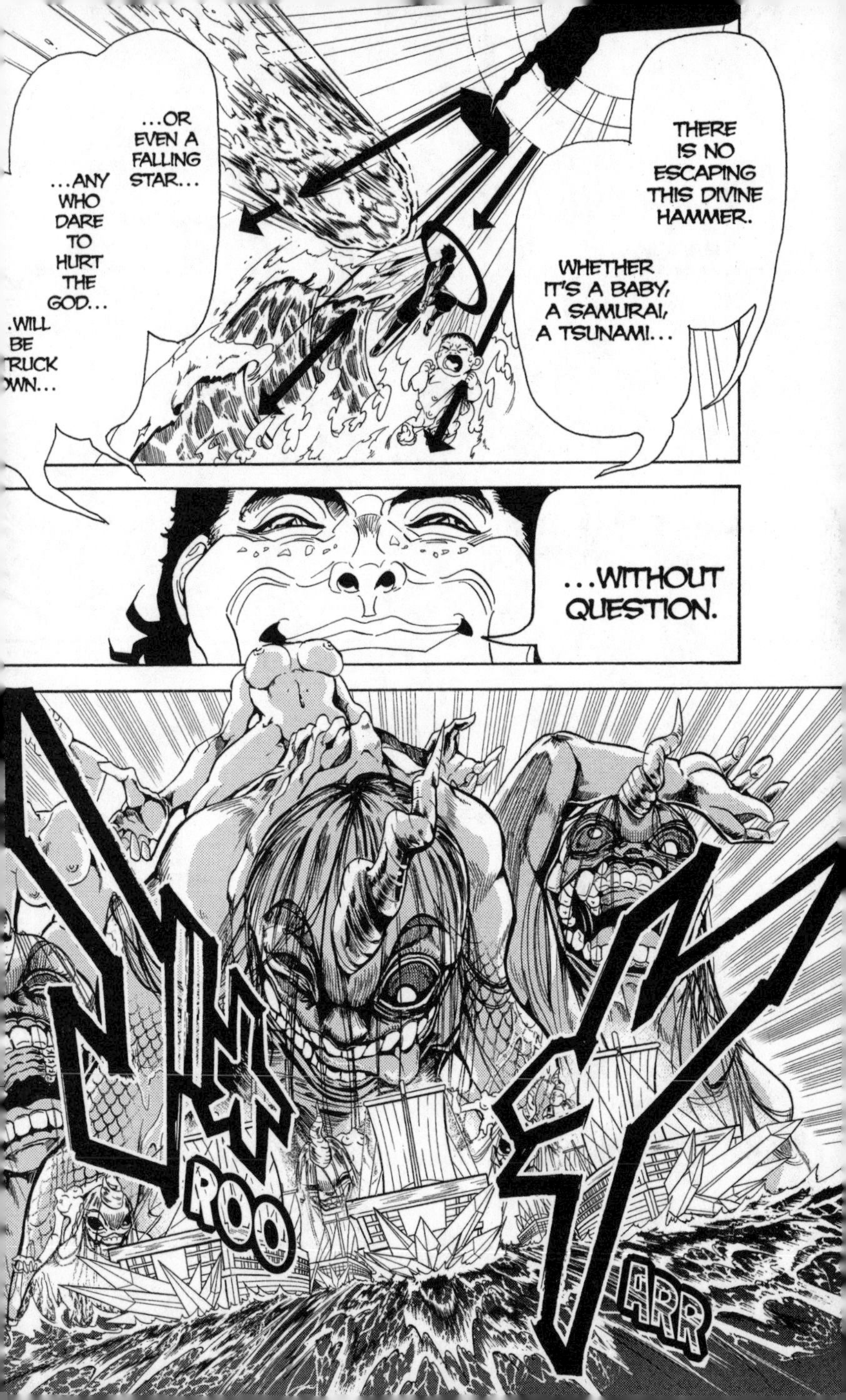
THERE IS NO ESCAPING THIS DIVINE HAMMER.
WHETHER IT'S A BABY, A SAMURAI, A TSUNAMI...
...OR EVEN A FALLING STAR...
...ANY WHO DARE TO HURT THE GOD...
.WILL BE TRUCK WN...
...WITHOUT QUESTION.
ROO
ARR

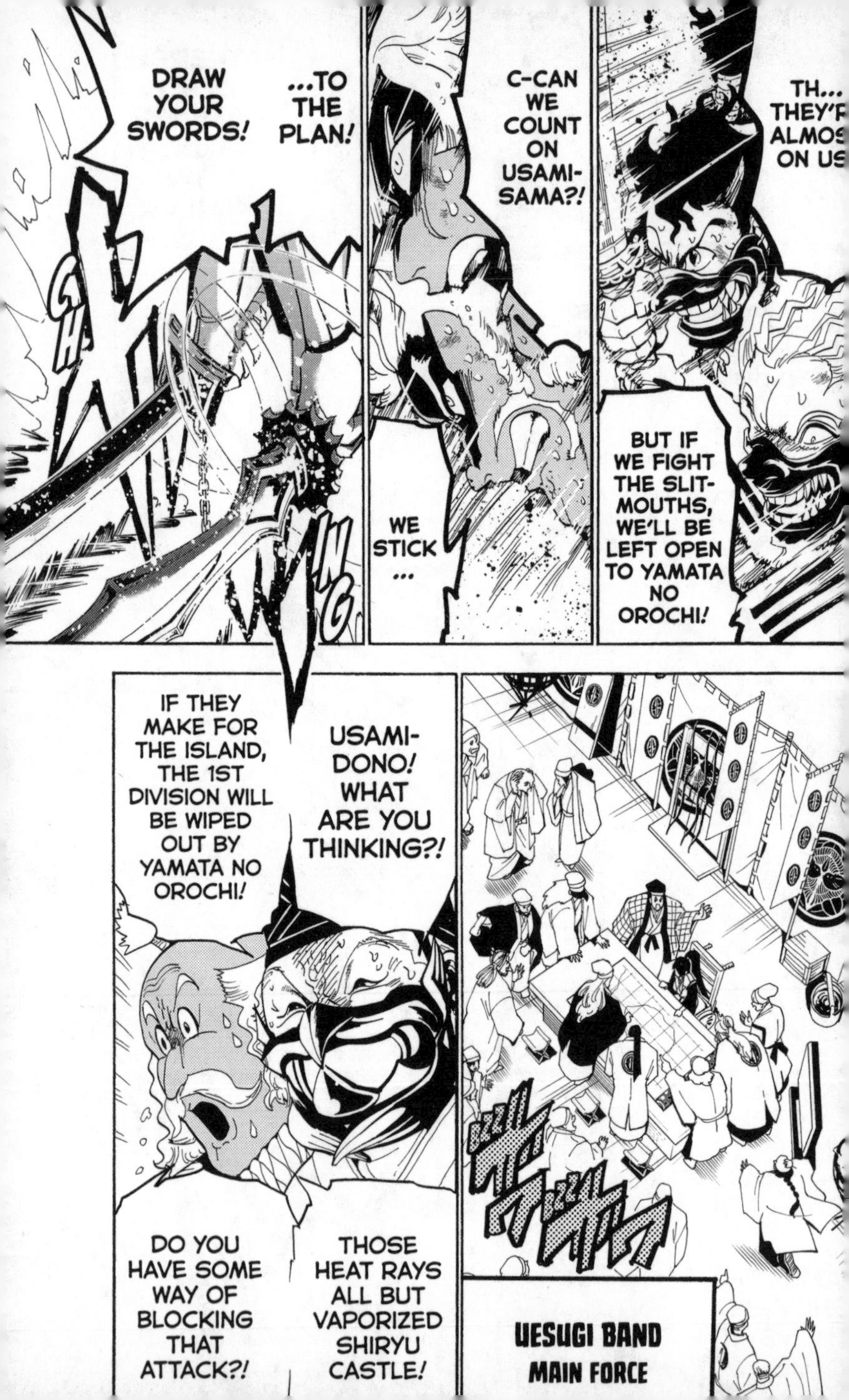
TH... THEY'R ALMOS ON US
BUT IF WE FIGHT THE SLIT-MOUTHS, WE'LL BE LEFT OPEN TO YAMATA NO OROCHI!
C-CAN WE COUNT ON USAMI-SAMA?!
WE STICK ...
...TO THE PLAN!
DRAW YOUR SWORDS!
UESUGI BAND MAIN FORCE
USAMI-DONO! WHAT ARE YOU THINKING?!
IF THEY MAKE FOR THE ISLAND, THE 1ST DIVISION WILL BE WIPED OUT BY YAMATA NO OROCHI!
THOSE HEAT RAYS ALL BUT VAPORIZED SHIRYU CASTLE!
DO YOU HAVE SOME WAY OF BLOCKING THAT ATTACK?!

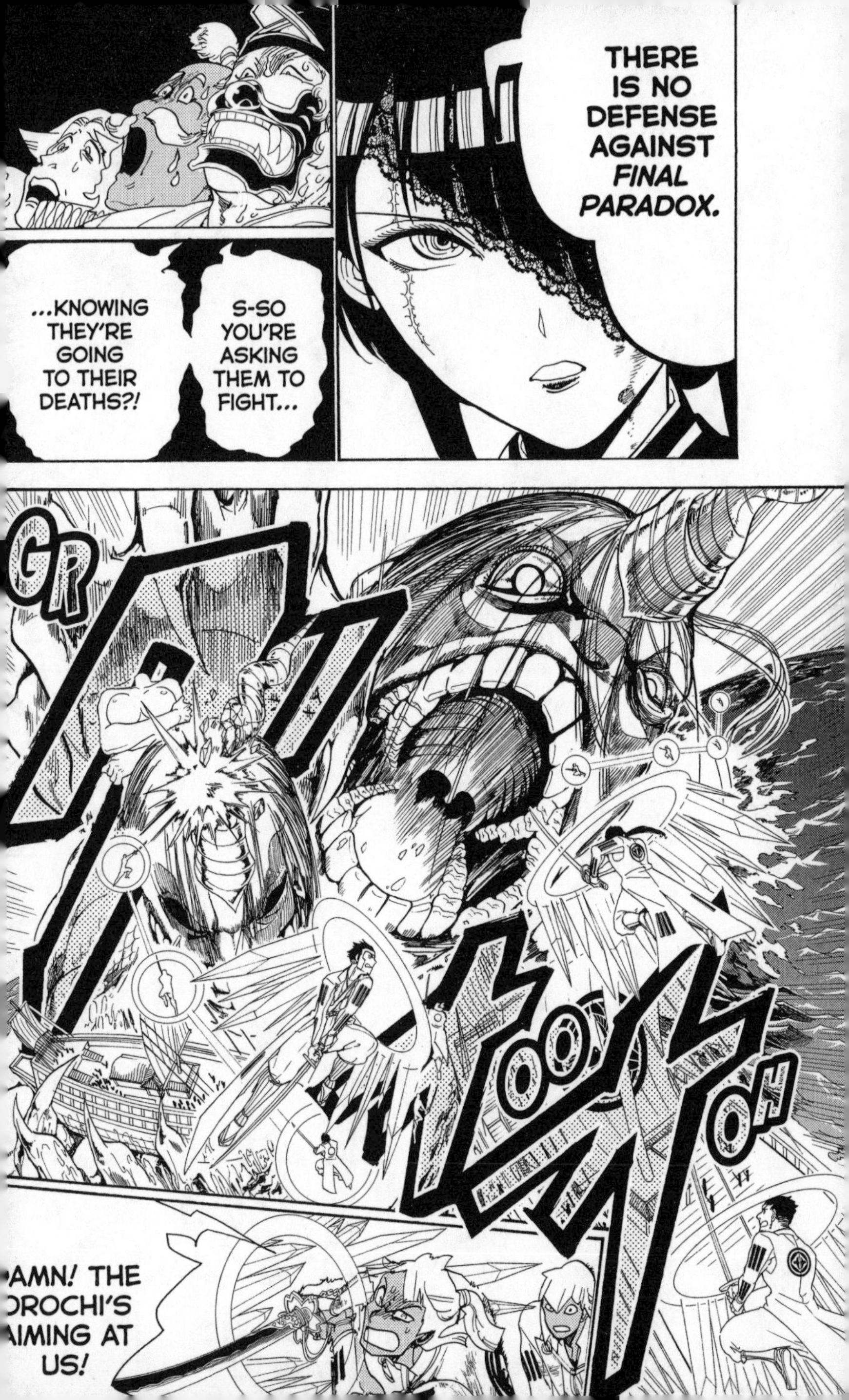
THERE IS NO DEFENSE AGAINST *FINAL PARADOX.*
S-SO YOU'RE ASKING THEM TO FIGHT...
...KNOWING THEY'RE GOING TO THEIR DEATHS?!
GR
AMN! THE OROCHI'S AIMING AT US!

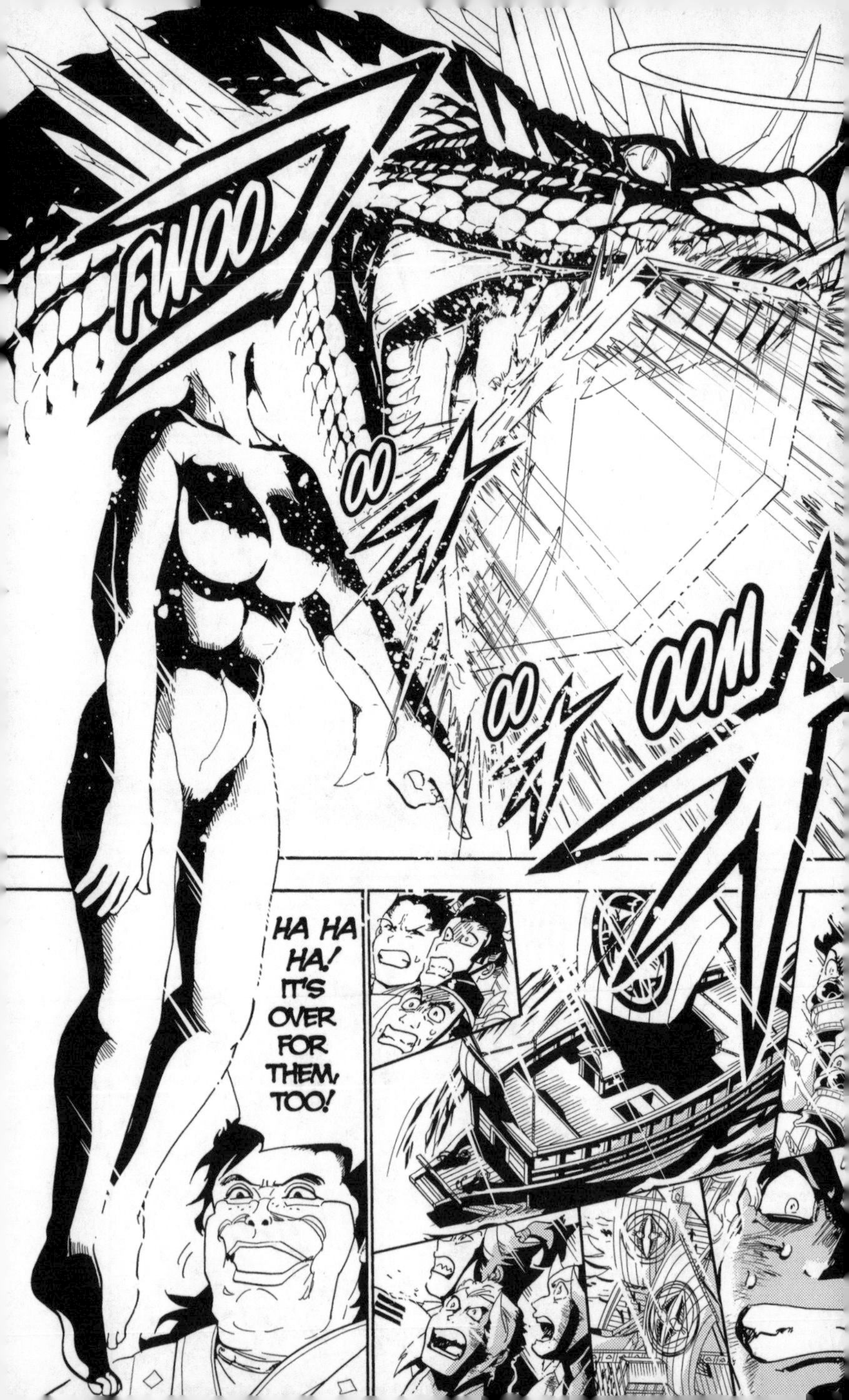
FWOO
OO
OO
OOM
HA HA HA! IT'S OVER FOR THEM, TOO!

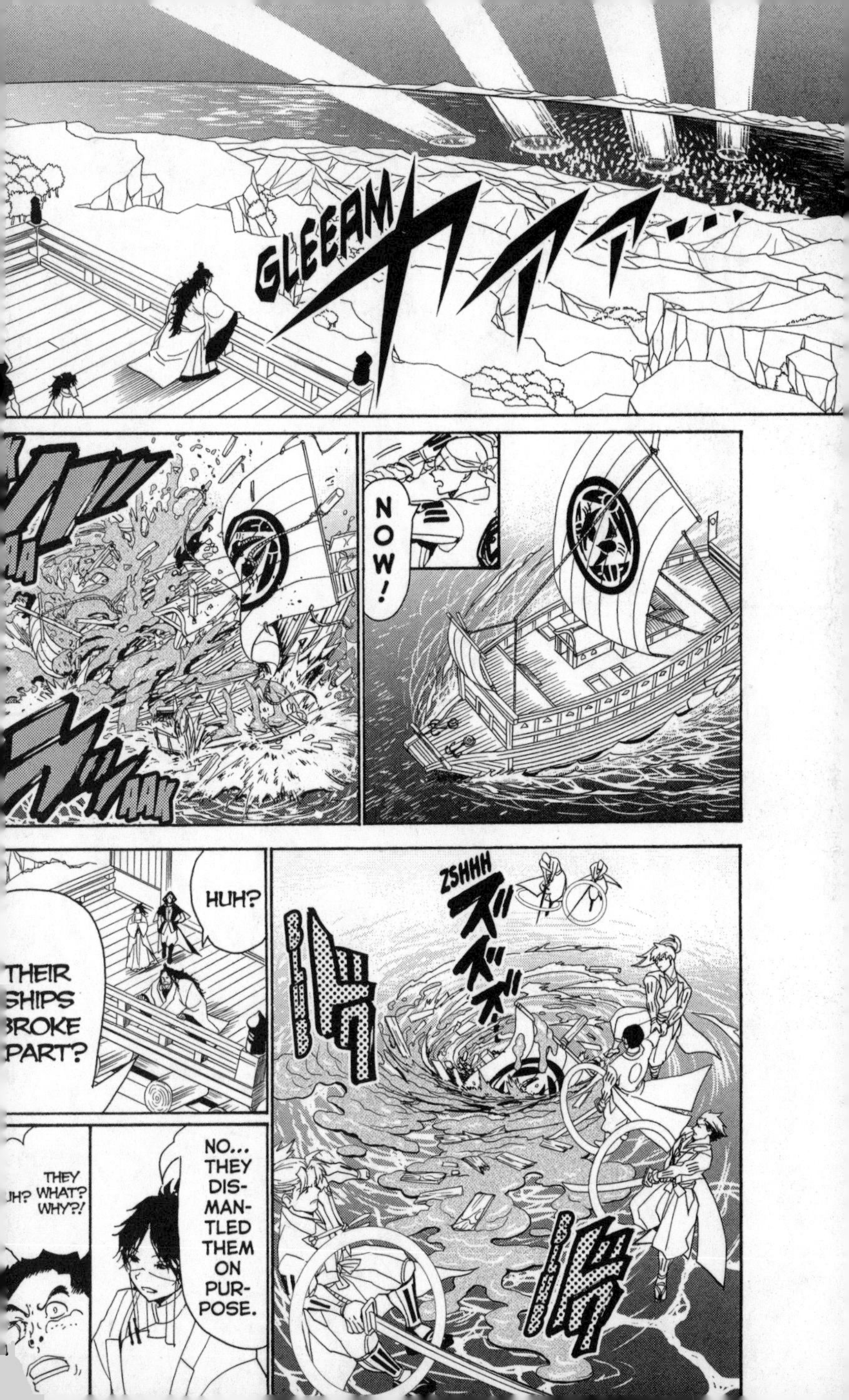
GLEEAM
NOW!
AAAK
HUH?
THEIR SHIPS BROKE PART?
ZSHHH
NO... THEY DIS-MAN-TLED THEM ON PUR-POSE.
THEY WHAT? WHY?!
UH?

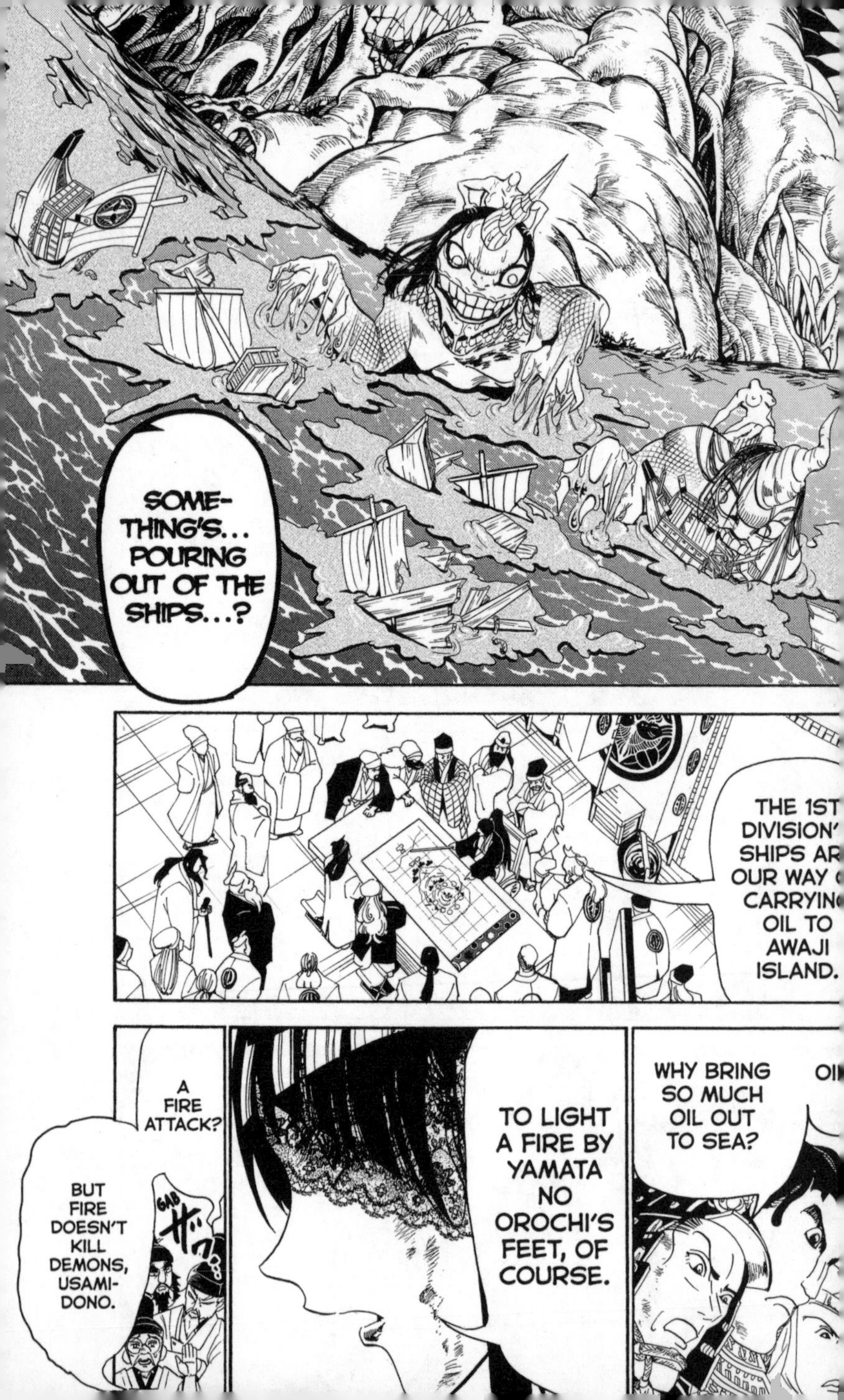
SOME-THING'S... POURING OUT OF THE SHIPS...?
THE 1ST DIVISION' SHIPS AR OUR WAY CARRYIN OIL TO AWAJI ISLAND.
OI
WHY BRING SO MUCH OIL OUT TO SEA?
TO LIGHT A FIRE BY YAMATA NO OROCHI'S FEET, OF COURSE.
A FIRE ATTACK?
BUT FIRE DOESN'T KILL DEMONS, USAMI-DONO.
GAB

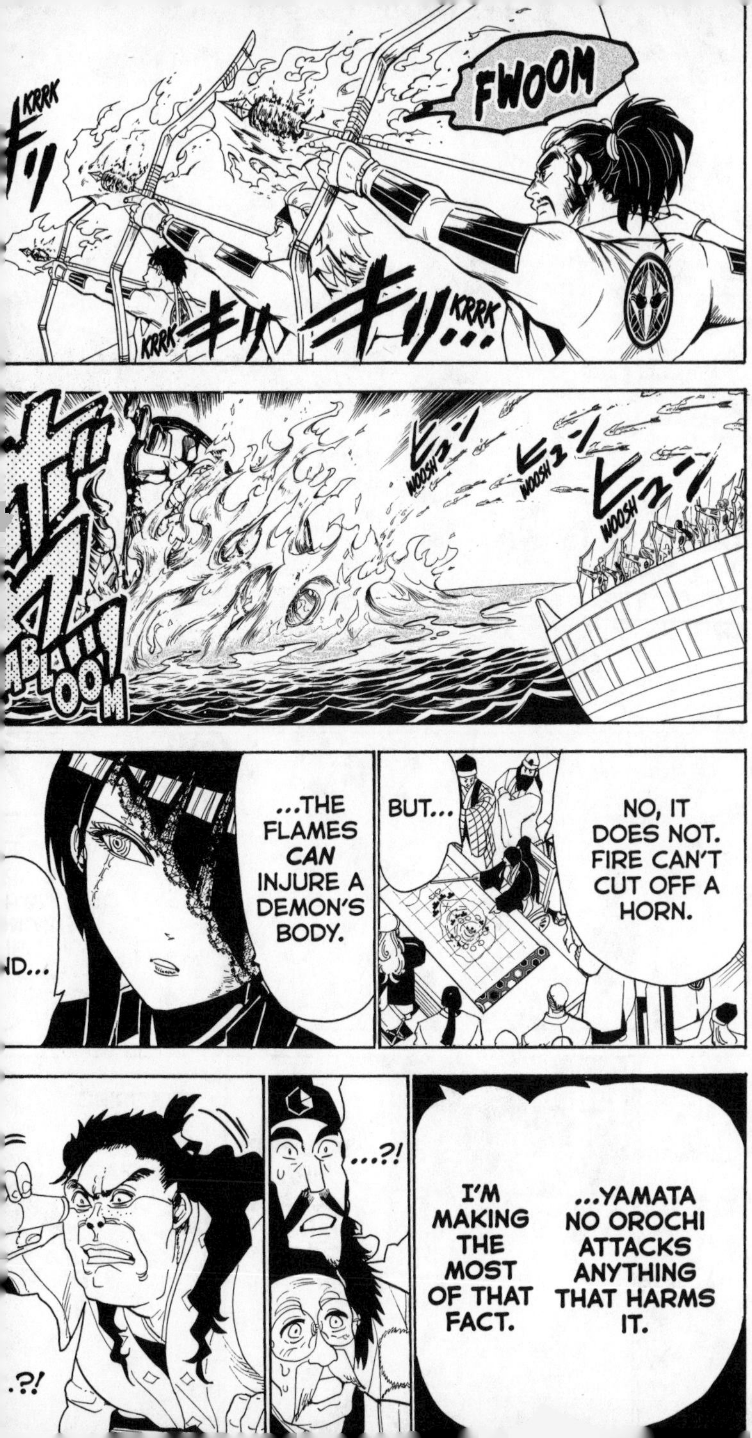
FWOOM
KRRK
KRRK
KRRK
WOOSH
WOOSH
WOOSH
BLOOOM
NO, IT DOES NOT. FIRE CAN'T CUT OFF A HORN.
BUT...
...THE FLAMES *CAN* INJURE A DEMON'S BODY.
...YAMATA NO OROCHI ATTACKS ANYTHING THAT HARMS IT.
I'M MAKING THE MOST OF THAT FACT.
...?!

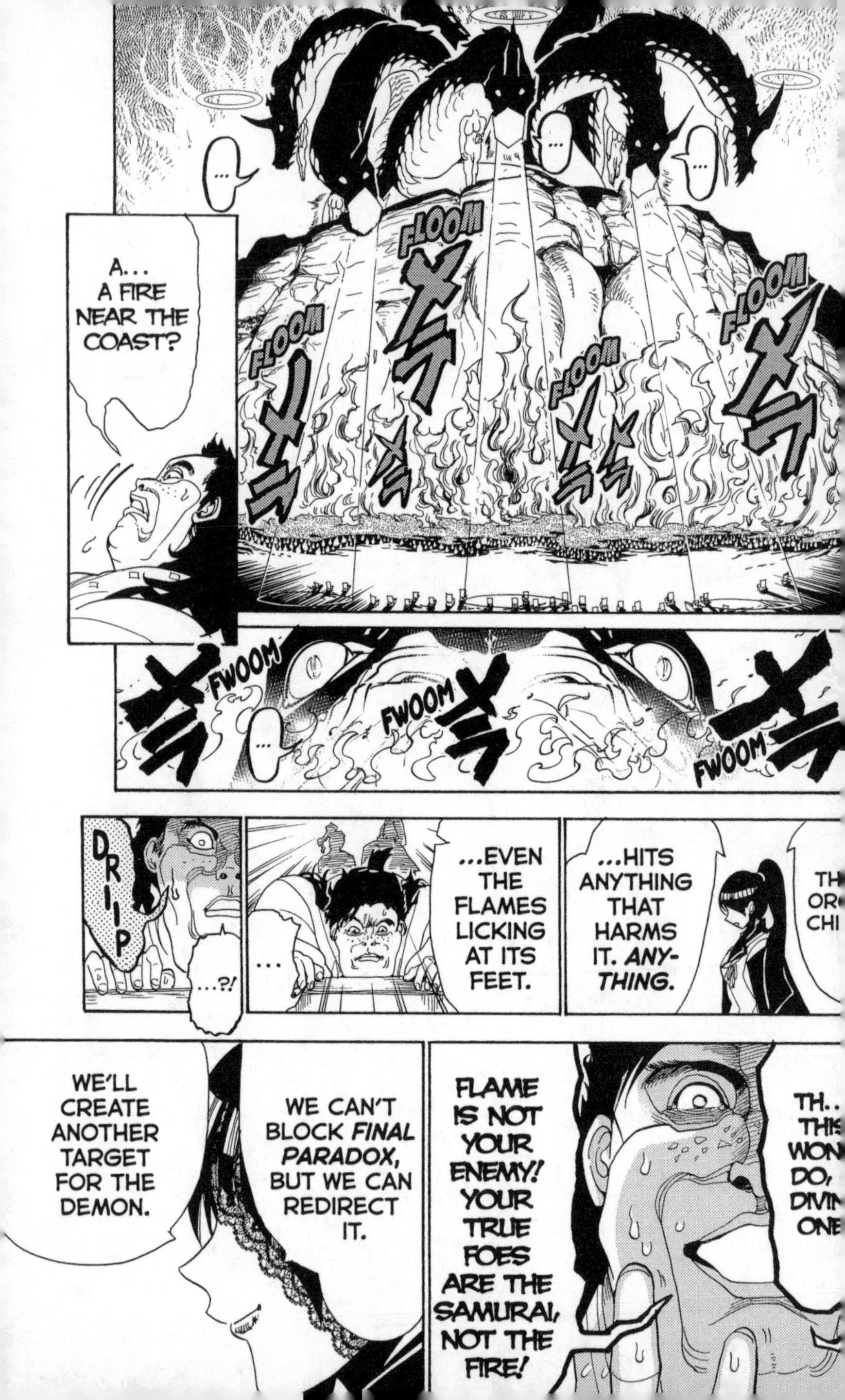
...
...
...
FLOOM
FLOOM
FLOOM
FLOOM
A... A FIRE NEAR THE COAST?
FWOOM
FWOOM
...
FWOOM
TH OR CHI
...HITS ANYTHING THAT HARMS IT. ANYTHING.
...EVEN THE FLAMES LICKING AT ITS FEET.
...
DRIP
...?!
TH.. THIS WON DO, DIVIN ONE
FLAME IS NOT YOUR ENEMY! YOUR TRUE FOES ARE THE SAMURAI, NOT THE FIRE!
WE CAN'T BLOCK FINAL PARADOX, BUT WE CAN REDIRECT IT.
WE'LL CREATE ANOTHER TARGET FOR THE DEMON.

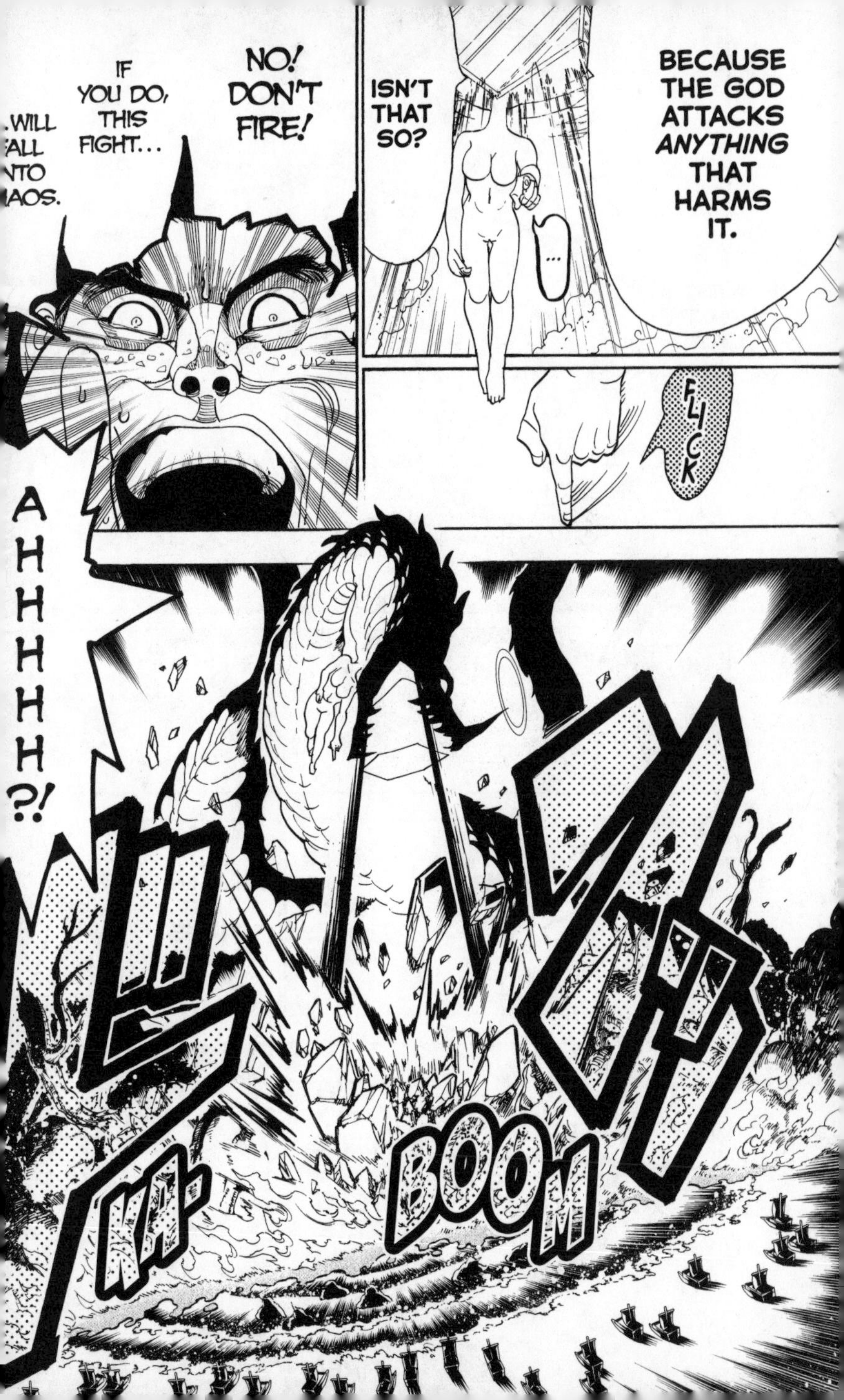

BECAUSE THE GOD ATTACKS *ANYTHING* THAT HARMS IT.
ISN'T THAT SO?
...
FLICK
NO! DON'T FIRE!
IF YOU DO, THIS FIGHT...
.WILL ALL NTO AOS.
AHHHHHH?!
KA-BOOM

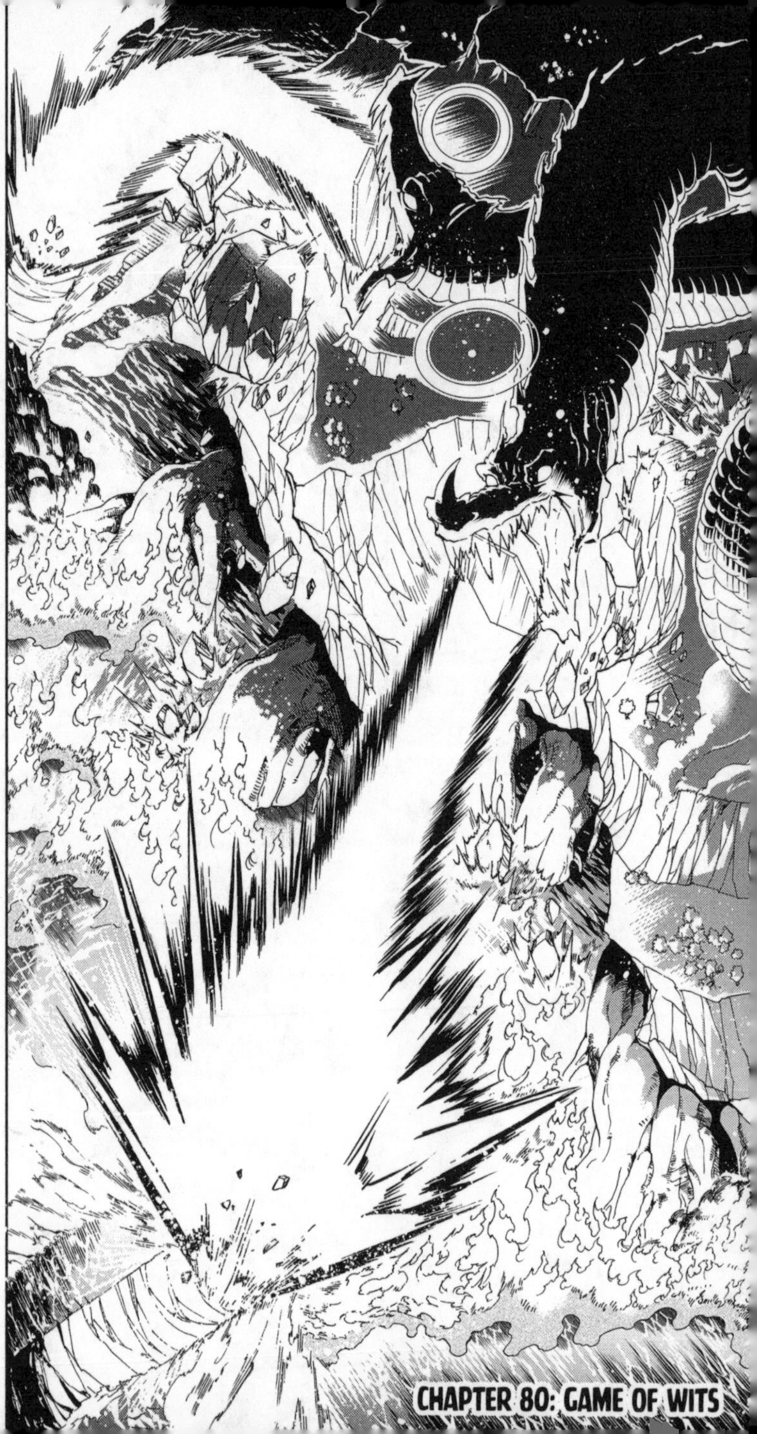

CHAPTER 80: GAME OF WITS

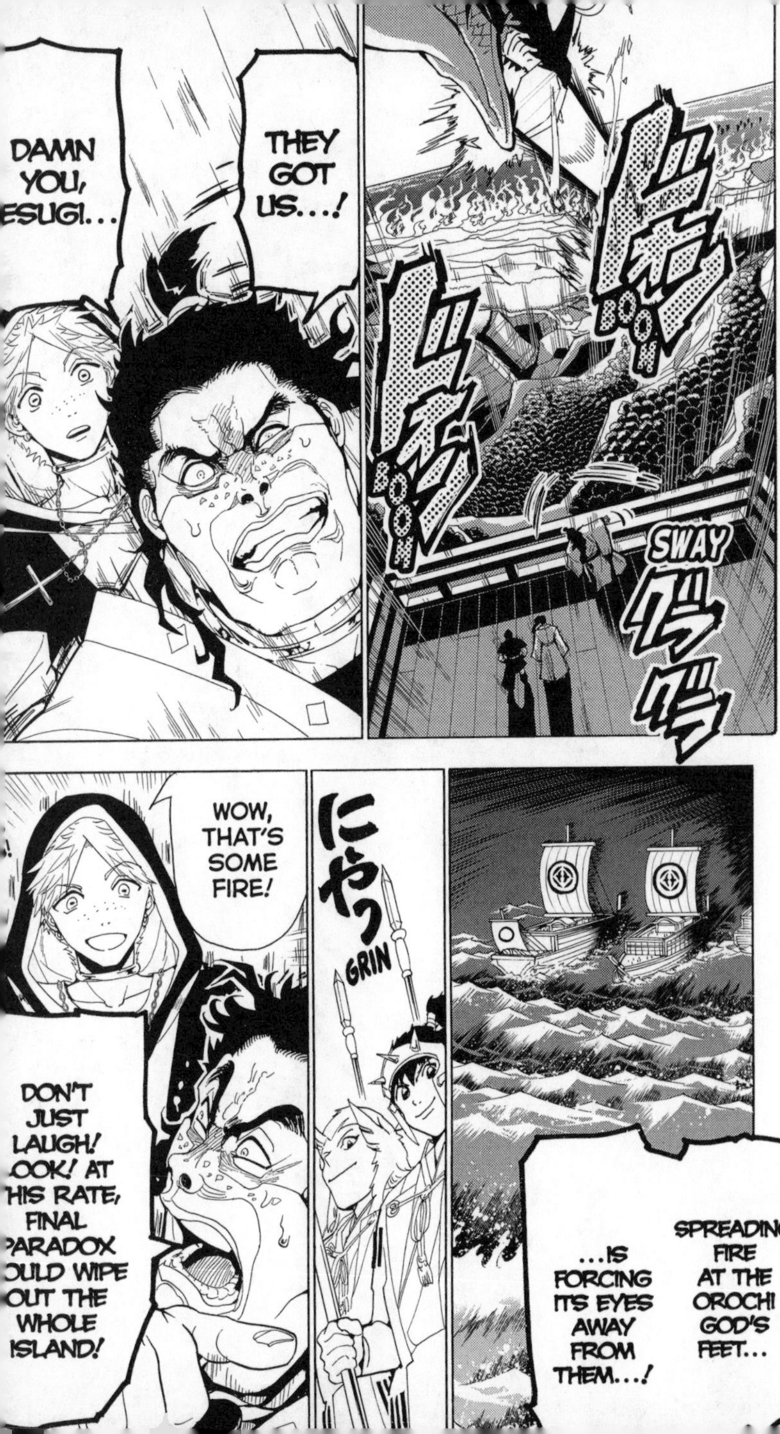
SWAY
グラグラ
THEY GOT US...!
DAMN YOU, ESUGI...
SPREADING FIRE AT THE OROCHI GOD'S FEET...
...IS FORCING ITS EYES AWAY FROM THEM...!
にやっ
GRIN
WOW, THAT'S SOME FIRE!
DON'T JUST LAUGH! OOK! AT HIS RATE, FINAL ARADOX OULD WIPE OUT THE WHOLE ISLAND!

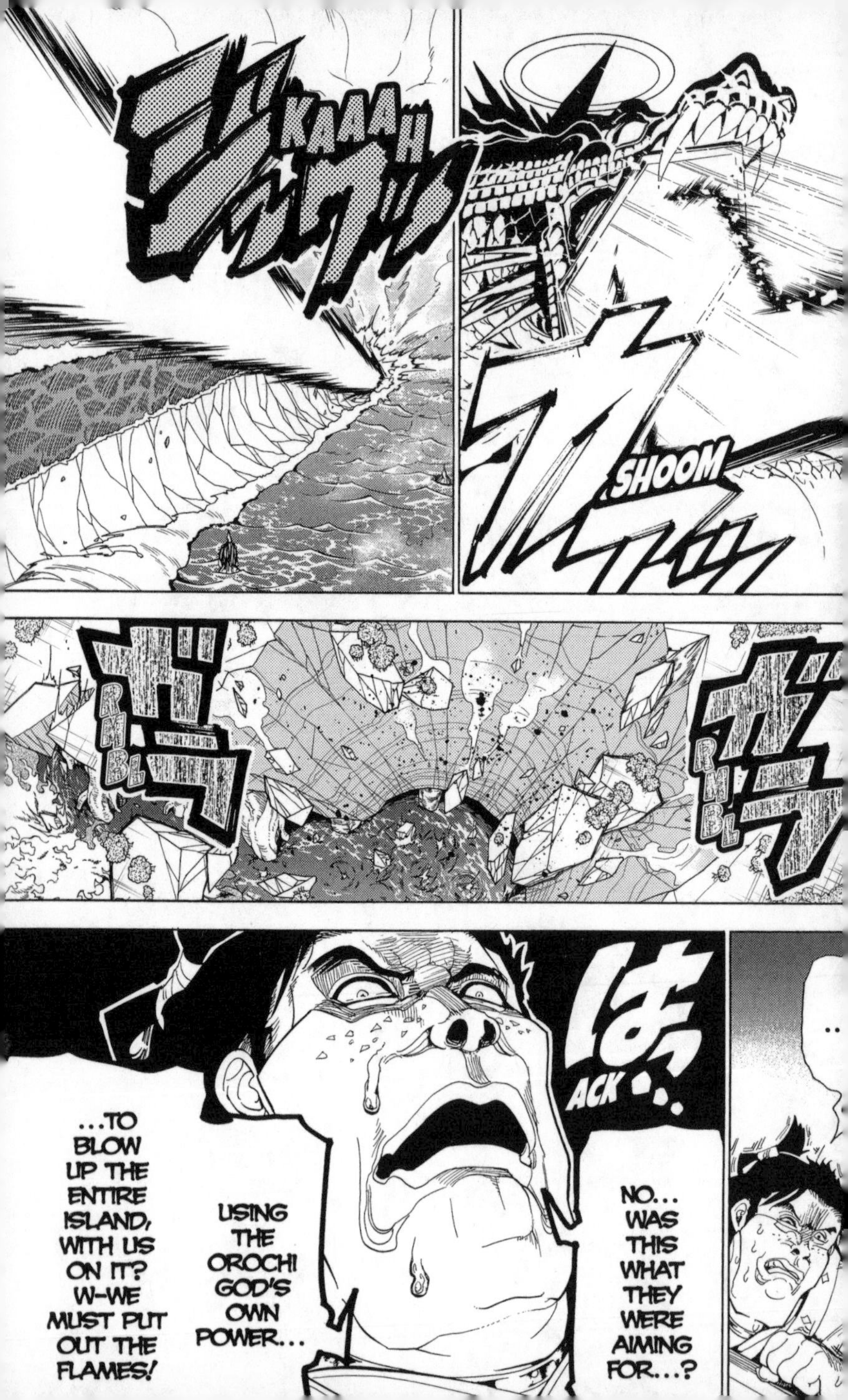
SHOOM
KAAAAH
RMBL
RMBL
..
ACK
NO... WAS THIS WHAT THEY WERE AIMING FOR...?
USING THE OROCHI GOD'S OWN POWER...
...TO BLOW UP THE ENTIRE ISLAND, WITH US ON IT? W-WE MUST PUT OUT THE FLAMES!

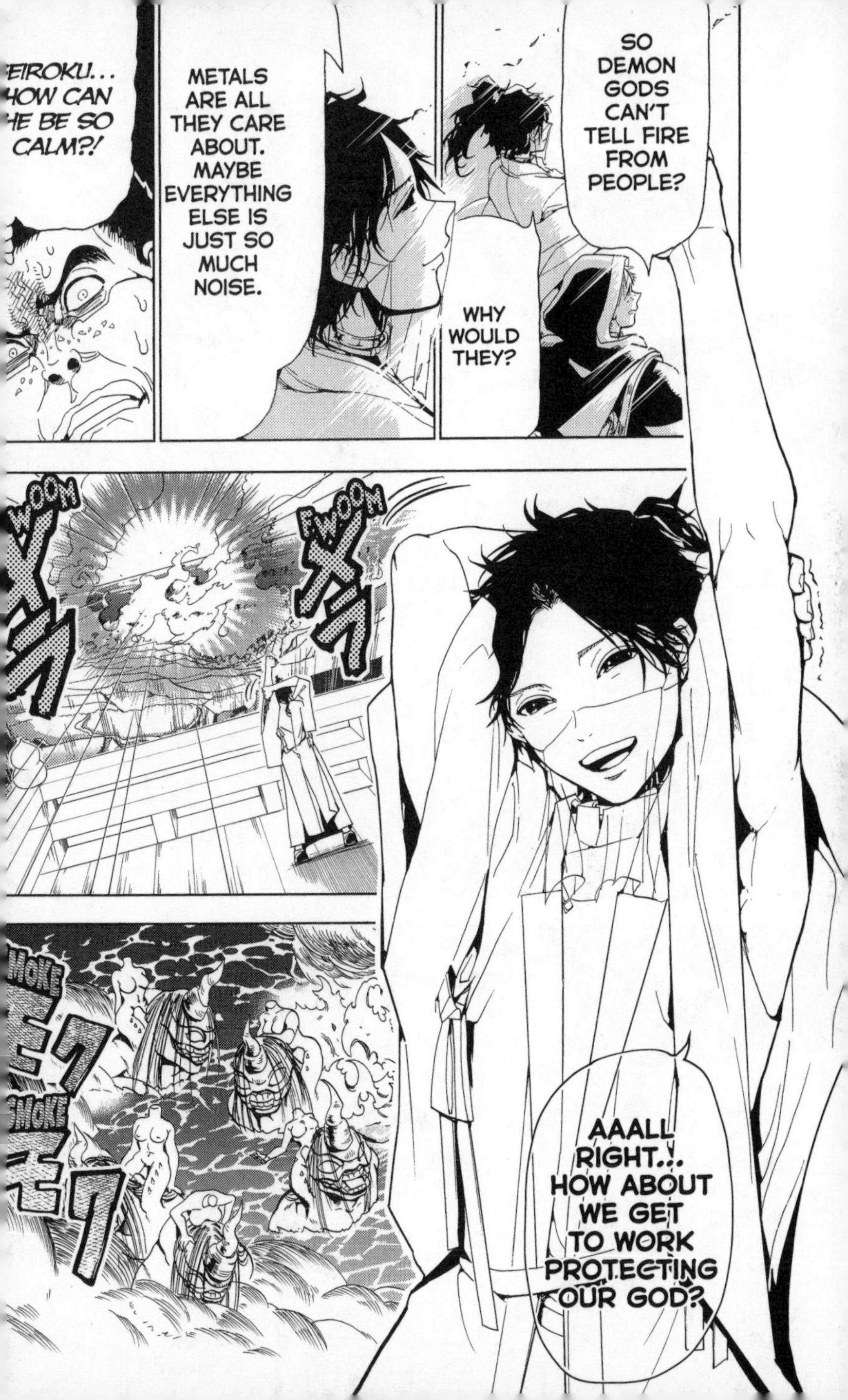

SO DEMON GODS CAN'T TELL FIRE FROM PEOPLE?
WHY WOULD THEY?
METALS ARE ALL THEY CARE ABOUT. MAYBE EVERYTHING ELSE IS JUST SO MUCH NOISE.
EIROKU... HOW CAN HE BE SO CALM?!
AAALL RIGHT... HOW ABOUT WE GET TO WORK PROTECTING OUR GOD?
FWOOM
FWOOM
SMOKE
SMOKE

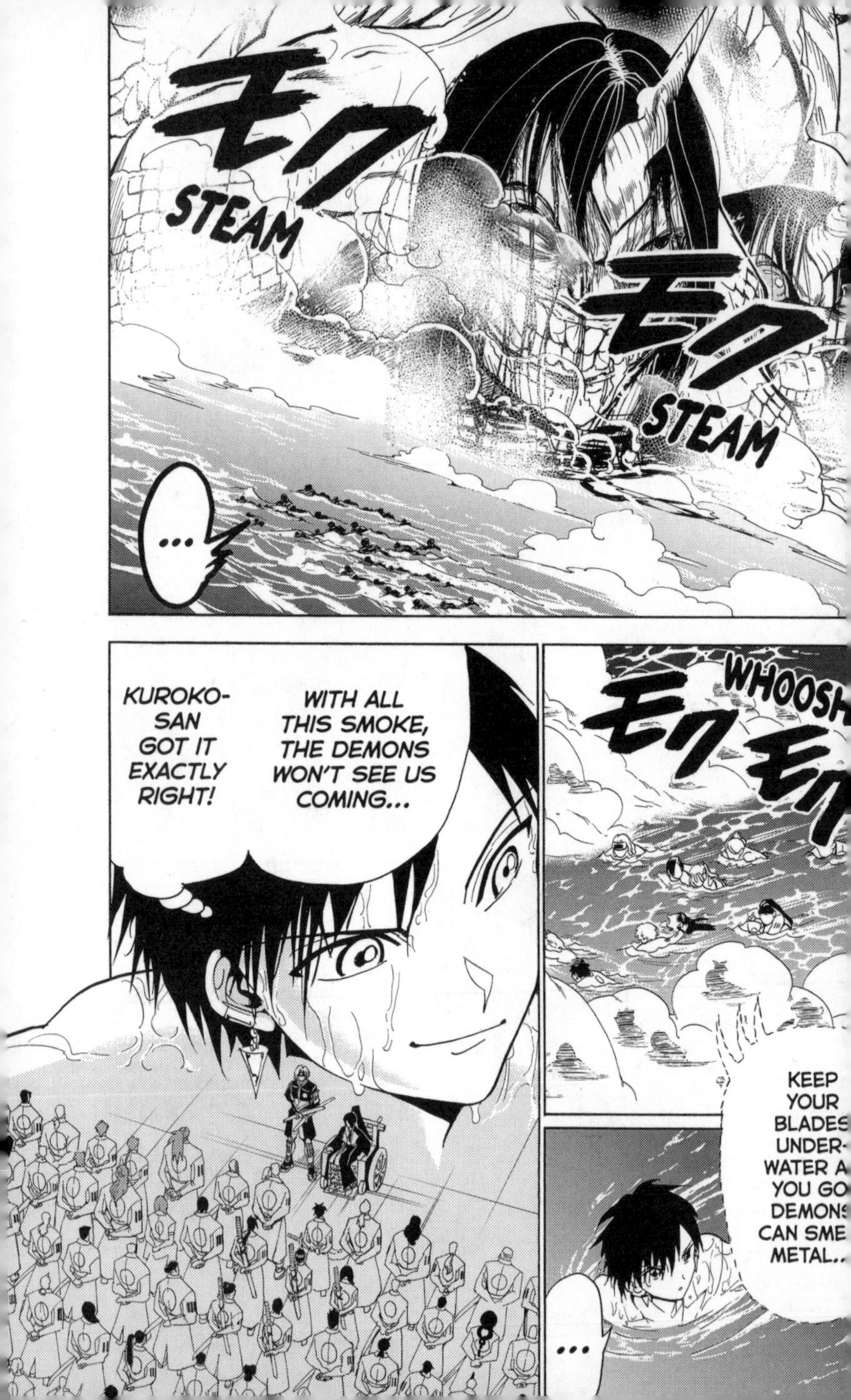

モク
STEAM
モク
STEAM
...
WHOOSH
モク
KEEP YOUR BLADES UNDER-WATER A YOU GO DEMONS CAN SME METAL..
...
KUROKO-SAN GOT IT EXACTLY RIGHT!
WITH ALL THIS SMOKE, THE DEMONS WON'T SEE US COMING...

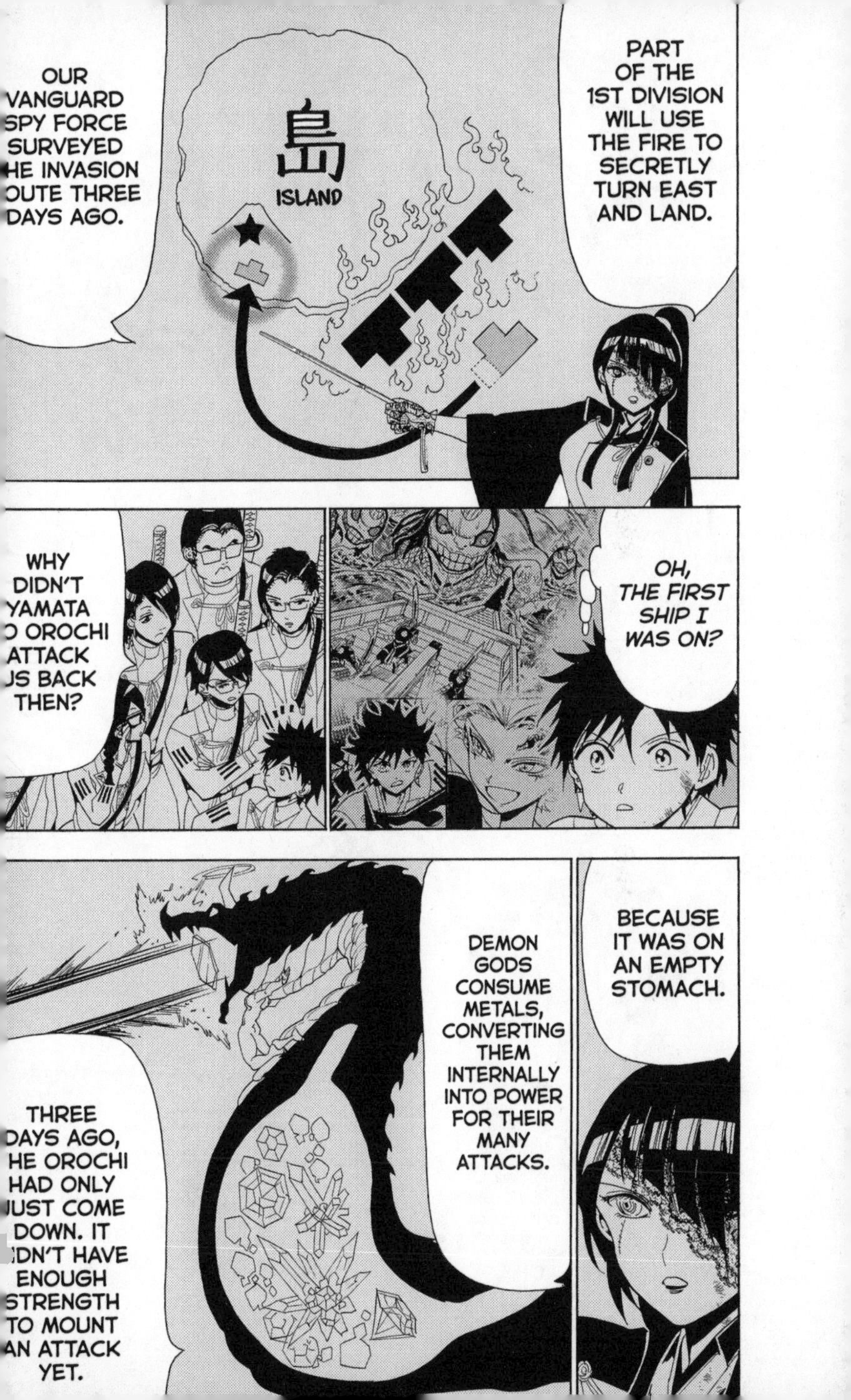

PART OF THE 1ST DIVISION WILL USE THE FIRE TO SECRETLY TURN EAST AND LAND.
島
ISLAND
OUR VANGUARD SPY FORCE SURVEYED HE INVASION OUTE THREE DAYS AGO.
OH, THE FIRST SHIP I WAS ON?
WHY DIDN'T YAMATA O OROCHI ATTACK JS BACK THEN?
BECAUSE IT WAS ON AN EMPTY STOMACH.
DEMON GODS CONSUME METALS, CONVERTING THEM INTERNALLY INTO POWER FOR THEIR MANY ATTACKS.
THREE DAYS AGO, HE OROCHI HAD ONLY JUST COME DOWN. IT IDN'T HAVE ENOUGH STRENGTH TO MOUNT AN ATTACK YET.

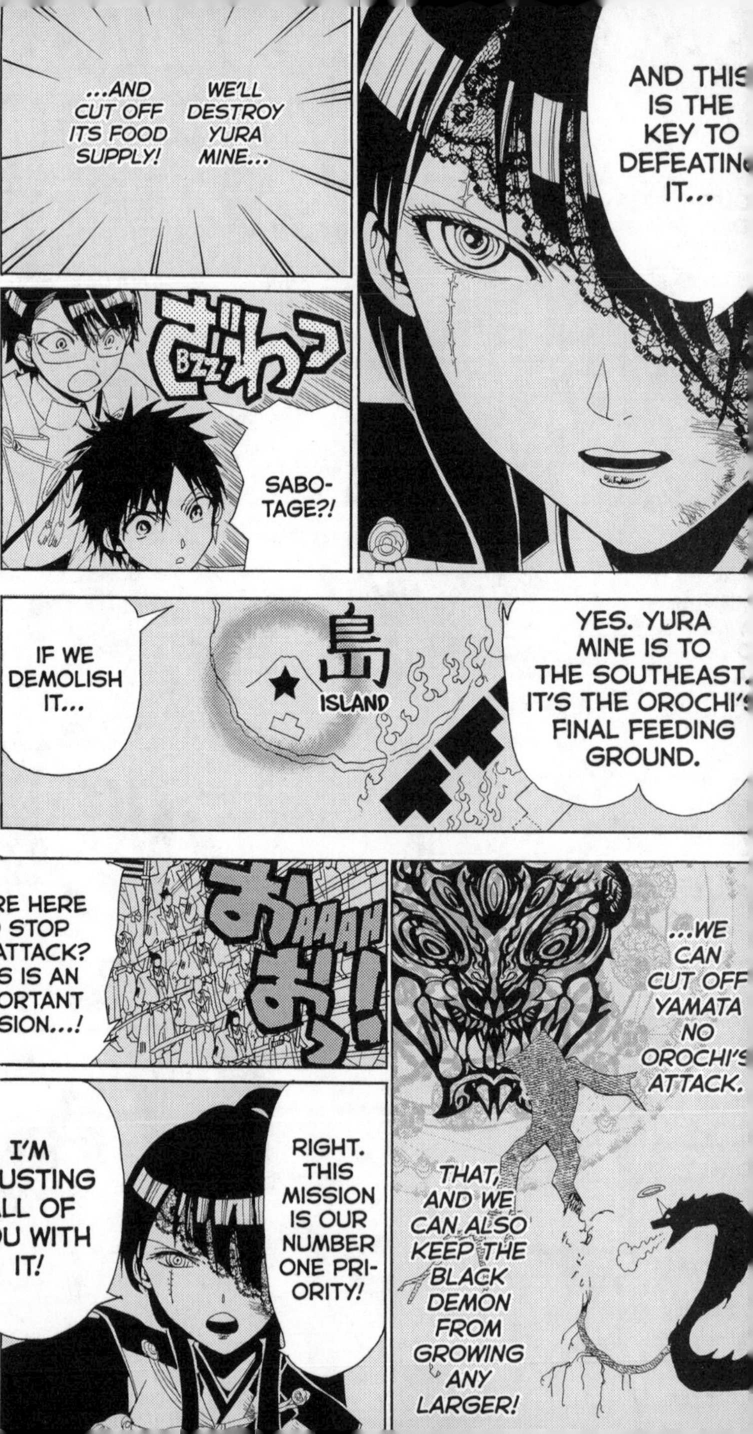
AND THIS IS THE KEY TO DEFEATIN IT...
WE'LL DESTROY YURA MINE...
...AND CUT OFF ITS FOOD SUPPLY!
BZZ
SABO-TAGE?!
YES. YURA MINE IS TO THE SOUTHEAST. IT'S THE OROCHI'S FINAL FEEDING GROUND.
島
ISLAND
IF WE DEMOLISH IT...
...WE CAN CUT OFF YAMATA NO OROCHI'S ATTACK.
THAT, AND WE CAN ALSO KEEP THE BLACK DEMON FROM GROWING ANY LARGER!
AAAAH
WE'RE HERE TO STOP ITS ATTACK? THIS IS AN IMPORTANT MISSION...!
RIGHT. THIS MISSION IS OUR NUMBER ONE PRIORITY!
I'M TRUSTING ALL OF YOU WITH IT!

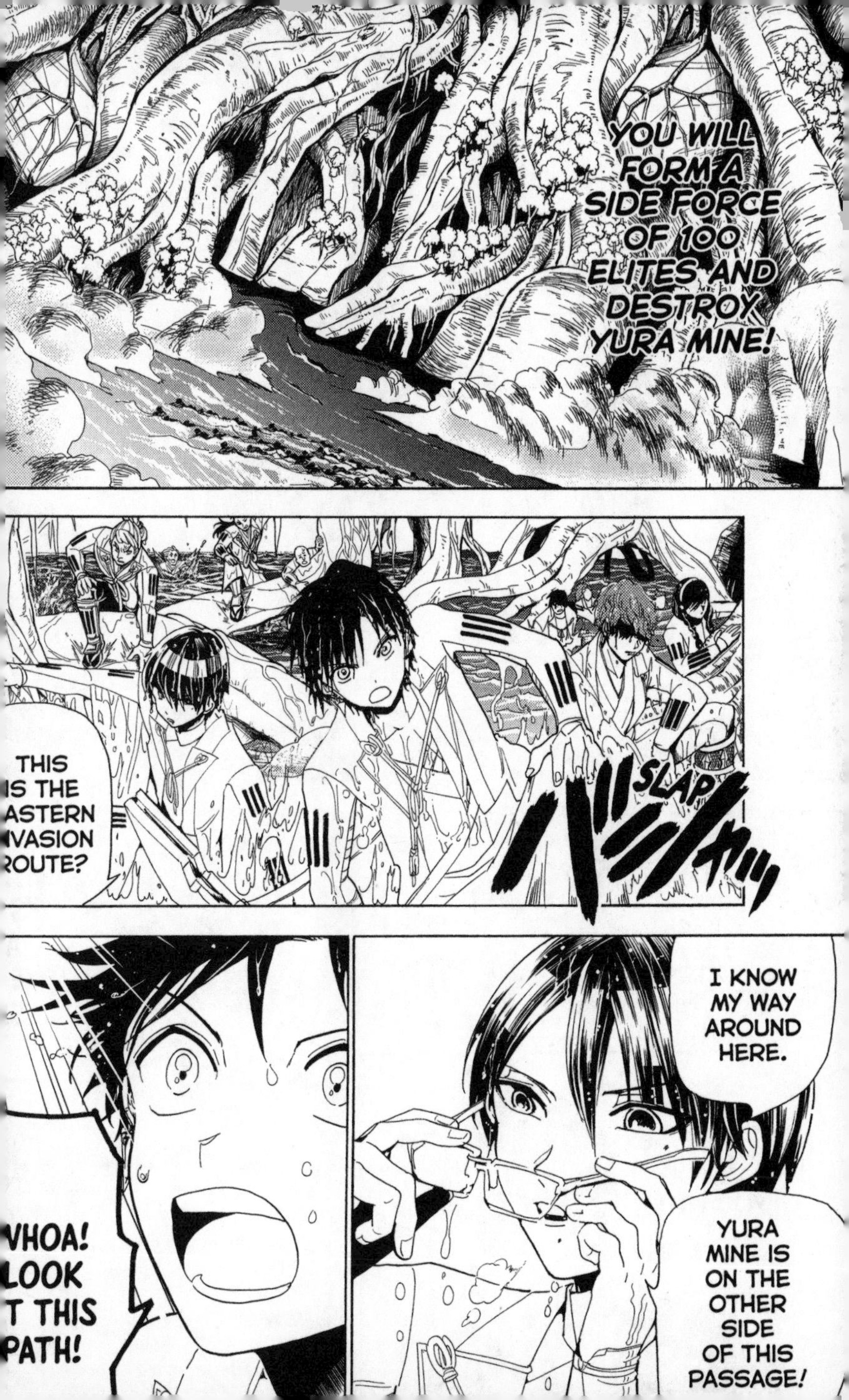
YOU WILL FORM A SIDE FORCE OF 100 ELITES AND DESTROY YURA MINE!
THIS IS THE ASTERN IVASION ROUTE?
SLAP
I KNOW MY WAY AROUND HERE.
YURA MINE IS ON THE OTHER SIDE OF THIS PASSAGE!
VHOA! LOOK T THIS PATH!

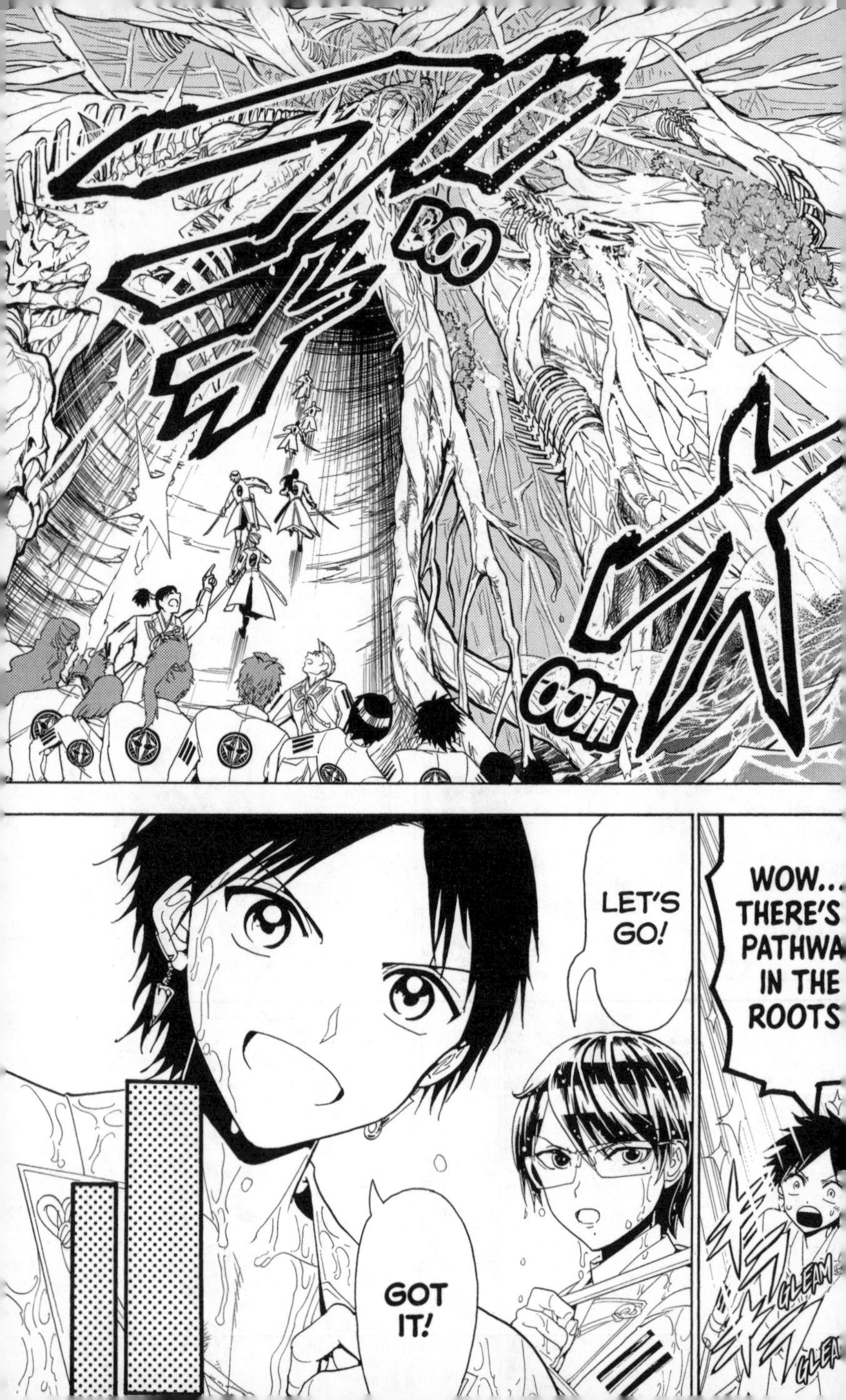
BOO
OOM
WOW... THERE'S PATHWA IN THE ROOTS
GLEAM
GLEA
LET'S GO!
GOT IT!

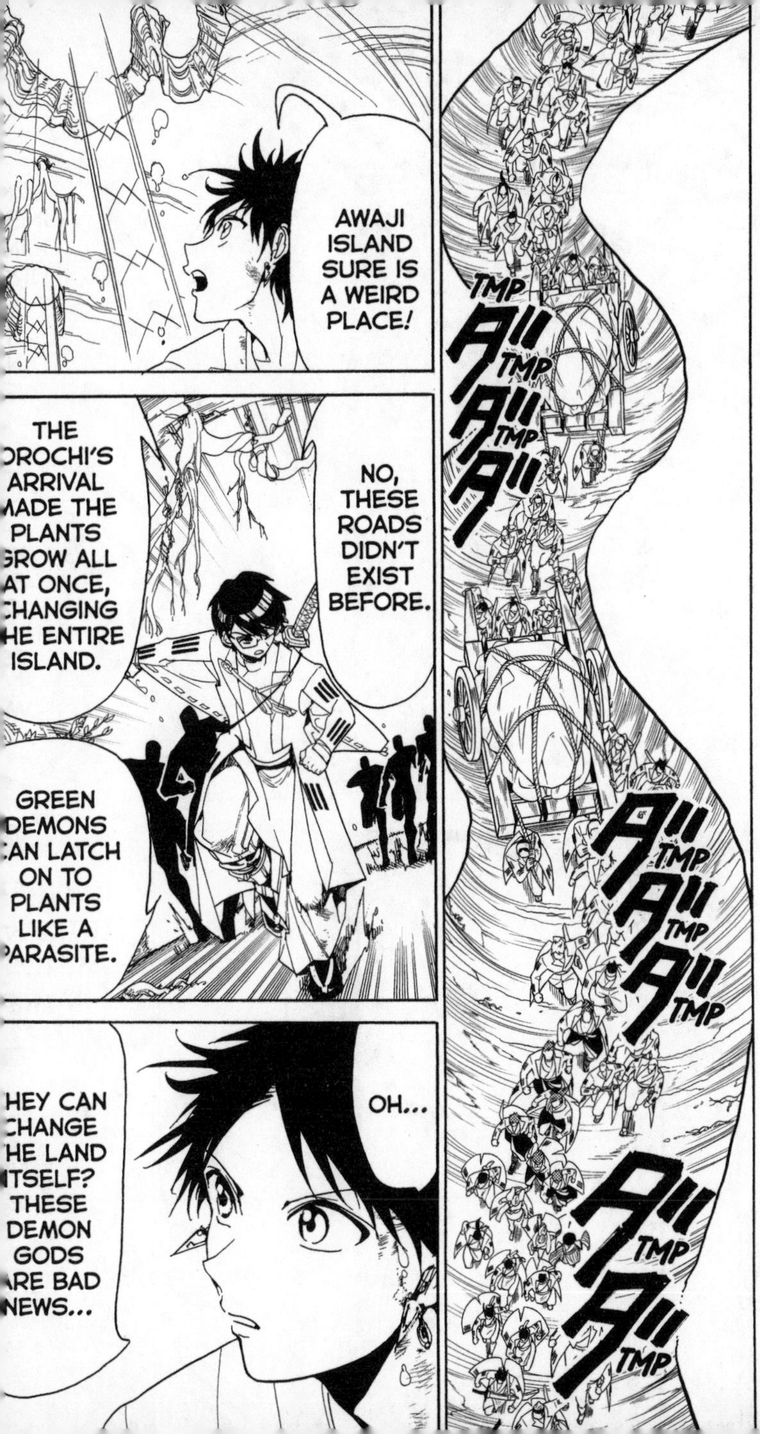

TMP
ダッ
TMP
ダッ
TMP
ダッ
ダッ
TMP
ダッ
TMP
ダッ
TMP
ダッ
TMP
ダッ
TMP
AWAJI ISLAND SURE IS A WEIRD PLACE!
NO, THESE ROADS DIDN'T EXIST BEFORE.
THE OROCHI'S ARRIVAL MADE THE PLANTS GROW ALL AT ONCE, CHANGING THE ENTIRE ISLAND.
GREEN DEMONS CAN LATCH ON TO PLANTS LIKE A PARASITE.
OH...
THEY CAN CHANGE THE LAND ITSELF? THESE DEMON GODS ARE BAD NEWS...

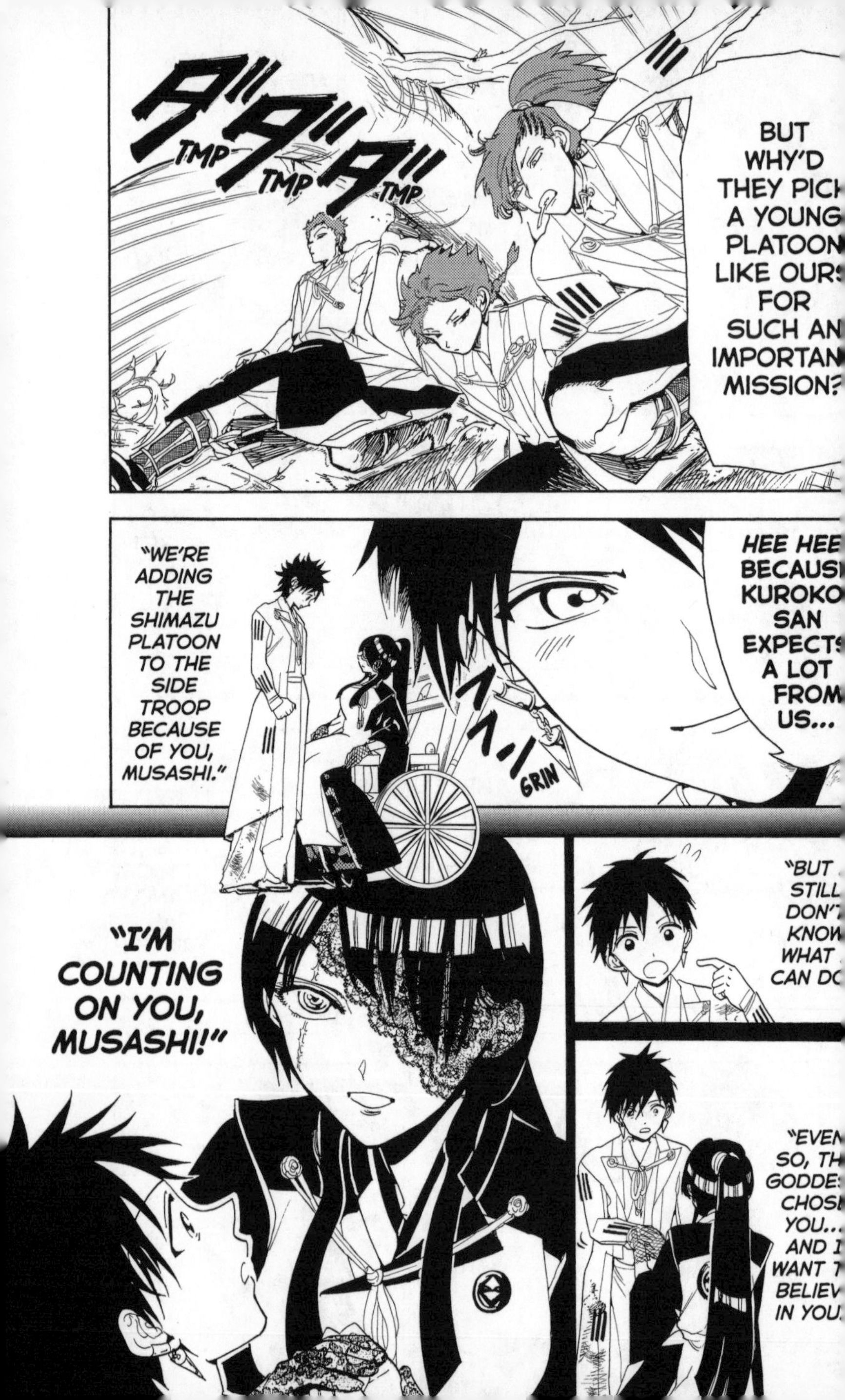
BUT WHY'D THEY PIC A YOUNG PLATOON LIKE OUR FOR SUCH AN IMPORTAN MISSION?
TMP
TMP
TMP
HEE HEE BECAUS KUROKO SAN EXPECT A LOT FROM US...
GRIN
"WE'RE ADDING THE SHIMAZU PLATOON TO THE SIDE TROOP BECAUSE OF YOU, MUSASHI."
"BUT STILL DON' KNOW WHAT CAN D
"EVEN SO, TH GODDE CHOS YOU... AND I WANT T BELIEV IN YOU.
"I'M COUNTING ON YOU, MUSASHI!"

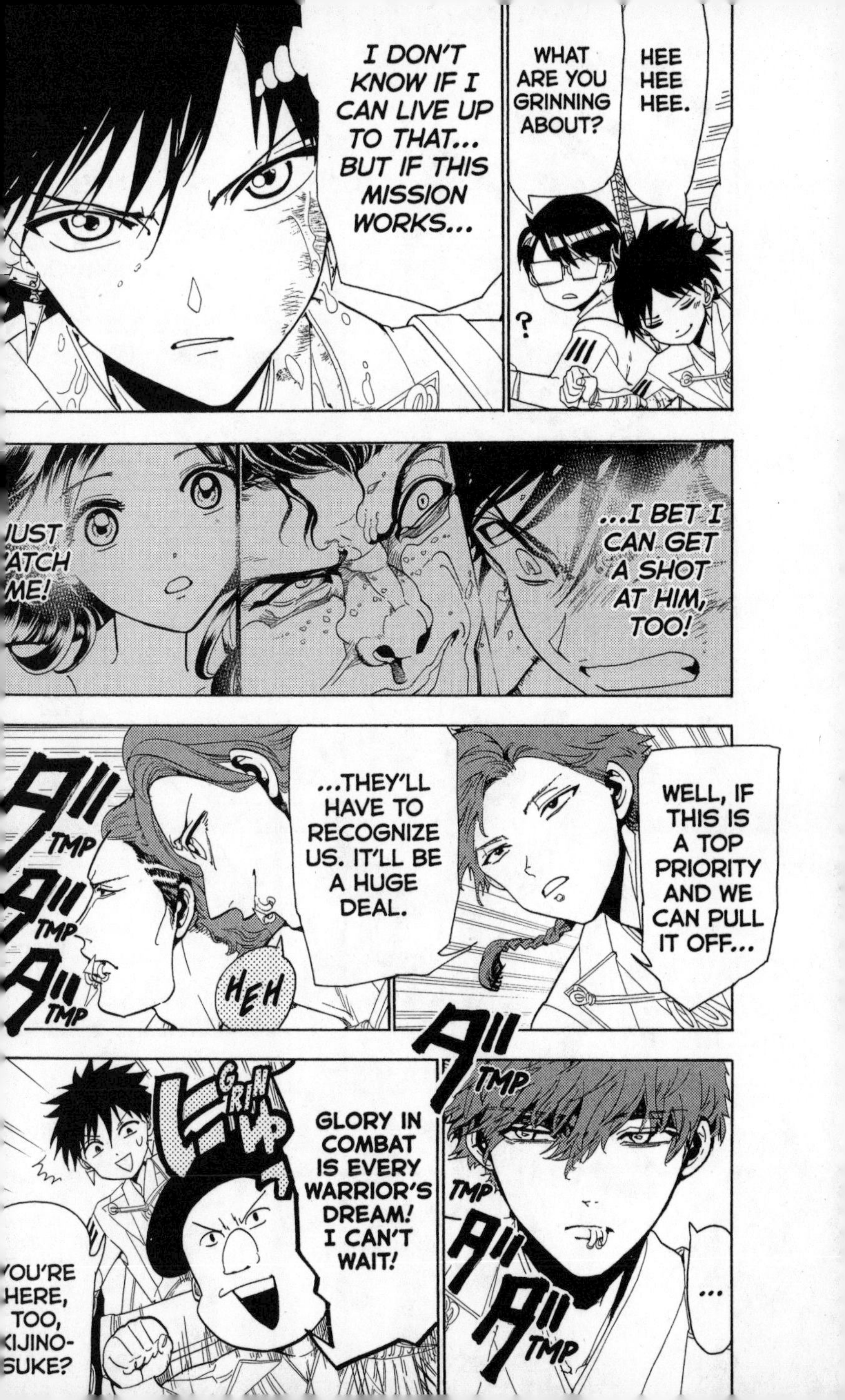

HEE HEE HEE.
WHAT ARE YOU GRINNING ABOUT?
?
I DON'T KNOW IF I CAN LIVE UP TO THAT... BUT IF THIS MISSION WORKS...
...I BET I CAN GET A SHOT AT HIM, TOO!
UST ATCH ME!
WELL, IF THIS IS A TOP PRIORITY AND WE CAN PULL IT OFF...
...THEY'LL HAVE TO RECOGNIZE US. IT'LL BE A HUGE DEAL.
HEH
TMP TMP TMP
TMP TMP TMP TMP
...
GRIN
GLORY IN COMBAT IS EVERY WARRIOR'S DREAM! I CAN'T WAIT!
OU'RE HERE, TOO, IJINO-SUKE?

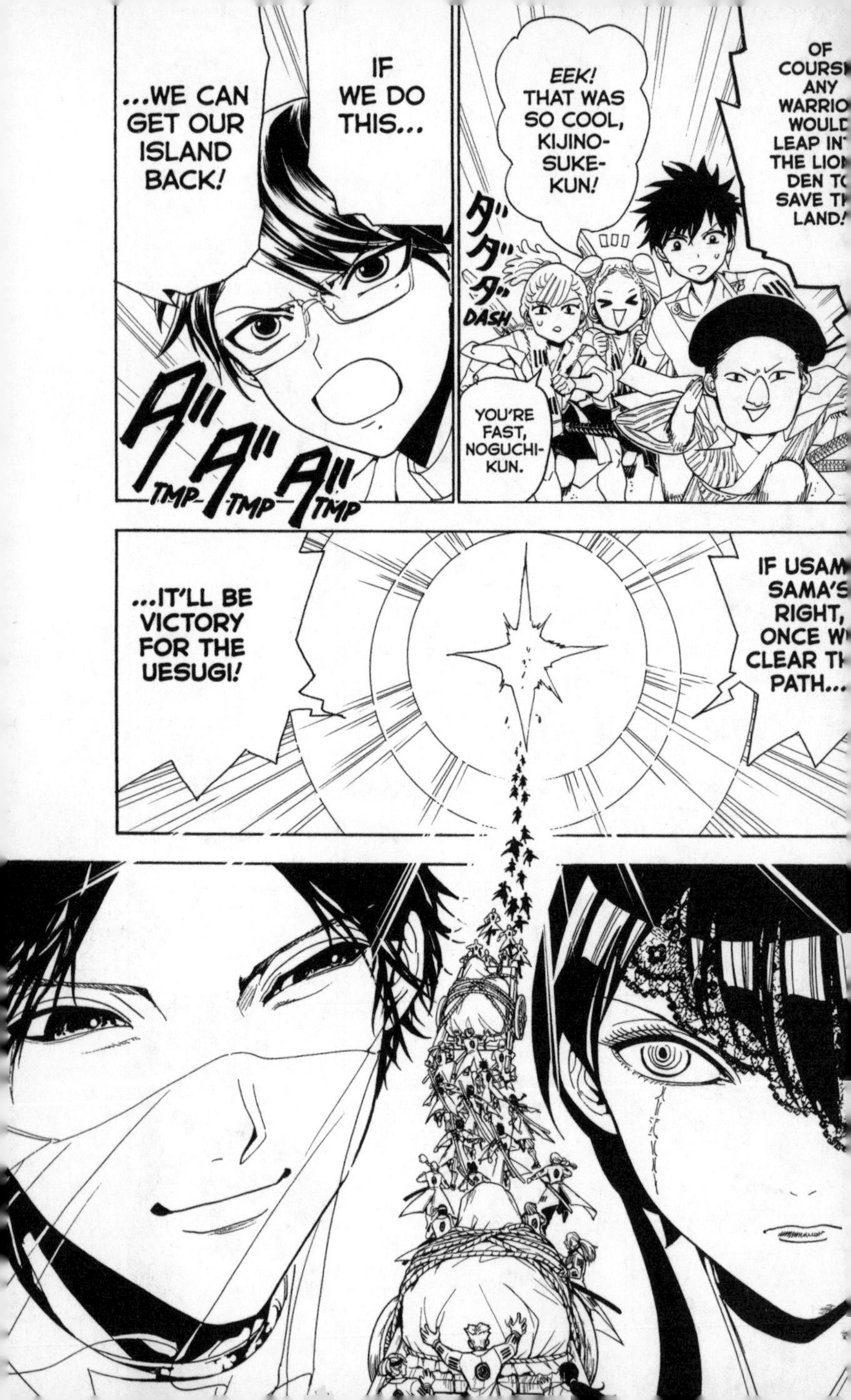
OF COURS ANY WARRIO WOULD LEAP INT THE LION DEN TO SAVE T LAND!
EEK! THAT WAS SO COOL, KIJINO-SUKE-KUN!
ダダダ
DASH
YOU'RE FAST, NOGUCHI-KUN.
IF WE DO THIS...
...WE CAN GET OUR ISLAND BACK!
TMP TMP TMP
IF USAM SAMA'S RIGHT, ONCE W CLEAR T PATH...
...IT'LL BE VICTORY FOR THE UESUGI!

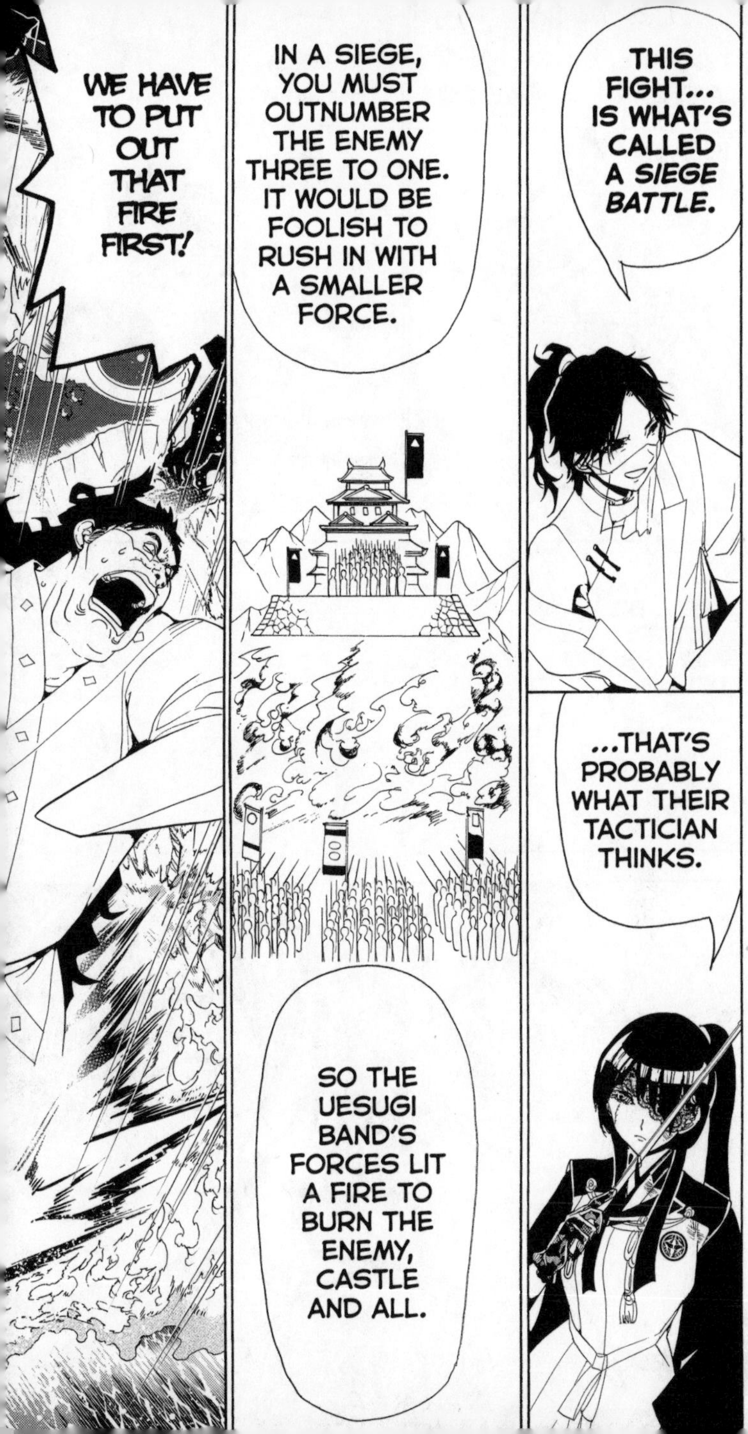
THIS FIGHT... IS WHAT'S CALLED A *SIEGE BATTLE*.
...THAT'S PROBABLY WHAT THEIR TACTICIAN THINKS.
IN A SIEGE, YOU MUST OUTNUMBER THE ENEMY THREE TO ONE. IT WOULD BE FOOLISH TO RUSH IN WITH A SMALLER FORCE.
SO THE UESUGI BAND'S FORCES LIT A FIRE TO BURN THE ENEMY, CASTLE AND ALL.
WE HAVE TO PUT OUT THAT FIRE FIRST!

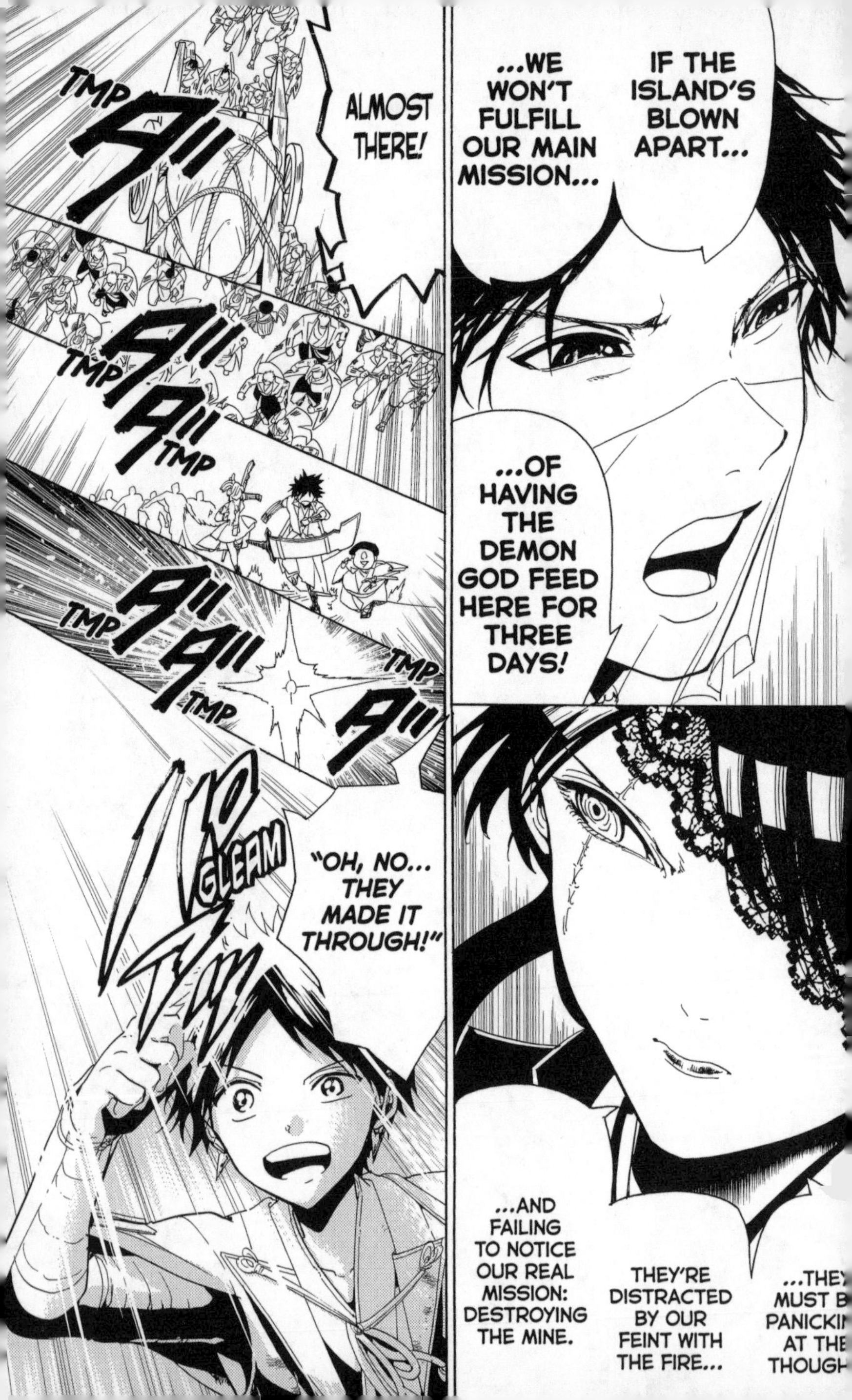
IF THE ISLAND'S BLOWN APART...
...WE WON'T FULFILL OUR MAIN MISSION...
...OF HAVING THE DEMON GOD FEED HERE FOR THREE DAYS!
...THE MUST B PANICKI AT THE THOUGH
THEY'RE DISTRACTED BY OUR FEINT WITH THE FIRE...
...AND FAILING TO NOTICE OUR REAL MISSION: DESTROYING THE MINE.
ALMOST THERE!
TMP
TMP
TMP
TMP
TMP
TMP
GLEAM
"OH, NO... THEY MADE IT THROUGH!"

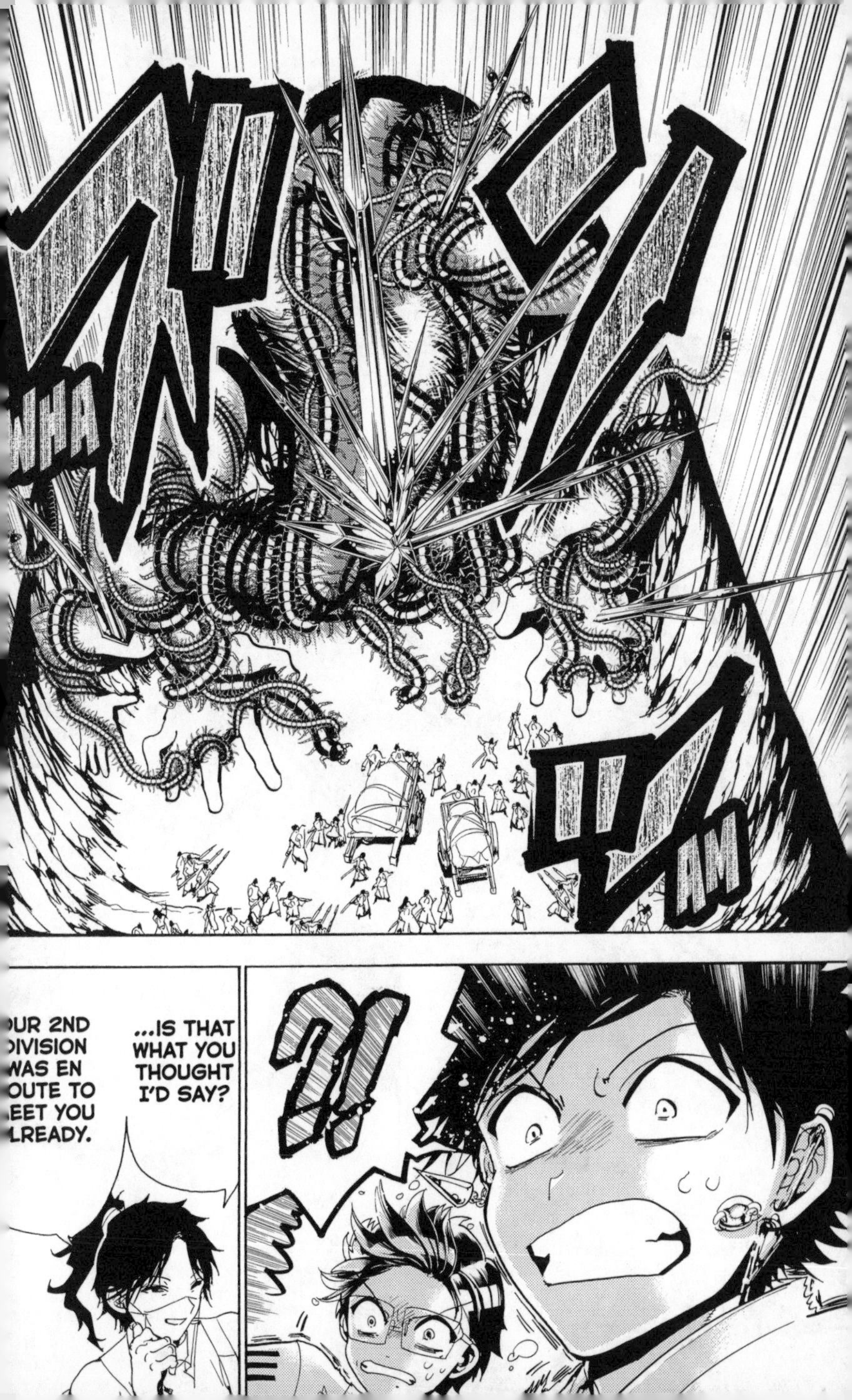
WHA
AM
?!
...IS THAT WHAT YOU THOUGHT I'D SAY?
OUR 2ND DIVISION WAS EN OUTE TO EET YOU LREADY.

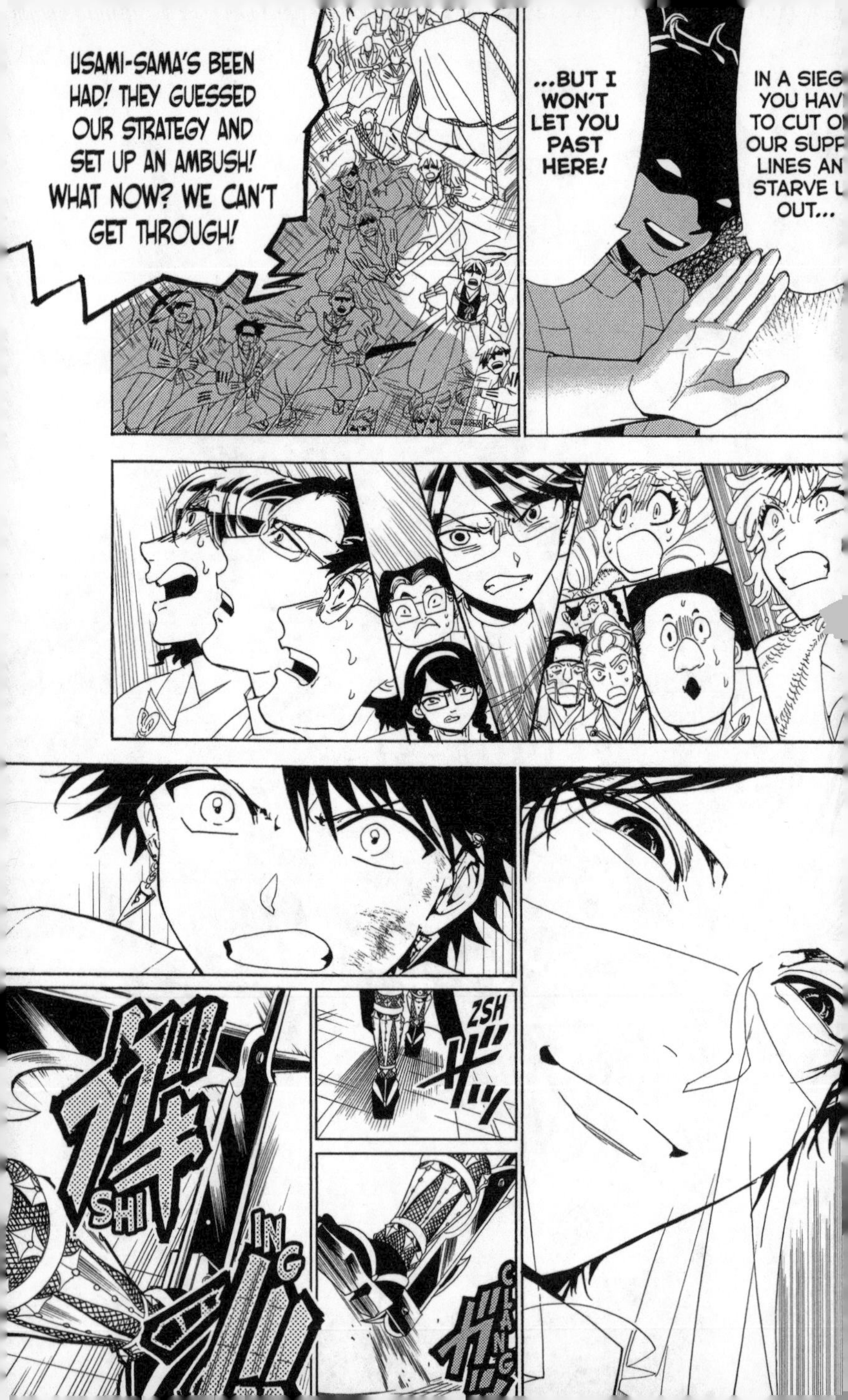
IN A SIEG YOU HAV TO CUT O OUR SUPP LINES AN STARVE L OUT...
...BUT I WON'T LET YOU PAST HERE!
USAMI-SAMA'S BEEN HAD! THEY GUESSED OUR STRATEGY AND SET UP AN AMBUSH! WHAT NOW? WE CAN'T GET THROUGH!
ZSH
CLANG
SHI
ING

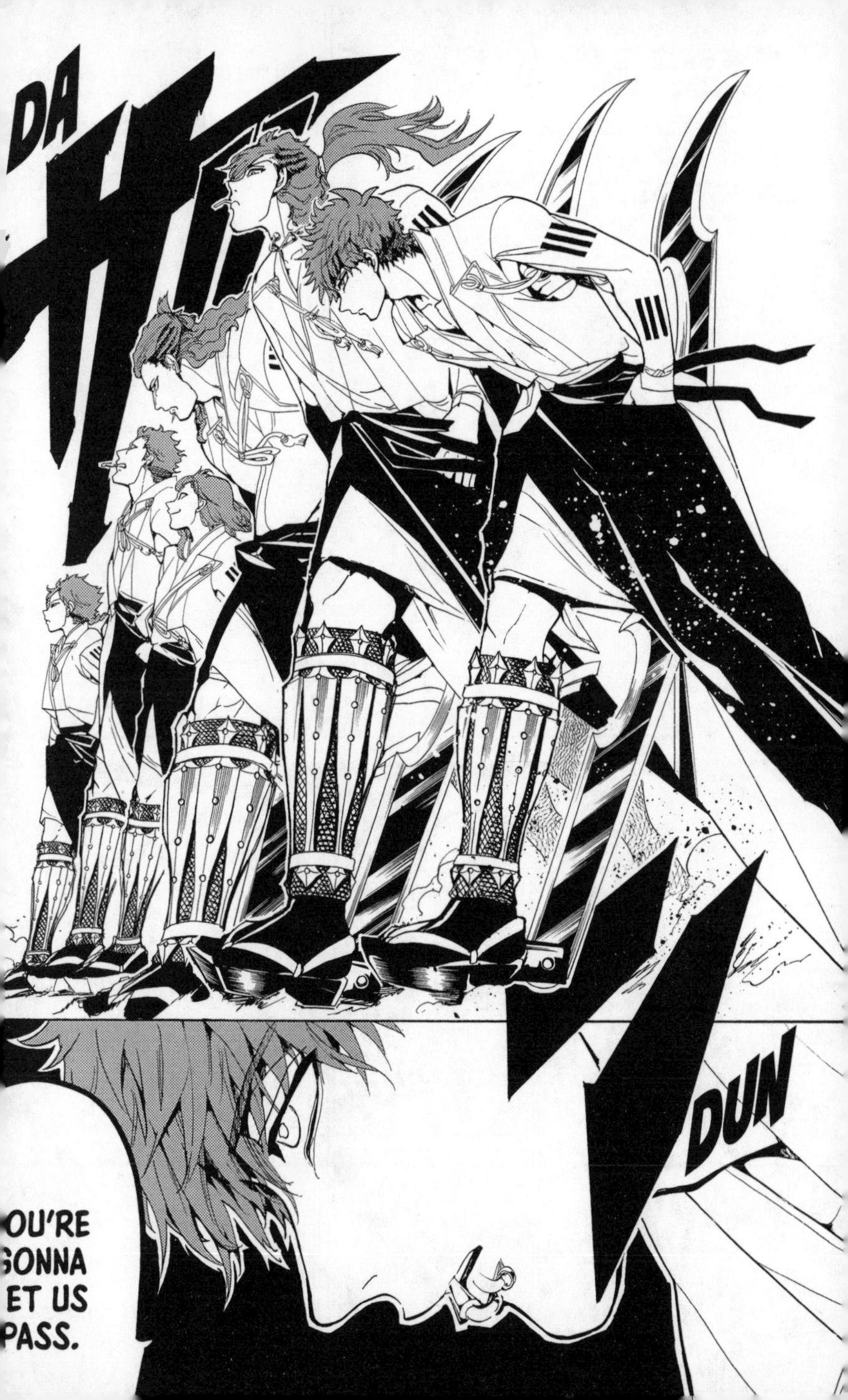
DA
DUN
OU'RE GONNA ET US PASS.

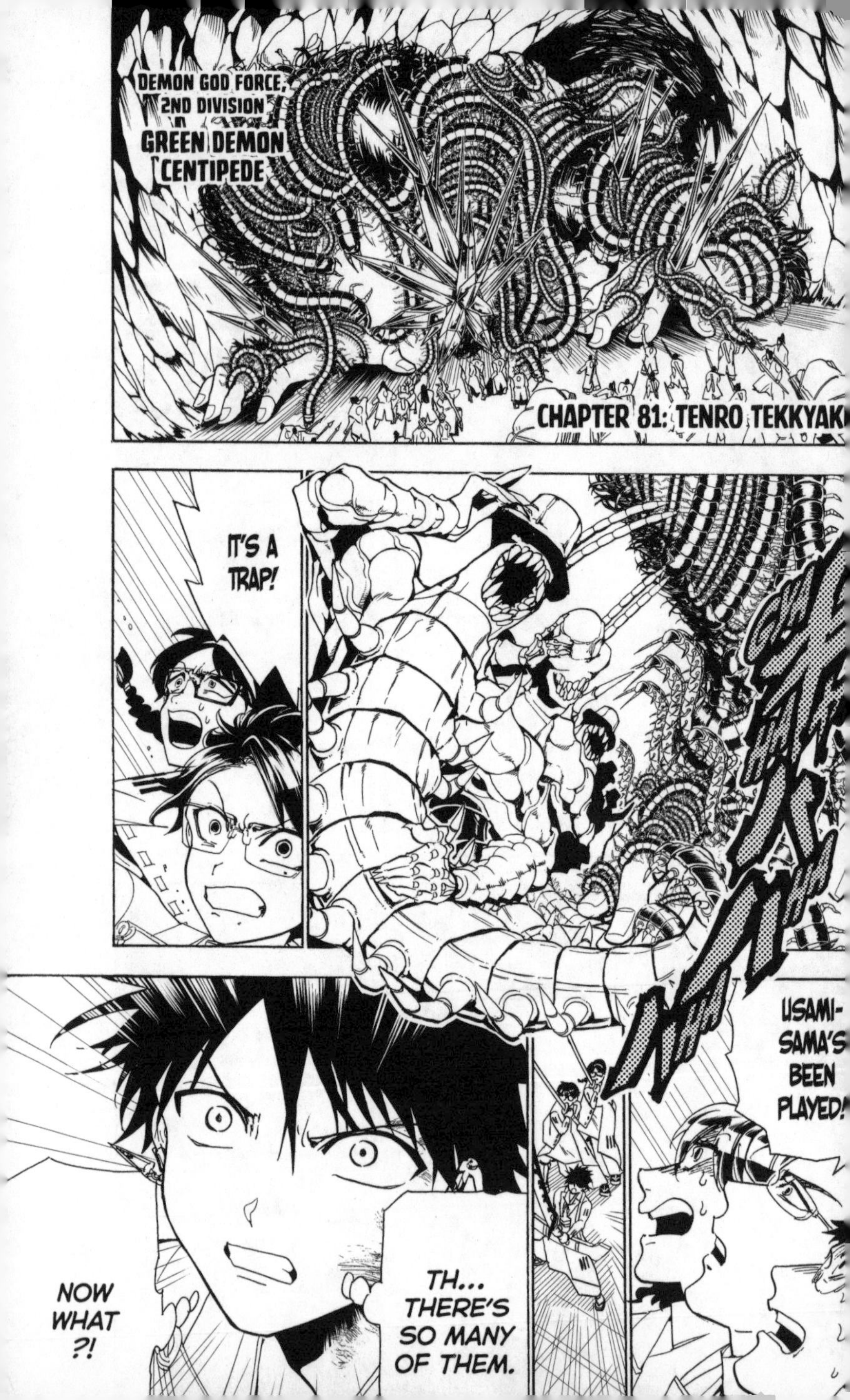
DEMON GOD FORCE, 2ND DIVISION
GREEN DEMON CENTIPEDE
CHAPTER 81: TENRO TEKKYAKU
IT'S A TRAP!
USAMI-SAMA'S BEEN PLAYED!
TH... THERE'S SO MANY OF THEM.
NOW WHAT?!

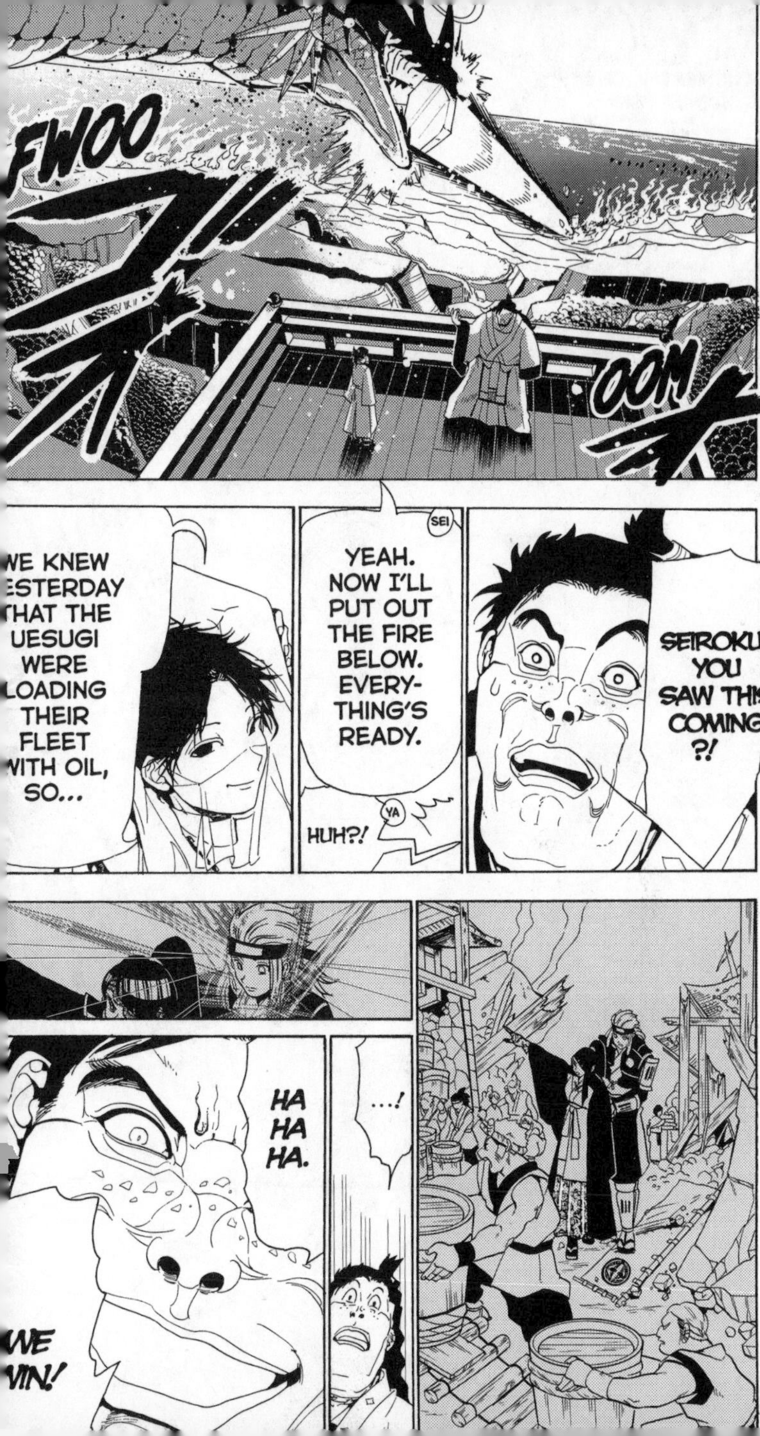
FWOO
OOM
SEIROKU! YOU SAW THIS COMING?!
SEI
YEAH. NOW I'LL PUT OUT THE FIRE BELOW. EVERY-THING'S READY.
YA
HUH?!
WE KNEW ESTERDAY THAT THE UESUGI WERE LOADING THEIR FLEET WITH OIL, SO...
...!
HA HA HA.
WE WIN!

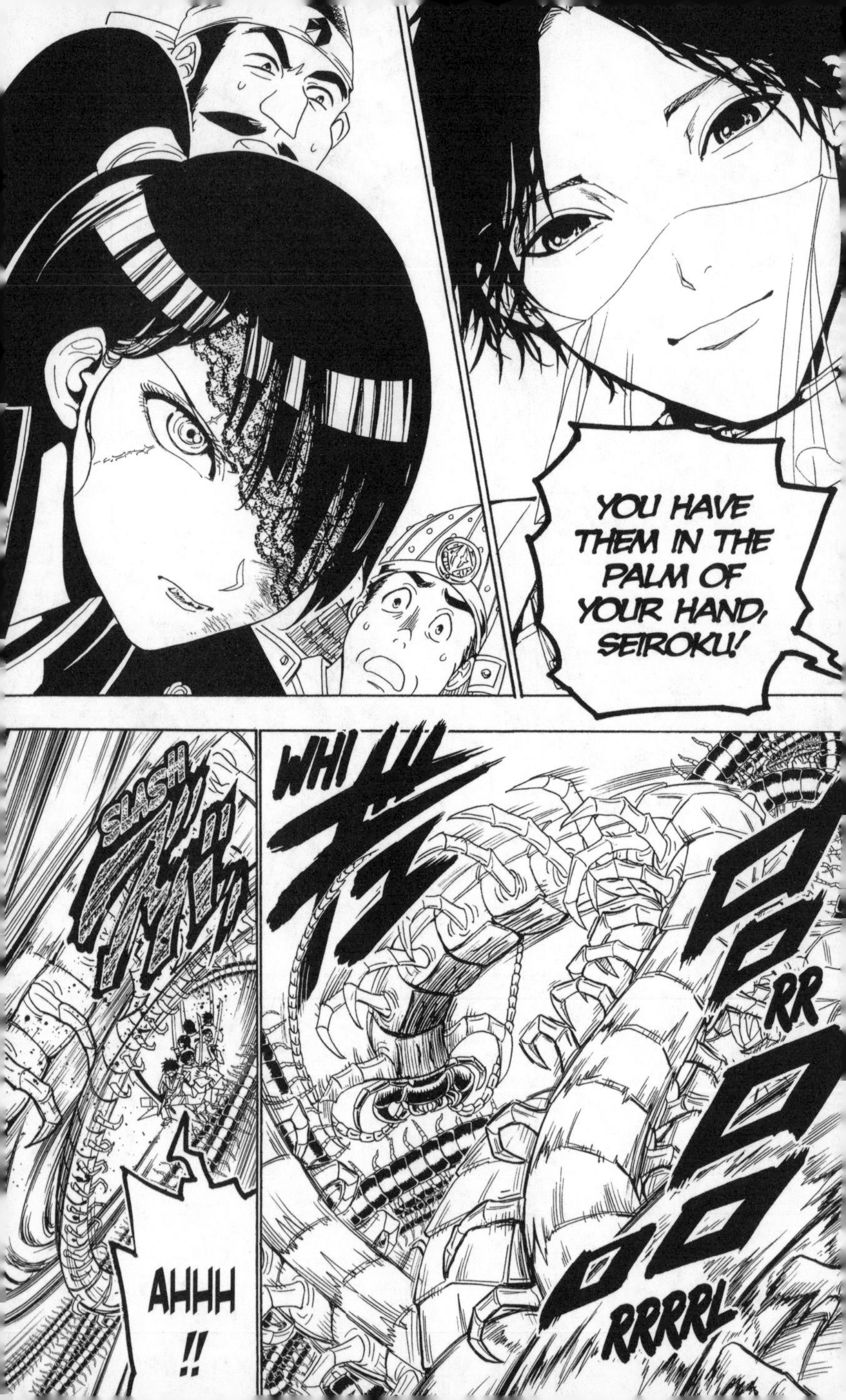
YOU HAVE THEM IN THE PALM OF YOUR HAND, SEIROKU!
WHI
RR
RRRRL
SLASH
AHHH!!

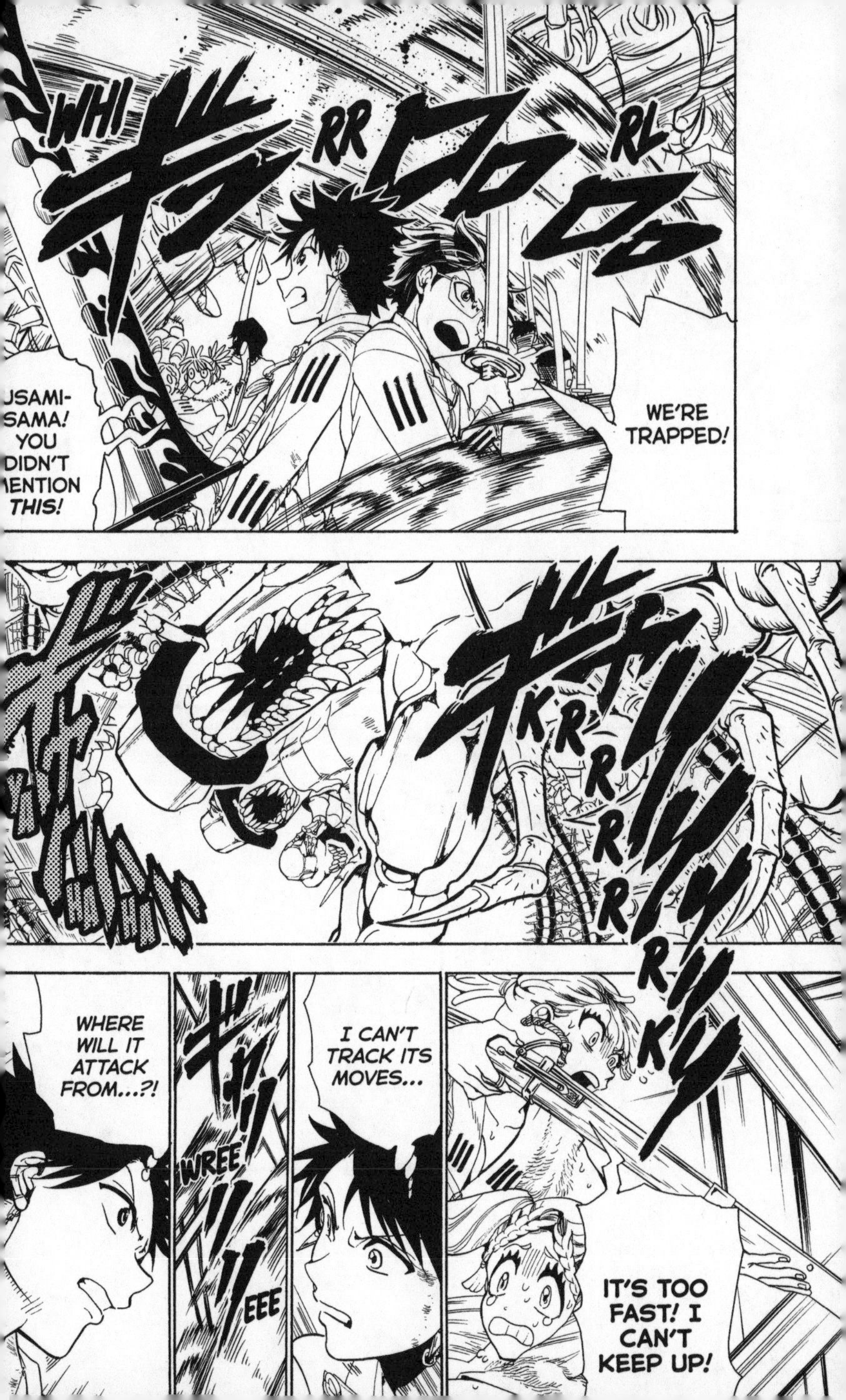

WHI RR RL
WE'RE TRAPPED!
USAMI-SAMA! YOU DIDN'T MENTION THIS!
KRRRRRRRK
IT'S TOO FAST! I CAN'T KEEP UP!
I CAN'T TRACK ITS MOVES...
WREE EEE
WHERE WILL IT ATTACK FROM...?!

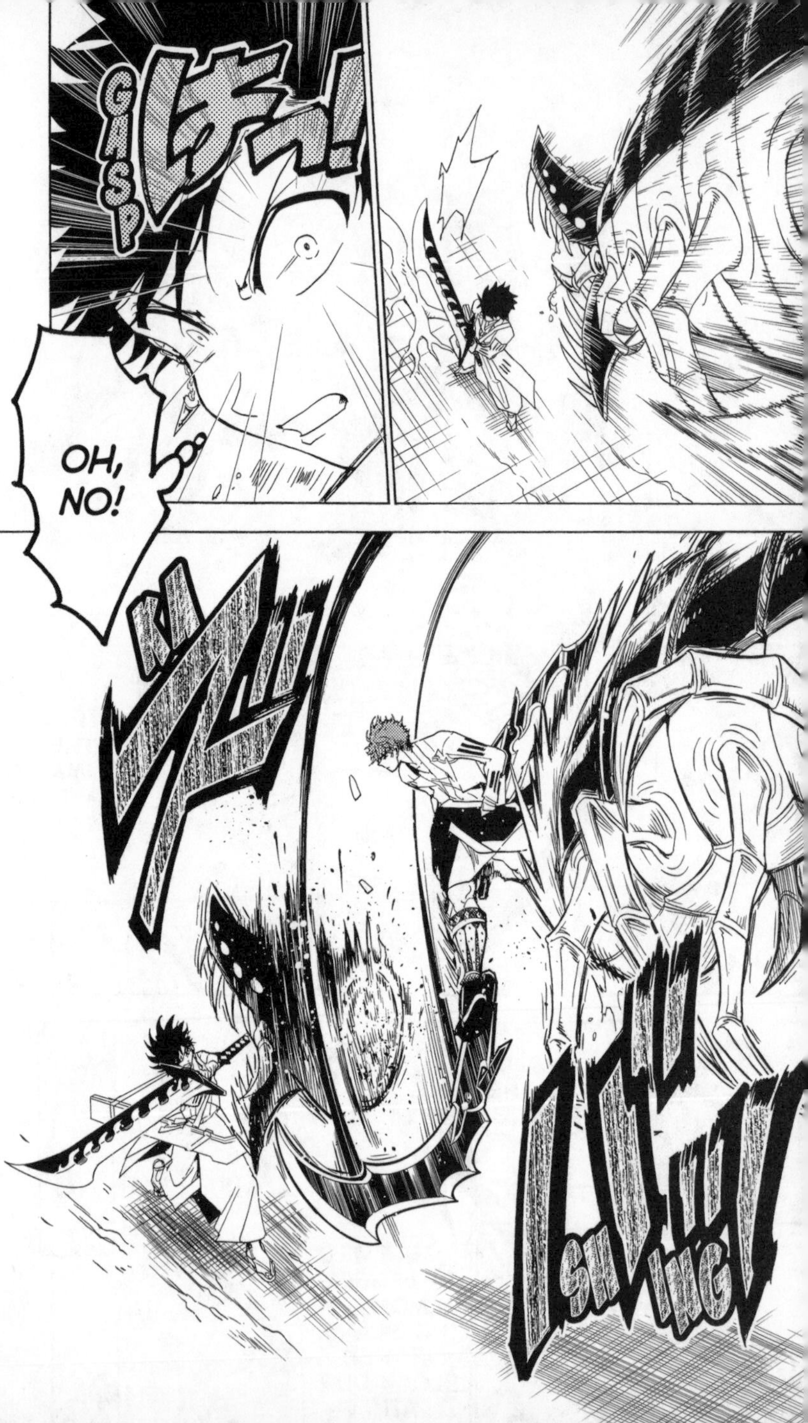
GASP
OH, NO!
SHING

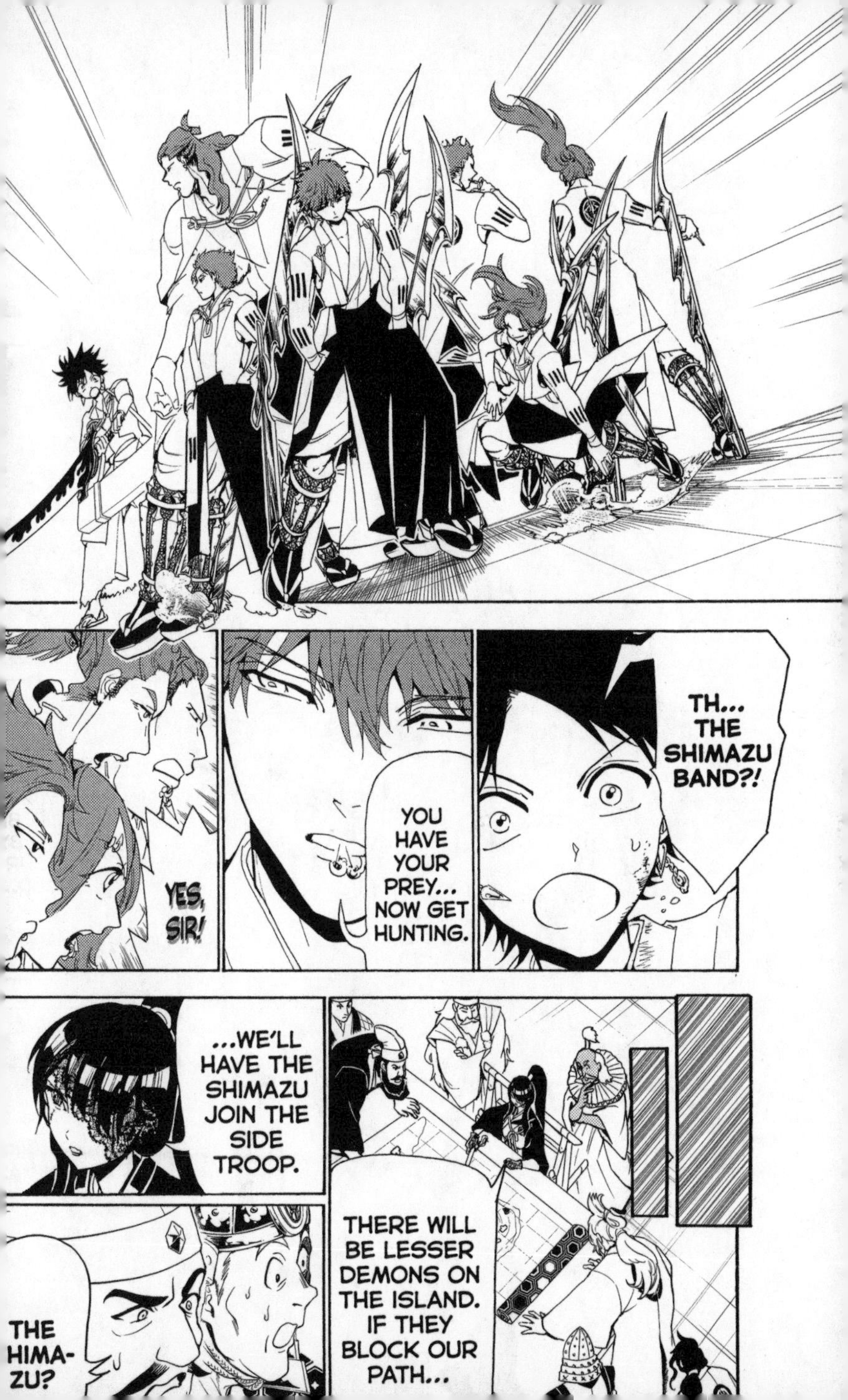
TH... THE SHIMAZU BAND?!
YOU HAVE YOUR PREY... NOW GET HUNTING.
YES, SIR!
THERE WILL BE LESSER DEMONS ON THE ISLAND. IF THEY BLOCK OUR PATH...
...WE'LL HAVE THE SHIMAZU JOIN THE SIDE TROOP.
THE HIMA-ZU?

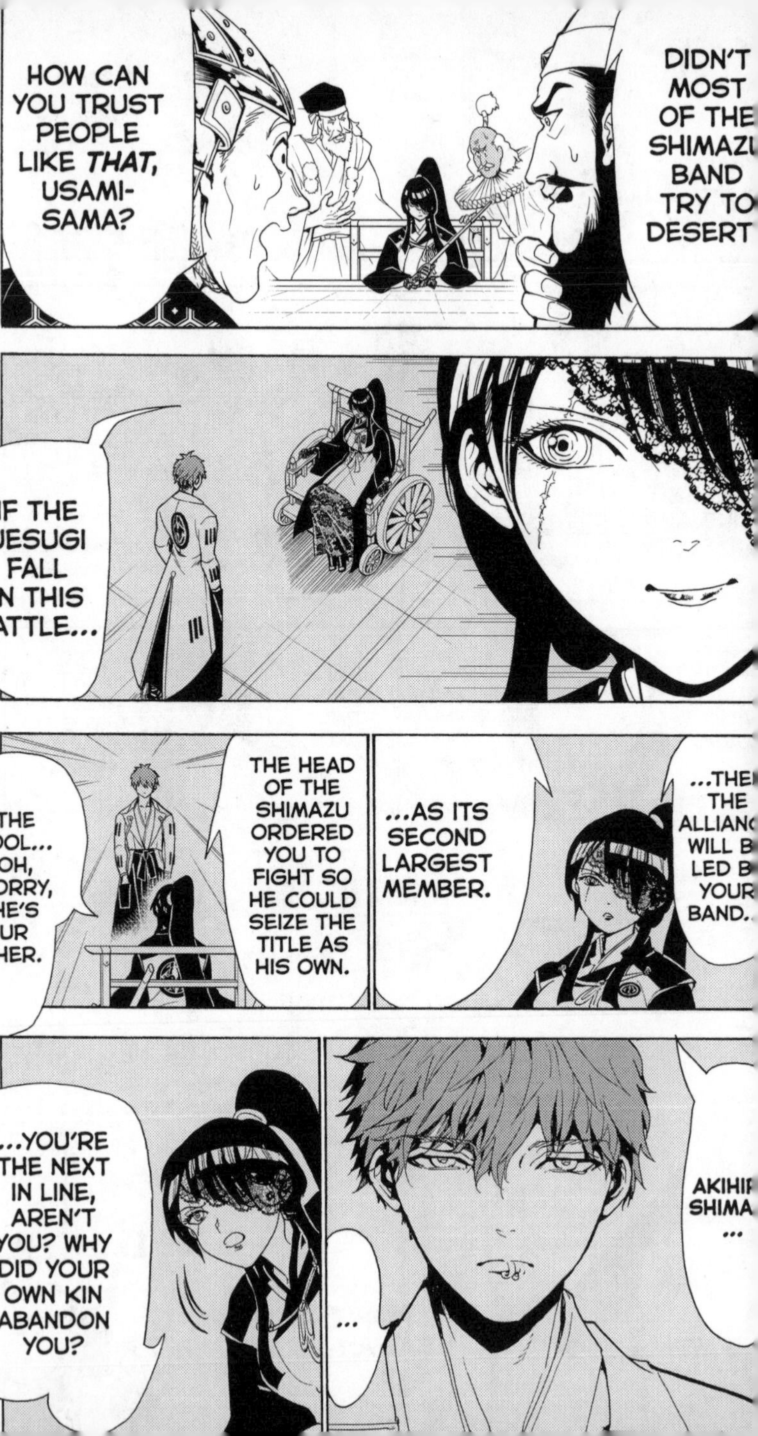

DIDN'T MOST OF THE SHIMAZU BAND TRY TO DESERT
HOW CAN YOU TRUST PEOPLE LIKE *THAT*, USAMI-SAMA?
IF THE UESUGI FALL IN THIS BATTLE...
...THE THE ALLIANC WILL B LED B YOUR BAND..
...AS ITS SECOND LARGEST MEMBER.
THE HEAD OF THE SHIMAZU ORDERED YOU TO FIGHT SO HE COULD SEIZE THE TITLE AS HIS OWN.
THE FOOL... OH, SORRY, HE'S YOUR FATHER.
AKIHIR SHIMA ...
...
...YOU'RE THE NEXT IN LINE, AREN'T YOU? WHY DID YOUR OWN KIN ABANDON YOU?

BECAUSE THE SHIMAZU CLAN...

...HAS TOO MANY HEIRS RIGHT NOW.

WHAT DO YOU MEAN?

THERE ARE SEVEN POTENTIAL SUCCESSORS IN ALL.

AND AS FOR THE SIX WHO GOT SENT TO AWAJI, FATHER DOESN'T LIKE ANY OF US.

HE SAID THAT WHOEVER TAKES THE DEMON'S HORN...

...WILL LEAD THE FAMILY.

WITHOUT SUPPORT FROM THE SHIMAZU ARMY?

THAT'S ASKING TOO MUCH...

YES.

IN OTHER WORDS...

...OUR OWN KIN...

...WON'T BAT AN EYE...

...IF WE FALL IN BATTLE.

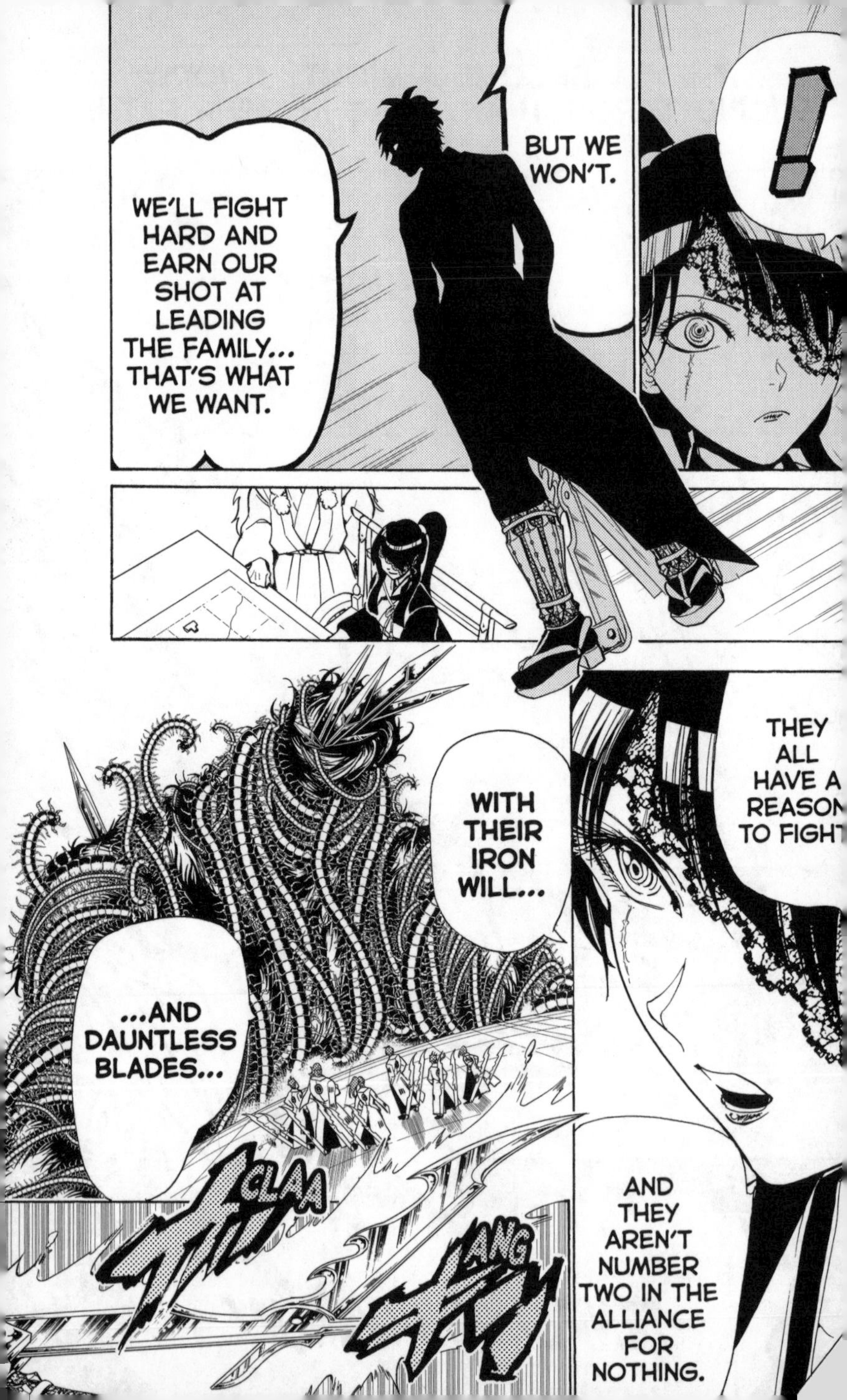
!
BUT WE WON'T.
WE'LL FIGHT HARD AND EARN OUR SHOT AT LEADING THE FAMILY... THAT'S WHAT WE WANT.
THEY ALL HAVE A REASON TO FIGHT
AND THEY AREN'T NUMBER TWO IN THE ALLIANCE FOR NOTHING.
WITH THEIR IRON WILL...
...AND DAUNTLESS BLADES...
CLAA
ANG

...THEY'LL BECOME A MIGHTY SWORD, SLICING THROUGH ANYTHING IN THEIR PATH!

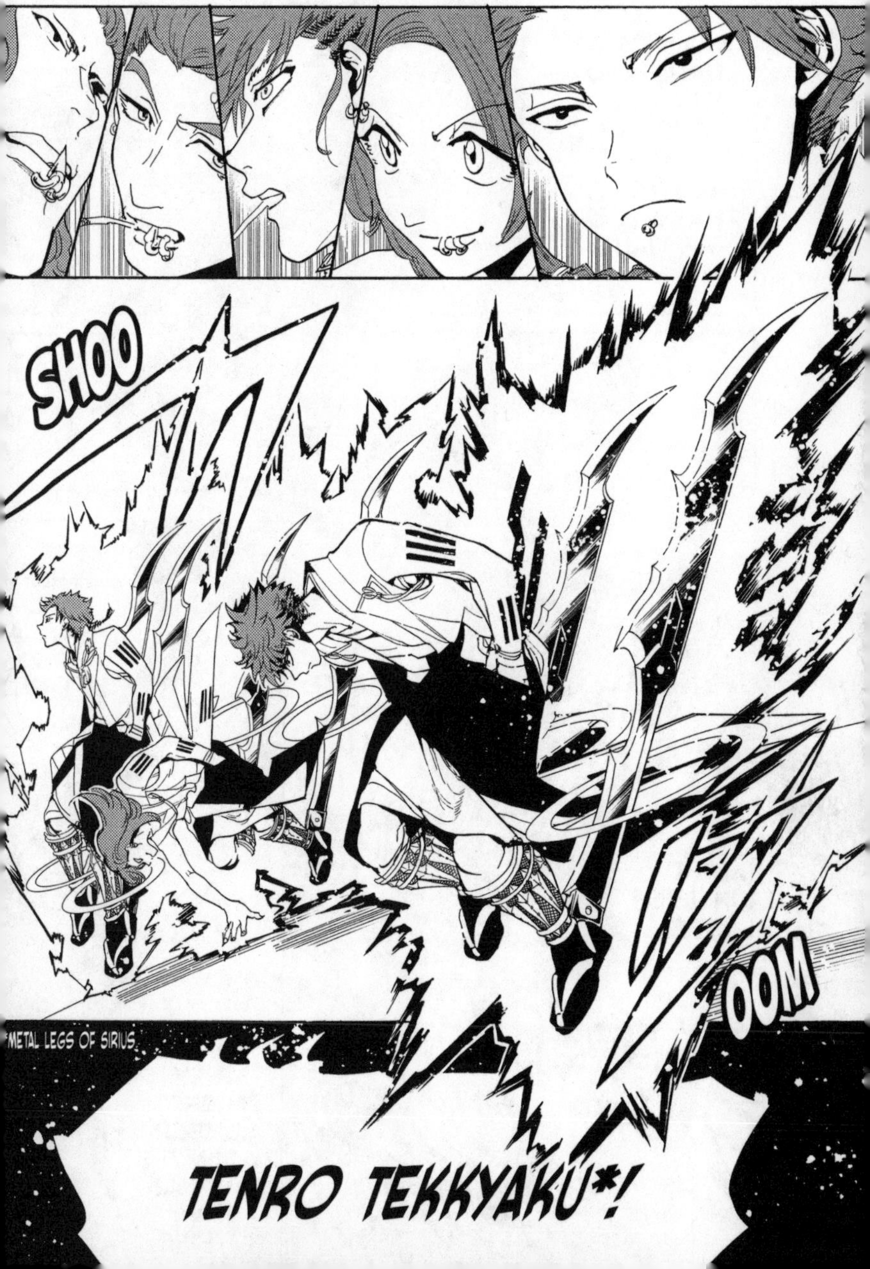

SHOO
OOM
TENRO TEKKYAKU*!
METAL LEGS OF SIRIUS

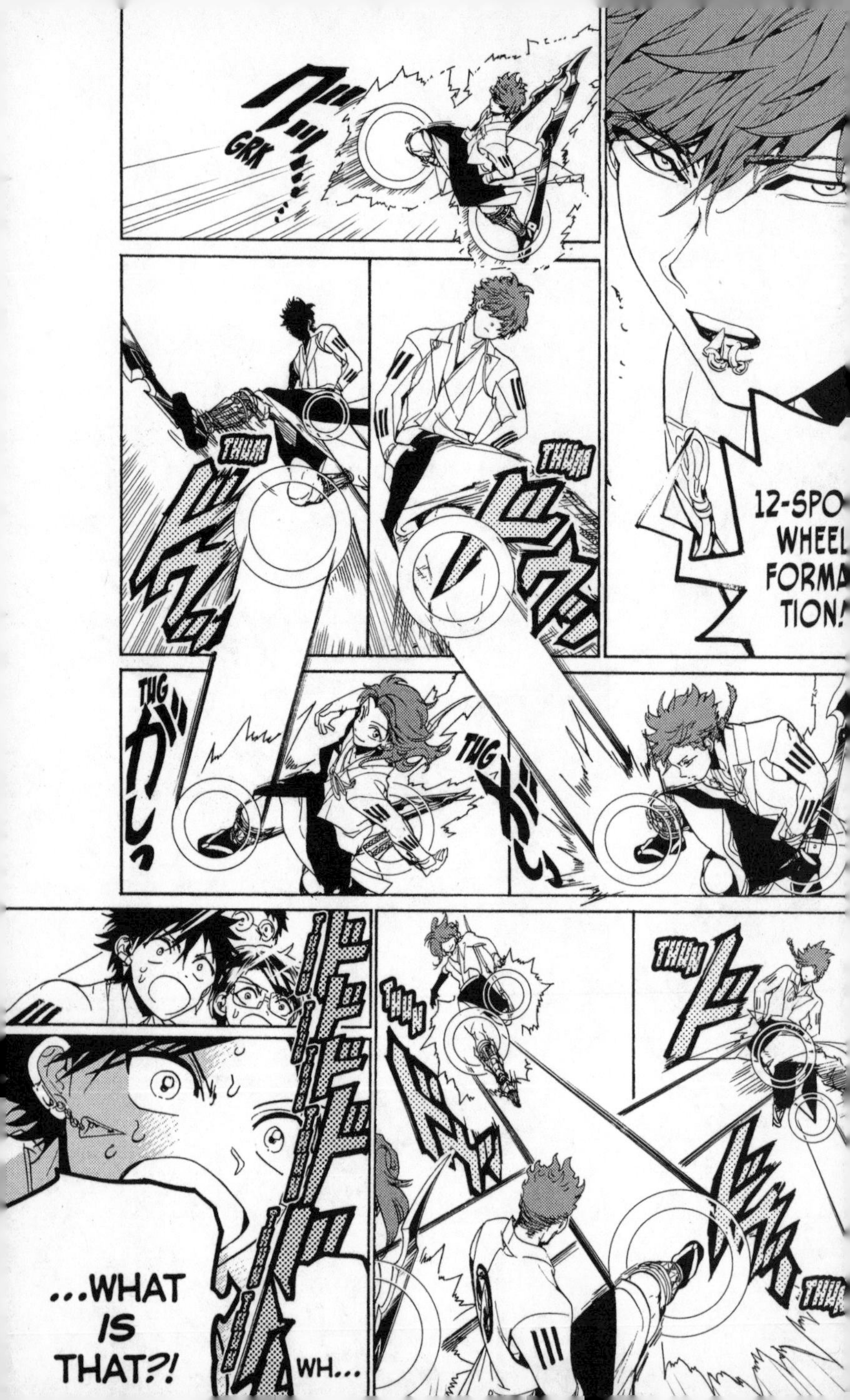
12-SPO WHEEL FORMA TION!
GRK
THUNK
THUNK
TUG
TUG
THUN
THUN
WH...
...WHAT IS THAT?!

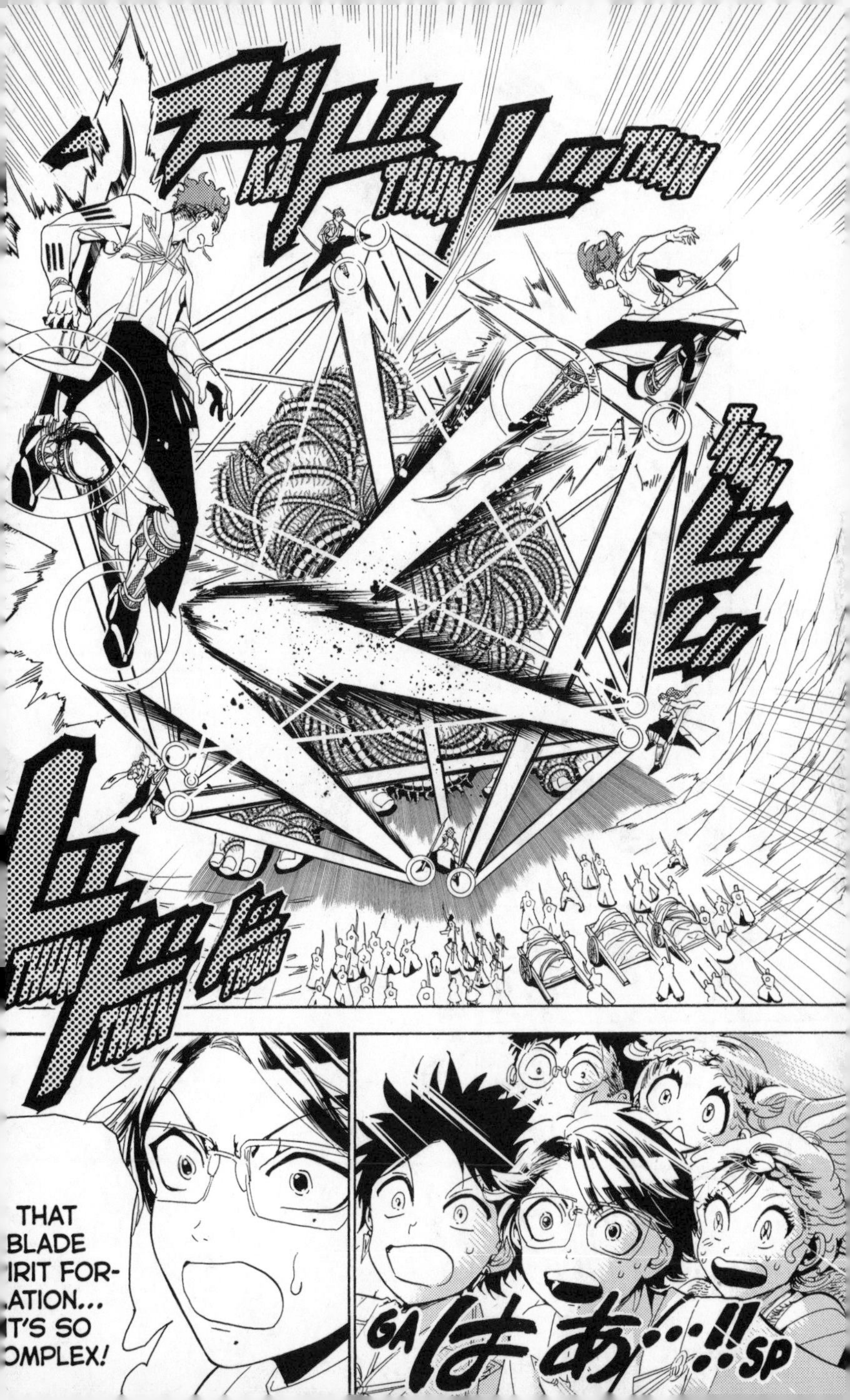
GA
はあ…!!
SP
THAT
BLADE
IRIT FOR-
ATION...
T'S SO
OMPLEX!

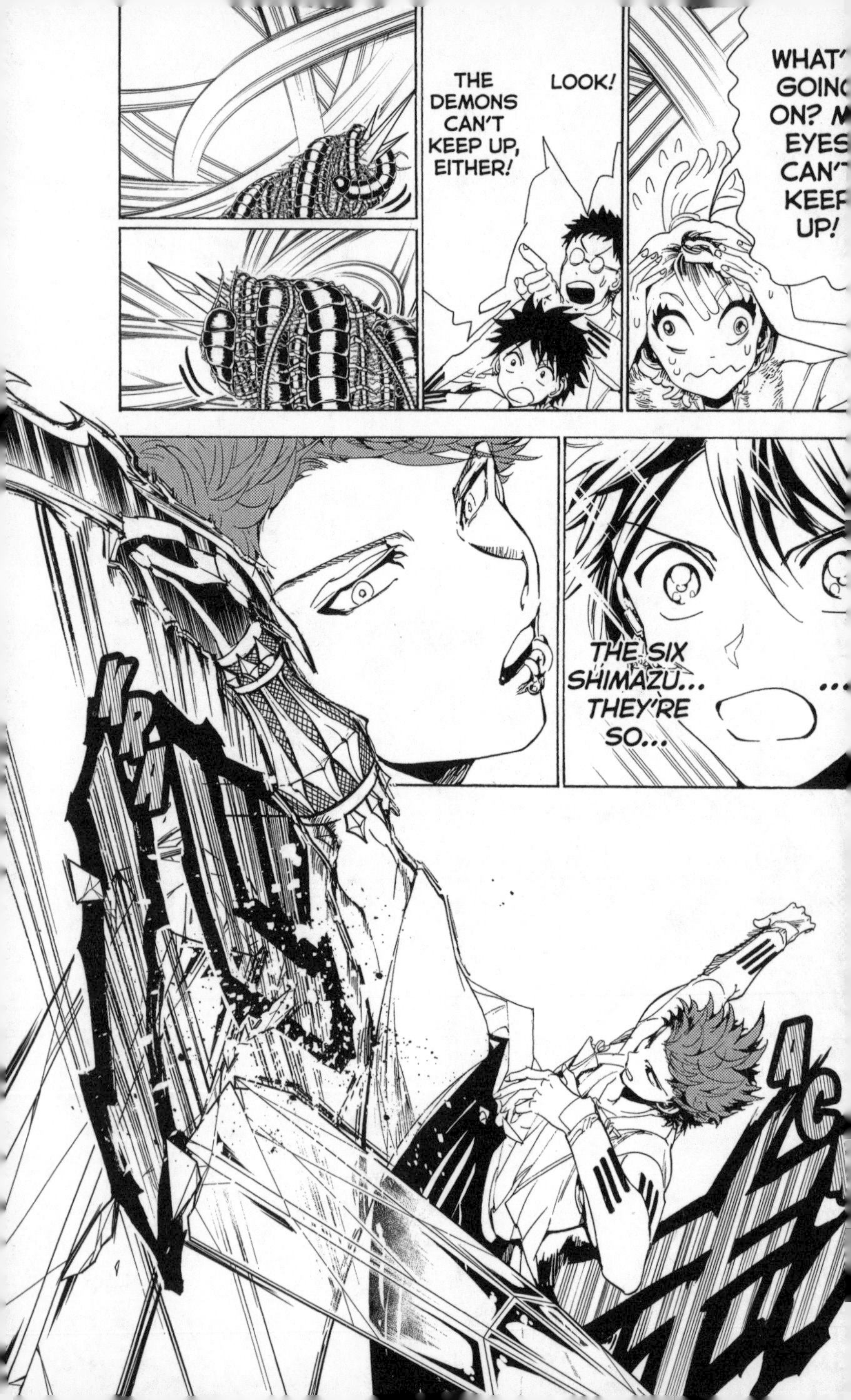

WHAT' GOING ON? M EYES CAN'T KEEP UP!
LOOK!
THE DEMONS CAN'T KEEP UP, EITHER!
THE SIX SHIMAZU... THEY'RE SO...
...

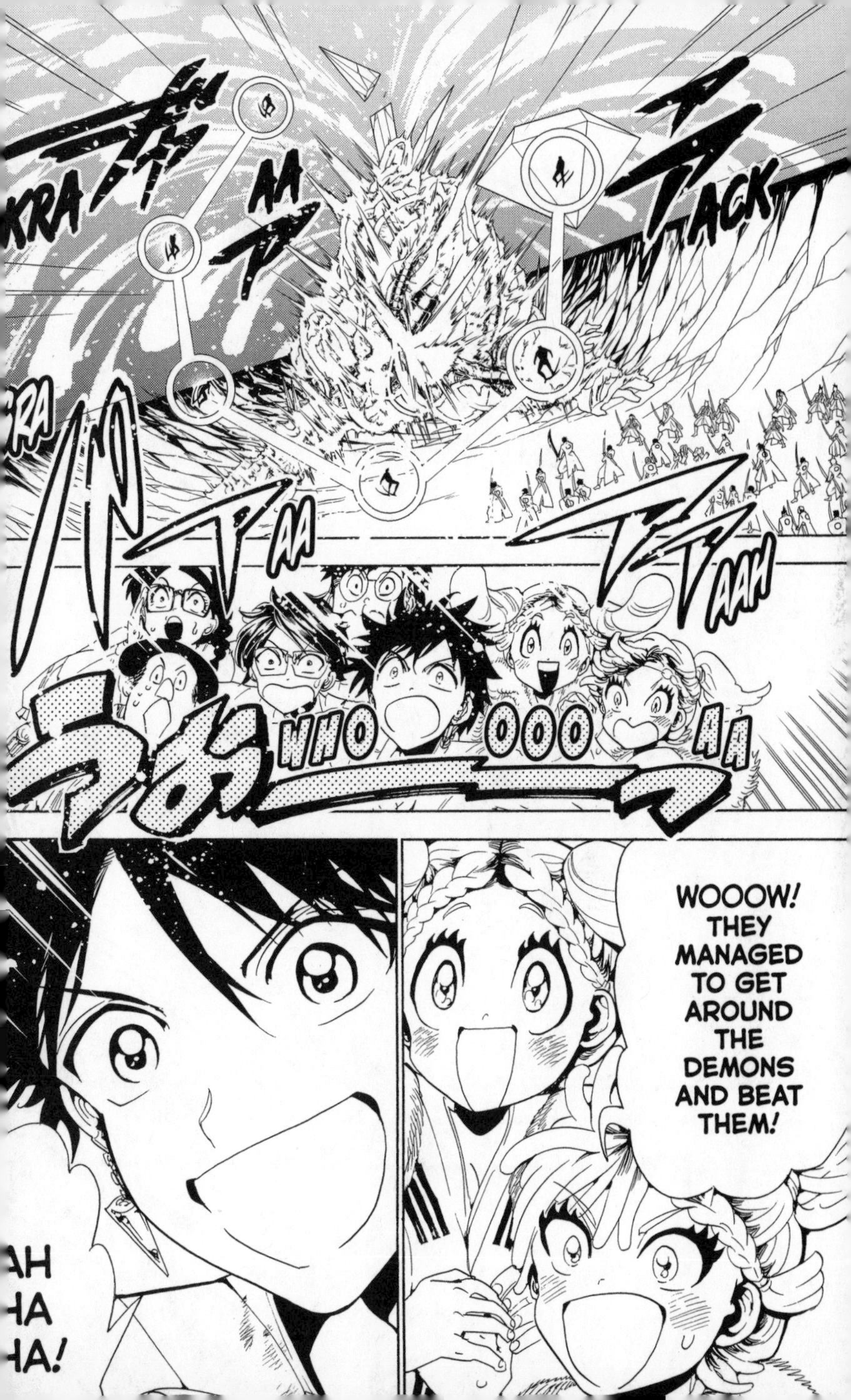
KRA
AA
ACK
RA
AA
AAH
WHO OOO AA
WOOOW! THEY MANAGED TO GET AROUND THE DEMONS AND BEAT THEM!
AH HA HA!

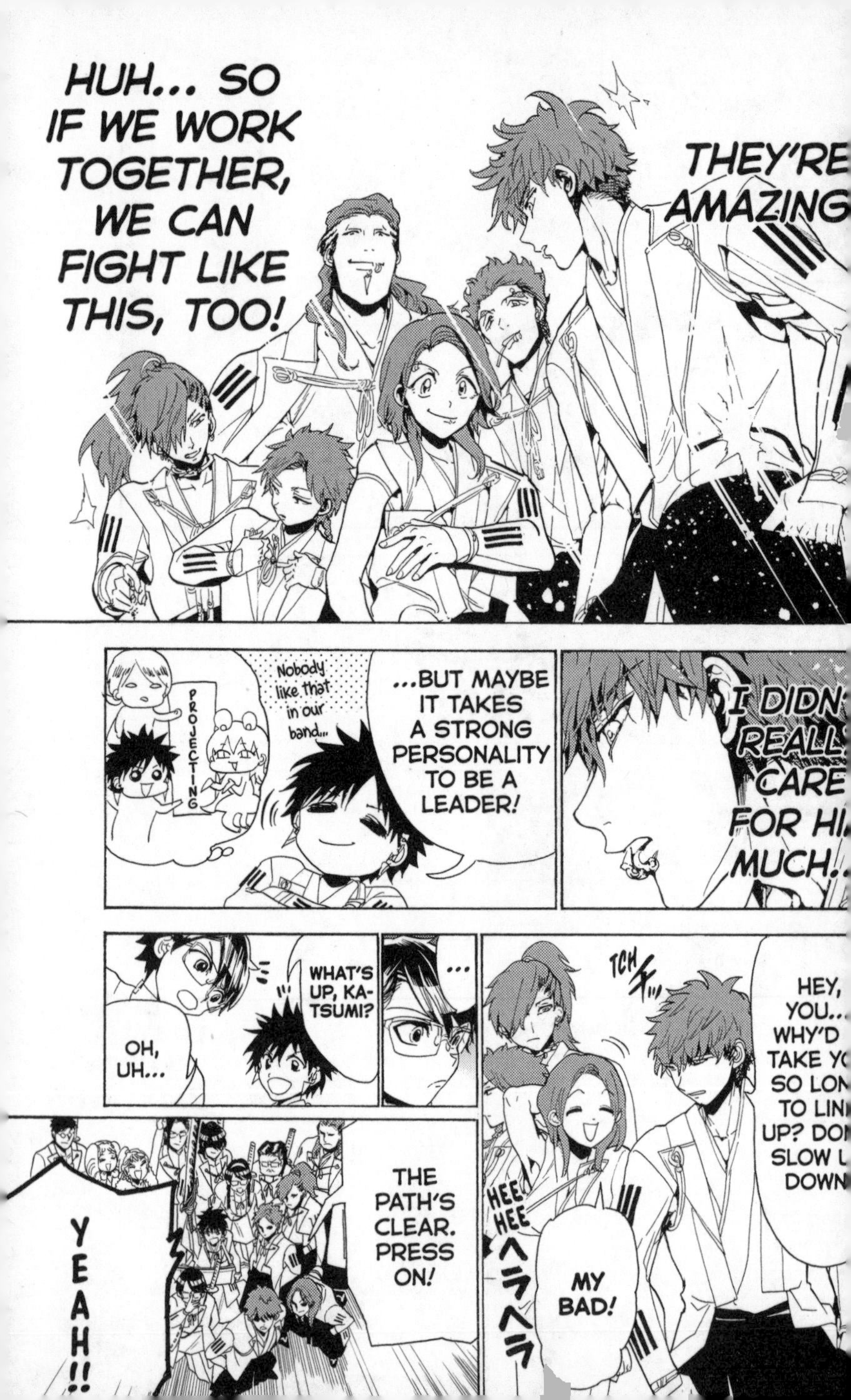

THEY'RE AMAZING
HUH... SO IF WE WORK TOGETHER, WE CAN FIGHT LIKE THIS, TOO!
I DIDN REALL CARE FOR HI MUCH..
...BUT MAYBE IT TAKES A STRONG PERSONALITY TO BE A LEADER!
Nobody like that in our band...
PROJECTING
HEY, YOU... WHY'D TAKE YO SO LON TO LIN UP? DO SLOW U DOWN
TCH
HEE HEE
MY BAD!
...
WHAT'S UP, KA-TSUMI?
OH, UH...
THE PATH'S CLEAR. PRESS ON!
YEAH!!

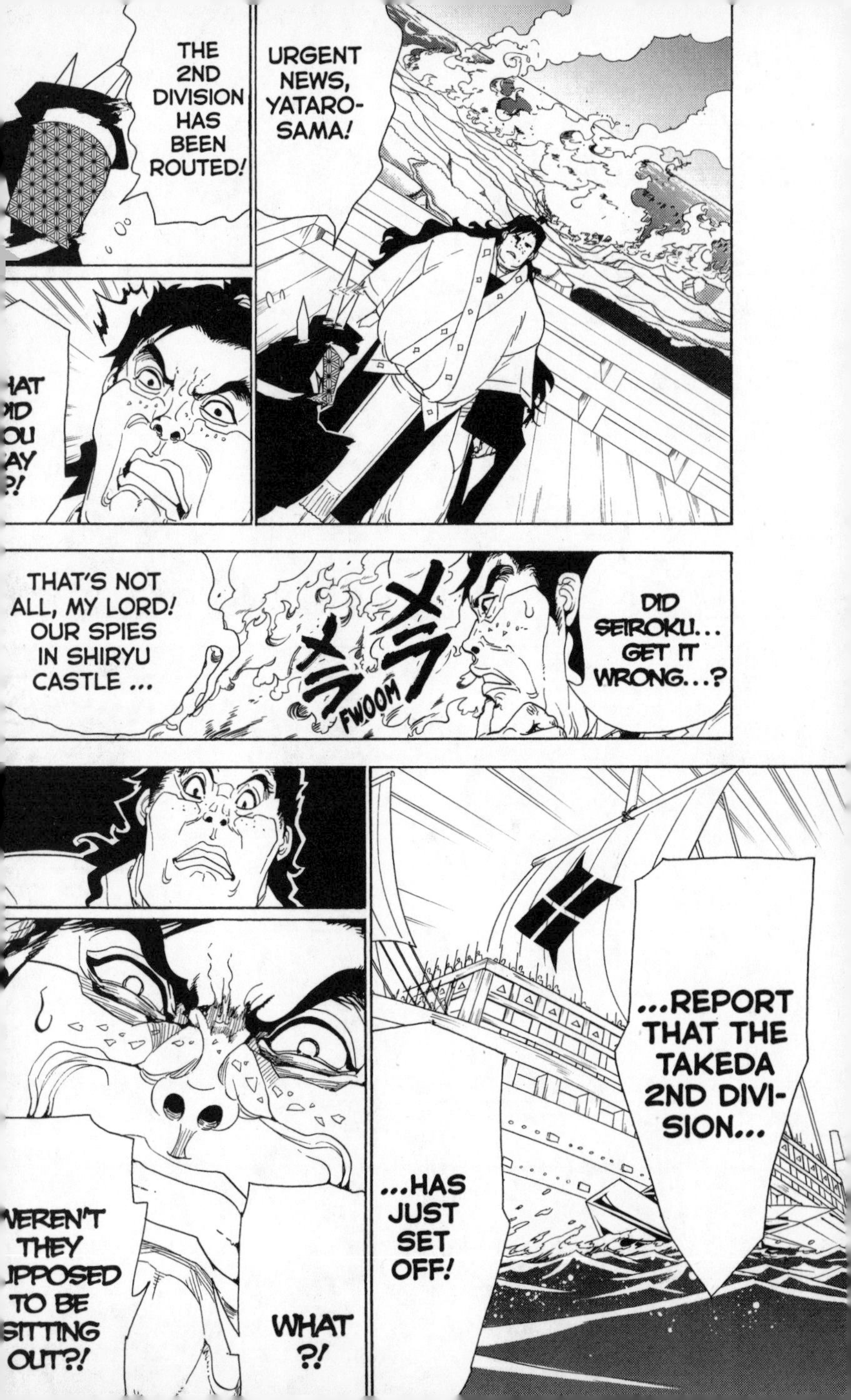
URGENT NEWS, YATARO-SAMA!
THE 2ND DIVISION HAS BEEN ROUTED!
HAT ID OU AY ?!
DID SEIROKU... GET IT WRONG...?
メラメラ
FWOOM
THAT'S NOT ALL, MY LORD! OUR SPIES IN SHIRYU CASTLE ...
...REPORT THAT THE TAKEDA 2ND DIVISION...
...HAS JUST SET OFF!
WHAT?!
VEREN'T THEY UPPOSED TO BE SITTING OUT?!

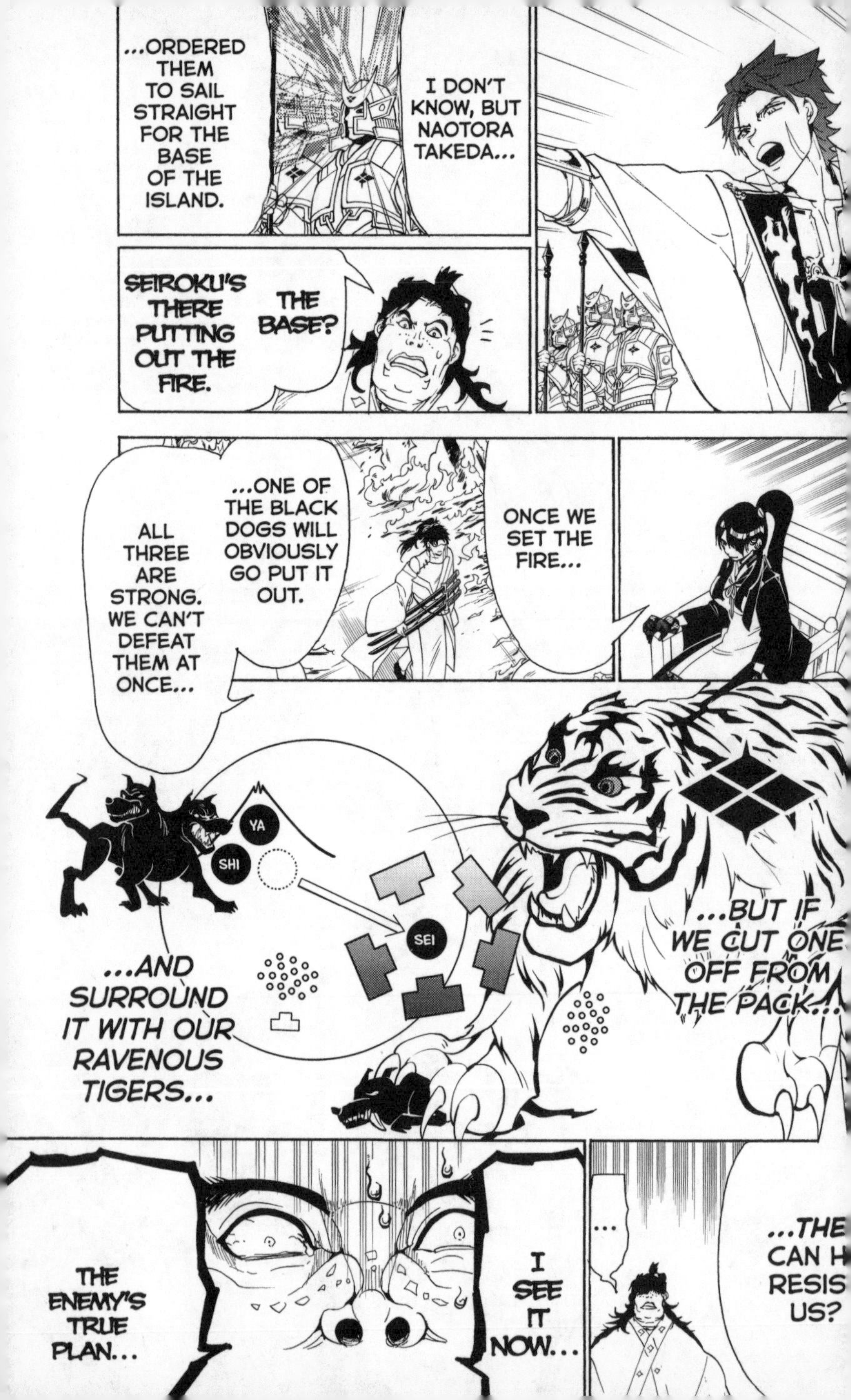

I DON'T KNOW, BUT NAOTORA TAKEDA...
...ORDERED THEM TO SAIL STRAIGHT FOR THE BASE OF THE ISLAND.
THE BASE?
SEIROKU'S THERE PUTTING OUT THE FIRE.
ONCE WE SET THE FIRE...
...ONE OF THE BLACK DOGS WILL OBVIOUSLY GO PUT IT OUT.
ALL THREE ARE STRONG. WE CAN'T DEFEAT THEM AT ONCE...
...BUT IF WE CUT ONE OFF FROM THE PACK...
YA
SHI
SEI
...AND SURROUND IT WITH OUR RAVENOUS TIGERS...
...THE CAN H RESIS US?
...
I SEE IT NOW...
THE ENEMY'S TRUE PLAN...

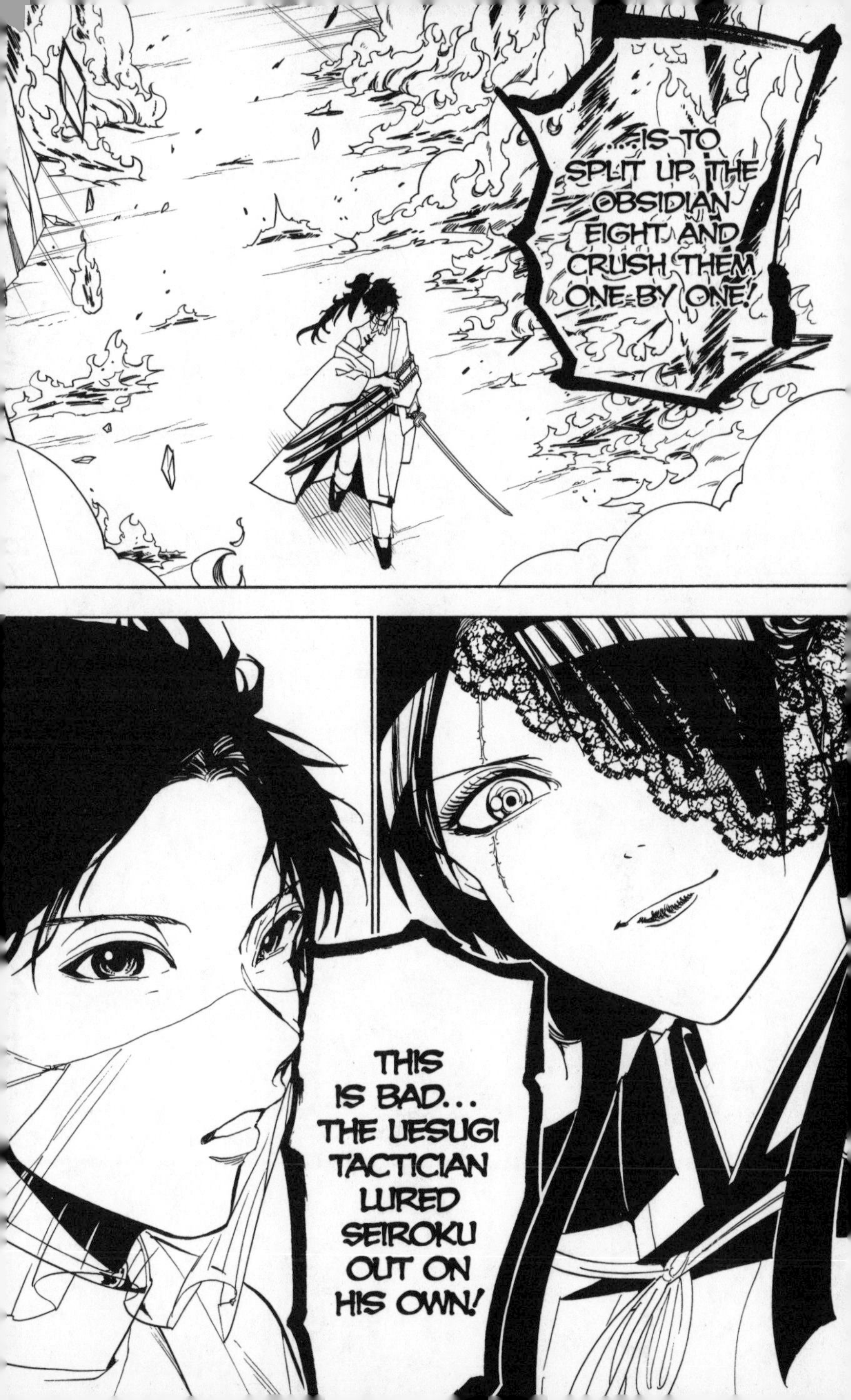
...IS TO SPLIT UP THE OBSIDIAN EIGHT AND CRUSH THEM ONE BY ONE!
THIS IS BAD... THE UESUGI TACTICIAN LURED SEIROKU OUT ON HIS OWN!

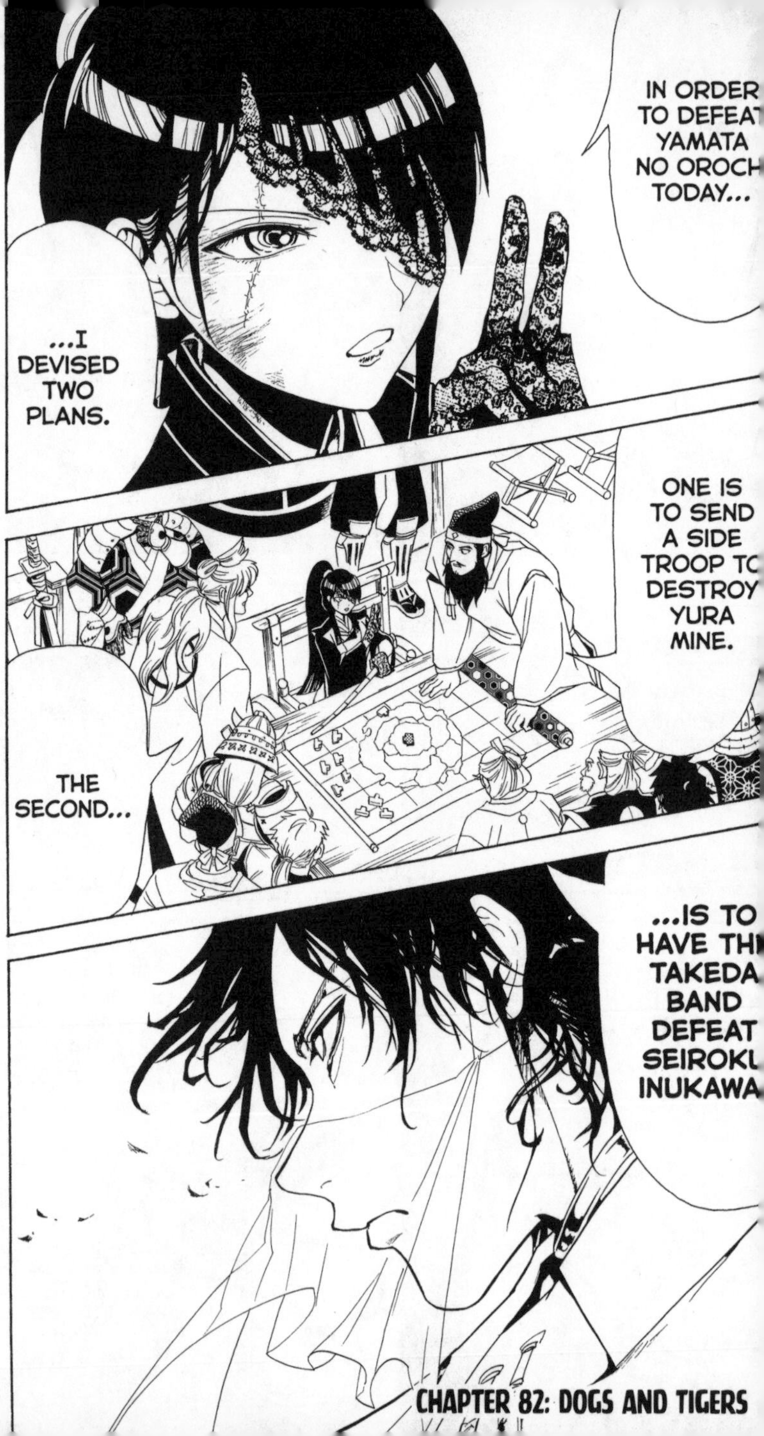
IN ORDER TO DEFEAT YAMATA NO OROCH TODAY...
...I DEVISED TWO PLANS.
ONE IS TO SEND A SIDE TROOP TO DESTROY YURA MINE.
THE SECOND...
...IS TO HAVE TH TAKEDA BAND DEFEAT SEIROKU INUKAWA
CHAPTER 82: DOGS AND TIGERS

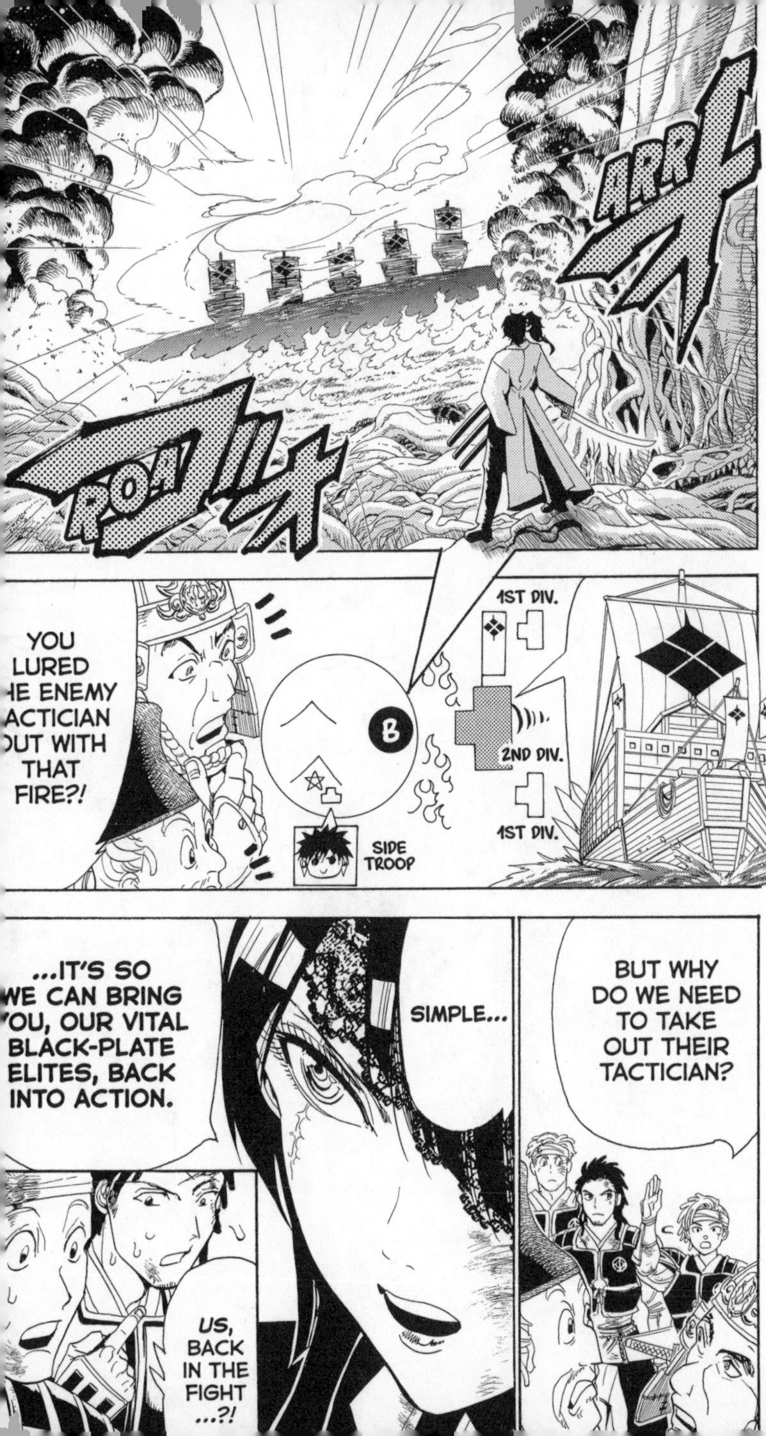
ARR!
ROA
1ST DIV.
2ND DIV.
1ST DIV.
B
SIDE TROOP
YOU LURED HE ENEMY ACTICIAN OUT WITH THAT FIRE?!
BUT WHY DO WE NEED TO TAKE OUT THEIR TACTICIAN?
SIMPLE...
...IT'S SO WE CAN BRING YOU, OUR VITAL BLACK-PLATE ELITES, BACK INTO ACTION.
US, BACK IN THE FIGHT ...?!

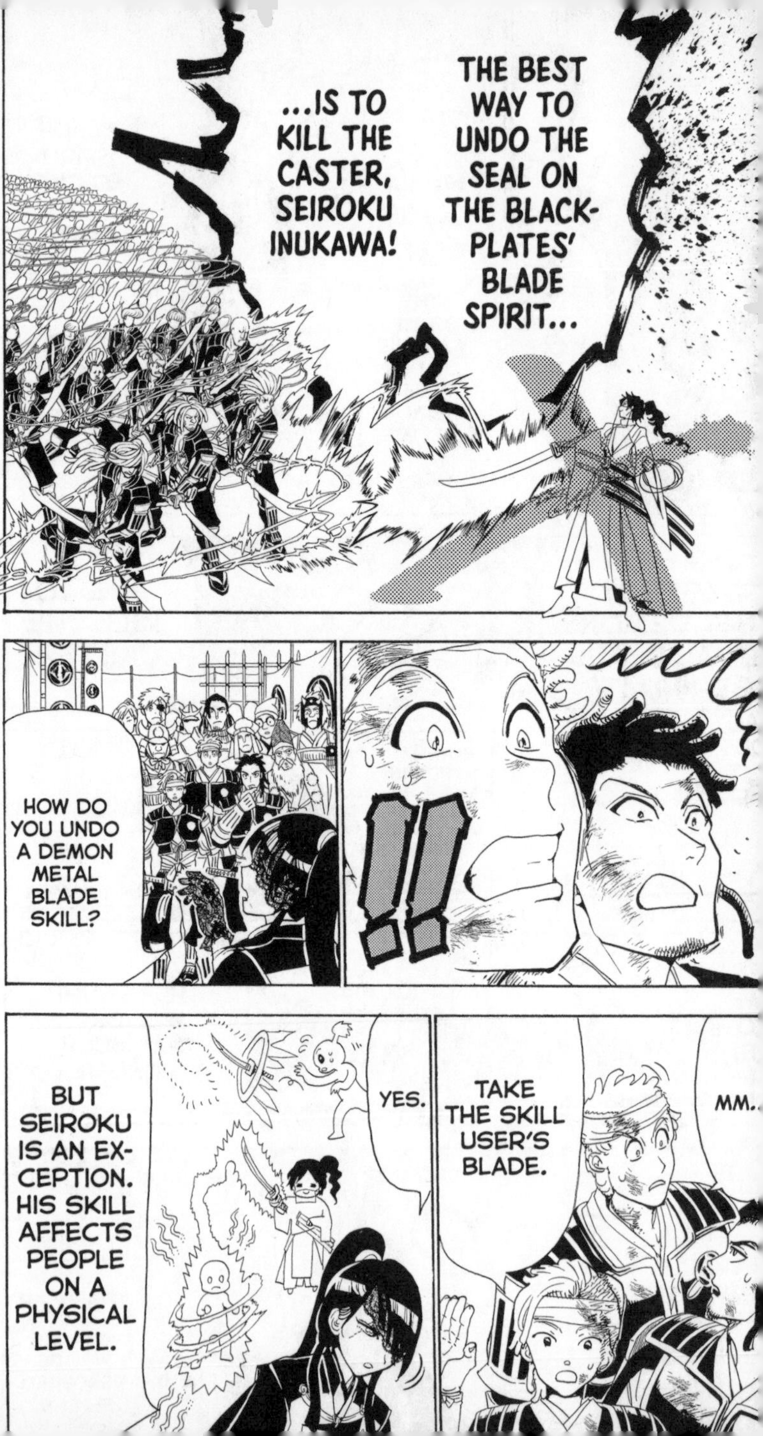
THE BEST WAY TO UNDO THE SEAL ON THE BLACK-PLATES' BLADE SPIRIT...
...IS TO KILL THE CASTER, SEIROKU INUKAWA!
!!
HOW DO YOU UNDO A DEMON METAL BLADE SKILL?
MM.
TAKE THE SKILL USER'S BLADE.
YES.
BUT SEIROKU IS AN EXCEPTION. HIS SKILL AFFECTS PEOPLE ON A PHYSICAL LEVEL.

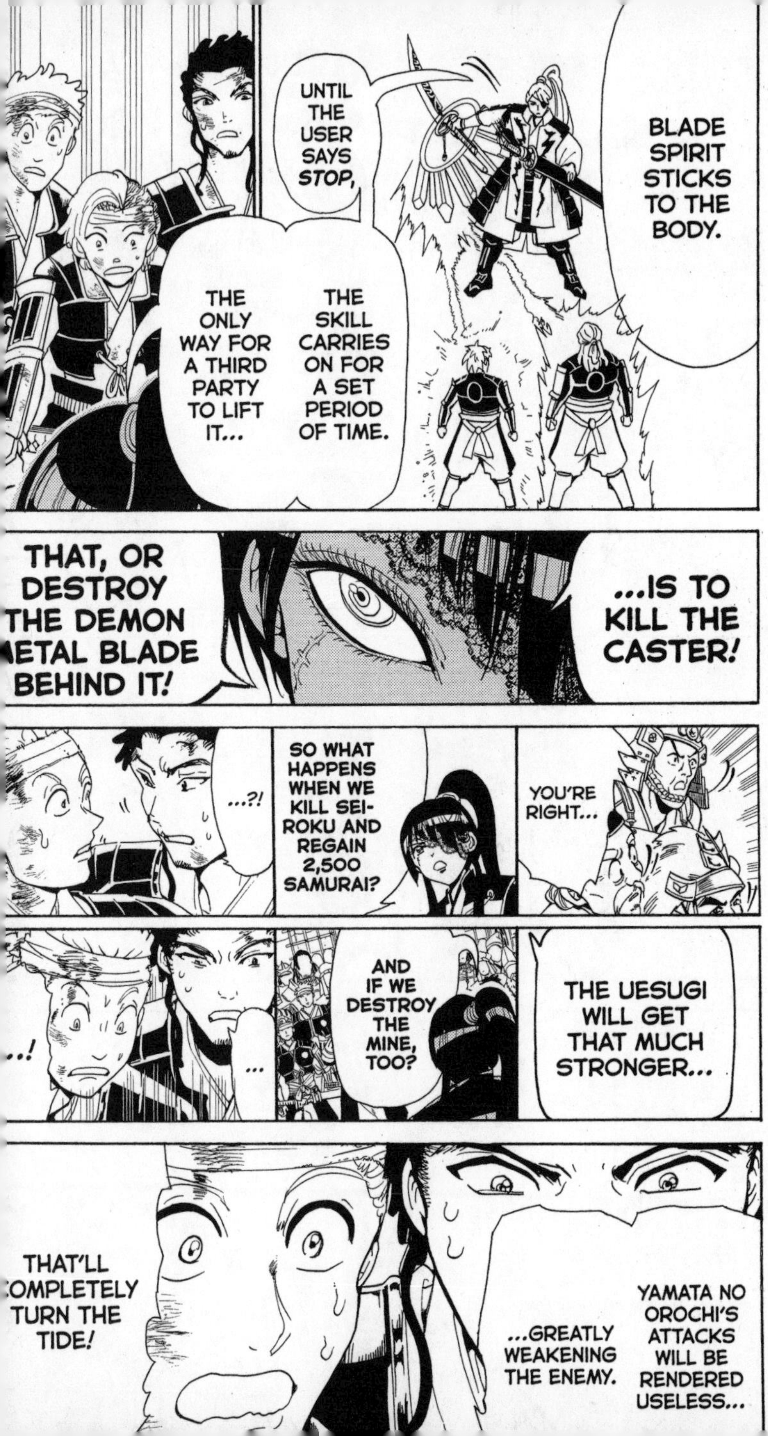
BLADE SPIRIT STICKS TO THE BODY.
UNTIL THE USER SAYS *STOP*,
THE SKILL CARRIES ON FOR A SET PERIOD OF TIME.
THE ONLY WAY FOR A THIRD PARTY TO LIFT IT...
...IS TO KILL THE CASTER!
THAT, OR DESTROY THE DEMON METAL BLADE BEHIND IT!
YOU'RE RIGHT...
SO WHAT HAPPENS WHEN WE KILL SEI-ROKU AND REGAIN 2,500 SAMURAI?
...?!
THE UESUGI WILL GET THAT MUCH STRONGER...
AND IF WE DESTROY THE MINE, TOO?
...
...!
YAMATA NO OROCHI'S ATTACKS WILL BE RENDERED USELESS...
...GREATLY WEAKENING THE ENEMY.
THAT'LL COMPLETELY TURN THE TIDE!

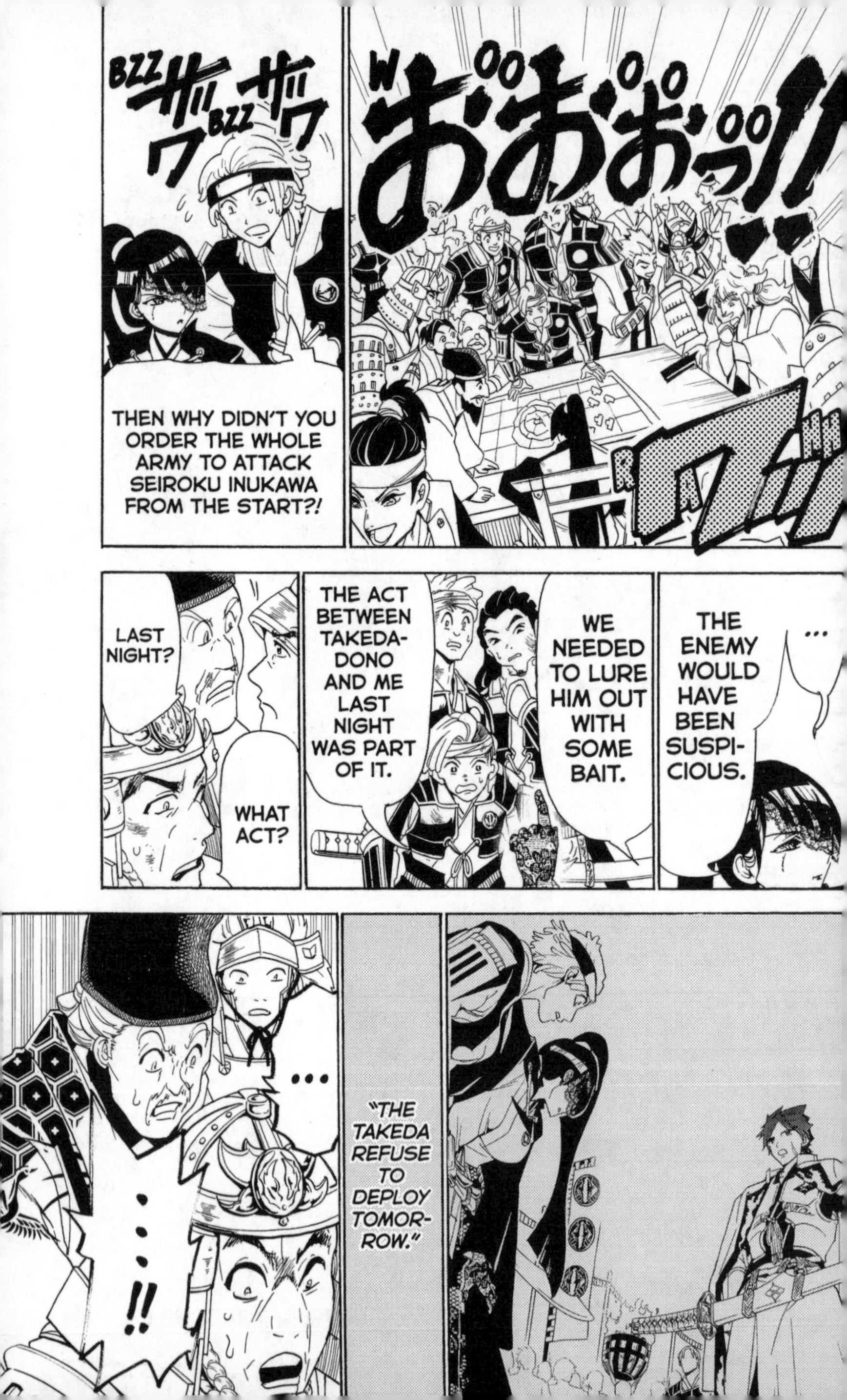
WOOOOO
BZZ BZZ
THEN WHY DIDN'T YOU ORDER THE WHOLE ARMY TO ATTACK SEIROKU INUKAWA FROM THE START?!
...
THE ENEMY WOULD HAVE BEEN SUSPICIOUS.
WE NEEDED TO LURE HIM OUT WITH SOME BAIT.
THE ACT BETWEEN TAKEDA-DONO AND ME LAST NIGHT WAS PART OF IT.
LAST NIGHT?
WHAT ACT?
"THE TAKEDA REFUSE TO DEPLOY TOMORROW."
...
...!!

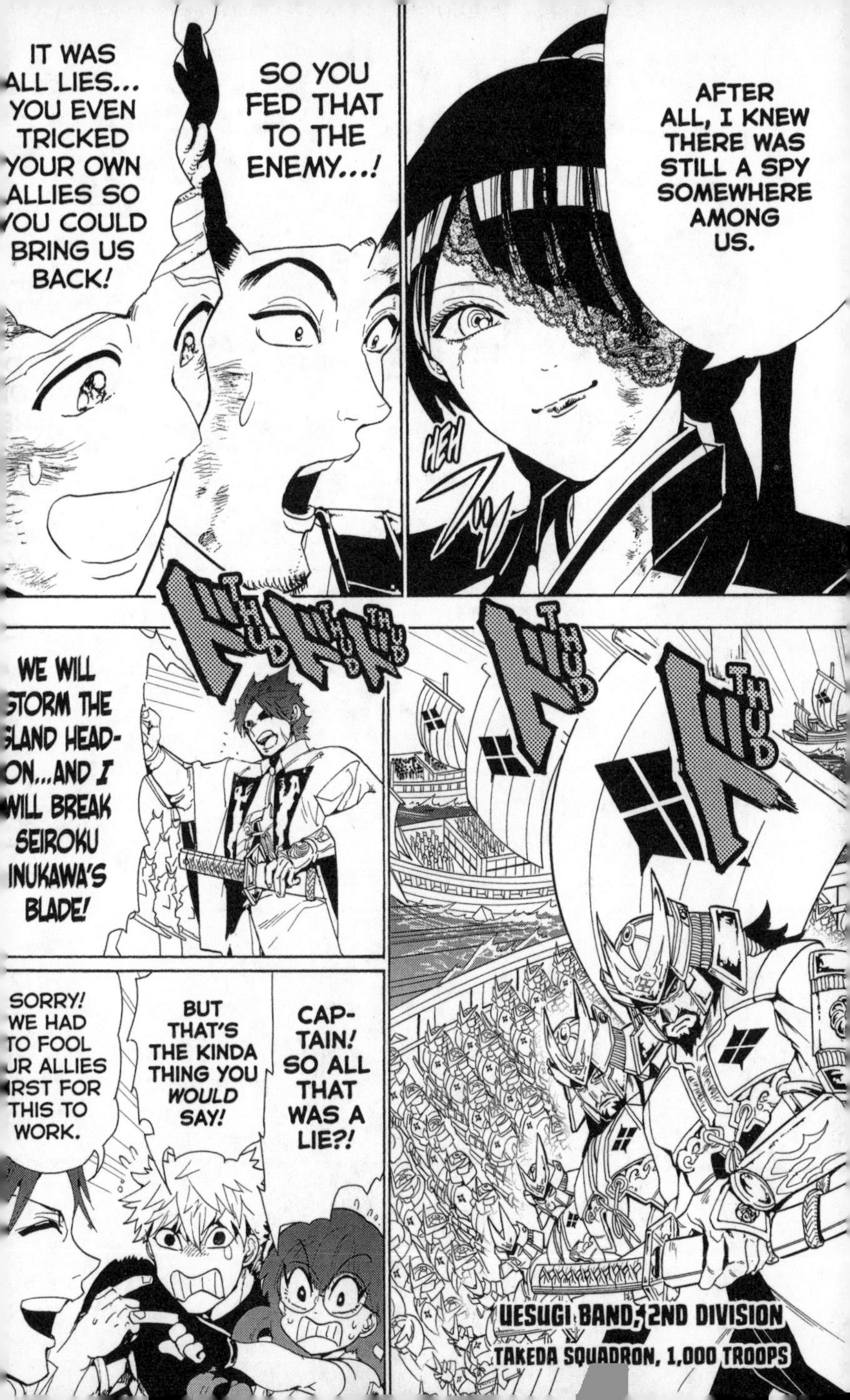
AFTER ALL, I KNEW THERE WAS STILL A SPY SOMEWHERE AMONG US.
HEH
SO YOU FED THAT TO THE ENEMY...!
IT WAS ALL LIES... YOU EVEN TRICKED YOUR OWN ALLIES SO YOU COULD BRING US BACK!
THUD
THUD
UESUGI BAND, 2ND DIVISION
TAKEDA SQUADRON, 1,000 TROOPS
THUD THUD!!
WE WILL STORM THE ISLAND HEAD-ON...AND I WILL BREAK SEIROKU INUKAWA'S BLADE!
CAP-TAIN! SO ALL THAT WAS A LIE?!
BUT THAT'S THE KINDA THING YOU WOULD SAY!
SORRY! WE HAD TO FOOL OUR ALLIES FIRST FOR THIS TO WORK.

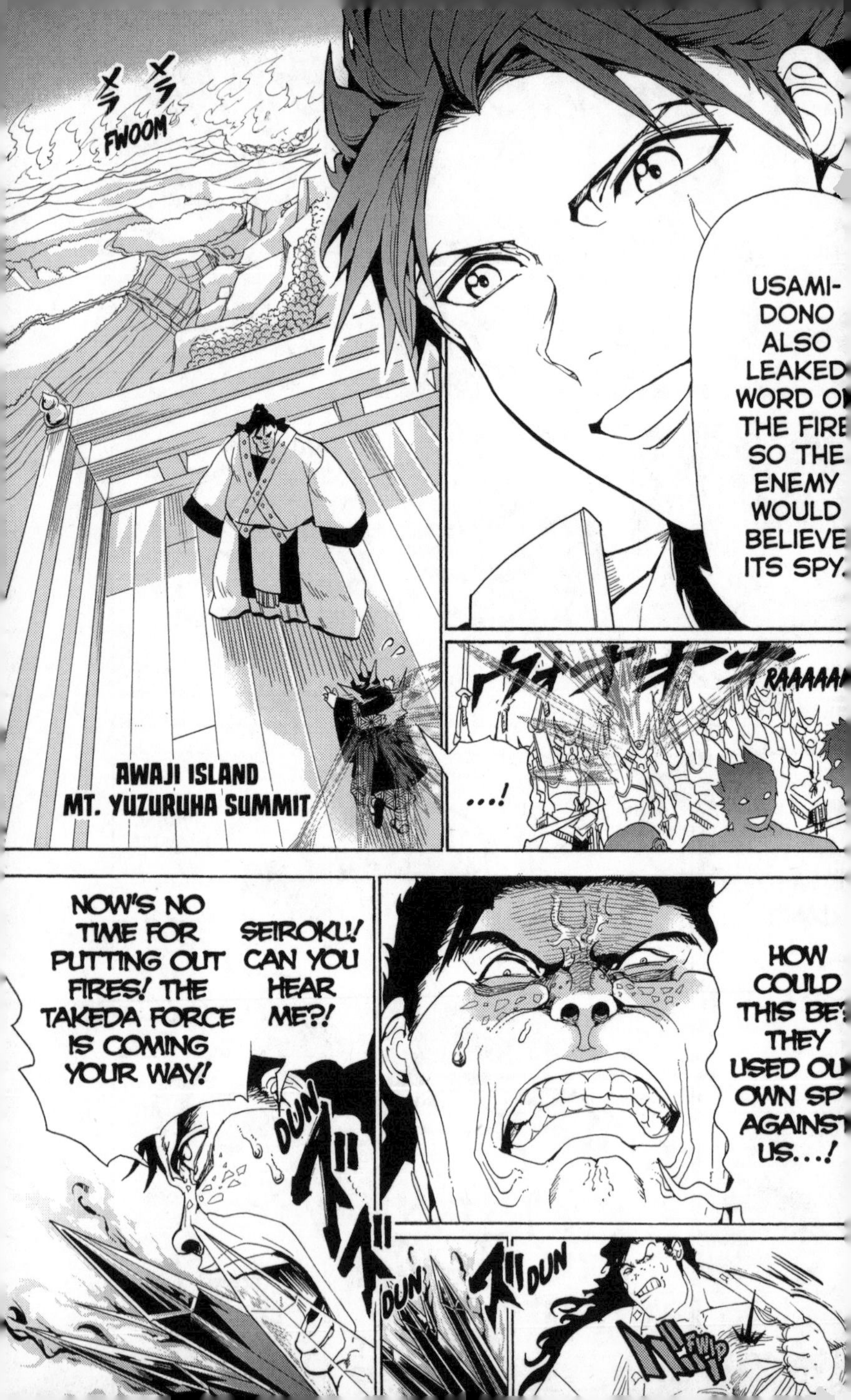
USAMI-DONO ALSO LEAKED WORD O THE FIRE SO THE ENEMY WOULD BELIEVE ITS SPY.
RAAAAA
...!
メラ メラ
FWOOM
AWAJI ISLAND MT. YUZURUHA SUMMIT
HOW COULD THIS BE THEY USED OU OWN SP AGAINST US...!
SEIROKU! CAN YOU HEAR ME?!
NOW'S NO TIME FOR PUTTING OUT FIRES! THE TAKEDA FORCE IS COMING YOUR WAY!
DUN
DUN
DUN
DUN
FWIP

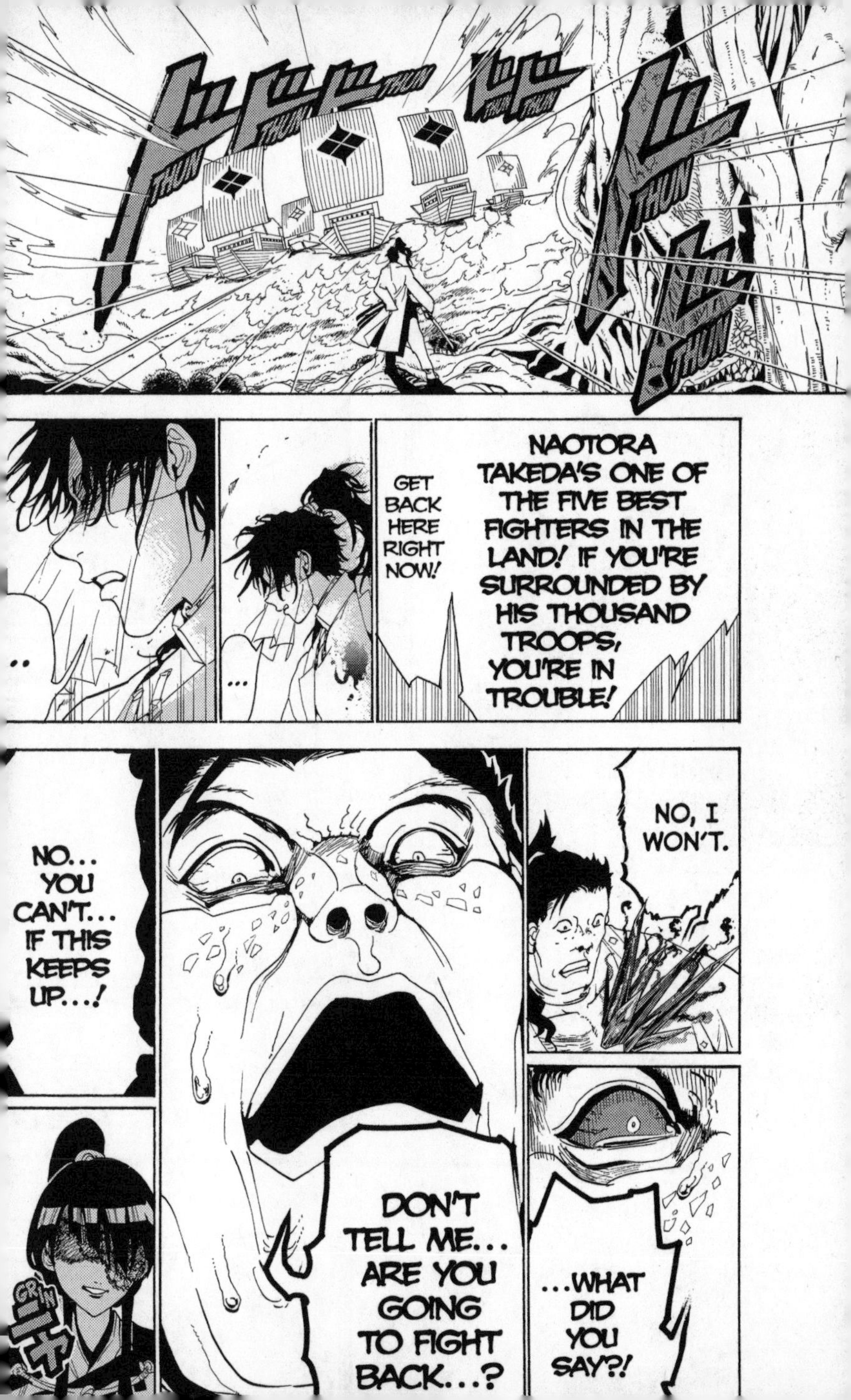
THUN
THUN
THUN
THUN
THUN
THUN
NAOTORA TAKEDA'S ONE OF THE FIVE BEST FIGHTERS IN THE LAND! IF YOU'RE SURROUNDED BY HIS THOUSAND TROOPS, YOU'RE IN TROUBLE!
GET BACK HERE RIGHT NOW!
...
..
NO, I WON'T.
...WHAT DID YOU SAY?!
DON'T TELL ME... ARE YOU GOING TO FIGHT BACK...?
NO... YOU CAN'T... IF THIS KEEPS UP...!
GRIN

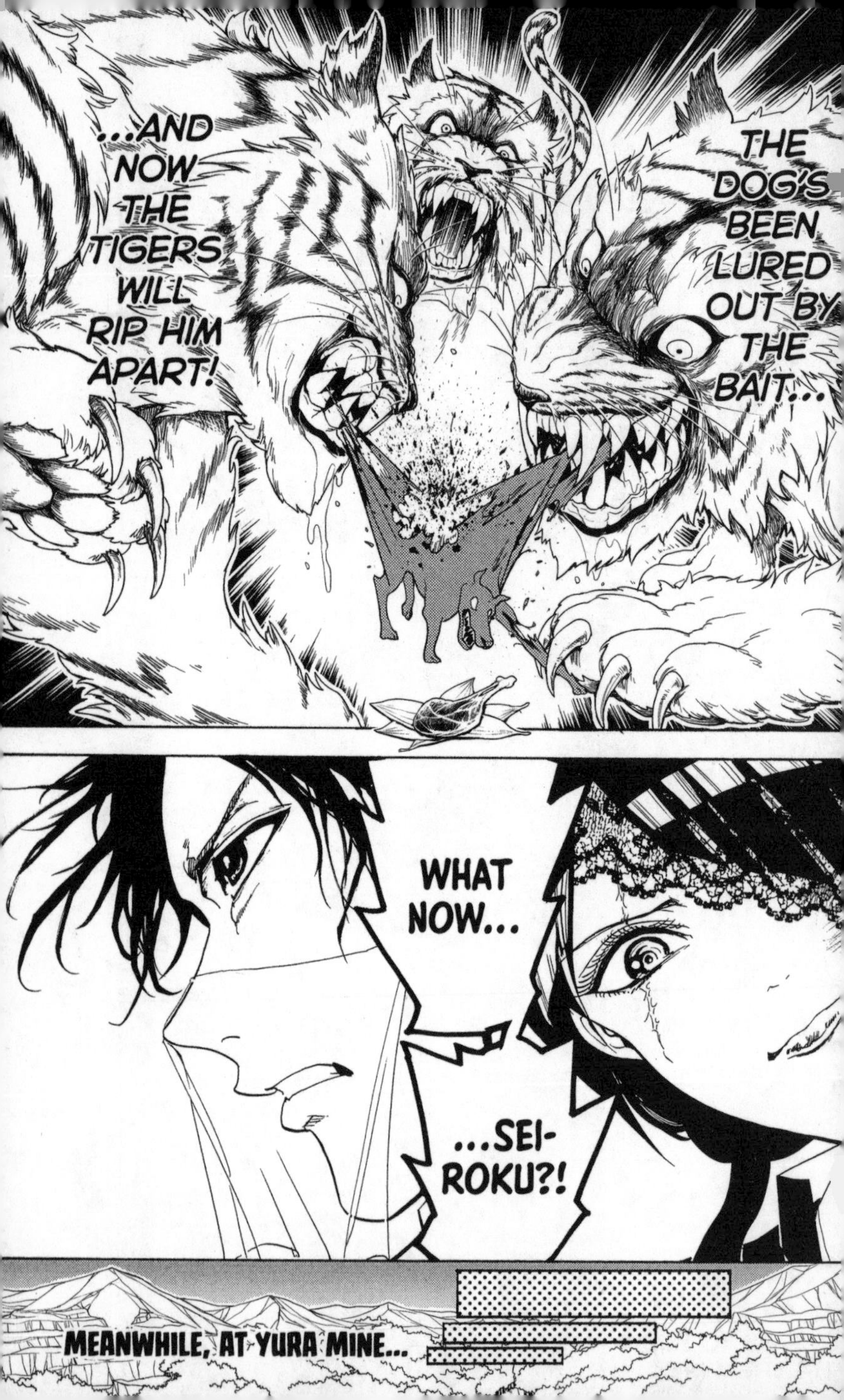
THE DOG'S BEEN LURED OUT BY THE BAIT...
...AND NOW THE TIGERS WILL RIP HIM APART!
WHAT NOW...
...SEI-ROKU?!
MEANWHILE, AT YURA MINE...

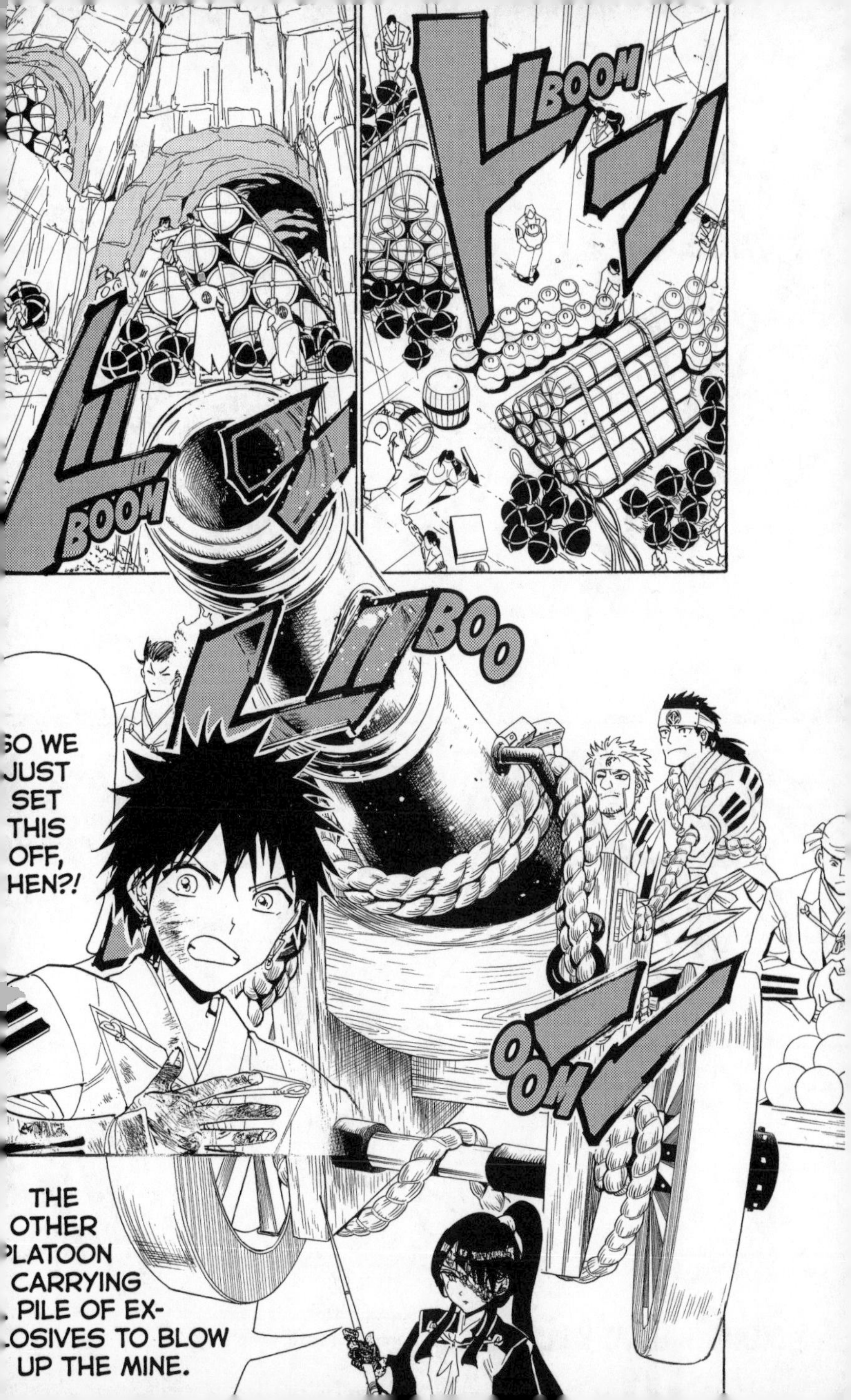
BOOM
BOOM
BOOOOM
SO WE JUST SET THIS OFF, HEN?!
THE OTHER PLATOON CARRYING PILE OF EX-LOSIVES TO BLOW UP THE MINE.

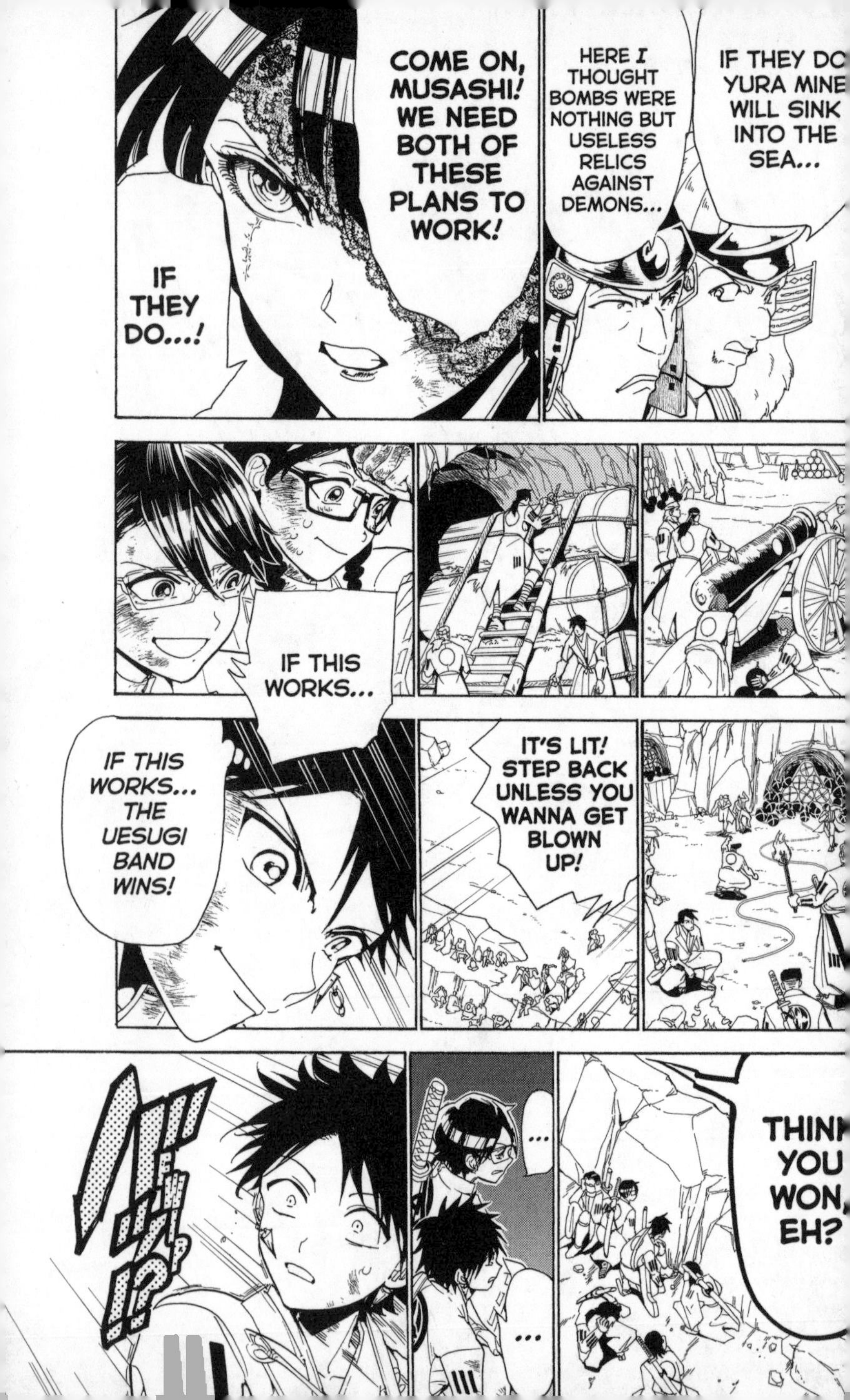
IF THEY DO YURA MINE WILL SINK INTO THE SEA...
HERE I THOUGHT BOMBS WERE NOTHING BUT USELESS RELICS AGAINST DEMONS...
COME ON, MUSASHI! WE NEED BOTH OF THESE PLANS TO WORK!
IF THEY DO...!
IF THIS WORKS...
IT'S LIT! STEP BACK UNLESS YOU WANNA GET BLOWN UP!
IF THIS WORKS... THE UESUGI BAND WINS!
THINK YOU WON, EH?
...
...

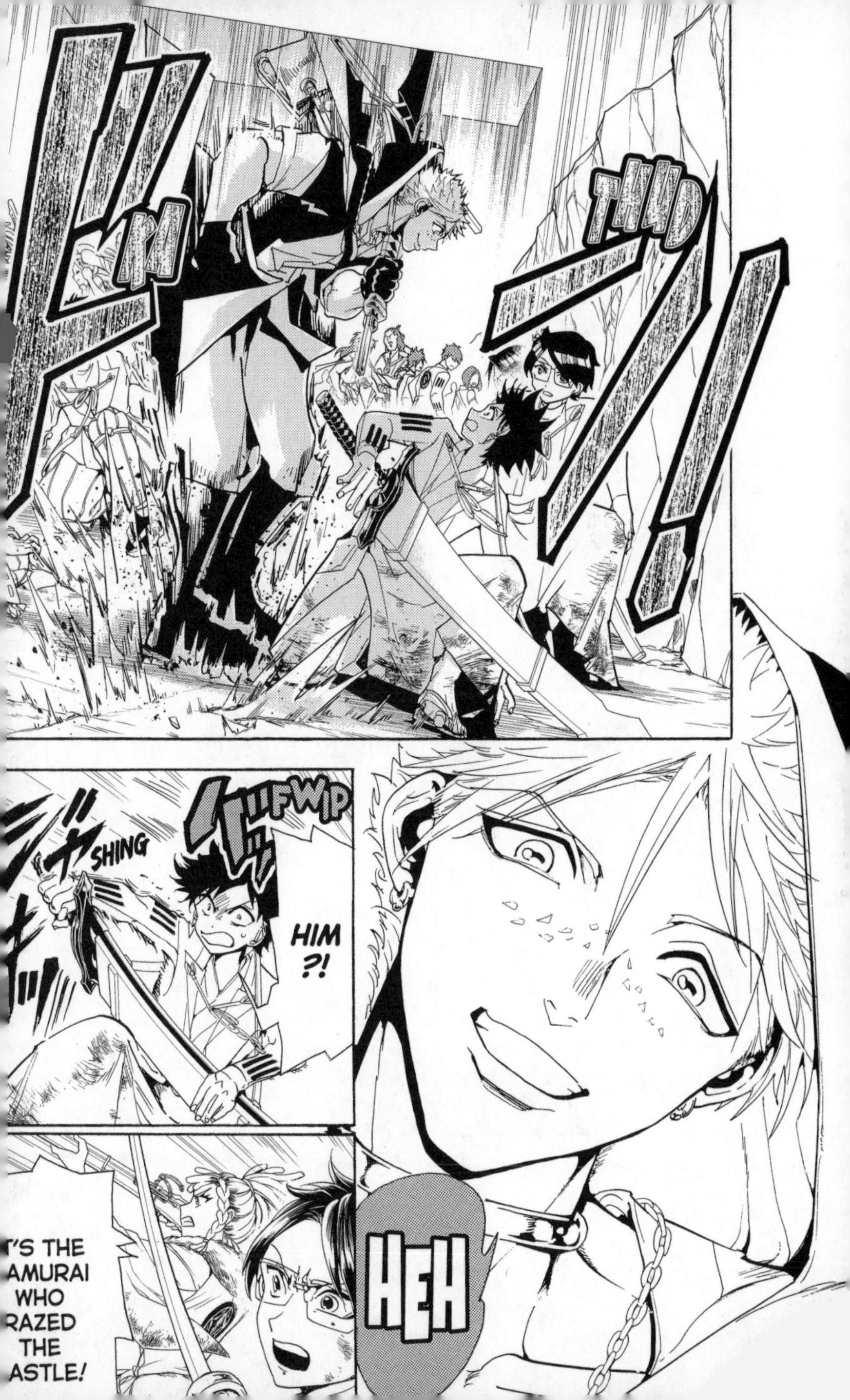
THUD
HEH
FWIP
SHING
HIM ?!
'S THE AMURAI WHO RAZED THE ASTLE!

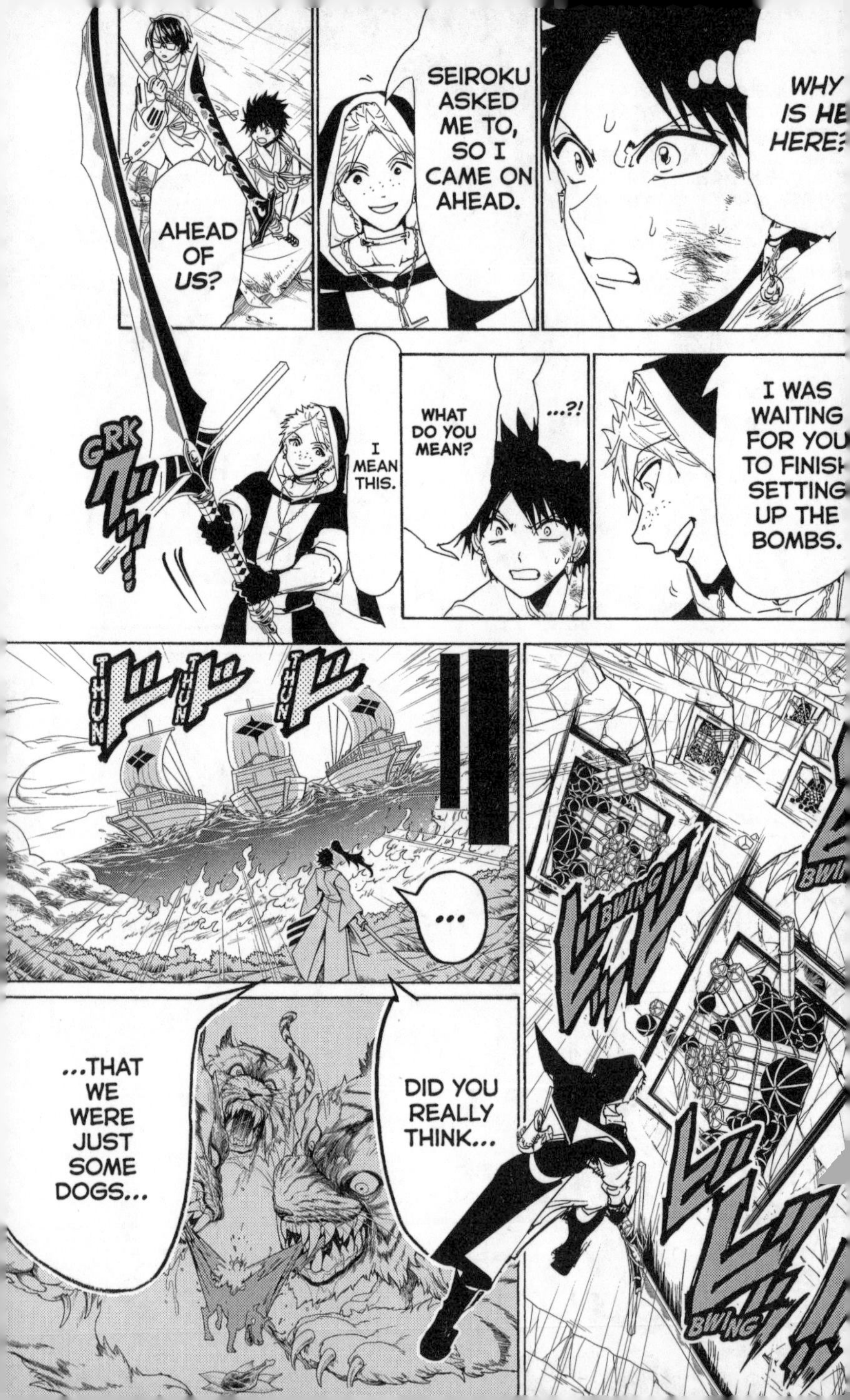
WHY IS HE HERE?
SEIROKU ASKED ME TO, SO I CAME ON AHEAD.
AHEAD OF US?
I WAS WAITING FOR YOU TO FINISH SETTING UP THE BOMBS.
...?!
WHAT DO YOU MEAN?
I MEAN THIS.
GRK
BWING
BWING
BWING
THUN
THUN
THUN
...
DID YOU REALLY THINK...
...THAT WE WERE JUST SOME DOGS...

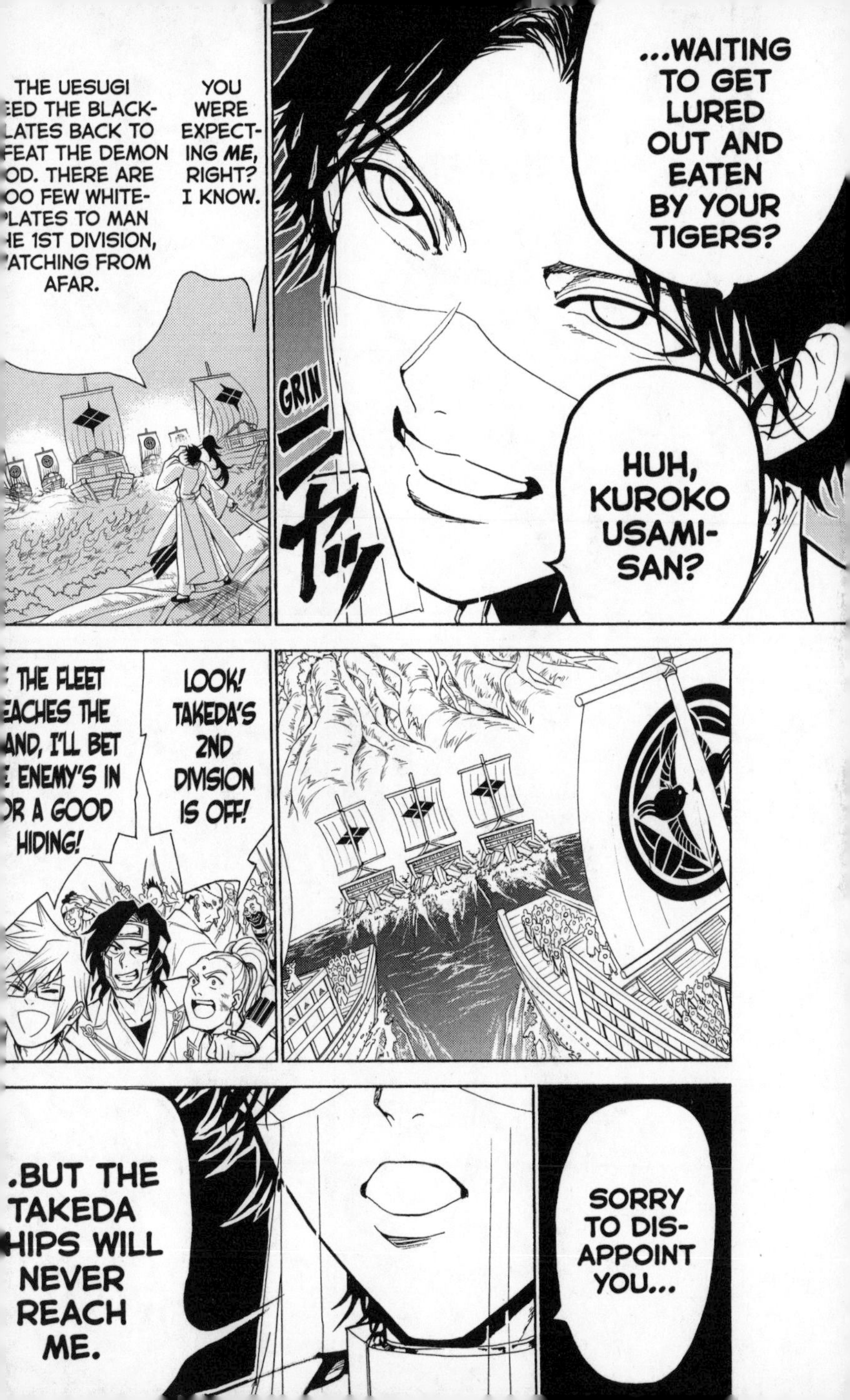
...WAITING TO GET LURED OUT AND EATEN BY YOUR TIGERS?
GRIN
HUH, KUROKO USAMI-SAN?
YOU WERE EXPECTING ME, RIGHT? I KNOW.
THE UESUGI EED THE BLACK-LATES BACK TO FEAT THE DEMON OD. THERE ARE OO FEW WHITE-LATES TO MAN HE 1ST DIVISION, ATCHING FROM AFAR.
LOOK! TAKEDA'S 2ND DIVISION IS OFF!
THE FLEET EACHES THE AND, I'LL BET E ENEMY'S IN OR A GOOD HIDING!
SORRY TO DIS-APPOINT YOU...
.BUT THE TAKEDA HIPS WILL NEVER REACH ME.

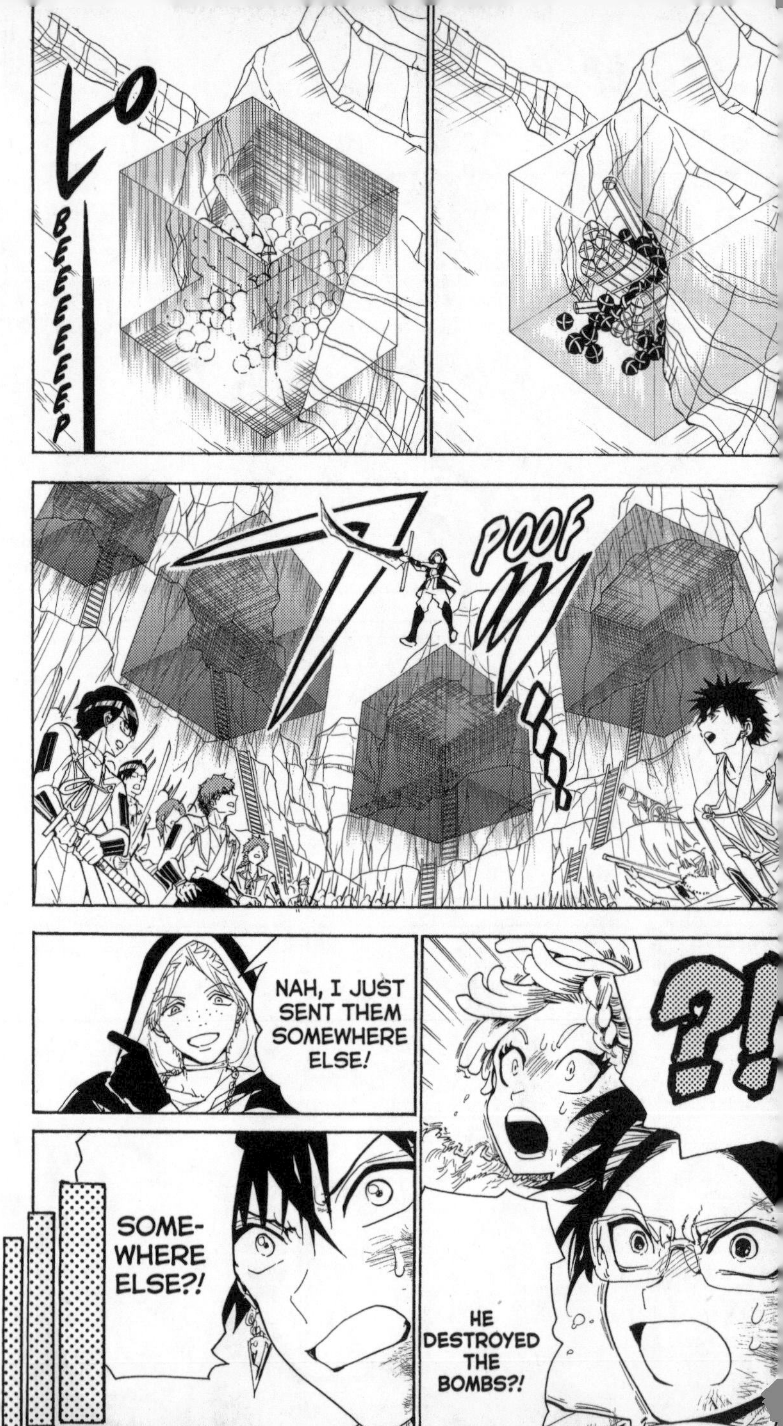
BEEEEEEEEP
POOF
?!
HE DESTROYED THE BOMBS?!
NAH, I JUST SENT THEM SOMEWHERE ELSE!
SOME-WHERE ELSE?!

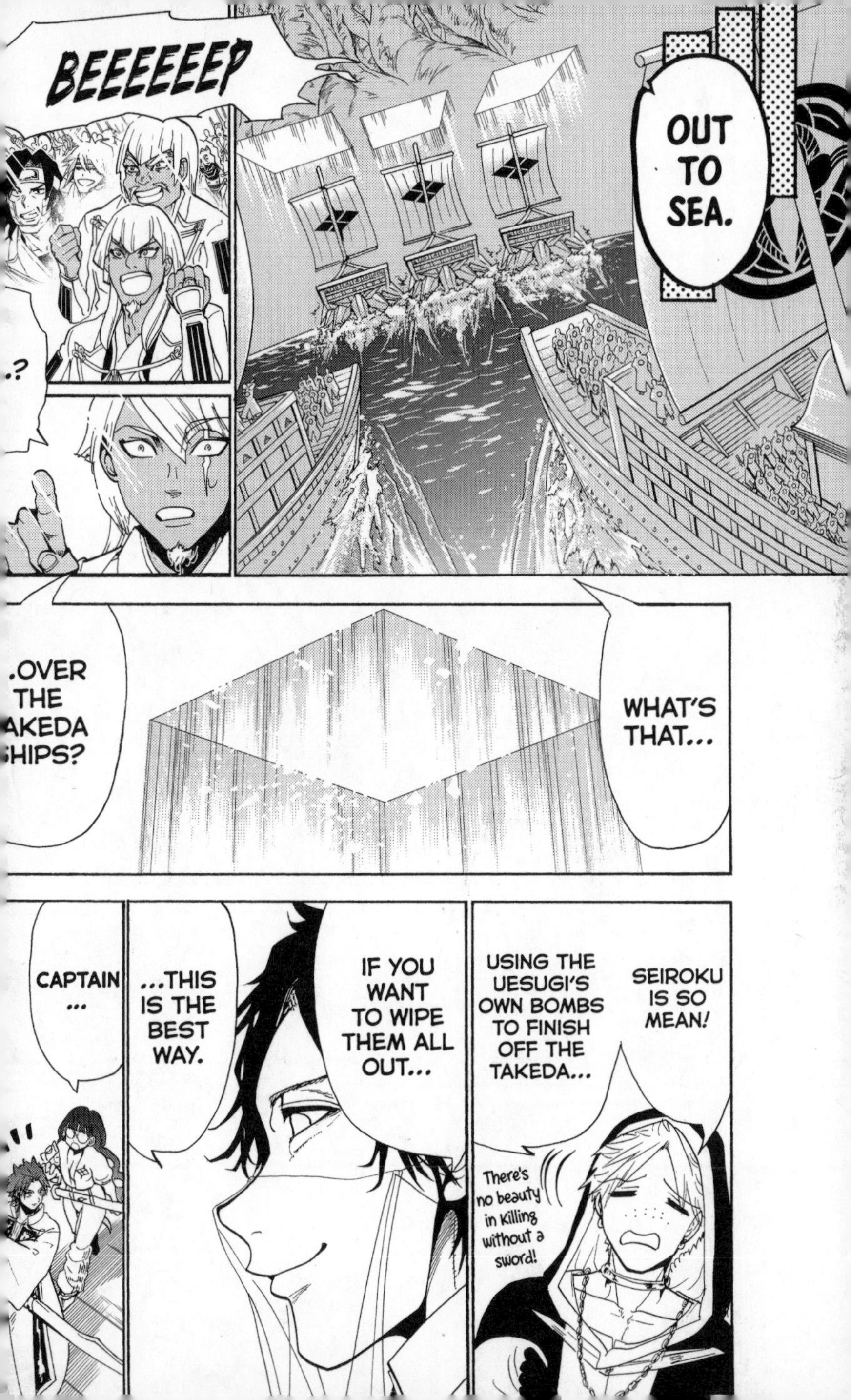
OUT TO SEA.
BEEEEEEEP
.?
WHAT'S THAT...
.OVER THE AKEDA HIPS?
SEIROKU IS SO MEAN!
USING THE UESUGI'S OWN BOMBS TO FINISH OFF THE TAKEDA...
There's no beauty in Killing without a sword!
IF YOU WANT TO WIPE THEM ALL OUT...
...THIS IS THE BEST WAY.
CAPTAIN ...

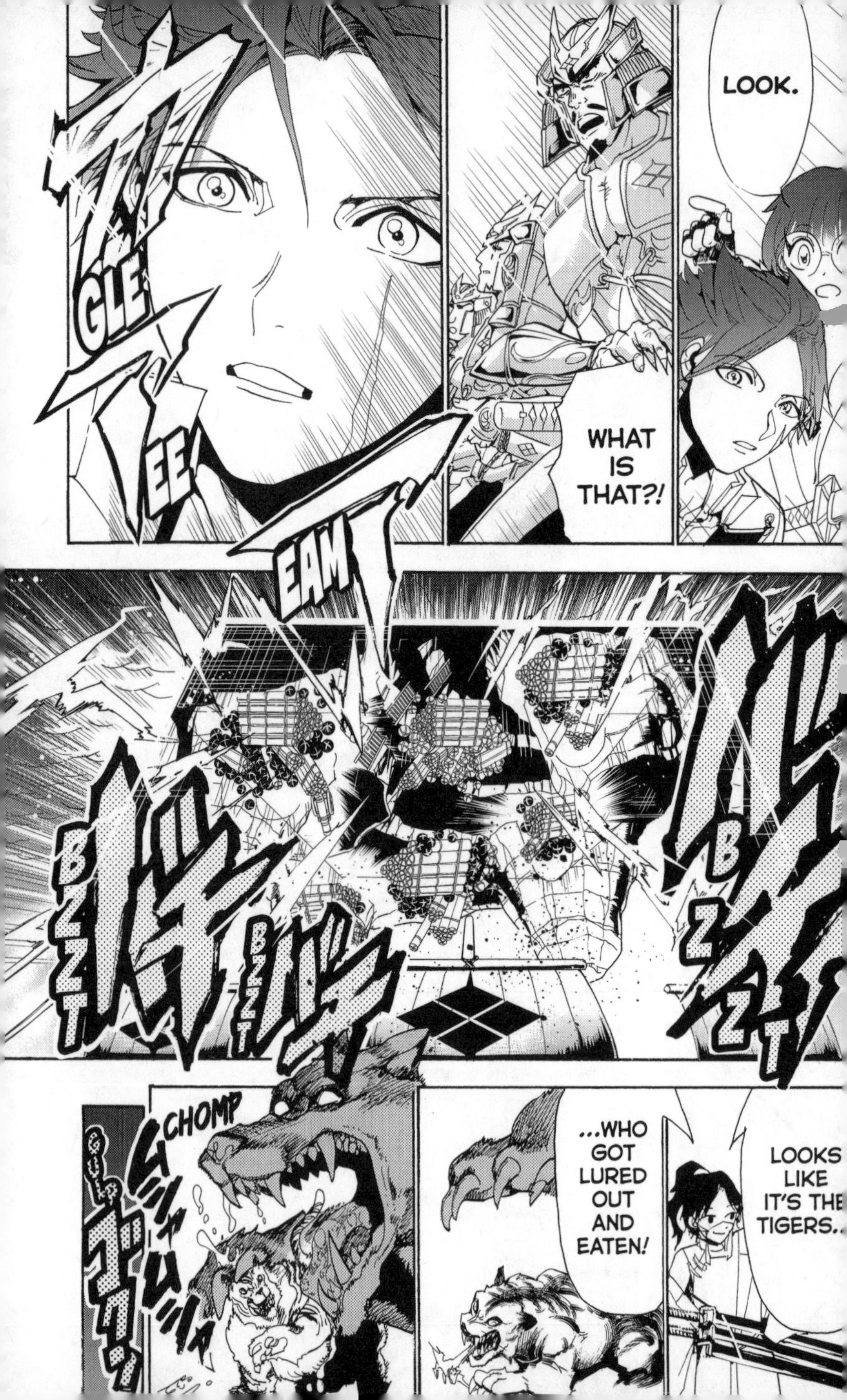
LOOK.
WHAT IS THAT?!
GLEEEAM
BZZZT
BZZT
BZZZT
LOOKS LIKE IT'S THE TIGERS...
...WHO GOT LURED OUT AND EATEN!
CHOMP
GULP

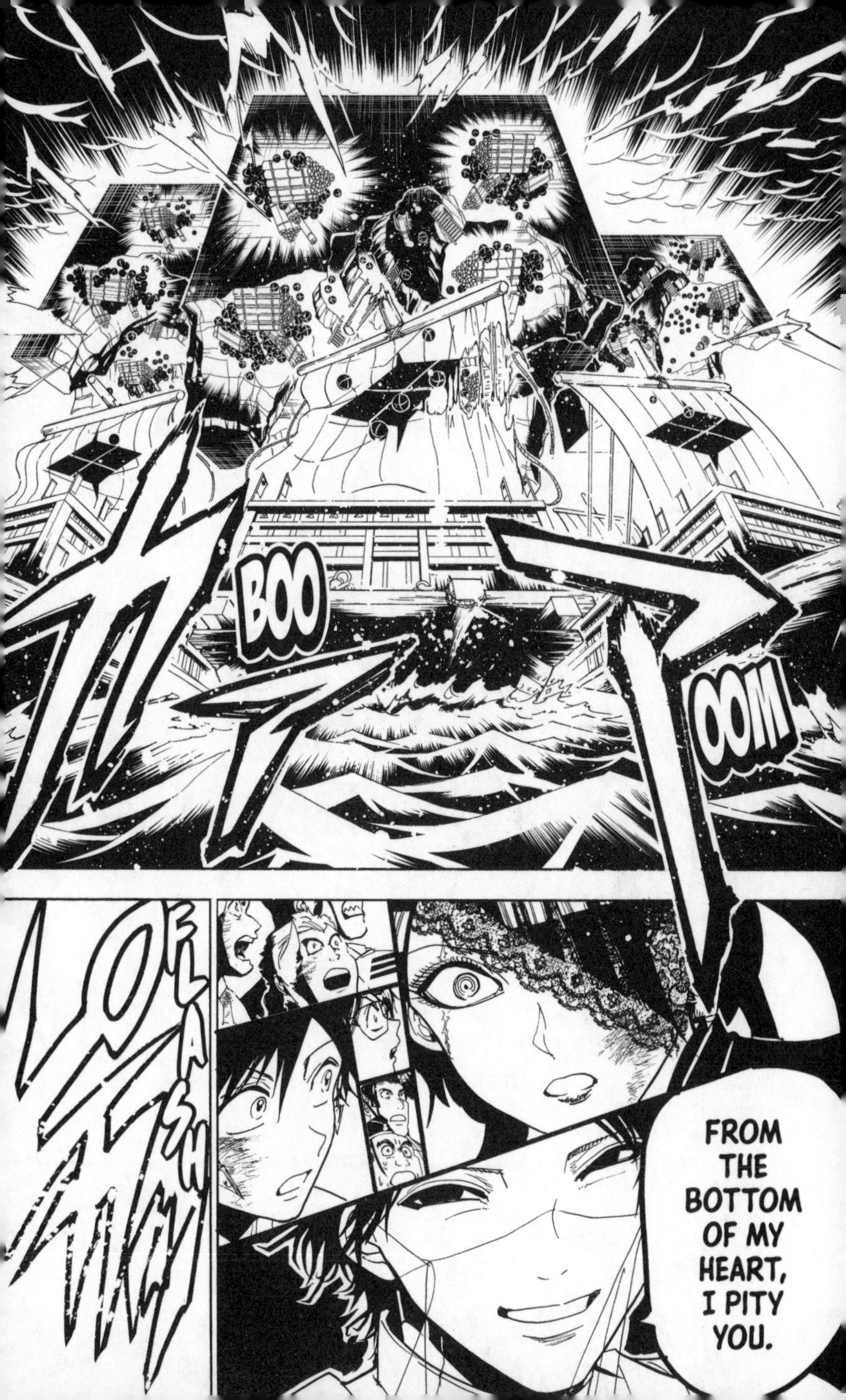
BOO
OOM
FROM THE BOTTOM OF MY HEART, I PITY YOU.
FLASH

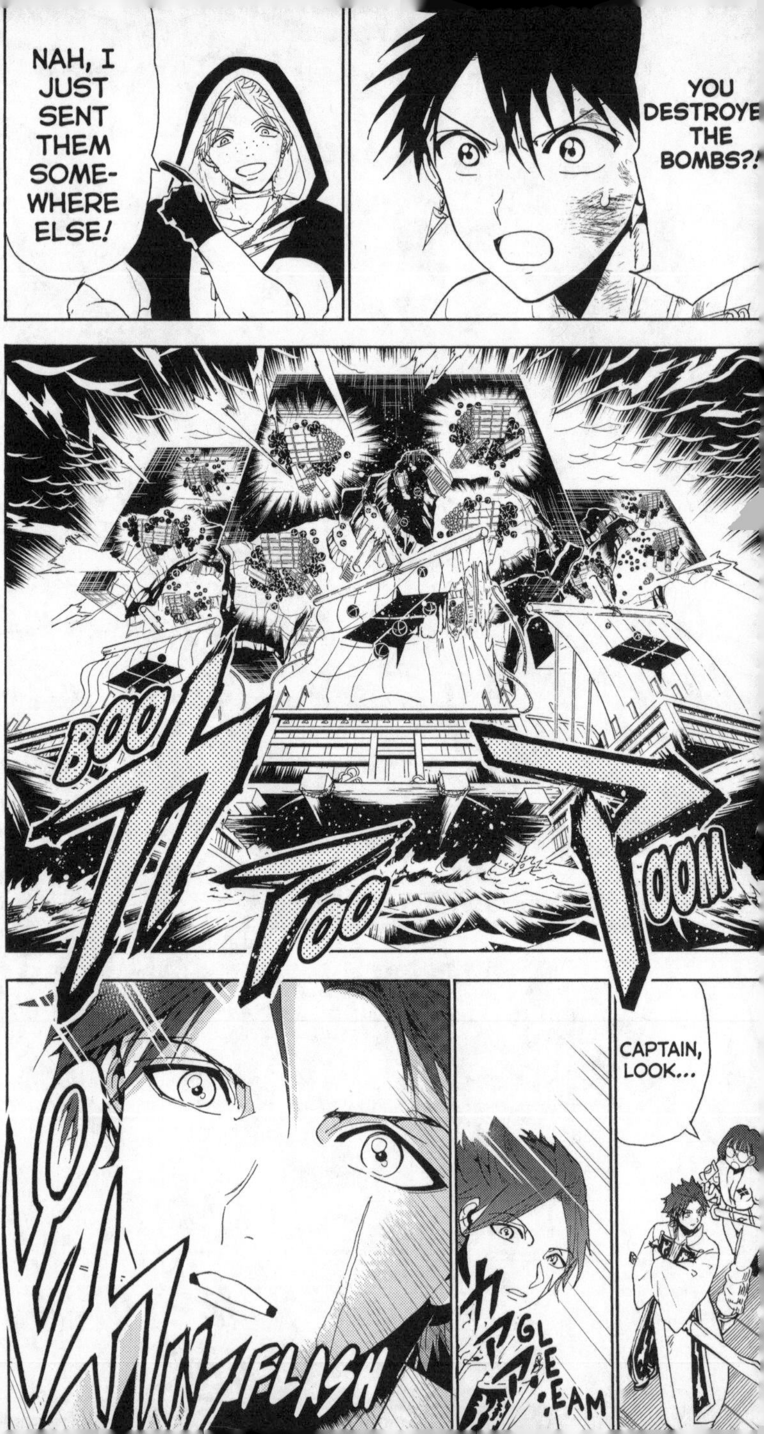
YOU DESTROYE THE BOMBS?!
NAH, I JUST SENT THEM SOME-WHERE ELSE!
BOO OO OOM
CAPTAIN, LOOK...
GLEAM
FLASH

CHAPTER 83: NAGGING SUSPICION

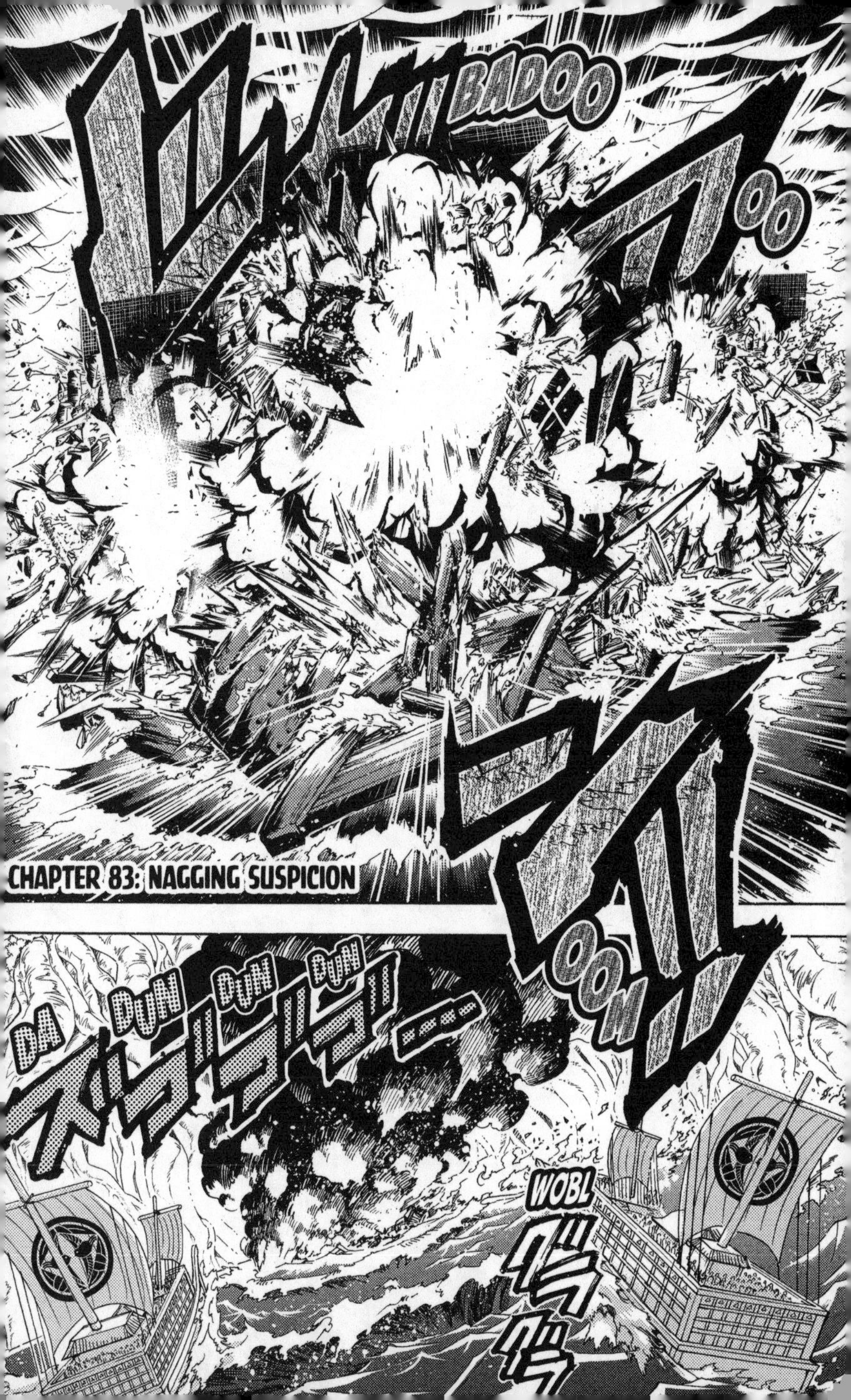
BADOO
OO
OOM
DA DUN DUN DUN
WOBL

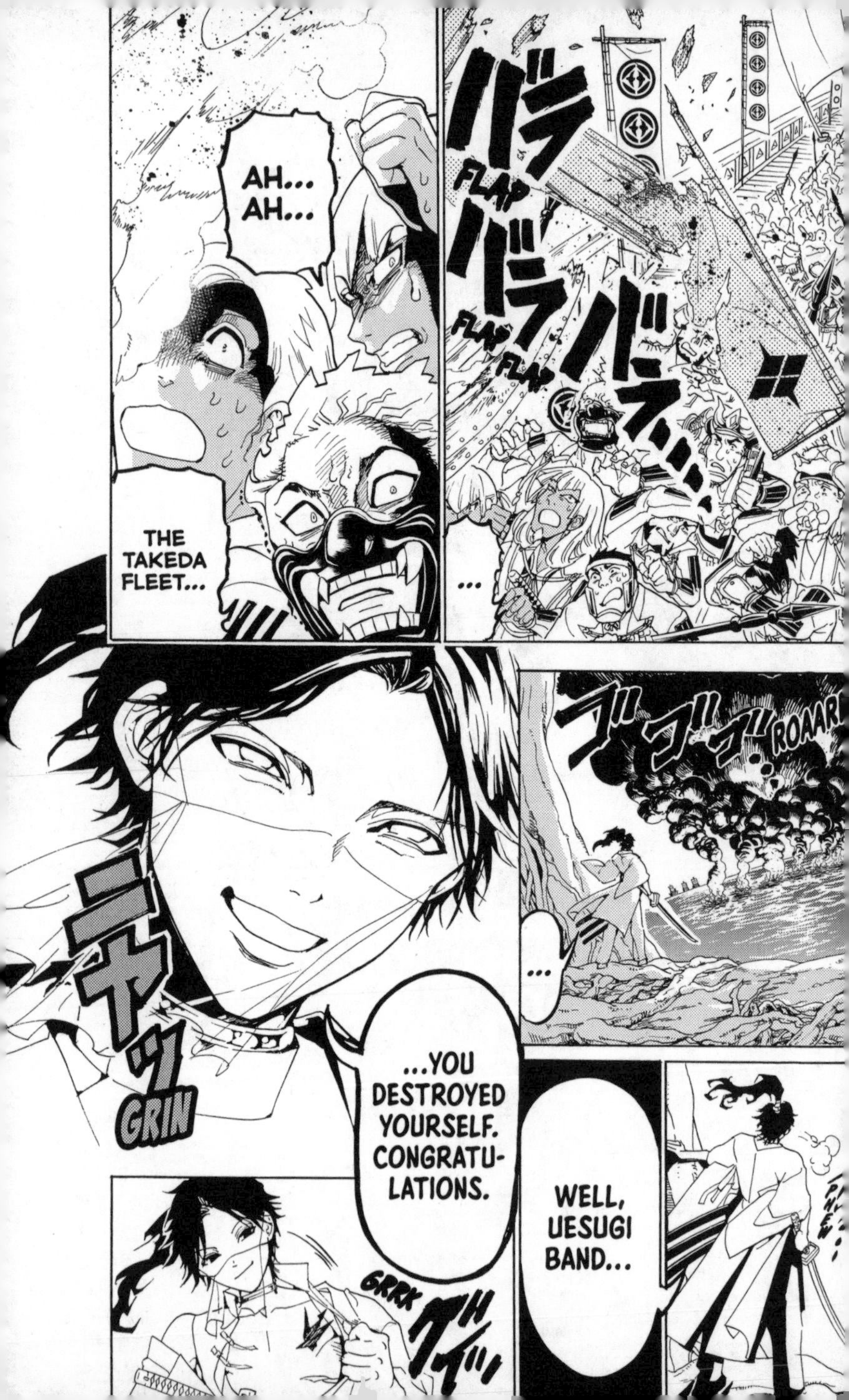

バラ
FLAP
バラ
FLAP
FLAP
バラ…
FLAP
...
AH... AH...
THE TAKEDA FLEET...
ゴゴゴ
ROAAR
...
ニヤッ
GRIN
...YOU DESTROYED YOURSELF. CONGRATULATIONS.
WELL, UESUGI BAND...
PHEW...
GRRK
グイッ

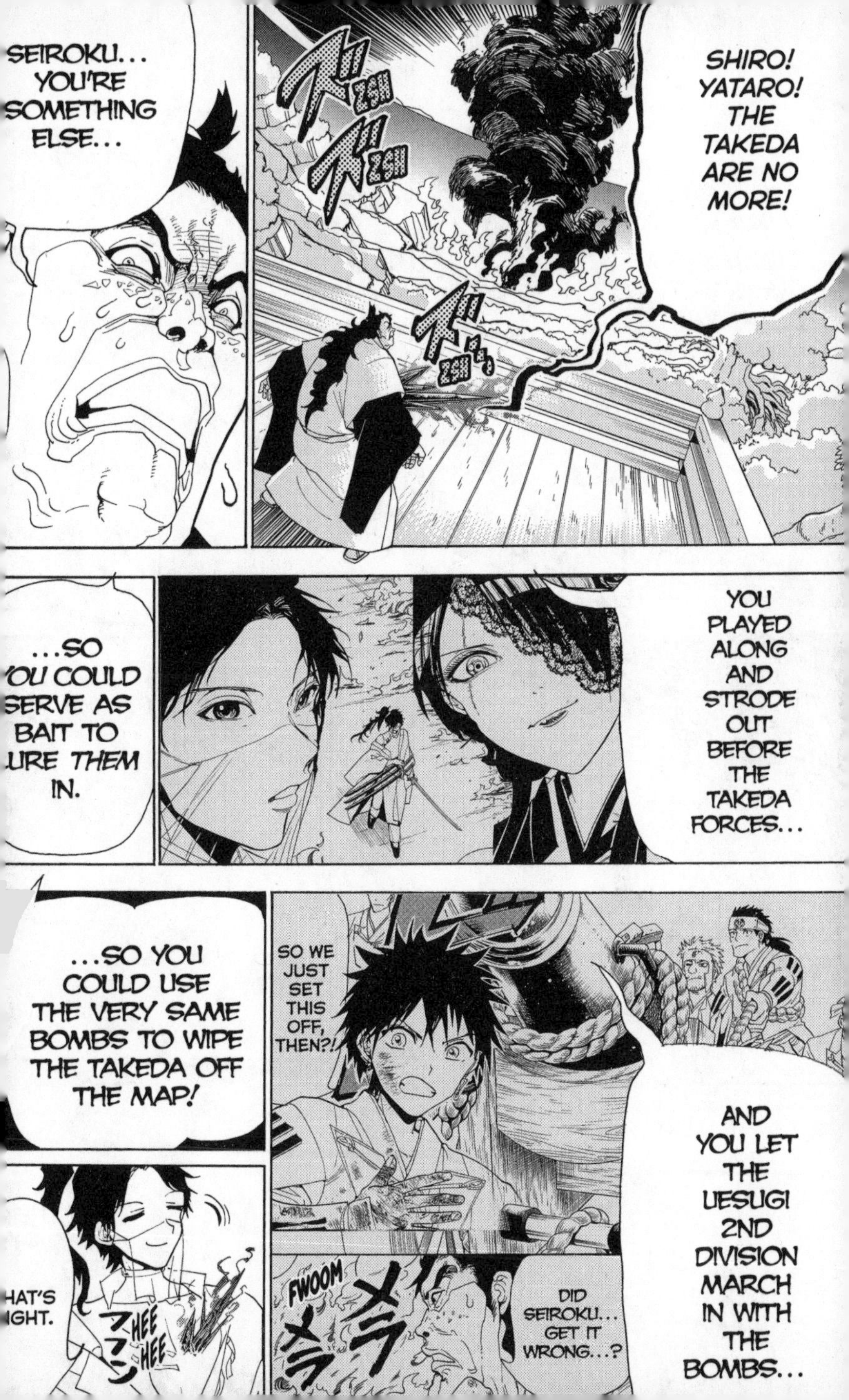
SHIRO! YATARO! THE TAKEDA ARE NO MORE!
ZSH
ZSH
ZSH
SEIROKU... YOU'RE SOMETHING ELSE...
YOU PLAYED ALONG AND STRODE OUT BEFORE THE TAKEDA FORCES...
...SO YOU COULD SERVE AS BAIT TO LURE THEM IN.
AND YOU LET THE UESUGI 2ND DIVISION MARCH IN WITH THE BOMBS...
SO WE JUST SET THIS OFF, THEN?!
DID SEIROKU... GET IT WRONG...?
FWOOM
...SO YOU COULD USE THE VERY SAME BOMBS TO WIPE THE TAKEDA OFF THE MAP!
HAT'S IGHT.
HEE HEE

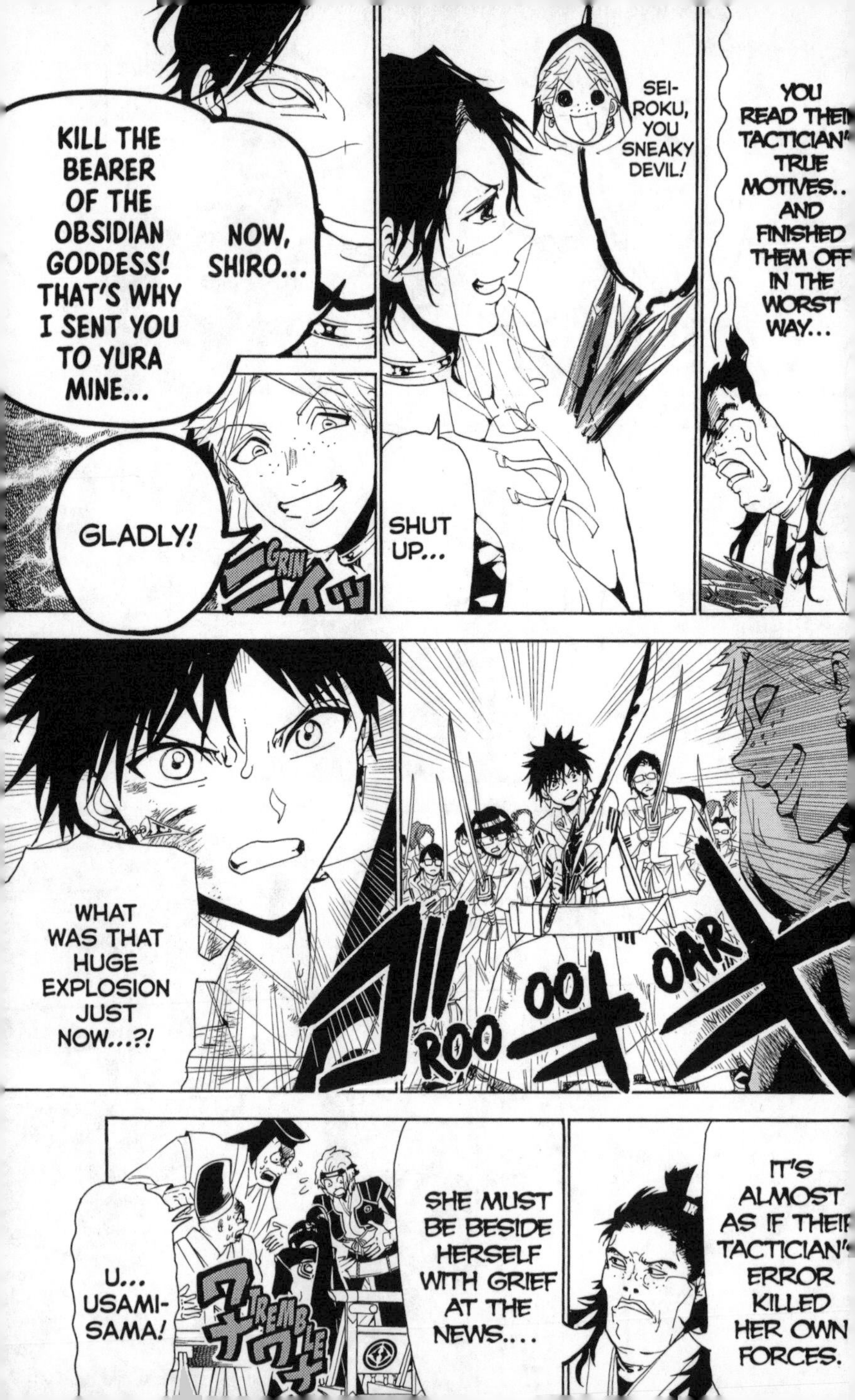
YOU READ THEI TACTICIAN' TRUE MOTIVES.. AND FINISHED THEM OFF IN THE WORST WAY...
SEI-ROKU, YOU SNEAKY DEVIL!
SHUT UP...
NOW, SHIRO...
KILL THE BEARER OF THE OBSIDIAN GODDESS! THAT'S WHY I SENT YOU TO YURA MINE...
GLADLY!
GRIN
ROO OO OAR
WHAT WAS THAT HUGE EXPLOSION JUST NOW...?!
IT'S ALMOST AS IF THEI TACTICIAN' ERROR KILLED HER OWN FORCES.
SHE MUST BE BESIDE HERSELF WITH GRIEF AT THE NEWS....
U... USAMI-SAMA!
TREMBLE

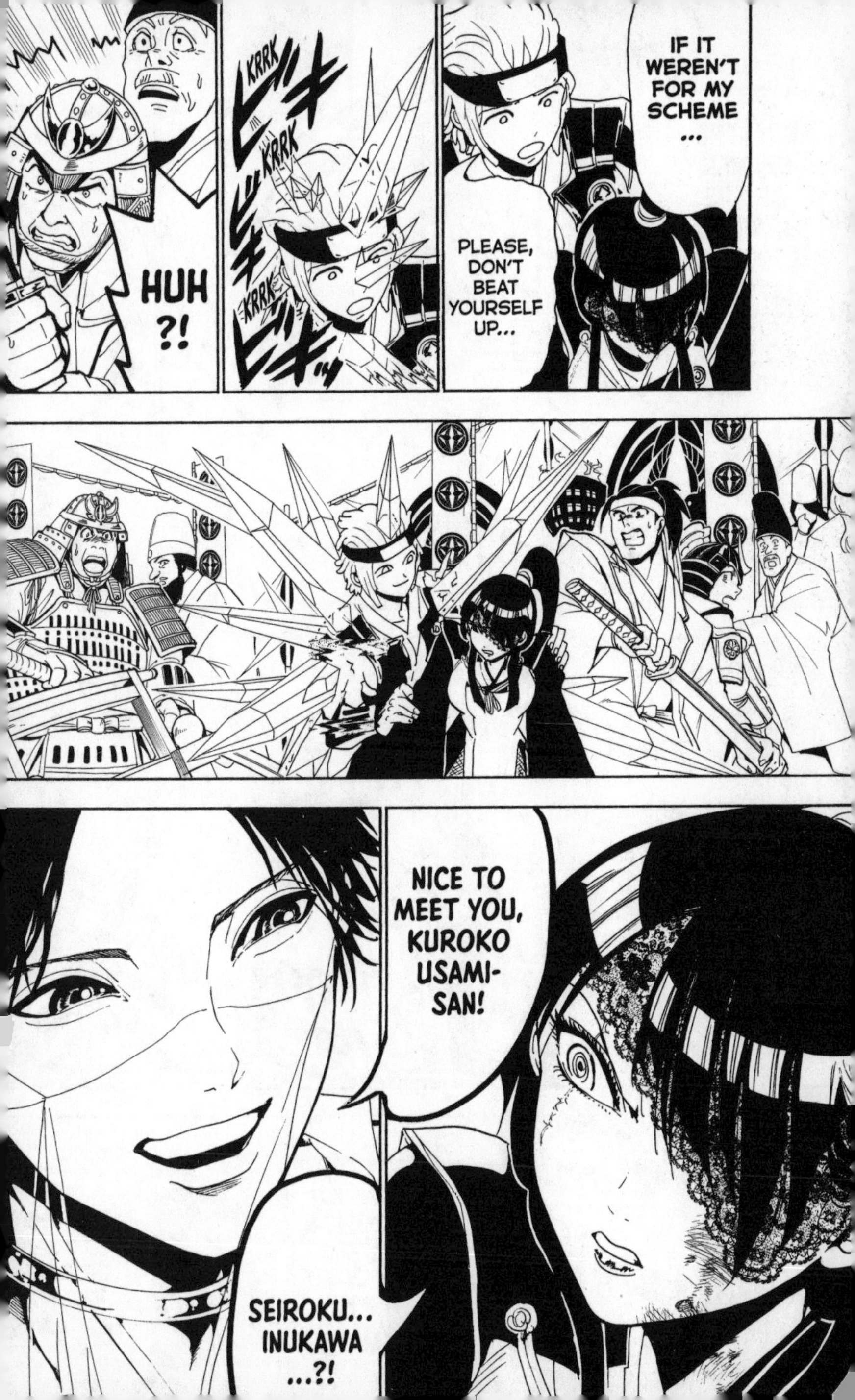
IF IT WEREN'T FOR MY SCHEME ...
PLEASE, DON'T BEAT YOURSELF UP...
KRRK
KRRK
KRRK
HUH ?!
NICE TO MEET YOU, KUROKO USAMI-SAN!
SEIROKU... INUKAWA ...?!

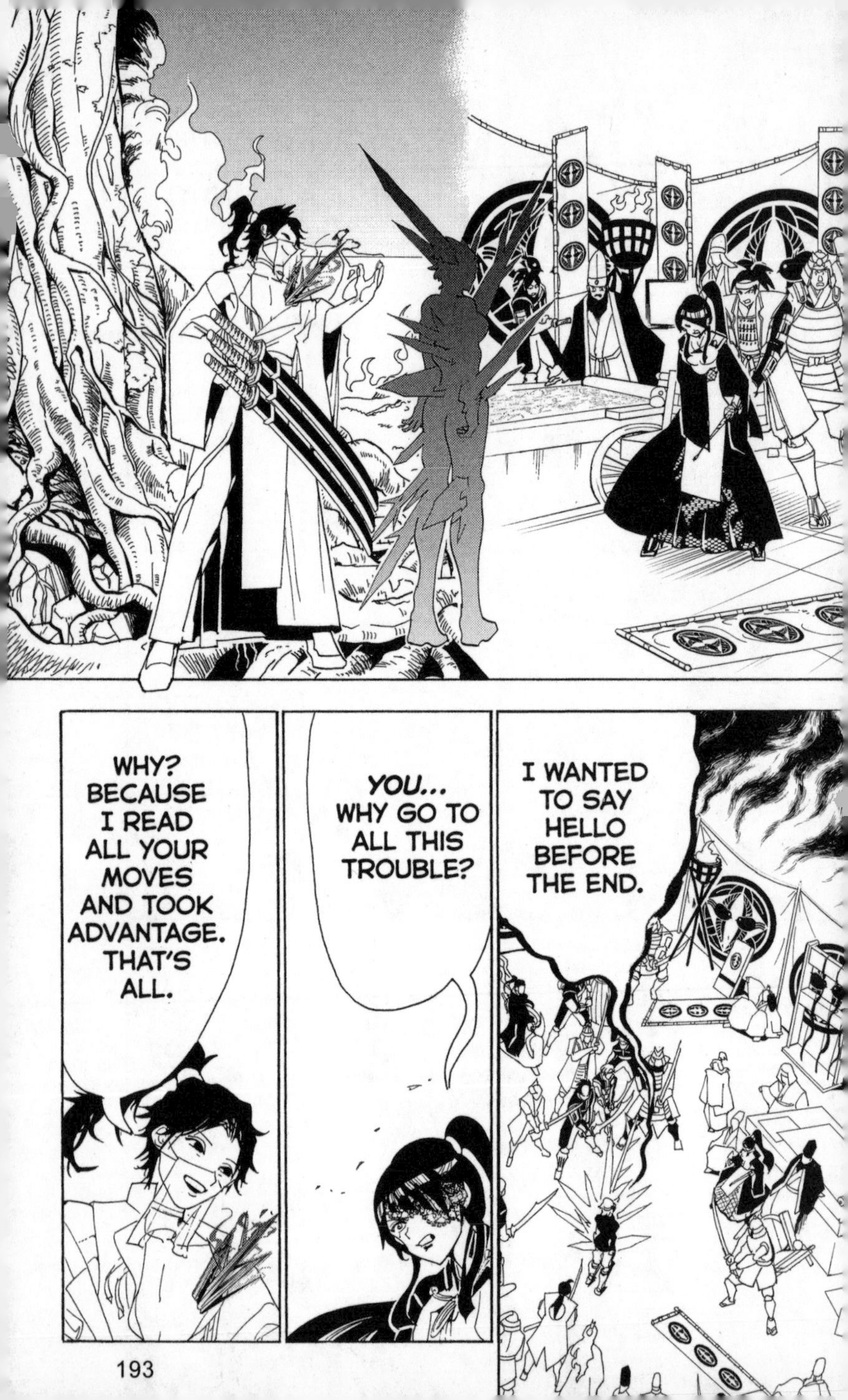
I WANTED TO SAY HELLO BEFORE THE END.
YOU... WHY GO TO ALL THIS TROUBLE?
WHY? BECAUSE I READ ALL YOUR MOVES AND TOOK ADVANTAGE. THAT'S ALL.

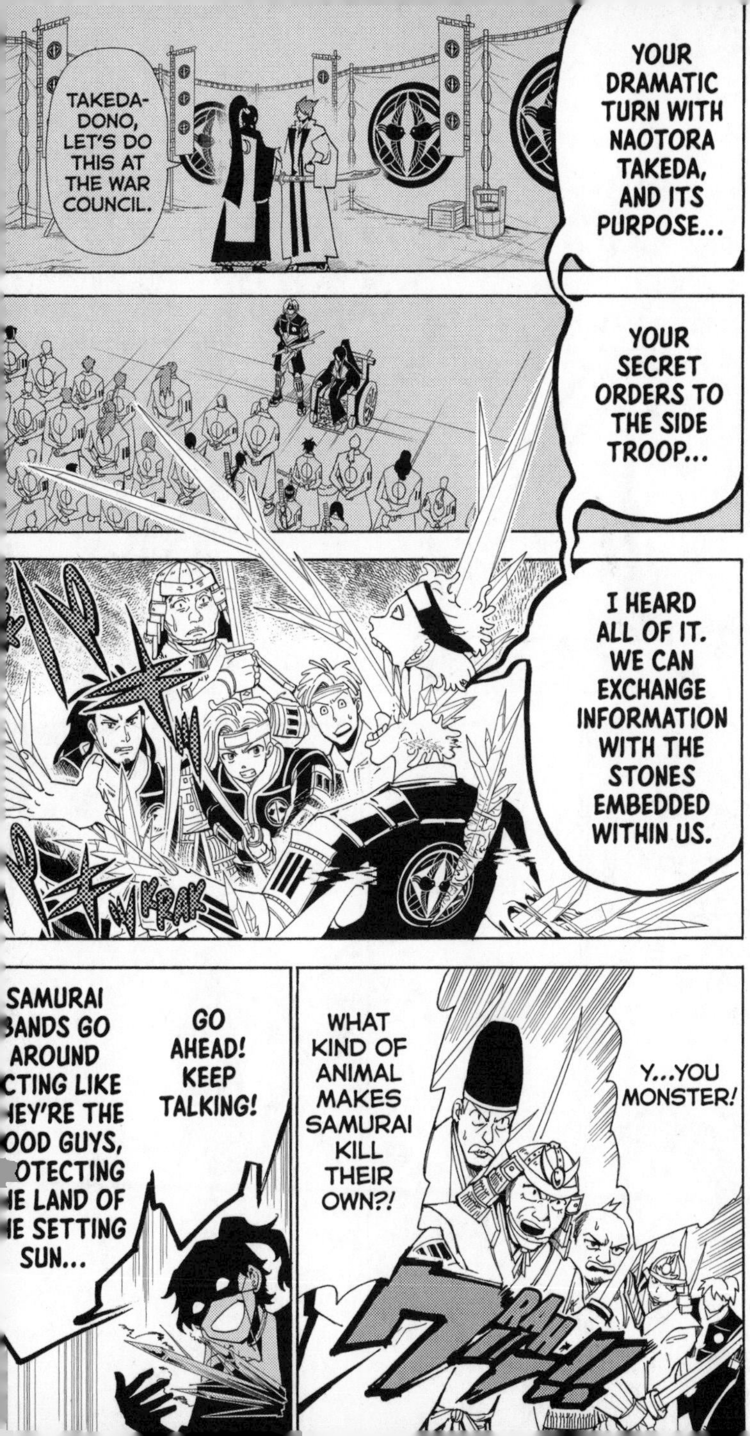
YOUR DRAMATIC TURN WITH NAOTORA TAKEDA, AND ITS PURPOSE...
TAKEDA-DONO, LET'S DO THIS AT THE WAR COUNCIL.
YOUR SECRET ORDERS TO THE SIDE TROOP...
I HEARD ALL OF IT. WE CAN EXCHANGE INFORMATION WITH THE STONES EMBEDDED WITHIN US.
KRAK
Y...YOU MONSTER!
WHAT KIND OF ANIMAL MAKES SAMURAI KILL THEIR OWN?!
RAH!
GO AHEAD! KEEP TALKING!
SAMURAI ANDS GO AROUND CTING LIKE EY'RE THE OOD GUYS, OTECTING E LAND OF E SETTING SUN...

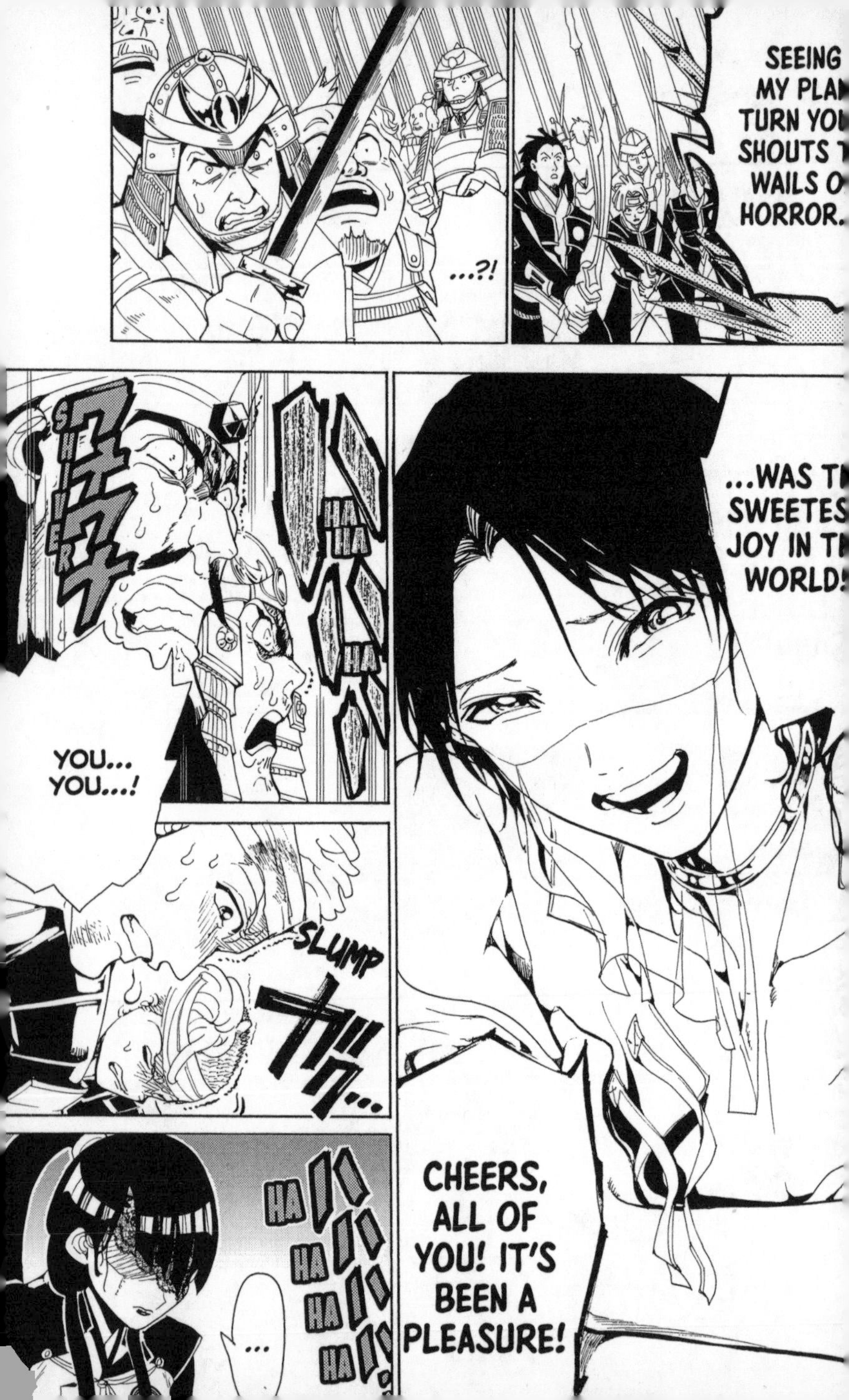
SEEING MY PLA TURN YOU SHOUTS T WAILS O HORROR.
...?!
...WAS T SWEETES JOY IN T WORLD!
CHEERS, ALL OF YOU! IT'S BEEN A PLEASURE!
SHIVER
HA HA HA
YOU... YOU...!
SLUMP
HA HA HA HA
...

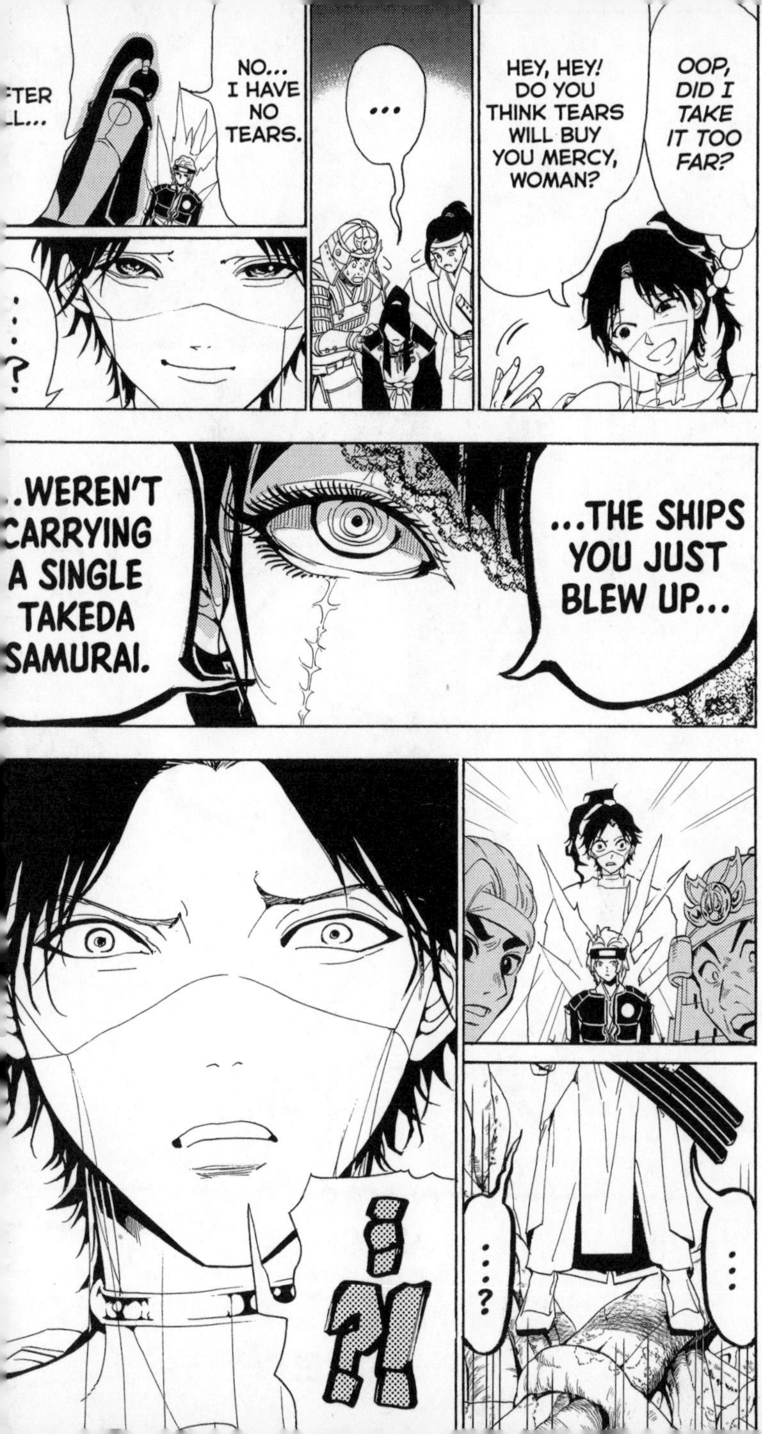
OOP, DID I TAKE IT TOO FAR?
HEY, HEY! DO YOU THINK TEARS WILL BUY YOU MERCY, WOMAN?
...
NO... I HAVE NO TEARS.
FTER LL...
...?
...THE SHIPS YOU JUST BLEW UP...
.WEREN'T CARRYING A SINGLE TAKEDA SAMURAI.
...
...?
?!

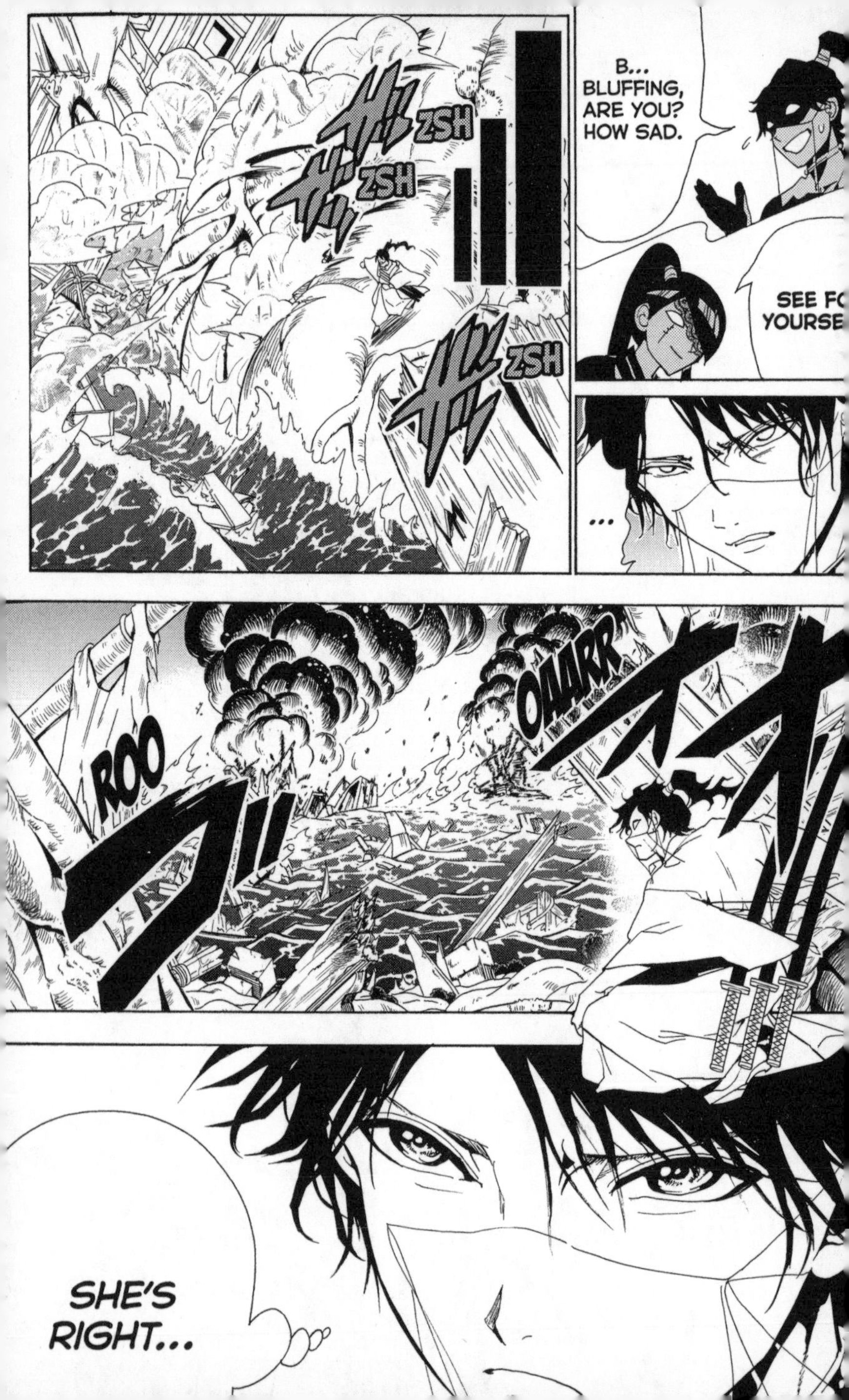
B... BLUFFING, ARE YOU? HOW SAD.
SEE FO YOURSE
...
ZSH
ZSH
ZSH
OAARR
ROO
SHE'S RIGHT...

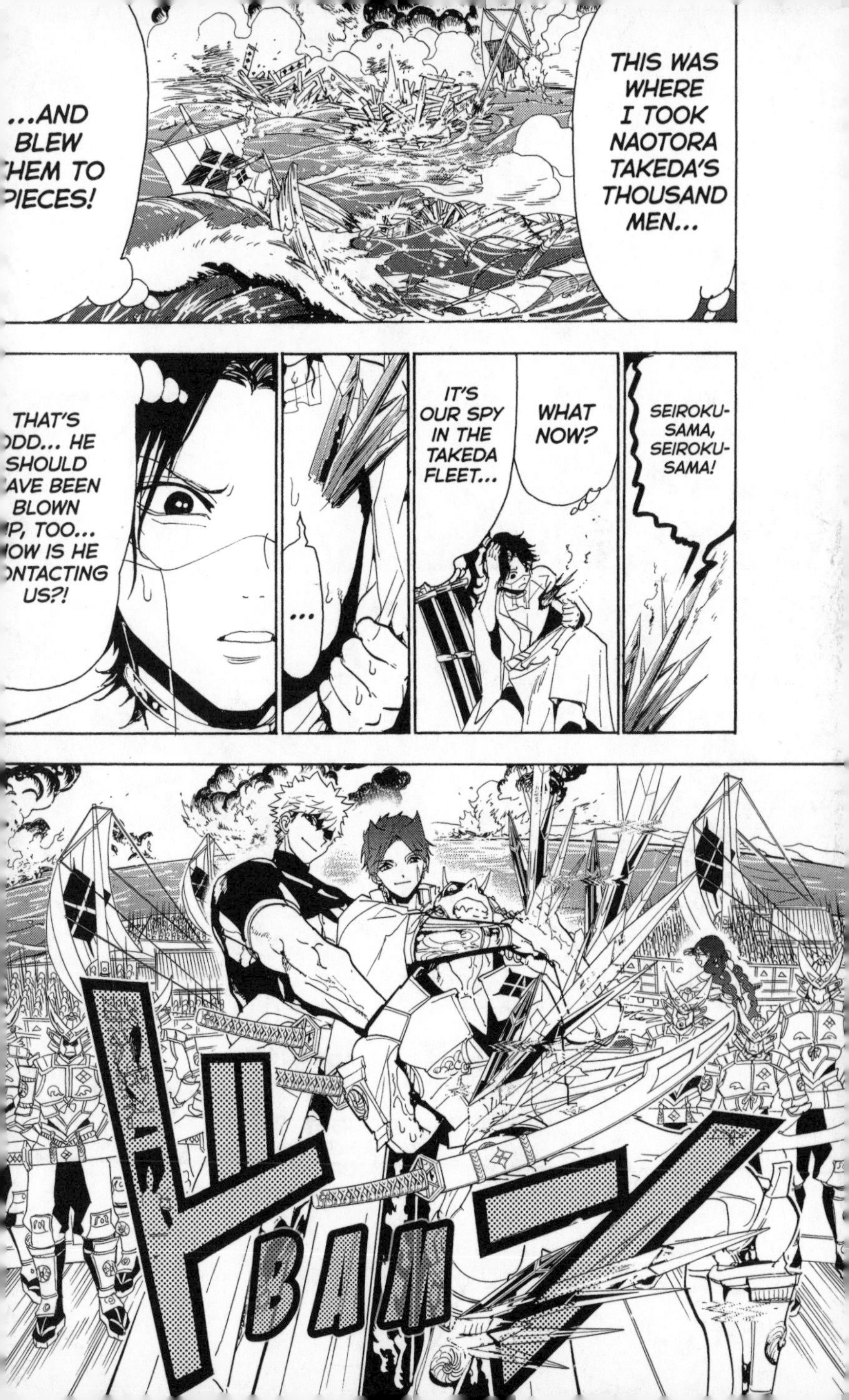
THIS WAS WHERE I TOOK NAOTORA TAKEDA'S THOUSAND MEN...
...AND BLEW THEM TO PIECES!
SEIROKU-SAMA, SEIROKU-SAMA!
WHAT NOW?
IT'S OUR SPY IN THE TAKEDA FLEET...
...
THAT'S ODD... HE SHOULD HAVE BEEN BLOWN UP, TOO... HOW IS HE CONTACTING US?!
BAN

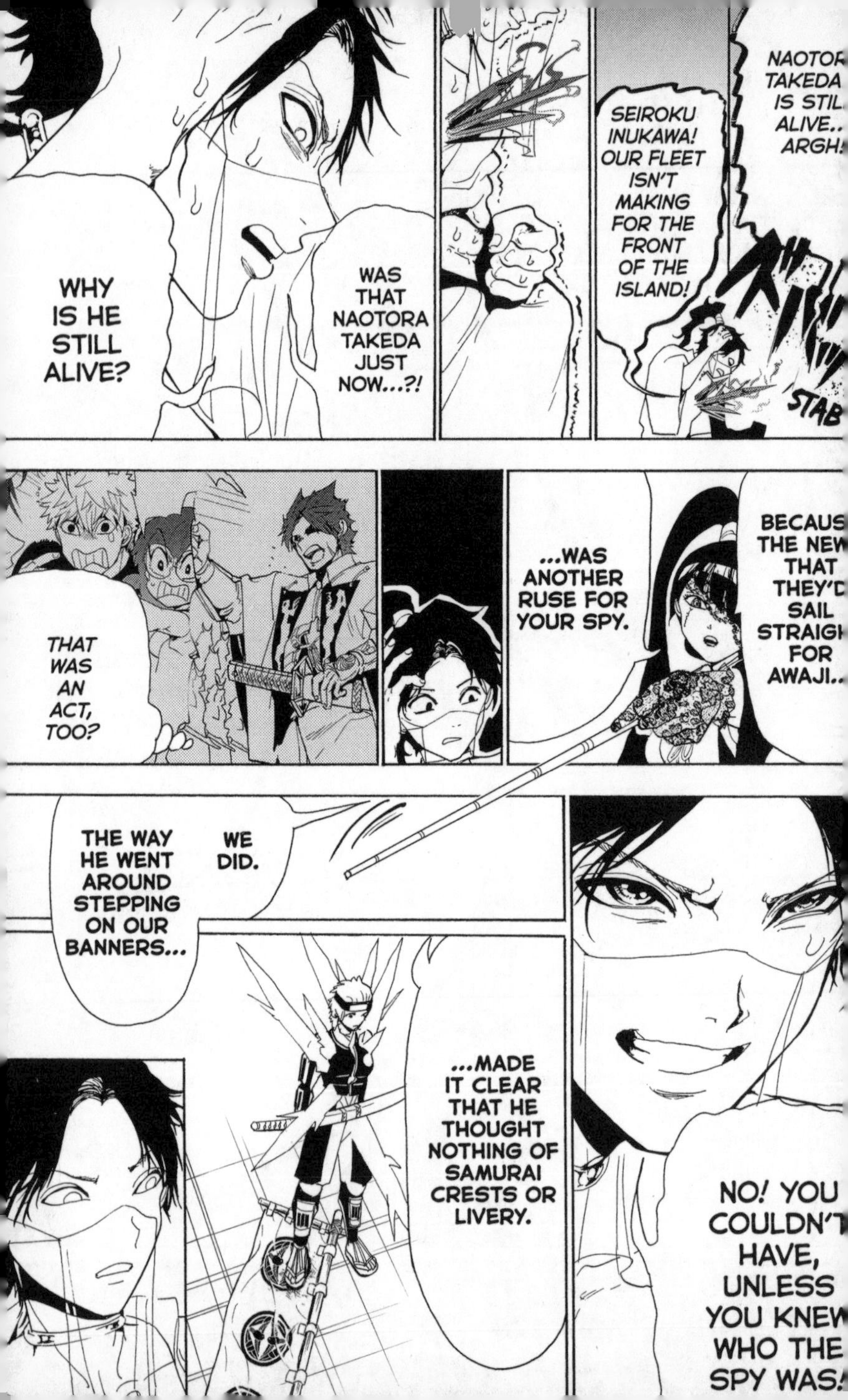

NAOTOR TAKEDA IS STIL ALIVE.. ARGH!
SEIROKU INUKAWA! OUR FLEET ISN'T MAKING FOR THE FRONT OF THE ISLAND!
STAB
WAS THAT NAOTORA TAKEDA JUST NOW...?!
WHY IS HE STILL ALIVE?
BECAUS THE NEW THAT THEY'D SAIL STRAIGH FOR AWAJI...
...WAS ANOTHER RUSE FOR YOUR SPY.
THAT WAS AN ACT, TOO?
NO! YOU COULDN'T HAVE, UNLESS YOU KNEW WHO THE SPY WAS!
WE DID.
THE WAY HE WENT AROUND STEPPING ON OUR BANNERS...
...MADE IT CLEAR THAT HE THOUGHT NOTHING OF SAMURAI CRESTS OR LIVERY.

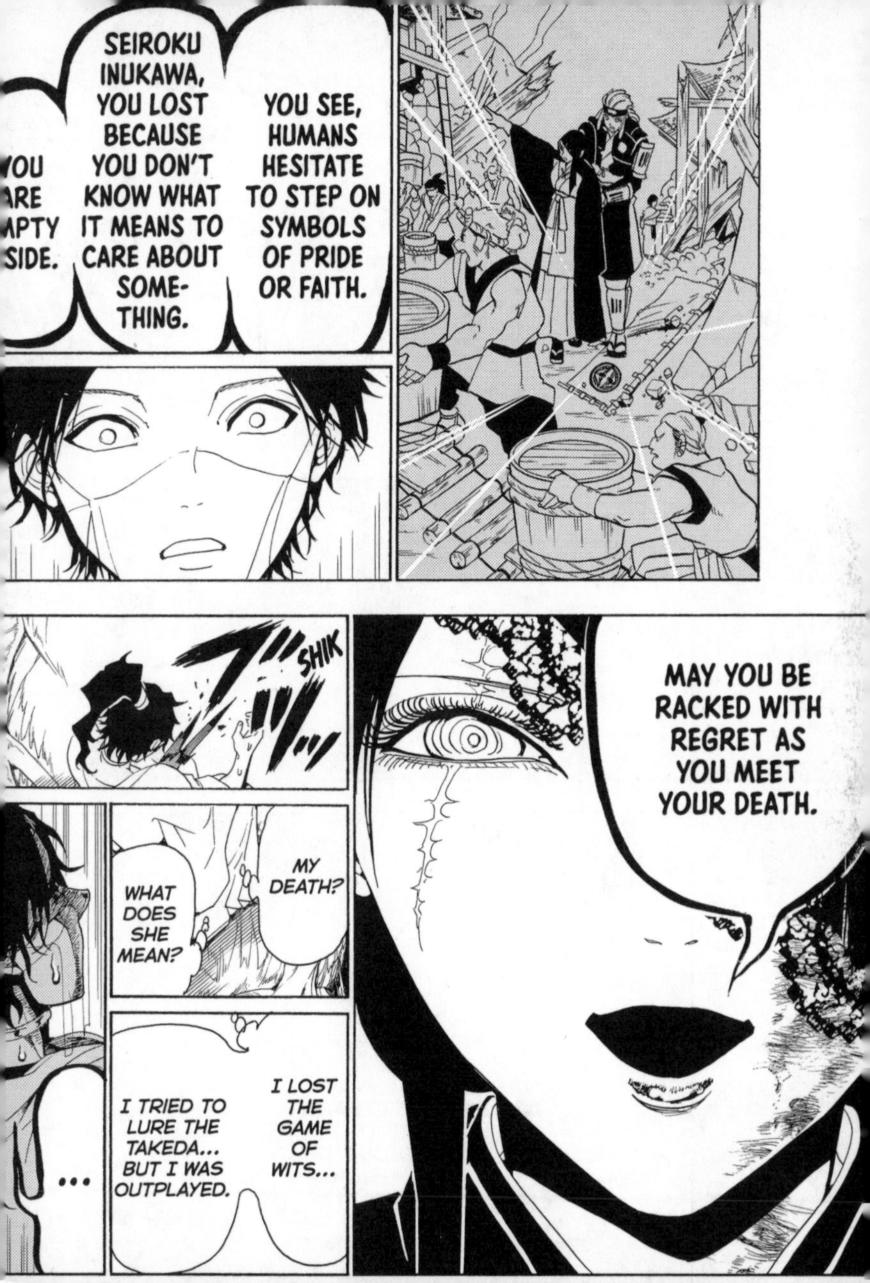
YOU SEE, HUMANS HESITATE TO STEP ON SYMBOLS OF PRIDE OR FAITH.
SEIROKU INUKAWA, YOU LOST BECAUSE YOU DON'T KNOW WHAT IT MEANS TO CARE ABOUT SOME-THING.
YOU ARE
MAY YOU BE RACKED WITH REGRET AS YOU MEET YOUR DEATH.
SHIK
MY DEATH?
WHAT DOES SHE MEAN?
I LOST THE GAME OF WITS...
I TRIED TO LURE THE TAKEDA... BUT I WAS OUTPLAYED.
...

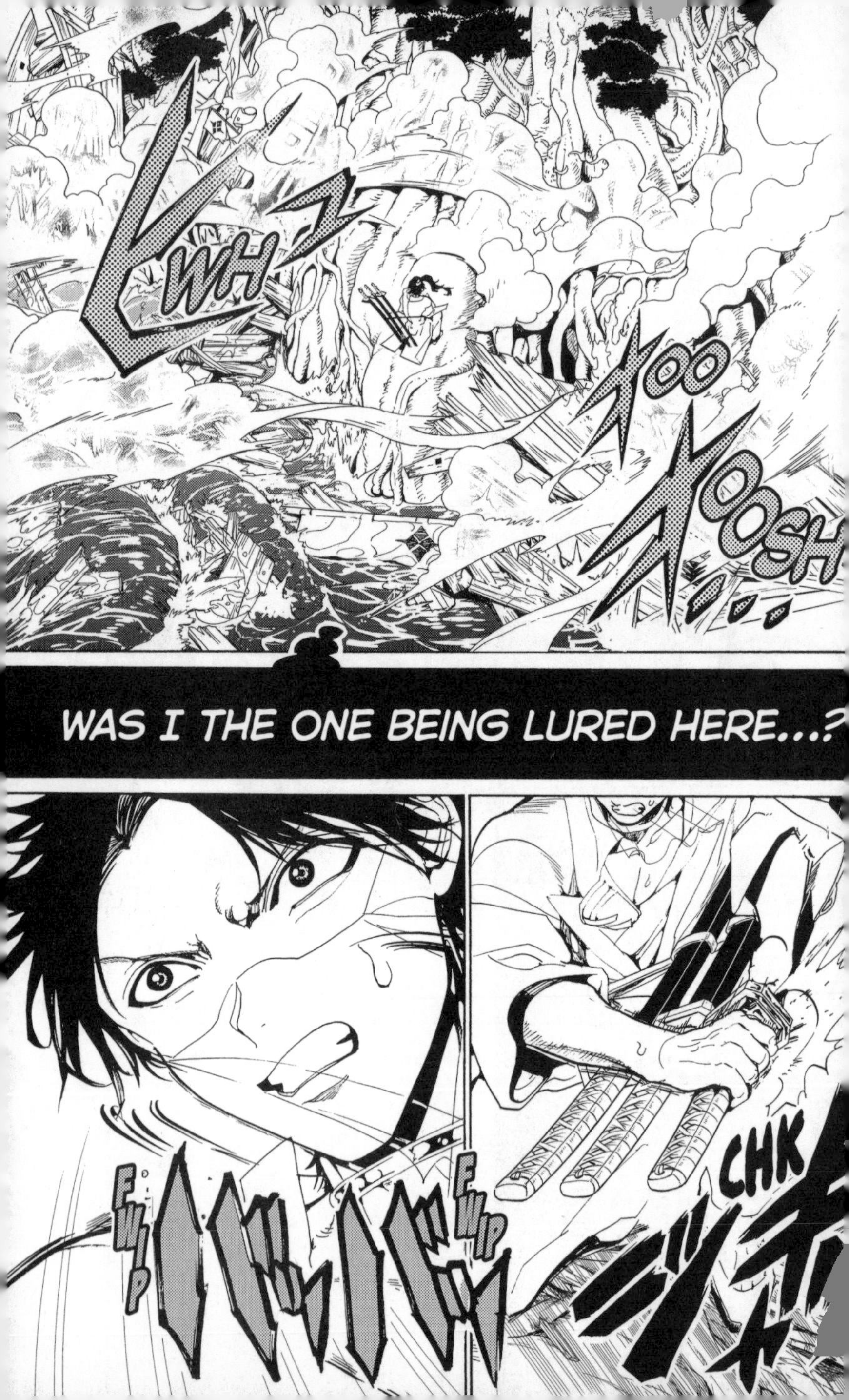

WOO
WOOSH
WH
WAS I THE ONE BEING LURED HERE...?
CHK
FWIP
FWIP

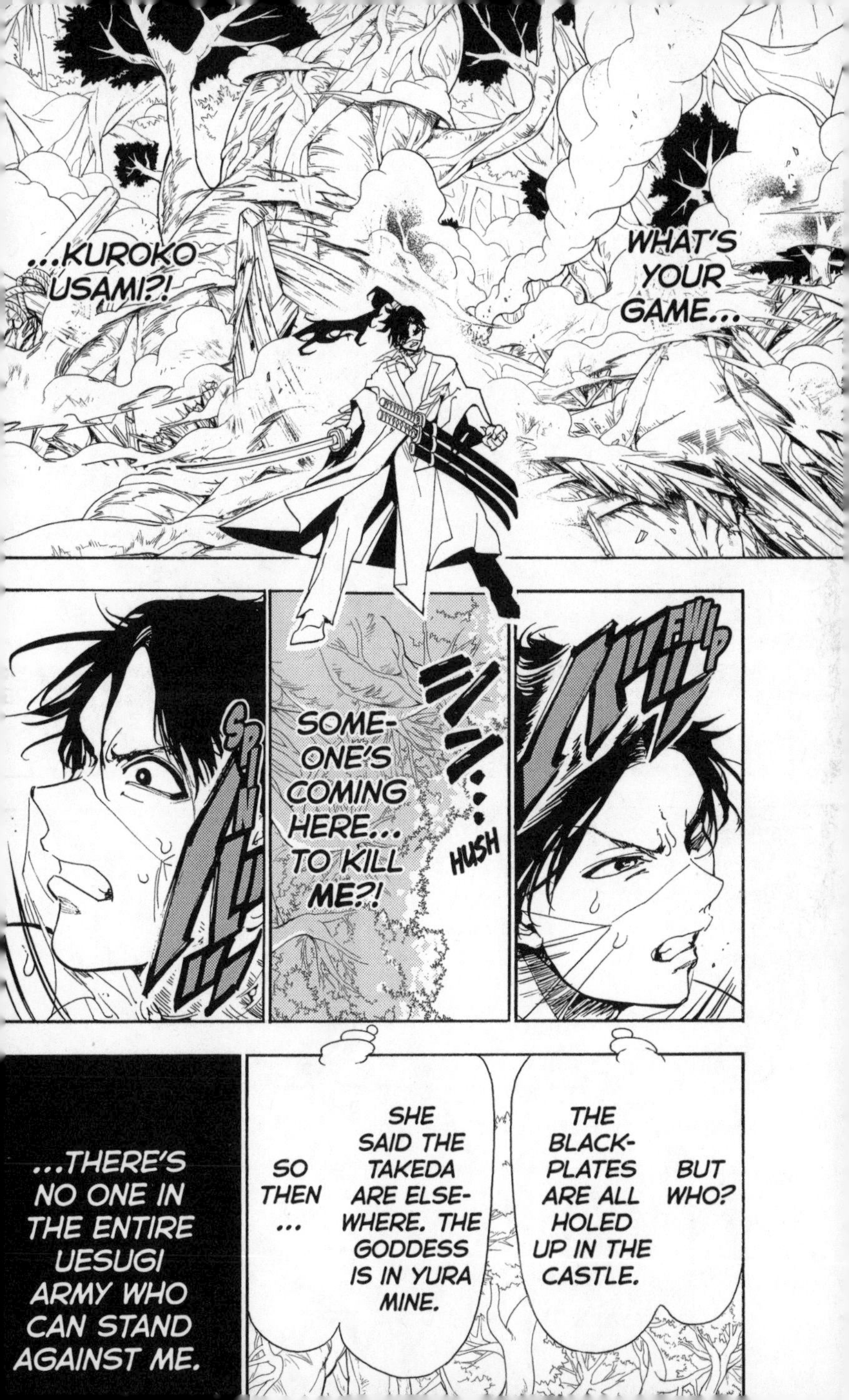
WHAT'S YOUR GAME...
...KUROKO USAMI?!
FWIP
SOME-ONE'S COMING HERE... TO KILL ME?!
HUSH
BUT WHO?
THE BLACK-PLATES ARE ALL HOLED UP IN THE CASTLE.
SHE SAID THE TAKEDA ARE ELSE-WHERE. THE GODDESS IS IN YURA MINE.
SO THEN ...
...THERE'S NO ONE IN THE ENTIRE UESUGI ARMY WHO CAN STAND AGAINST ME.

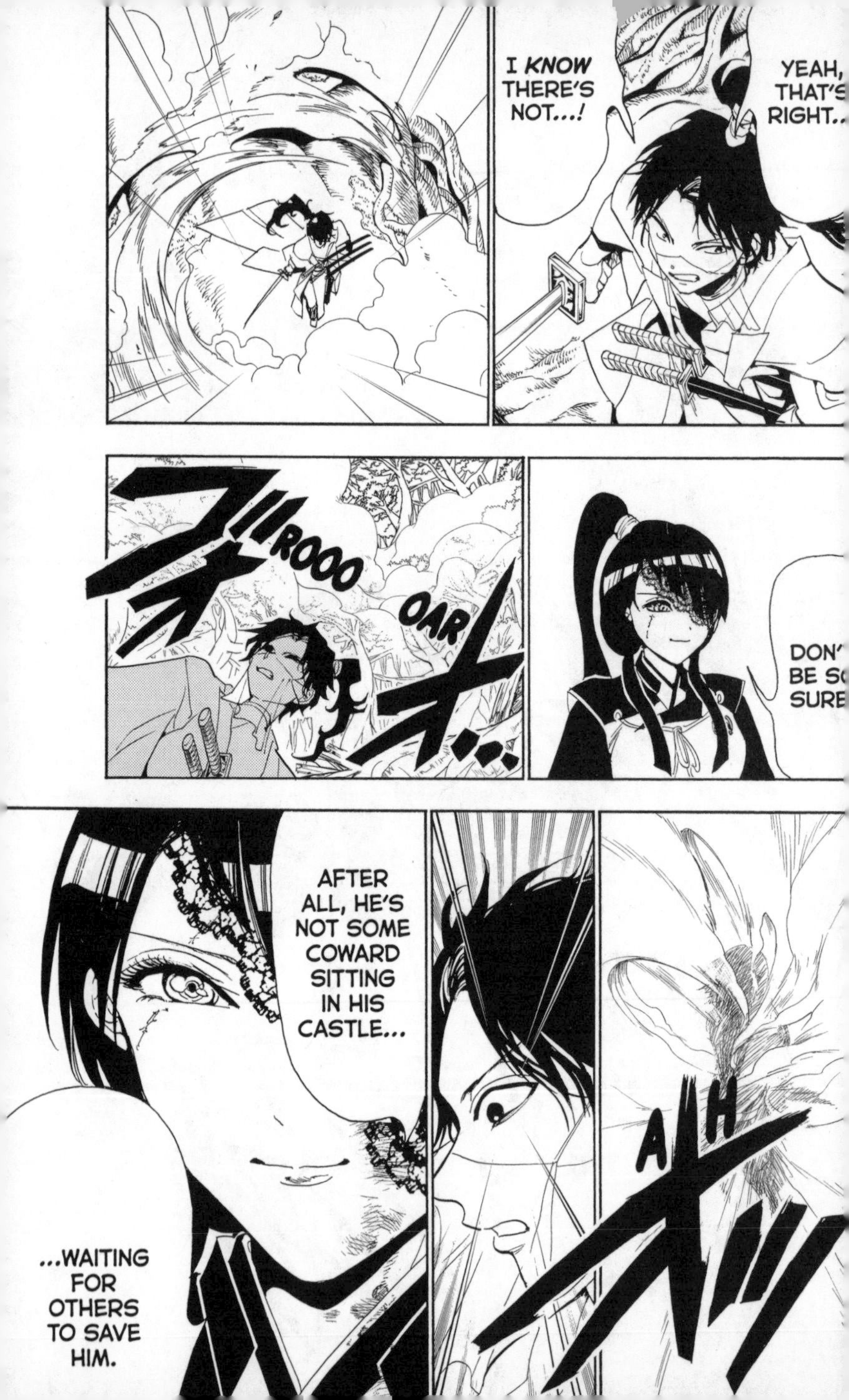
YEAH, THAT'S RIGHT..
I KNOW THERE'S NOT...!
DON' BE S SURE
ROOO
OAR
AH
AFTER ALL, HE'S NOT SOME COWARD SITTING IN HIS CASTLE...
...WAITING FOR OTHERS TO SAVE HIM.

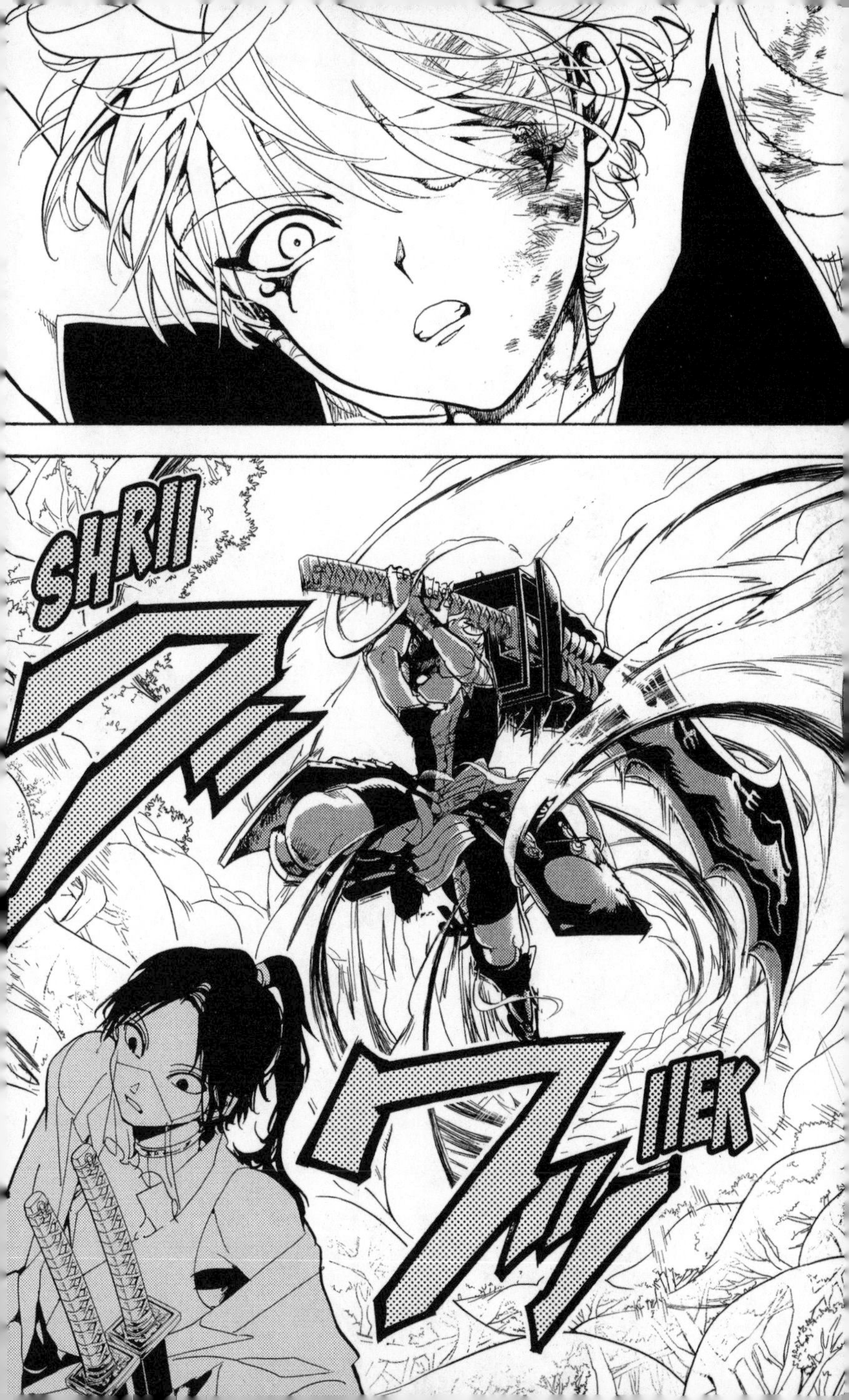
SHRII
IIEK

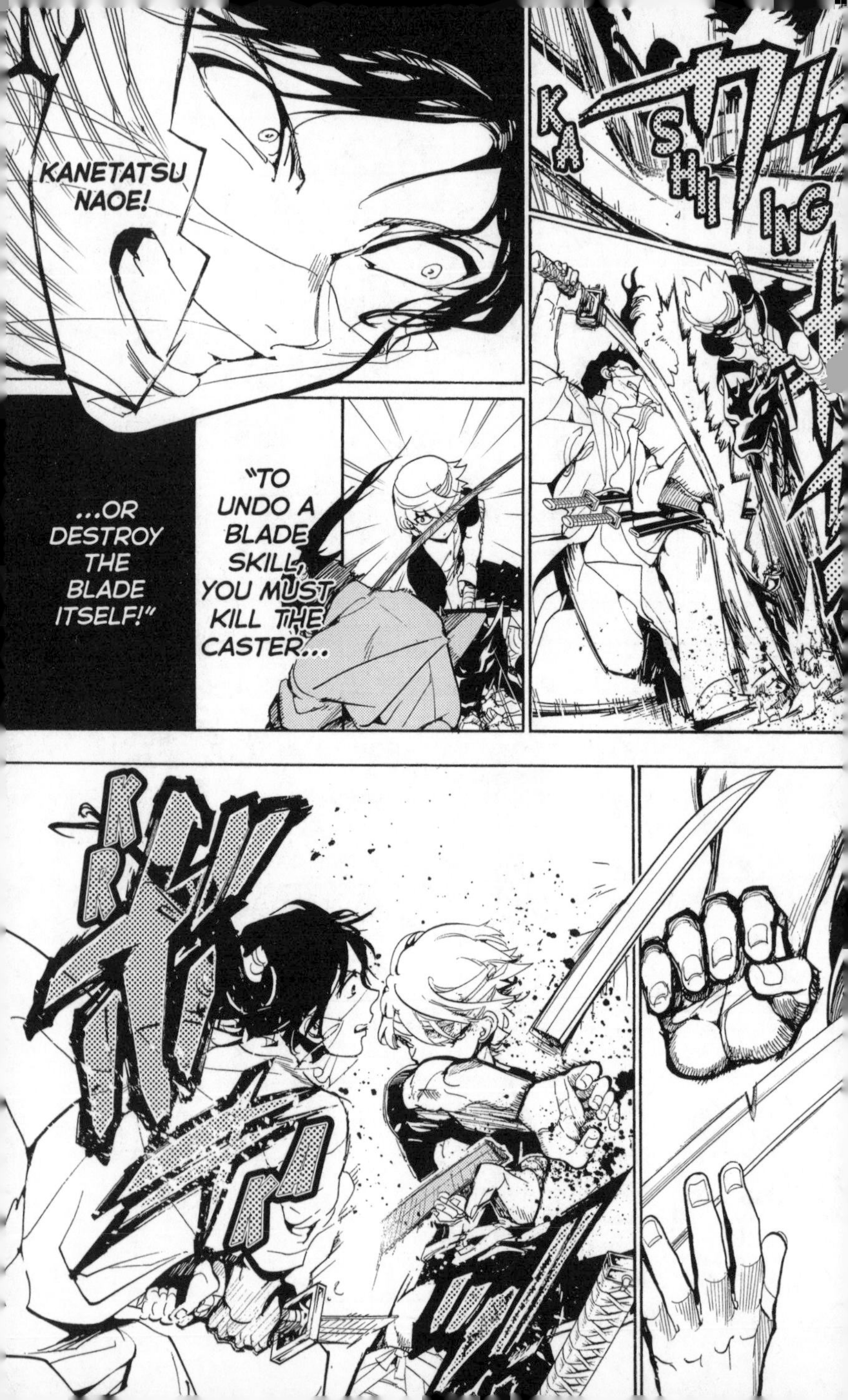
KASHIING
KANETATSU NAOE!
"TO UNDO A BLADE SKILL, YOU MUST KILL THE CASTER...
...OR DESTROY THE BLADE ITSELF!"

ORIENT VOLUME 9 BONUS CHAPTER

USAMI-SAN WANTS TO GO SHOPPING

DIDN'T YOU HAVE SOME SPIKY, BRIGHT RED DRESS ON LAST WEEK?

HMPH! IT'S THE LATEST FROM *LILY AND ARLEQUIN.*

KUROKO, YOUR WARDROBE'S AMAZING AS ALWAYS...

BRAND-NAME

BRAND-NAME

Where do they sell all that?

LIMITED-EDITION

BRAND-NAME

...WAS AT A LOSS FOR WORDS.

UH... THAT'S A GOOD COLOR FOR HIDING BLOOD SPATTERS!

I MEAN, I HARDLY KNOW HOW TO COMMENT ANYMORE. EVEN THAT CHATTER-BOX, MASAKI...

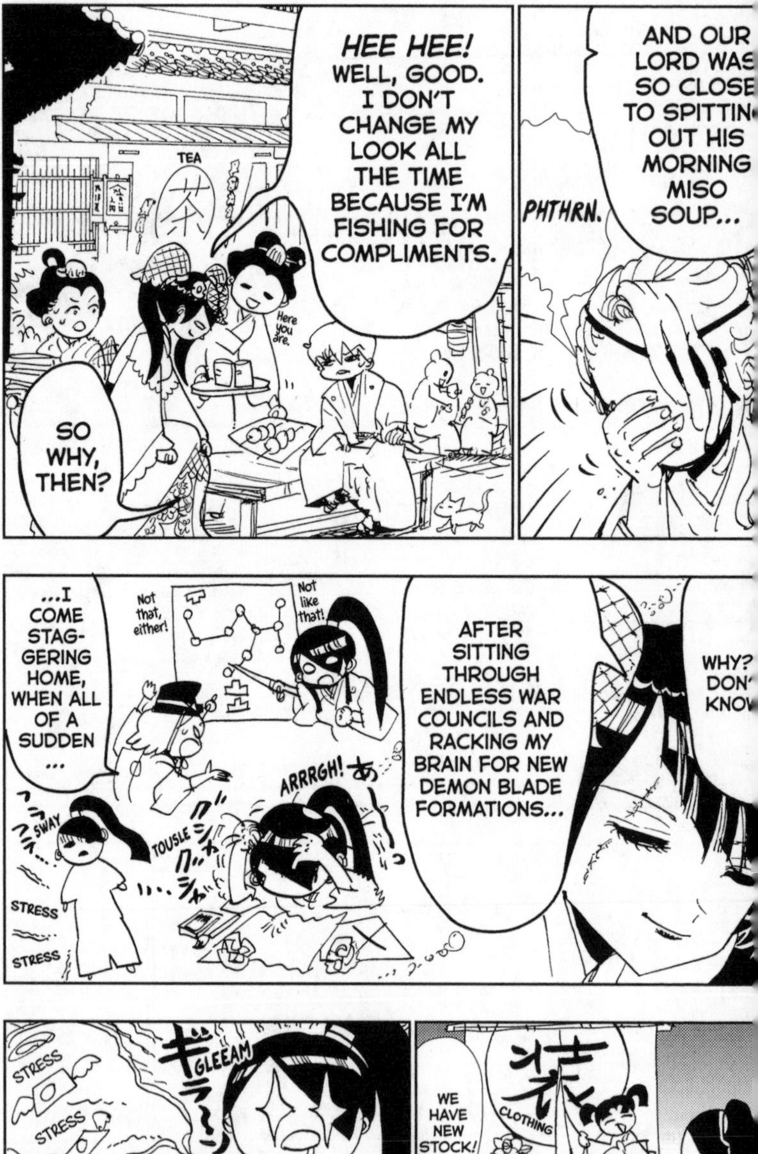
AND OUR LORD WAS SO CLOSE TO SPITTIN OUT HIS MORNING MISO SOUP...
PHTHRN.
HEE HEE! WELL, GOOD. I DON'T CHANGE MY LOOK ALL THE TIME BECAUSE I'M FISHING FOR COMPLIMENTS.
TEA
Here you are.
SO WHY, THEN?
WHY? DON' KNOW
AFTER SITTING THROUGH ENDLESS WAR COUNCILS AND RACKING MY BRAIN FOR NEW DEMON BLADE FORMATIONS...
...I COME STAGGERING HOME, WHEN ALL OF A SUDDEN ...
Not that, either!
Not like that!
ARRRGH!
SWAY
TOUSLE
STRESS
STRESS
WE HAVE NEW STOCK!
CLOTHING
GLEEAM
STRESS
STRESS
PANT
PANT
PURSE

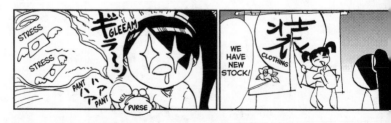

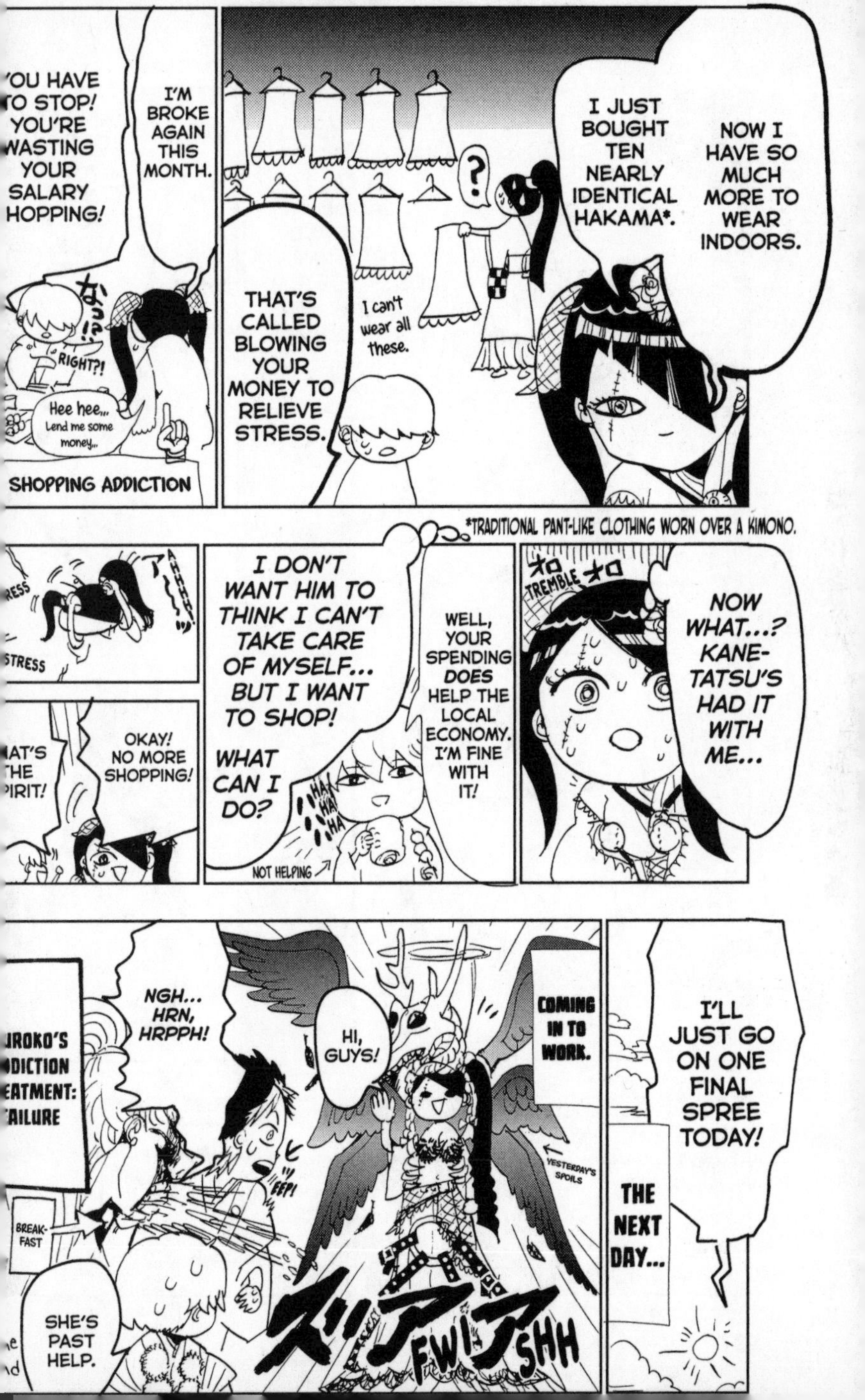
I JUST BOUGHT TEN NEARLY IDENTICAL HAKAMA*. NOW I HAVE SO MUCH MORE TO WEAR INDOORS.
?
THAT'S CALLED BLOWING YOUR MONEY TO RELIEVE STRESS.
I can't wear all these.
I'M BROKE AGAIN THIS MONTH.
'OU HAVE TO STOP! YOU'RE WASTING YOUR SALARY HOPPING!
なっ!?
RIGHT?!
Hee hee... Lend me some money...
SHOPPING ADDICTION
*TRADITIONAL PANT-LIKE CLOTHING WORN OVER A KIMONO.
オロ TREMBLE オロ
NOW WHAT...? KANE-TATSU'S HAD IT WITH ME...
I DON'T WANT HIM TO THINK I CAN'T TAKE CARE OF MYSELF... BUT I WANT TO SHOP!
WHAT CAN I DO?
WELL, YOUR SPENDING DOES HELP THE LOCAL ECONOMY. I'M FINE WITH IT!
HA HA HA
NOT HELPING
RESS
STRESS
AHHHH!
OKAY! NO MORE SHOPPING!
AT'S THE PIRIT!
THE NEXT DAY...
I'LL JUST GO ON ONE FINAL SPREE TODAY!
COMING IN TO WORK.
HI, GUYS!
YESTERDAY'S SPOILS
NGH... HRN, HRPPH!
EEP!
BREAK-FAST
FWISHH
SHE'S PAST HELP.
UROKO'S ADDICTION TREATMENT: FAILURE

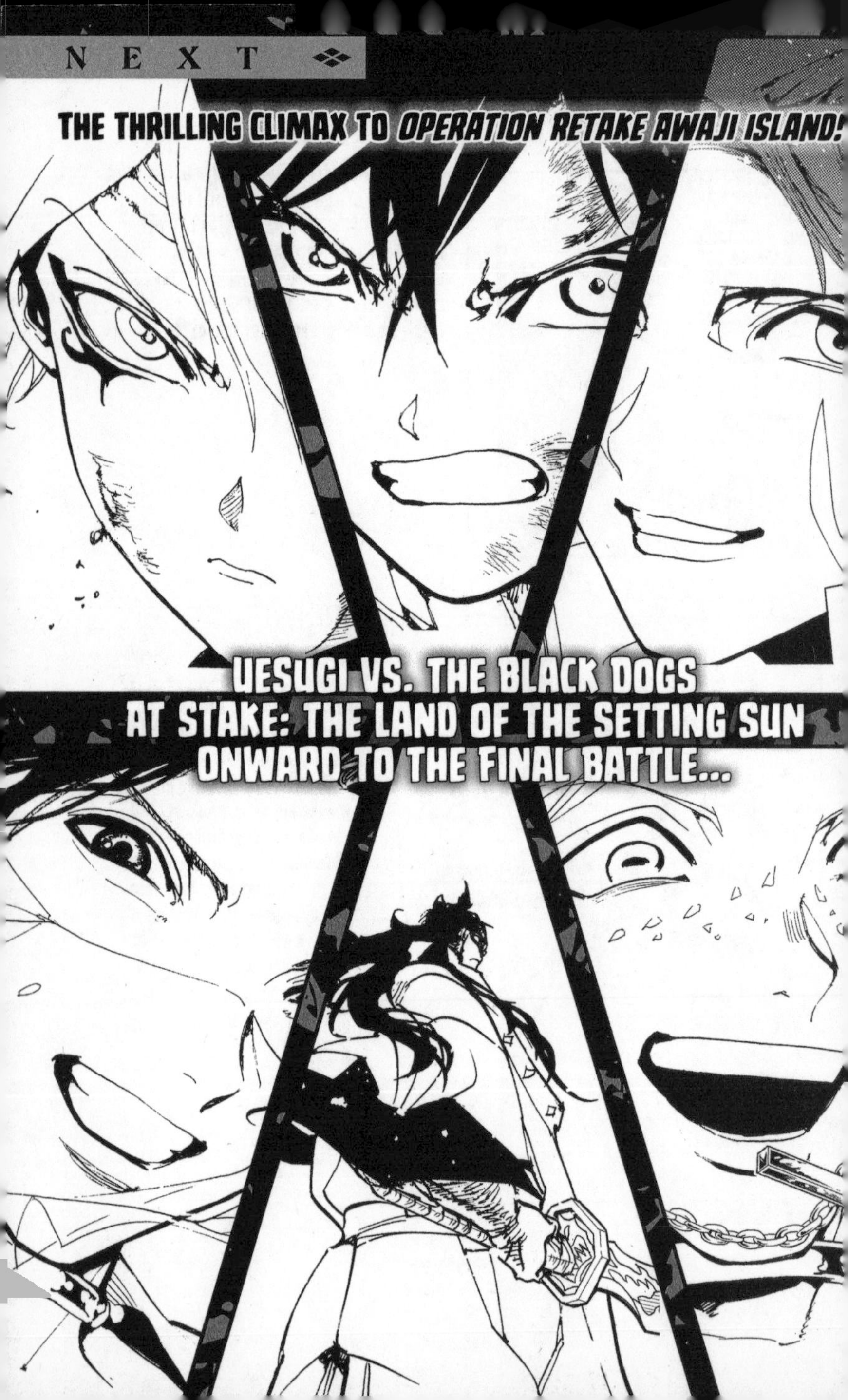
NEXT
THE THRILLING CLIMAX TO *OPERATION RETAKE AWAJI ISLAND!*
UESUGI VS. THE BLACK DOGS
AT STAKE: THE LAND OF THE SETTING SUN
ONWARD TO THE FINAL BATTLE...

Translation Notes

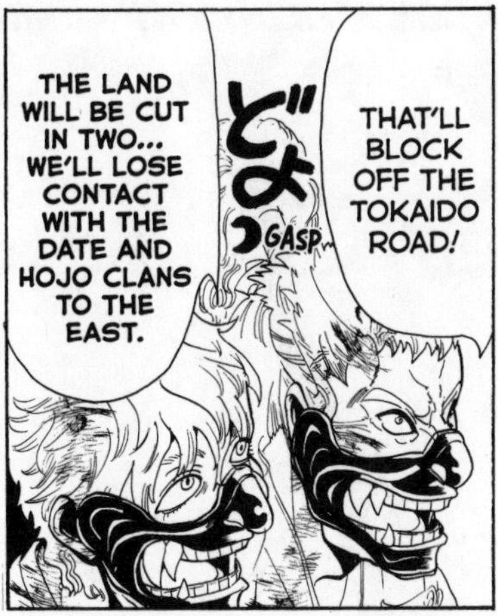
THAT'LL BLOCK OFF THE TOKAIDO ROAD!
どよっ
GASP
THE LAND WILL BE CUT IN TWO... WE'LL LOSE CONTACT WITH THE DATE AND HOJO CLANS TO THE EAST.

Pg. 74, Tokaido Road

The Tokaido (Eastern Sea Road) was the most important of the five major land routes during the Tokugawa period (1603–1867). Running primarily along the southern coast of Japan, the Tokaido carried countless merchants, tradesmen, samurai, and others to and from Edo (present-day Tokyo).

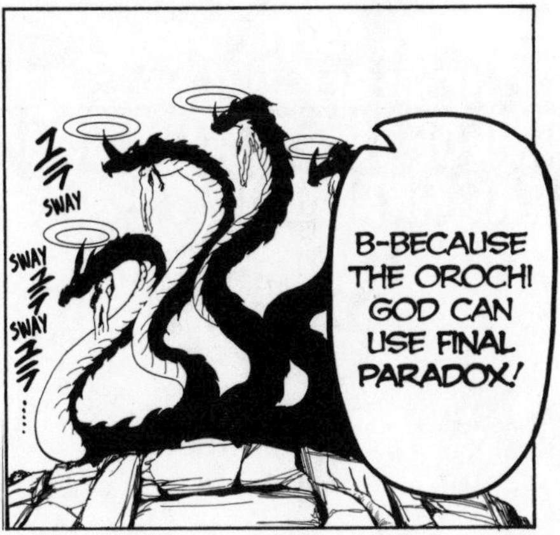
B-BECAUSE THE OROCHI GOD CAN USE FINAL PARADOX!
SWAY
SWAY
SWAY

Pg. 122, Final Paradox

This word for "paradox" (矛楯; yokotate) is a combination of the words for "spear" and "shield." According to a story from the Chinese Warring States period, a merchant from Chu State boasted that his shields were so strong that nothing could pierce them, and his spears so sharp that they could pierce anything. Overhearing this, a passerby asked the merchant what would happen if he used his spear to pierce his shield. The merchant found himself stumped by the paradox.

Translation Notes

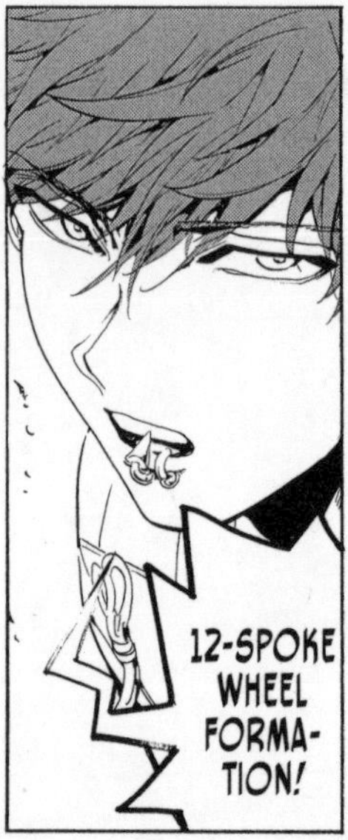
12-SPOKE WHEEL FORMA-TION!

Pg. 161, wheel formation

The *Koyo Gunkan*, a military record of the Takeda Clan written in the 16th or 17th century, claims that renowned daimyo Takeda Shingen employed a "rolling wheel formation" against his rival, Uesugi Kenshin. This moving spiral allowed fresh troops to rotate out with weary or wounded troops while maintaining pressure on the enemy.

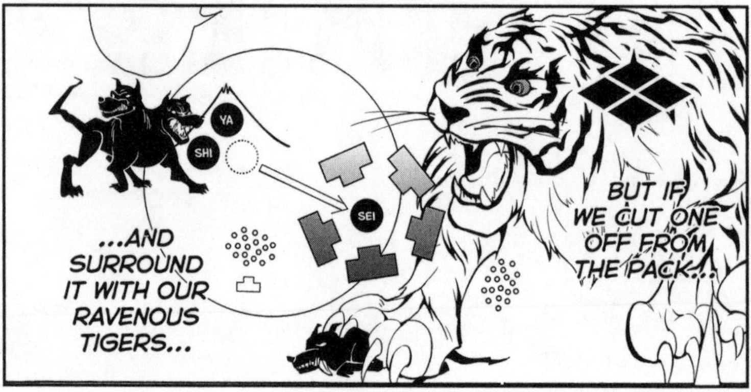
BUT IF WE CUT ONE OFF FROM THE PACK...
YA
SHI
SEI
...AND SURROUND IT WITH OUR RAVENOUS TIGERS...

Pg. 167, ravenous tigers

The second kanji in the name Naotora (尚虎) means "tiger." Hence, Naotora Takeda's forces are described here as "ravenous tigers."

ORIENT

Young characters and steampunk setting, like *Howl's Moving Castle* and *Battle Angel Alita*

Beyond the Clouds © 2018 Nicke / Ki-oon

A boy with a talent for machines and a mysterious girl whose wings he's fixed will take you beyond the clouds! In the tradition of the high-flying, resonant adventure stories of Studio Ghibli comes a gorgeous tale about the longing of young hearts for adventure and friendship!

A SMART, NEW ROMANTIC COMEDY FOR FANS OF *SHORTCAKE CAKE* AND *TERRACE HOUSE*!

KC KODANSHA COMICS

A romance manga starring high school girl Meeko, who learns to live on her own in a boarding house whose living room is home to the odd (but handsome) Matsunaga-san. She begins to adjust to her new life away from her parents, but Meeko soon learns that no matter how far away from home she is, she's still a young girl at heart — especially when she finds herself falling for Matsunaga-san.

PERFECT WORLD

Rie Aruga

A TOUCHING NEW SERIES ABOUT LOVE AND COPING WITH DISABILITY

An office party reunites Tsugumi with her high school crush Itsuki. He's realized his dream of becoming an architect, but along the way, he experienced a spinal injury that put him in a wheelchair. Now Tsugumi's rekindled feelings will butt up against prejudices she never considered — and Itsuki will have to decide if he's ready to let someone into his heart...

"Depicts with great delicacy and courage the difficulties some with disabilities experience getting involved in romantic relationships... Rie Aruga refuses to romanticize, pushing her heroine to face the reality of disability. She invites her readers to the same tasks of empathy, knowledge and recognition."
—Slate.fr

"An important entry [in manga romance]... The emotional core of both plot and characters indicates thoughtfulness... [Aruga's] research is readily apparent in the text and artwork, making this feel like a real story."
—Anime News Network

The boys are back, in 400-page hardcover that are as pretty and badass as they are!

Saiyuki © Kazuya Minakura / Ichijii

SAIYUKI

THE ORIGINAL SERIES

KAZUYA MINEKURA

"AN EDGY COMIC LOOK AT AN ANCIENT CHINESE TALE." —YAL

Genjo Sanzo is a Buddhist priest in the city of Togenkyo, which is being ravaged by yokai spirits that have fallen out of balance with the natural order. His superiors send him on a journey far to the west to discover why this is happening and how to stop it. His companions are three yokai with human souls. But this is no day trip — the four will encounter many discoveries and horrors on the way.

FEATURES NEW TRANSLATION, COLOR PAGES, AND BEAUTIFUL WRAPAROUND COVER ART!

omething's Wrong With Us

NATSUMI ANDO

The dark, psychological, sexy shojo series readers have been waiting for!

A spine-chilling and steamy romance between a Japanese sweets maker and the man who framed her mother for murder!

Following in her mother's footsteps, Nao became a traditional Japanese sweets maker, and with unparalleled artistry and a bright attitude, she gets an offer to work at a world-class confectionary company. But when she meets the young, handsome owner, she recognizes his cold stare...

KC/ KODANSHA COMICS

The adorable new odd-couple cat comedy manga from the creator of the beloved *Chi's Sweet Home*, in full color!

Praise for Chi's Sweet Home

"Nearly impossible to turn away... a true all-ages title that anyone, young or old, cat lover or not, will enjoy. The stories will bring a smile to your face and warm your heart."

—School Library Journal

Sue & Tai-chan

Konami Kanata

Sue is an aging housecat who's looking forward to living out her life in peace... but her plans change when the mischievous black tomcat Tai-chan enters the picture! Hey! Sue never signed up to be a catsitter! *Sue & Tai-chan* is the latest from the reigning meow-narch of cute kitty comics, Konami Kanata.

KC
KODANSHA
COMICS

THE SWEET SCENT OF LOVE IS IN THE AIR! FOR FANS OF OFFBEAT ROMANCES LIKE *WOTAKOI*

Sweat and Soap © Kintetsu Yamada / Kodansha Ltd.

In an office romance, there's a fine line between sexy and awkward... and that line is where Asako — a woman who sweats copiously — meets Koutarou — a perfume developer who can't get enough of Asako's, er, scent. Don't miss a romcom manga like no other!

The beloved characters from
Cardcaptor Sakura return in a brand new,
reimagined fantasy adventure!

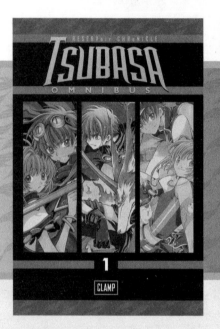

"[*Tsubasa*] takes readers on a fantastic ride that only gets more exhilarating with each successive chapter." —Anime News Network

In the Kingdom of Clow, an archaeological dig unleashes an incredible power, causing Princess Sakura to lose her memories. To save her, her childhood friend Syaoran must follow the orders of the Dimension Witch and travel alongside Kurogane, an unrivaled warrior; Fai, a powerful magician; and Mokona, a curiously strange creature, to retrieve Sakura's dispersed memories!

One of CLAMP's biggest hits returns
in this definitive, premium, hardcover
20th anniversary collector's edition!

"A wonderfully
entertaining story
that would be a
great installment ir
anybody's manga
collection."
— Anime News Networ

"CLAMP is an all-
female manga-
creating team whos
feminine touch sho
in this entertaining
sci-fi soap opera."
— Publishers Weekly

Chobits © CLAMP·ShigatsuTsuitachi CO.,LTD./Kodansh

Poor college student Hideki is down on his luck. All he wants is a
good job, a girlfriend, and his very own "persocom"—the latest
and greatest in humanoid computer technology. Hideki's luck
changes one night when he finds Chi—a persocom thrown out
in a pile of trash. But Hideki soon discovers that there's much
more to his cute new persocom than meets the eye.

KC
KODANSHA
COMICS

Orient 9 is a work o[f] ...
places, and incidents are the ...
or are used fictitiously. Any re[s] ...
persons, living or dead, is en[...] ...

A Kodansha Comics Trade Paperback Original
Orient 9 copyright © 2020 Shinobu Ohtaka
English translation copyright © 2022 Shinobu Ohtaka

Published in the United States by Kodansha Comics, an imprint of
Kodansha USA Publishing, LLC, New York.

Publication rights for this English edition arranged through
Kodansha Ltd., Tokyo.

First published in Japan in 2020 by Kodansha Ltd., Tokyo.

ISBN 978-1-64651-427-4

Printed in the United States of America.

www.kodansha.us

9 8 7 6 5 4 3 2 1
Translation: Kevin Gifford
Lettering: Belynda Ungurath
Editing: Andres Oliver
Kodansha Comics edition cover design by Phil Balsman
YKS Services LLC/SKY Japan, INC.

Publisher: Kiichiro Sugawara

Director of publishing services: Ben Applegate
Director of publishing operations: Dave Barrett
Associate director of publishing operations: Stephen Pakula
Publishing services managing editors: Alanna Ruse, Madison Salters
Production managers: Emi Lotto, Angela Zurlo
Logo and character art ©Kodansha USA Publishing, LLC